SELECTED

LETTERS

OF

Friedrich

Nietzsche

SELECTED

LETTERS

OF

Friedrich
Nietzsche

Edited and Translated by
CHRISTOPHER MIDDLETON

Hackett Publishing Company, Inc.
Indianapolis/Cambridge

Friedrich Nietzsche: 1844–1900

Copyright © 1969 by The University of Chicago
Reprinted 1996 by Hackett Publishing Company, Inc.

02 01 00 99 98 97 96   1 2 3 4 5 6 7

For further information please address

   Hackett Publishing Company, Inc.
   P.O. Box 44937
   Indianapolis, Indiana 46244-0937

Library of Congress Cataloging-in-Publication Data

Nietzsche, Friedrich Wilhelm, 1844–1900.
       [Correspondence. English. Selections]
       Selected letters of Friedrich Nietzsche/edited and translated by
   Christopher Middleton.
            p.   cm.
       Originally published: Chicago: University of Chicago Press, 1969.
       Includes bibliographical references and index.
       ISBN 0-87220-359-X (cloth: alk. paper)
       ISBN 0-87220-358-1 (pbk.: alk. paper)
       1. Nietzsche, Friedrich Wilhelm, 1844–1900—Correspondence.
   2. Philosophers—Germany—Correspondence.   I. Middleton, Christopher.
   II. Title.
   B3316.A4   1996
   193—dc21
       [B]   96-46577
                                                                 CIP

The paper used in this publication meets the minimum requirements of American
National Standard for Information Sciences—Permanence of Paper for Printed
Library Materials, ANSI Z39.48-1984.

∞

Contents

Pages 354–57 are a reproduction of Nietzsche's letter (No. 118
in this volume) to Malwida von Meysenbug, August, 1883,
from Nationale Forschungs- und Gedenkstätten
(Goethe- und Schiller-Archiv), Weimar

Preface

I have usually retained the German titles of works by Nietzsche and by other authors and composers, except when the context prompted an ad hoc or standard English title. The standard English titles of works by Nietzsche mentioned in letters or annotations are as follows:

Die Geburt der Tragödie	*The Birth of Tragedy*
Die Zukunft unserer	*The Future of Our Educational*
Bildungsanstalten	*Institutions*
Unzeitgemässe Betrachtungen	*Thoughts out of Season* (or
	Untimely Meditations)
Menschliches, Allzumenschliches	*Human, All-Too-Human*
Morgenröte	*The Dawn of Day*
Die fröhliche Wissenschaft	*The Joyful Wisdom*
Also sprach Zarathustra	*Thus Spake Zarathustra*
Jenseits von Gut und Böse	*Beyond Good and Evil*
Zur Genealogie der Moral	*The Genealogy of Morals*
Der Fall Wagner	*The Case of Wagner*
Götzen-Dämmerung	*Twilight of the Idols*
Der Antichrist	*The Antichrist*
Ecce Homo	*Ecce Homo*
Nietzsche contra Wagner	*Nietzsche contra Wagner*

Quotations from the writings of Nietzsche are from the edition by Karl Schlechta, *Werke in drei Bänden* (Munich: Carl Hanser Verlag, 1954–56), which includes the *Nietzsche Index* (1965).

My sources for the letters have been, principally, the three following works: (1) F. Nietzsche, *Briefe*, vols. 1–4, in the *Historisch-Kritische Gesamtausgabe* (Munich: C. H. Beck), vol. 1 (1850–65), edited by Wilhelm Hoppe and Karl Schlechta, 1938; vols. 2–4 (1865–69, 1869–73, 1873–77), edited by Wilhelm Hoppe, 1938–42. The notes to these volumes provided me with many details. The volumes contain 1,020 letters of the period 1850–77. (2) *Werke in drei Bänden*, vol. 3, edited by Karl Schlechta, pp. 929–1352.

vii

This was my main source for letters of the period 1878–89, though for the same period I also used the _Briefwechsel mit Franz Overbeck_ (see below). Schlechta's annotation of the letters is slight. I used his notes for several matters of fact, but have added a large number of my own. His edition contains 278 letters from the period 1861–89. (3) _Nietzsche in seinen Briefen und Berichten der Zeitgenossen_, edited by Alfred Baeumler (Leipzig: Alfred Kröner Verlag, 1932), pp. 527. This compilation was used for filling various gaps in the two works cited above.

In order to avoid selecting, for the period 1878–89, only from existing selections, I have referred to _Gesammelte Briefe_ (Leipzig: Insel Verlag, 1907) in 5 volumes. The reliability of this edition being dubious, all texts used have been the ones established by Hoppe and Schlechta after the death of Elisabeth Förster-Nietzsche, except for those letters in _Nietzsche in seinen Briefen_ which do not appear in _Werke in drei Bänden_, vol. 3. Pedantry or no, and at the risk of too much deference to Schlechta's often sweeping verdicts, I have not included letters whose authenticity is doubtful, with one exception, which I include as an example of a faked letter, showing how and why Elisabeth tampered with her brother's correspondence.

Other collections: _F. Nietzsches Briefwechsel mit Franz Overbeck_ (Leipzig: Insel Verlag, 1916) and _F. Nietzsches Briefwechsel mit Erwin Rohde_ (Leipzig: Insel Verlag, 1923). Both of these have gaps in the texts of some letters, but they have been remedied in those which appear in _Werke in drei Bänden_, vol. 3. C. A. Bernoulli, _Overbeck und Nietzsche_, 2 vols. (Jena: Eugen Diederichs Verlag, 1907): this immense compilation includes letter material by and about Nietzsche. An early German selection also exists: _Nietzsches Briefe_, selected and edited by Richard Oehler (Leipzig: Insel Verlag, 1915; 2d enlarged edition 1917).

The following are collections of letters to Nietzsche: Peter Gast, _Briefe an Friedrich Nietzsche_, 2 vols. (Munich, 1923–24); _Die Briefe Carl von Gersdorffs an Friedrich Nietzsche_, 3 vols. (Weimar, 1934–36), vol. 4, edited by Erhart Thierbach (Weimar, 1937), containing Gersdorff's letters about Nietzsche to Rohde, Wagner, Cosima Wagner, Elisabeth Förster-Nietzsche, and Carl Fuchs. _Cosima Wagners Briefe an Friedrich Nietzsche_, 2 parts (Weimar, 1938–41), edited by Erhart Thierbach. All except a few of Nietzsche's letters to Cosima were destroyed by fire at Bayreuth.

There exist in English the following three collections: _Selected Letters of Friedrich Nietzsche_, edited by Oscar Levy, translated by Anthony M. Ludovici (London: William Heinemann, 1921); _The Nietzsche-Wagner Correspondence_, edited by Elisabeth Förster-Nietzsche, translated by Caroline V. Kerr (New York: Boni and Liveright, 1921); _Nietzsche: Unpublished Letters_, translated and edited by Kurt F. Leidecker (New York: Philosophical

Library, 1959)—containing seventy-five letters of the period 1861–89, but defective translations in defective English. In French: *La vie de Frédéric Nietzsche, d'après sa correspondance: Textes choisis et traduits par Georges Walz* (Paris: Les éditions Rieder, 1932)—274 letters, detailed biographical preface, excellent apparatus.

Nietzsche's punctuation in his letters tended to be idiosyncratic. His dashes, ellipses, and parentheses have been retained to a large extent. But in order to facilitate reading, dashes between sentences have been largely eliminated. In most instances, dashes within sentences were retained, also ellipses within sentences and at the ends of sentences: these usually indicate an implied aside, or some kind of break in thought. Ellipses in square brackets (as in the footnotes) indicate an editorial cut in the text cited. A few square-bracketed words occur in the text, in lieu of annotation. One long dash in brackets indicates an earlier editorial cut from the text of a letter, which cannot be remedied.

The division of the letters into four periods is based on Nietzsche's own analysis of his life, as suggested in letter No. 110 (February 11, 1883). For convenience, biographical notes for each period are printed at the start of each period. The Epilogue gives details of Nietzsche's breakdown and of the years which ensued.

I want to thank James Hynd, William Arrowsmith, and Donald Carne-Ross for help with quotations and references in Greek and Latin, and the National Translation Center for a grant which made this work possible.

Introduction

Nietzsche has had an incalculably immense impact on European writing and thought since 1900. During the early 1930's, when his thought was lending itself to Nazi distortions, Thomas Mann and Hermann Broch, among German writers, turned against him as a representative "bourgeois esthete" of the later nineteenth century. Mann connected him with the "guilt of the intellect, its unpolitical disregard of the actual world, surrender to the esthetic enjoyment of its own audacities. . . . In those secure bourgeois times, nobody realized how easily a people can be made to believe that there are no longer any iniquities which cry out to heaven."[1] Nonetheless, Nietzsche's nihilism was so symptomatic, his quest of the naked truth so single-minded, his character as a writer and thinker so exhilarating, that Mann used him as a model for his fabulous artificer of the age, the composer Adrian Leverkühn, in his novel *Doktor Faustus*. This ambiguity is also found in Broch's remarkable essay "Evil in the Value System of Art" (1933). Nietzsche may not be of this age, Broch wrote, since he was a creature of the bourgeois "estheticizing" nineteenth century. But his discovery and analysis of the problem of value are as crucial as Kierkegaard's: they meant the end of an outworn metaphysics, and they anticipated "the immense tension between good and evil, the almost unbearably tense polarizations which mark this age and give it its extremist character, this pressure on people to incorporate into their lives both the highest ethical challenge and a reality which has terrors that often surpass comprehension—so that life may be lived at all."[2] A third writer, Gottfried Benn—whose Nietzschean fixation had made him a radio puppet of Nazi ideology at the time Mann and Broch were writing the sentences quoted—argued as late as 1950 that Nietzsche was in fact innocent of social and political crimes committed in his name:

Politicians . . . are people who, when they get rhetorical, hide behind minds and behind intellectuals whom they do not understand. . . . Yet it is a remarkable fact that,

1. Thomas Mann, "Leiden an Deutschland," in *Tagebuchblätter 1933–34* (Stockholm: Fischer Verlag, 1946), p. 151.
2. Hermann Broch, *Gesammelte Werke: Essays,* vol. 1: *Dichten und Erkennen* (Zurich: Rhein Verlag, 1955), pp. 313–14.

in a certain period of his work (*Zarathustra*) he was dominated by Darwinistic ideas, believed in the selection of the fittest, the struggle for existence which only the hardest survive, but he took over these ideas for the coloring of his vision, it was not granted to him to ignite his vision with the images of saints. He would certainly not have welcomed the blond beast who came out of this. As a human being he was impecunious, immaculate, pure—a great martyr and a great man. I might add: for my generation he was the earthquake of an epoch and the greatest genius of the German language since Luther.³

Even to his most penetrating critics, like Georg Lukacs, Nietzsche remains something of an enigma.⁴ His books are highly idiosyncratic, born of questioning in the face of pain and death, a kind of crystallized spray from massive brain waves. He is obviously one of the great moribunds of the nineteenth century—kindred spirit to Kierkegaard, Leopardi, Amiel, Baudelaire, Dostoevski, and (not least) Wagner. Going further back, there is his acknowledged and obviously chemical sympathy for Hölderlin. One might hope that his letters would reveal the man behind the immoralist, behind the visionary, behind the terrorist of metaphysical revolt, who had such delicately beautiful hands and such a famous mustache. Yet he was a reticent man, in his conversation as in his letters. The letters are like aerial photography of a subterranean labyrinth.

Until about 1876, when he was thirty-two, Nietzsche's letters do contain protestations of friendship: with Gersdorff, with Rohde, with the motherly Malwida von Meysenbug. It was to be a system of friends, with a spiritual center in Bayreuth, that should regenerate and transform German society, in the names of Schopenhauer and Wagner. As late as 1884, he is dreaming of a "Brotherhood of the *Gaya Scienza*" to be assembled in Nice. But after 1876, he becomes steadily more conscious of his isolation: of the strangeness of his mind, the "incommunicability of the heart." To Wagner in November, 1872, he writes of his existing "in the midst of a solar system of loving friendship." Yet in the same month he writes to Malwida: "Why on earth did I not write to you for such a long time? That is what I ask myself in amazement, without finding good reasons or even excuses. But I have often found it most difficult to decide on writing to those of whom I am thinking most. Yet I do not understand it. . . . There is much that is irrational, and only forgetting can help one against it." Eleven months before his breakdown, there is a momentary lifting of the iron mask of self-imposed (and self-creating) isolation: "The perpetual lack of a really refreshing and *healing human love*, the absurd isolation which it entails, making almost any

3. Gottfried Benn, *Gesammelte Werke*, 1 (Wiesbaden: Limes Verlag, 1959), 482–83.

4. Georg Lukacs, *Die Zerstörung der Vernunft* (Berlin: Aufbau Verlag, 1955).

residue of a connection with people merely something that wounds one—that is all very bad indeed and right only in itself, having the right to be necessary." Five months later, he is writing: ". . . a great emptiness around me. Literally, there is no one who could understand my situation. The worst thing is, without a doubt, not to have heard for ten years a single word that actually got through to me. . . ."

His experiences during the second half of 1882 certainly enforced this isolation, which *Zarathustra* sublimates. He even goes so far as to say, in February, 1883: "All my human relationships have to do with a mask of me, and I must perpetually be the victim of living a completely hidden life." Yet this was all part of his gestalt as a human being. It was the context of what he called "the vehemence of my inner pulsations"—the presence and the preponderance in the "scale of my experiences and circumstances . . . of notes that have a rarer, remoter, and thinner pitch than the normal ones in the middle" (1887). This kind of finesse, which he cultivated (as Kafka later cultivated his own eccentricity), is noticed as early as 1871, when he writes, "Everything that is left over and cannot be grasped in terms of musical relations does of course disgust and horrify me." The total heterodoxy of his last writings is torn from this humanly almost untenable situation. It "drips with blood," as he wrote of *Zarathustra II* in 1883. That heterodoxy is the fruit of the terror and joy of seeking the antithesis while still trapped in the human shell. Remy de Gourmont, whose writings in the early 1900's are permeated with Nietzsche, seems to have derived from him his own intellectual imperative: "We must lodge contradictory ideas in the hotel of our brain, and possess enough disinterested intelligence, enough ironic force, to impose peace on them."[5] De Gourmont is no less Nietzsche's unavowed apostle when he writes, in 1904, "Truth is only a statue of shadow, but to reach it man takes a thousand troubles, one of which perhaps is fertile."[6]

Nietzsche's revolt against a petrified morality could not have been so deep and so audacious without this alienation. And the letters do show that this was no revolt without objectives, that there is nothing to be against if you are not for something, and that you are finished if it is only yourself you are for. The objectives and their dangers were defined as follows in 1876: "Since the belief that a God directs the fate of the world has disappeared . . . mankind itself must set up universal goals embracing the whole earth. . . . If mankind is not to destroy itself through the conscious possession of such universal rule, it must first of all attain to an unprecedented knowledge of the preconditions of culture, as a scientific standard for uni-

5. "Epilogues" (1913), in: *Selections*, edited and translated by Richard Aldington (London: Chatto and Windus, 1932), p. 149.

6. *Selections*, pp. 116–17.

versal goals. Herein lies the tremendous task facing the great minds of the coming century."[7] Since then, much has been written with a view to defining these preconditions of culture. Everywhere the collectives are gathering to hear them discussed. The explosion we live in—with historical time pushed back behind the Sumerians, and space being made available for our emptiness —has not made in the interim any exact knowledge of these preconditions a source of saving action.

The startling thing about Nietzsche is of course the immense wealth of ideas, questions, definitions of *new* feelings—the delicate orchestration of his deep intuitions—which flowed from his brain in this context of isolation, not in spite of his genius for lacking contact with people but because of it. Stylistically too, with people he is often formal, defensive, masked, gropingly or atrociously histrionic; frequently writing of the physical torments which visited him year after year, he rarely bares his tormented heart. Only in naked relation to the idea does his prose become incandescent.

His relations with women are symptomatic here. He calls himself "a man not racked by the passions" (1875). To Rohde, on this friend's engagement, he wrote: "You *needed* so badly a completely trusting soul. . . . For me it is different, heaven knows, or does not know. It does not seem to be all that necessary, except on rare days" (1876). The centerpiece here is, inevitably, the 1882 relation with Lou Salomé. This was a complicated affair, and not the least of its complications was Nietzsche's well-authenticated lack of sex appeal. This may have saved him in the end from a worse fate; but it lent his approach to Lou a high-flown oddness, and perhaps a lack of candor. Socrates talking to Theodota in Xenophon's *Memorabilia* is an antithesis which most sharply defines Nietzsche's desperateness here. His intentions not only ran counter to all the prejudices of his society and family, but also drove him probably closer to death, to the desire for death, than any of his physical torments had done. In 1876, six years before this, he writes to the young Livonian Mathilde Trampedach a proposal of marriage which is no less helplessly gauche than his application, five years previously, for a chair in philosophy: "Muster all the courage of your heart, so as not to be afraid of the question I am going to ask you: Will you be my wife? I love you and feel that you already belong to me." Only with older women does he seem to have been more relaxed—sometimes with Malwida, and, during his last stays at Sils Maria, with Fräulein Mansurov and the Fynns (not documented by letters). His sister was his Xanthippe. The fight with her was long and excruciating, punctuated by reconciliations made (it would seem) on his part simply to keep Elisabeth quiet, so that he could concentrate

---

7. Friedrich Nietzsche, *Werke in drei Bänden*, 1 (Munich: Carl Hanser Verlag, 1954), 465–66 (=*Menschliches, Allzumenschliches*, vol. 1, section 25).

on the work that mattered. The selection of letters documents this conflict fairly closely. Did either of them ever understand the other? There comes in 1884 a surprising moment in a letter to Malwida (one which Elisabeth was later to suppress): "There can be no reconciliation between a vindictive anti-Semitic goose and me. Beyond that, I am showing as much forbearance as possible, because I know what can be said to excuse my sister and what is at the back of her (to me) so despicable and undignified behavior: love."

Nietzsche's letters do not tell us many of the things that we might like to know about him: what psychological motives directed his thinking, how he perceived physical objects in his world, what it was like when the storms of ideas and images attacked him, and how he observed people. He put his whole mind, all his complexity and candor, into his books. Most of his letters were signals of his presence, a singular and towering presence, but were not carefully wrought self-revelations, like Rilke's, and they were not marvels of feeling, observation, and fun, like the letters of Eduard Mörike. In making my selection, which amounts to about one-tenth of his total output, I kept two needs in mind. The first was to enable the reader to feel that he was in Nietzsche's presence. Here the snag was Nietzsche's reticence. Constantly self-concerned as he is, he seldom takes us down the darker galleries of his labyrinth, and the periods may end in cryptic dots when he is doing just that. He is the master of a kind of definitive silence. I also wanted to present this perceptible Nietzsche as transparently as possible—his gestalt, evolving and perennial. The second need was for letters which mark the stresses and turnings of his life, and which reveal something of his life's design. Among letters of biographical interest, the ones preferred were those which give an inkling of those "moods" which he cultivated from start to finish, and which shaped the transformations of his thought. When in doubt about overlappings and repetitions, I chose the letter which spoke most reflectively or with some special accent.

Nietzsche's main concerns being ideas, philosophy, history, morals, music, and literature, my problem was to assemble a representative body of complete letters, showing how and what he thought about these concerns. I omit certain letters which are striking only on account of a single vivid detail (some details, from an additional twenty-seven letters, went into the footnotes); inclusion of complete letters for the sake of single details in them would have made the book boring and diffuse. I had to draw the line somewhere. I regret depriving the reader of some details, all the same. One is even tempted to think that the demonic concentration of Nietzsche's mind makes even the most casual utterances pregnant. And even if one does not think of his mind in this way, it is good to know, for instance, that in

November, 1879, he was recommending that Overbeck read *Tom Sawyer;* that he defined, in November, 1886, the freedoms of the *philosophus radicalis* as "freedom from profession, wife, children, society, country, faith, and so on, and so on," and declared that, at the same time, he suffered acutely from these deprivations because he was "fortunately a living being, and not just an analyzing machine and an objectifying apparatus"; and that in June, 1887, he fled from a Schumann concert in Chur, exasperated by the "softening of sensibility" in this music, calling it "a sea of fizzy lemonade." Nevertheless, I believe that the selection presents a ground plan of the labyrinth. It is designed for readers whose interests are, broadly, cultural ones; and it will do more than simply whet the appetite for an understanding of Nietzsche's thought on cultural matters, in his time, under its conditions. The selection, together with the footnotes, also presents, I believe, a coherent picture of Nietzsche as a letter writer. It might be doubted, all the same, whether this is a complete picture, because a large number of his letters are dull and perfunctory, and such letters were not included, although this dullness does have something to do with the case. I realize that some letters which I found dull might seem less so to other people, especially to those who believe that he was preeminently demonic and ironic and incapable of dullness. However, I think that my restraint on this count has not been overzealous, and that any omissions here do not deprive the reader of materials essential to the gestalt.

In his letters Nietzsche is a character unknown to many people, including philosophers and historians of ideas. He is a character of whom little sign can be found in those accounts of his work which keep occurring in studies of our lethal civilization and its ideological premises. He is battling with a little old tailor over an unpaid-for pair of new trousers before going out into the rain for his first meeting with Wagner. On an April stroll, he is being invited to buy shares in a company to exploit the healthful waters at Pasugg. He is being photographed, "executed" by the "one-eyed Cyclops," "eternalized anew as a pirate, or a prominent tenor, or a boyar." He is excoriating the "miserable mysticism" of Romundt: "He keeps weirdly pondering the inception of sentience, synthetic unity of apperception—the Lord Jesus Christ preserve us!" He is prostrate in a darkened room on the outskirts of Basel, crippled by months of headache, certain of death. He is a helplessly confused, half-blind victim of steam locomotion at the Chiasso railway station. He is patrolling the streets of Nice after an earthquake and ridiculing the hotel dwellers, all terrified with the exception of "an old, very pious lady who is convinced that the good Lord is not entitled to do her any harm." He is walking in the Turin arcades, clad in his light overcoat, which is lined with blue, the owner of two pairs of laceable shoes and some immense English winter gloves. He is being served *ossobuchi* from the cuisine of his future royal cook, and then eating ice cream as the Galleria Subalpina orchestra strikes up, once again, the overture to *The Barber of Seville*. Finally, he is at his table in his cheap Turin lodging, his nose as close as ever to the page, raving as he writes to Burckhardt in his pointed, vertical, Gothic hand: "I . . . make my own tea and do my own shopping, suffer from torn boots, and thank heaven every moment for the *old* world, for which human beings have not been simple and quiet enough."

I

1861-69

*Student
Years;
Schopenhauer
and
Wagner*

I · 1861–69: *Student Years; Schopenhauer and Wagner*

1844–58

October 15, 1844: Friedrich Wilhelm Nietzsche born to Karl Ludwig Nietzsche (born 1813) and Franziska, *née* Oehler (born 1826), at Röcken in Saxony. 1846: July 10—Elisabeth Nietzsche born. 1848: birth of a brother (died 1850). 1849: death of Karl Ludwig Nietzsche. 1850: family moves to Naumburg.

1858–64

School years at Schulpforta. Friendship with Paul Deussen (1859) and with Carl von Gersdorff (1861). 1861: Gustav Krug acquaints N with piano score of Wagner's *Tristan*. From the Schulpforta medical records: "N is a robust, compact human being with a noticeably fixed look in his eyes, short-sighted and often troubled by shifting headache. His father died young, of brain-softening, and was born to elderly parents; the son was born at a time when the father was already unwell. No bad symptoms yet, but the antecedents should be taken into account."

1864 (October)–1865 (October)

Studies at Bonn University: two semesters of theology and classical philology. June, 1865: Gürzenich music festival in Cologne.

1865 (October)–1867 (October)

Studies classical philology under Friedrich Wilhelm Ritschl at Leipzig University. Late October/early November, 1865: discovers Schopenhauer in Rohn's antiquarian bookshop. December: founds Classical Society (Philologischer Verein). 1866: beginning of friendship with Erwin Rohde. Summer: discovers F. A. Lange's *Geschichte des Materialismus*. Pro-Prussian mood in Austro-Prussian war. Summer 1867: walking-tour with Rohde in the Böhmerwald (dated August, 1866, by Schlechta). Music festival—"Zukunftsmusik"—at Meiningen in Thuringia.

1867 (October)–1868

One-year military service in mounted artillery, stationed in Naumburg. Training interrupted by injury in March, 1868. Convalescence. Plans for dissertation on 'the concept of the organic since Kant'. Project for studying in Paris, with Rohde, during 1869.

3

1868 (October)–1869 (April)

Return to Leipzig. October 28: hears Wagner's *Tristan* and *Meistersinger* overtures. Meets Wagner on November 8. *De Laertii Diogenis fontibus* (I–II and III–IV). "What I am afraid of is not the terrible shape behind my chair, but its voice: also not the words, but the horribly unarticulated and inhuman tone of that shape. Yes, if only it spoke as human beings do." January, 1869: offered professorship at Basel University, where he arrives in April. The appointment includes teaching at the Pädagogium (school).

1 · *Letter to my friend, in which I recommend that he read my favorite poet*

October 19, 1861

Dear friend:

A few remarks in your last letter about Hölderlin surprised me greatly, and I feel moved to take issue with you on behalf of this my favorite poet.[1] I shall repeat to you your hard and even unjust words (perhaps you have already even changed your mind): "I do not understand at all how Hölderlin can be your favorite poet. On me, at least, these vague half-mad utterances of a disrupted, broken mind made only a sad and at times repulsive impression. Unclear talk, sometimes the ideas of a lunatic, violent outbreaks against Germany, deification of the pagan world, now naturalism, now pantheism, now polytheism, all confused—these things have set their mark on his poems, though of course in accomplished Greek meters." Accomplished Greek meters! My God! Is that all the praise you can offer? These poems (to consider their form alone) spring from the purest, most susceptible sensibility; these poems, whose naturalness and originality eclipse the art and formal skill of Platen; these poems, now moving with the most sublime rhythms of the ode, now fading into the most delicate sounds of sorrow; can you find for these poems no better word of praise than the shallow everyday "accomplished"? And indeed that is not the worst injustice. Unclear talk, sometimes the ideas of a lunatic! These contemptuous words show me, first, that you are caught up in the common inane prejudice against Hölderlin, and,

---

1. This letter appears among N's autobiographical fragments, and is fictitious. But it may well have originated in a dispute with one of his friends, Deussen or Gersdorff, at Schulpforta. N would have read Hölderlin in the two-volume edition by Christoph Schwab, 1846. Hölderlin had died in 1843, one year before N's birth.

second, that you have nothing but a vague notion of his work, insofar as you have not read either his poems or his other works. Altogether you seem to believe that he wrote only poems. So you do not know his *Empedocles* then, this most important dramatic fragment, in whose melancholy tones reverberates the future of the unhappy poet, his grave of long madness, and not as you say in unclear talk but in the purest Sophoclean language and with an inexhaustible fullness of profound ideas. Also you do not know *Hyperion*, in which the harmonious movement of his prose, the sublimity and beauty of the characters, made upon me an impression like that of the wave beat of a troubled sea. Indeed, this prose is music, soft melting sounds interrupted by painful dissonances, finally expiring in dark mysterious funeral songs. But what I have said concerns mainly the outer form only; allow me to add now a few words about the fullness of Hölderlin's ideas, which you seem to regard as confusion and obscurity. Even if your reproach does apply to a few poems of his madness, and sometimes even in the previous ones the depth of mind is wrestling with the advancing night of madness, yet by far the greatest number are altogether priceless pearls of our literature. I would only refer you to such poems as "The Homecoming," "The Fettered River," "Sunset," "The Blind Singer," and I shall even quote to you the last strophes of the "Evening Fantasy," in which the deepest melancholy and longing for tranquility are expressed.[2]

> In the evening sky a springtime comes into flower;
> Countless the roses blossom, and tranquil seems
> The golden world; O take me up there,
> Crimson clouds! and may in the high places
>
> My love and sorrow vanish in light and air!—
> Yet, as if banished by foolish prayer the magic
> Flees away. Darkness comes and lonely
> Under the sky, as ever and ever, I am.
>
> Now come, gentle slumber! Too much the heart
> Craves for, but at last, youthfulness, you fade!
> You restless one, you dreamer!
> Serene and peaceful will be my age then.

In other poems, especially in "Remembrance" and "The Journey,"[3] the poet raises us up to the purest ideal spheres, and we feel with him that this was the element where he was at home. And last, a whole series of poems is noteworthy, in which he tells the Germans bitter truths which are, unfortunately, only too firmly grounded. In *Hyperion* too, he flings sharp and cutting words

---

2. German titles: "Rückkehr in die Heimat," "Der gefesselte Strom," "Sonnenuntergang," "Der blinde Sänger," "Abendphantasie."
3. "Andenken," "Die Wanderung."

at German "barbarism." Yet this abhorrence of reality is compatible with the greatest love of his country, and this love Hölderlin did have in high degree. But he hated in Germans the mere specialist, the philistine.

In the unfinished tragedy *Empedocles*, the poet unfolds his own nature to us. Empedocles' death is a death from divine pride, from scorn of man, from being sated with the earth, and from pantheism. Whenever I have read it, the whole work has always moved me profoundly; there is a divine loftiness in this Empedocles. In Hyperion, on the other hand, though he too seems to be bathed in the transfiguring radiance, all is dissatisfaction and unfulfillment; the characters which the poet conjures up are "airy images, which resound around us, awakening nostalgia, delighting us, but also arousing unsatisfied longing." But nowhere has the longing for Greece been revealed in purer tones; nowhere, either, is the kinship of soul between Hölderlin, Schiller, and Hegel, his close friend, more plain to see.

I have been able to touch on all too little this time, but I must leave it to you, dear friend, to piece together an image of the unhappy poet from the features I have indicated. That I do not disprove the reproaches you make regarding his contradictory religious views, this you must ascribe to my knowing all too little philosophy, which demands in high degree a close consideration of that phenomenon. Perhaps you will one day take the trouble to examine this point more closely and, by illuminating it, to shed some light on the causes of his breakdown, which of course would hardly have its roots only in this.

You will certainly forgive me for using at times excessively hard words against you, in my enthusiasm; I only hope—and do regard this as the purpose of my letter—that it will move you to an understanding and to an unprejudiced evaluation of this poet, whose very name is hardly known to most of his countrymen.

Your friend,
F. W. Nietzsche

2 · *To Elisabeth Nietzsche*   Bonn, Sunday after Whitsun
                                   [June 11, 1865]

Dear Lisbeth:

After your last so graceful letter, interwoven with girlish poems, it would be unjust and ungrateful of me to make you wait any longer for a reply, especially since I have rich materials this time and am only too glad to "chew over" with you in spirit the joys I have had.

First, however, I must touch on a part of your letter in which the pastoral coloring is as pronounced as the Lama-like warmth of heart.[4] Do not worry, dear Lisbeth. If the will is as good and as determined as you say in your letter, our dear uncles will not have much trouble. As for your principle, that the truth is always on the more difficult side, I concede this to you in part. Nonetheless, it is difficult to understand that two times two does not equal four; but does that make it any the more true?

On the other hand, is it really so difficult simply to accept everything in which one has been brought up, which has gradually become deeply rooted in oneself, which holds true among relatives and among many good people, which does moreover really comfort and elevate man? Is that more difficult than to take new paths, struggling against habituation, uncertain of one's independent course, amid frequent vacillations of the heart, and even of the conscience, often comfortless, but always pursuing the eternal goal of the true, the beautiful, the good?

Is it then a matter of acquiring the view of God, world, and atonement in which one can feel most comfortable? Is it not, rather, true that for the true researcher the result of his research is of no account at all? Do we, in our investigations, search for tranquility, peace, happiness? No—only for the truth, even if it were to be frightening and ugly.

One last remaining question. If we had believed since youth that all salvation came not from Jesus but from another—say, from Mohammed—is it not certain that we would have enjoyed the same blessings? To be sure, faith alone gives blessing, not the objective which stands behind the faith. I write this to you, dear Lisbeth, only in order to counter the most usual proofs of believing people, who invoke the evidence of their inner experiences and deduce from it the infallibility of their faith. Every true faith is indeed infallible; it performs what the believing person hopes to find in it, but it does not offer the least support for the establishing of an objective truth.

Here the ways of men divide. If you want to achieve peace of mind and happiness, then have faith; if you want to be a disciple of truth, then search.

Between, there are many halfway positions. But it all depends on the principal aim.

Forgive me for this boring and not exactly fertile discussion. You will often have told yourself these things, and always better and more beautifully than I have done.

4. "Lama" was N's nickname for his sister.

On this earnest foundation I shall now build—and the building will be all the jollier. I have wonderful days to tell you about this time.

On Friday, June 2, I traveled across to Cologne for the Rhineland Music Festival.[5] On the same day the international exhibition was opened there. During these days Cologne looked like a great metropolis. An unending turmoil of languages and costumes; an awful number of pickpockets and other crooks; all hotels full, even their remotest rooms; the city most gracefully decorated with flags—that was the outer impression. As a singer I received my white and red silken breast ribbon and went to the rehearsal. Unfortunately you do not know the Gürzenich hall, but on my last holidays I gave you a fabulous idea of it by comparing it with the Naumburg stock exchange. Our choir consisted of 182 sopranos, 154 altos, 113 tenors, and 172 basses.[6] In addition, an orchestra of about 160 players, including 52 violins, 20 violas, 21 cellos, and 14 double basses. Seven of the best male and female solo singers had been brought in. The whole company was conducted by Hiller. Of the ladies, many were distinguished by their youth and beauty. For the three main concerts they all appeared in white, with blue shoulder ribbons and with natural or artificial flowers in their hair. Each held a beautiful bouquet in her hand. We gentlemen all wore evening dress with white waistcoats. On the first evening we all sat together deep into the night, and I finally fell asleep beside an old Franconian in an armchair and woke in the morning folded up just like a penknife.[7] In addition I have been suffering since my last holidays from severe rheumatism in the left arm. The next night I slept in Bonn again. The first big concert was on Sunday—*Israel in*

5. N's visit to Cologne for the music festival occurred four months after the episode, during a February visit, which he described to Paul Deussen. Thomas Mann used Deussen's account in his *Doktor Faustus*, elaborating the episode and placing it in Leipzig. Deussen wrote: "One day in February, 1865, N had traveled to Cologne by himself, had been shown the sights by a guide, and eventually asked the latter to take him to a restaurant. But the guide takes him to a house of ill repute. 'I found myself,' N told me the next day, 'suddenly surrounded by half a dozen apparitions in tinsel and gauze, who were looking at me expectantly. I stood there speechless for a while. Then I went instinctively to the piano—as the only being in that company which had a soul—and struck a few chords. They unfroze me, and I ran out of the place.' From this and everything else that I know of N, I am inclined to think that one can apply to him the words which Steinhart dictated to us in a Latin biography of Plato: *Mulierem nunquam attigit* [*He never touched a woman*]." (P. Deussen, *Erinnerungen an F. N.*, Leipzig, 1901, p. 24.) This does not square with Richard Blunck's fairly well-founded contention that N was twice treated for a syphilitic infection later the same year in Leipzig (R. Blunck, *F. N.: Kindheit und Jugend*, Munich-Basel, 1953). During this same period, N complains of severe "rheumatic pains." Cf. also note to No. 186.

6. N himself was a bass. Ferdinand Hiller (1811–85), who conducted, was the regular conductor of the City of Cologne orchestra.

7. "Franconia" was the name of the student fraternity to which N belonged at Bonn.

Egypt, by Händel. We sang with inimitable enthusiasm, the temperature standing at fifty degrees Réaumur. The Gürzenich hall was sold out for all three days. Tickets for each concert cost between two and three talers. The performance was perfect, in everyone's judgment. There were scenes which I shall never forget. When Staegemann and Julius Stockhausen, the "king of all basses," were singing their famous heroes' duet, an amazing storm of applause broke out, bravos eight times over, flourishes from the trumpets, people yelling for an encore. All three hundred ladies flung their three hundred bouquets into the singers' faces, who were quite literally veiled in a cloud of flowers. The scene was repeated when they sang the duet *da capo.*

In the evening we gentlemen from Bonn were setting off to visit the bars together, but were invited by the Cologne Men's Choral Society to dine at the Gürzenich restaurant and stayed there amid carnivalesque toasts and singing, in which the Cologne people blossom forth, amid four-part choruses and mounting enthusiasm. At three in the morning I got away with two acquaintances; and we wandered through the city, ringing doorbells, but found nowhere to sleep, even the post office did not accept us—we wanted to sleep in the delivery vans—till finally a night porter opened the Hotel du Dôme for us. We collapsed on the benches in the dining room and were asleep in two seconds. Outside, the sky was brightening. After an hour and a half the house boy came and woke us, for the room had to be cleaned. We left in a state of humorous desperation, walked across the railway station toward Deutz, had breakfast, and went in very subdued voice to the rehearsal, where I fell asleep with great enthusiasm (and obbligato trumpets and drums). I was all the more lively at the afternoon performance from six to eleven, for my favorite things were performed: Schumann's *Faust* music and the A Major Symphony of Beethoven. In the evening I was longing for somewhere to sleep, and wandered around to about thirteen hotels, where everything was full or overfull. Finally, in the fourteenth, after the owner had assured me that all rooms were full here as well, I told him cold-bloodedly that I would stay here and that he had better find me a bed. And it was done—camp beds were set up in the dining room, costing twenty groschen for the night.

On the third day the last concert took place at last, in which a number of smaller things were performed. The best moment was the performance of the symphony by Hiller, with its epigraph, "Spring Must Come." The musicians were unusually excited, for we all thought most highly of Hiller. After every movement there was immense jubilation and after the last a similar scene, only even more so. Hiller's podium was covered with wreaths and bouquets. One of the musicians placed a laurel wreath on

Hiller's head, and the orchestra played a threefold flourish. The old man covered his face and wept, which profoundly moved the ladies.

One lady I will mention especially—Mme Szarvadi of Paris, a piano soloist. Imagine a small person, still young, all fire, rather ugly, interesting, with black curly hair.

The last night, in complete lack of the *nervus rerum*, I spent again with the old Franconian, this time, moreover, on the floor, which was not very nice. In the morning I traveled back to Bonn.

"It was the true artistic life," as a lady said to me.

One returns with arrant irony to one's books, to textual criticism, and to other things.

It is definite that I shall go to Leipzig. The fight between Jahn and Ritschl is still raging.[8] Both parties threaten each other with annihilating publications. Deussen will probably go to Leipzig as well.

For the school festival (May 21) we former Schulpforta students at Bonn sent a telegram to the College of Teachers and received a very friendly reply.

Today we have a former Schulpforta students' excursion to Königswinter. Our red caps with gold braid look very good indeed.

Soon I shall be writing to dear Rudolf, who wrote me such a friendly letter. Give my warmest regards to our dear aunt and uncle.[9]

Fritz

3 · *To Carl von Gersdorff*   Naumburg, April 7, 1866[10]

Dear friend:

Sometimes there come those quiet meditative moments in which one stands above one's life with mixed feelings of joy and sadness, like those lovely summer days which spread themselves expansively and comfortably across the hills, as Emerson so excellently describes them.[11] Then nature becomes

8. Refers to the quarrel between these two eminent classical scholars over administrative and personal matters. Jahn was at Bonn, Ritschl now at Leipzig.

9. Ida and Moritz Schenkel. Rudolf was the brother of Moritz Schenkel, who was Protestant pastor at Cainsdorf, near Dresden.

10. N moved to Leipzig University in October, 1865. Gersdorff, whom he had met at Schulpforta in 1861, was also at Leipzig at this time. (Gersdorff, born the same year as N, died in 1904.)

11. N's relation to Emerson is discussed in E. Baumgarten, *Das Vorbild Emersons im Werk und Leben Ns*, Heidelberg, 1957. In this passage, N blends Emerson and Schopenhauer (e.g., "pure, contemplative, impartial eye"); he had begun to read Schopenhauer toward the end of October or in early November, 1865.

perfect, as he says, and we ourselves too; then we are set free from the spell of the ever watchful will; then we are pure, contemplative, impartial eye. In this mood, for which I long above all others, I take up my pen to answer your friendly and thoughtful letter. Our common fears have been fused into a small residue: we have seen once more how, by a few strokes of the pen, perhaps only by the whims of a few individuals, the destinies of countless people are determined, and we gladly leave it for the pious ones to thank their God for these whims.[12] It may be that this reflection will make us want to laugh when we see each other in Leipzig again.

From the most personal point of view, I had already accustomed myself to the military idea. Often I wanted to be lifted up and carried away from my monotonous work; I was greedy for the opposites, of excitement, of a tempestuous lust for life, of enthusiasm. For, however much I have exerted myself, it has become plainer to me day by day that one cannot simply pull such a work out of the hat. During the vacation I have learned—relatively—a great deal; by the end of the vacation, my Theognis has progressed by at least a semester's work. I have made several illuminating discoveries, which will come to enrich my *Quaestiones Theogn.* I am walled in by books—thanks to Corssen's uncommon kindness. I must mention also Volkmann, who has freely helped me, especially with the whole Suidas literature, in which he is the leading expert.[13] I have become so familiar with this field that I have independently enlarged it by recently finding the evidence why the *Violarium* of Endocia does not go back to Suidas but to Suidas's chief source, an epitome of Hesychius Milesius (lost, of course). For my Theognis, this is of startling significance, as I shall show you later sometime. I am also in daily expectation of a letter from Dr. Dilthey in Berlin, a student of Ritschl's, who is better informed than anyone else about Theognis. I was completely open with him, and concealed neither my findings nor my scholastic status. I hope that, back in Leipzig, I shall be able to start committing myself to paper; I have collected practically all my material. There is of course no denying that I hardly understand this trouble which I have imposed upon myself, which takes me away from myself (from Schopenhauer also—it is often the same thing), which will result in exposing myself to the judgment of people and will perhaps compel even me to put on the mask of a learnedness that I do not possess. One loses something, in any

12. Refers to the continuing quarrel between Prussia and Austria over the duchies of Holstein and Schleswig. The Austrians had been encouraging agitation for the Augustenburg faction in Holstein. Bismarck was negotiating with Italy and France, with a view to isolating Austria and provoking war to establish Prussian domination of a unified Germany.

13. Wilhelm Corssen and Dietrich Volkmann were teachers at Schulpforta who had taken a great interest in N.

case, by getting into print. Some delays and annoyances did not fail to
present themselves. The Berlin Library did not want to lend the sixteenth-
and seventeenth-century editions of Theognis. I requested a quantity of
necessary books from the Leipzig Library through Roscher.[14] But Roscher
wrote that his conscience would not allow him to pass on books which were
out in his name. Which conscience I would not dream of reproaching, but
it was inconvenient enough.

Three things are my relaxations, but infrequent ones: my Schopenhauer, Schumann's music, and then solitary walks. Yesterday a magnificent
storm was in the sky, I hurried out to a nearby hilltop, called Leusch (perhaps you can tell me what that means), found a hut up there, a man who was
slaughtering two kids, and his young son. The storm broke with immense
force, with wind and hail. I felt an incomparable elation, and I knew for certain that we can rightly understand nature only when we have to run to her,
away from our troubles and pressures. What to me were man and his un-
quiet will! What were the eternal "Thou shalt," "Thou shalt not"! How
different the lightning, the wind, the hail, free powers, without ethics! How
fortunate, how strong they are, pure will, without obscurings from the
intellect!

On the other hand, I have found examples enough to show how ob-
scured the intellect in men often is. Recently I was talking to a person who
plans to go out soon as a missionary—to India. I asked him a few questions;
he had not read any Indian books, had not heard of the Oupnek'hat,[15] and
had decided not to have anything to do with the Brahmins—because they
would be well trained in philosophy. Holy Ganges!

Today I heard an intelligent sermon by Wenkel, on Christianity, the
"faith which has overcome the world," intolerably arrogant vis-à-vis other
peoples who are not Christians, and yet very clever. He repeatedly replaced
the word "Christianity" by another, which always gave a right sense, even
for our way of thinking. If the sentence "Christianity has overcome the
world" is replaced by "The feeling of sin—briefly, a metaphysical need—
has overcome the world," and this does not offend us, one must only be con-
sistent and say, "The true Indians are Christians" as well as "The true
Christians are Indians." But at root the interchanging of such established
words and concepts is not really honest, for it utterly confuses weaker
minds. If Christianity means "Belief in an historical event or in an historical
person," then I'll have nothing to do with Christianity. But if it means

14. Wilhelm Roscher (1845–1923) was a fellow student at Leipzig, son of Wilhelm Roscher, professor of economics there.

15. This is an early translation of fifty Upanishads, into Latin, by Anquetil
Duperron (Strasbourg, 1801); translated into German in 1808.

simply the need for redemption, then I can value it highly, and do not even object to its attempt to discipline philosophers, who are too few in comparison with the mass of those needing redemption though made of the same stuff—yes, even if all those who practice philosophy were to be followers of Schopenhauer! But only too often there lurks behind the mask of the philosopher the lofty majesty of the "will," which seeks to realize its own self-glorification. If the philosophers ruled, then τὸ πλῆθος would be lost; if the mass rules, as it does now, it still behoves the philosopher, *raro in gurgite vasto*, δίχα ἄλλων, like Aeschylus, φρονέειν.[16]

At the same time it is of course extremely vexing for us to restrain our still young and strong Schopenhauerian thoughts, to leave them only half expressed, and to have always on our hearts the burden of this unhappy difference between theory and practice. I know no consolation for this; on the contrary, I need consolation. I feel that we must judge the heart of the matter more mildly. That too is something that lurks in this collision.

With this, dear friend, goodbye, my best wishes to your relatives, as mine send you theirs; and it is agreed, when we meet again, we shall smile—and rightly so.[17]

Your friend
Friedrich Nietzsche

4 · *To Franziska and Elisabeth Nietzsche*

[Leipzig, end of June, 1866]

Dear Mamma and Lisbeth:

I hope you receive a newspaper, so that you will have eagerly followed the decisive events of the past weeks.[18] The dangers which surround Prussia are extremely great; it is quite impossible for its program to be realized through

---

16. τὸ πλῆθος, "mass of the people." The Latin quotation is from Vergil, *Aen.* I. 118: "Apparent rari nantes in gurgite vasto" ("Only a few swimmers appear in the vast ocean"); the Greek is adapted from Aeschylus, *Agamemnon*, 757 f.: δίχα δ' ἄλλων μονόφρων εἰμί ("Separate from others, I think my own thoughts").

17. An allusion to *Julius Caesar*, Act V, sc. 1 (just before the Battle of Philippi)· Brutus: "If we do meet again, why, we shall smile! / If not, why then, this parting was well made." To which Cassius replies: ". . . If we do meet again, we'll smile indeed. . . ."

18. Refers to the war between Prussia and Austria. Prussian troops occupied Holstein on June 7; Austria succeeded in mobilizing many German states, including Saxony, against Prussia but was no match for Bismarck's military tactics. Prussia overran all obstacles and defeated Austria decisively at Königsgrätz in Bohemia on July 3.

a complete victory. To found the unified German state in this revolutionary way is an audacity on Bismarck's part; courage and ruthless consistency he has, but he underestimates the moral forces among the people. Nonetheless, the latest moves are excellent; above all, he has known how to place a large, if not the largest, part of the guilt on Austria.

Our situation is quite simple. When a house is on fire, one does not ask first whose fault it is; one puts it out. Prussia is on fire. It is now a matter of saving what one can. That is the general feeling.

The moment the war began, all secondary considerations receded. I am just as much an enraged Prussian as, for example, my cousin is an enraged Saxon. But for all of Saxony it is an especially difficult time. Their country entirely in enemy hands. Their army docile and inactive. Their king far away from his people. Another king and a prince have simply been finished off. That is the latest declaration of the princedom "by God's grace." It makes it understandable that old Gerlach with a few Westfalian bumpkins should curse about the union between crowned (Victor Eman [-uel]) and uncrowned democracy.[19]

Ultimately the Prussian way of getting rid of princes is the easiest in the world. It is a great piece of luck that Hanover and Kurhessen did not join with Prussia, or we would never have got rid of these fellows. So we are living in the Prussian city of Leipzig. Today a state of war was declared throughout Saxony. Gradually it comes to be like living on an island, for telegraphic and postal communications and the railways are constantly upset. Communication with Naumburg, as with anywhere in Prussia, is of course normal. But it is hardly possible to send a letter, for example, to Deussen in Tübingen.

All the same, lectures continue. When I returned recently from Naumburg, a letter from Ritschl was waiting, in which he told me that the collation from Rome has arrived. The Paris one arrives at the end of this week.

Yet I am always conscious that the day is close on which I shall be drafted. Moreover, it is now dishonorable to sit at home while the fatherland is beginning a life-and-death struggle.

Go sometime to the *Landamt* and ask for exact information as to

19. Ernst Ludwig von Gerlach was a member of the Prussian parliament and a strong opponent of Bismarck. The king who was far away was the Saxon Johann, who had fled to Bohemia. King Georg V, Hanover, had been forced to abdicate after the Prussian annexation of Hanover (Battle of Langensalza, June 27). The deposed prince was Friedrich-Wilhelm I, Kurfürst of Hessen. "Crowned democracy" is a reference to Bismarck's commercial treaty with Italy (November, 1865).

when the one-year volunteers are to be drafted, and let me know the details soon.

The most enjoyable thing that Leipzig offers is Hedwig Raabe, who continues to play to a full house at a time when, for example, receipts at the Dresden theater are only six talers a day.

Goodbye for now and send me the laundry and news soon. Greetings to you both.

F. W. N.

Continuation

Since the letter was not sent, you'll hardly be enraged to have an addition to it. I have been ill for three days, but am better again today. The heat must have done me no good. But that does not matter. The important thing is that our soldiers have won their first biggish victory. The day before yesterday, in the evening, it was announced by our city commandant, who at once had a huge black-and-white flag hoisted over his hotel. The mood of the people is very divided. They believe the miserable Viennese lies, which say that these last encounters have meant equal losses for the Prussians, they talk of 15,000 Prussian prisoners being taken. What nonsense. In Vienna, of course, all telegrams are falsified and switched around, so as to encourage the masses.

Incidentally, I am delighted at the brilliant collapse ($\pi\alpha\pi\pi\alpha\xi$) of the Naumburg-Zeitz conservatives at the last election. We want no egoists in the House, who, in order to promote their own interests, act nicely, talk meaninglessly, wag their servile tails, and explode with obsequiousness like puffballs. And they made a great stink.

I received your letter, with Gersdorff's, and can relieve you of fears. As if you were any safer than I am in Leipzig! I am staying here now and really would not like during this time to be in a sleepy newspaperless hole with its *Kreuzzeitung* exhalations all around.[20]

I am really worried on account of Gersdorff's elder brother. The Ziethen hussars were the first to be involved in the fighting, and it is said that they suffered heavy losses. Our Gersdorff is hoping to become an officer in three months at the least, unless silly cadets get preferred to him.

So, keep well; when Lama celebrates her birthday, I hope to come to Naumburg. But please write first about the draft question.

20. The *Kreuzzeitung* was the *Neue Preussische Zeitung*, which had been founded by Gerlach.

5.   *To Carl von Gersdorff*   [Naumburg, end of August, 1866]

Dear friend:

"No letter in the mail for me" is what you will often have been wondering. But there is one from me; only it is still in the awful mail and has not been delivered yet. "Be still, my heart!"

The longer the time has been in which you have heard nothing from me and the more ungrateful I must be seeming for not answering with a single line your penultimate letter, which was as affectionate as it was richly thoughtful—all because the Nürnberg field post swallowed my letter up without ever disgorging it—so much the more do I feel the need to make reparation for the fault of the mail and to disburden myself of the apparently quite justified reproach of ingratitude. It is very bitter for me to know that you are on active service, chagrined by the failure of plans, by an environment which has few comforts, by mind-killing activities, and, on top of it all, by the negligence of a friend. For it cannot seem otherwise to you. Enough that I blush, as one often blushes, without feeling conscious of guilt, at the thought of sinking lower for some reason in the estimation of others, especially of others who are dear to one.

Unfortunately I can tell you only little, trivial things about my experiences. My work is finished, and Ritschl has it; I completed it in three parts, and stayed in Leipzig until the finishing touch—my signature—had been put to it. I have never written anything so reluctantly; in the end I reeled off the material in the most monotonous way; yet Ritschl was well satisfied with the one part he has read. It will probably be published in October. Ritschl wants to read the work carefully; Wilhelm Dindorf also has asked permission to do so. I shall probably negotiate with the latter. He asked me, through Ritschl, if I would like to work on an Aeschylus lexicon, from the standpoint of the latest Aeschylus criticism. Naturally for a good fee. I have been thinking that I can learn much from this, that I could become closely familiar with Aeschylus, that I would have in my hands the Dindorf collation of the Codex Mediceus (the only one which German scholars consider complete), that I would be comfortably able—would even need—to prepare one play, perhaps the *Choephorae*, for a future lecture. And after all these considerations, I accepted the project. Only I must first prove my competence by working out a test passage during this vacation. Actually such a work is not uninteresting in the case of Aeschylus; one is compelled to exercise continuous stringent criticism vis-à-vis the mass of conjectures. Dindorf estimated a book of at least sixty sheets. After the holidays I shall start financial negotiations with Teubner—if I am taken on. Ritschl is becoming more and more friendly toward me.

Consequently I shall stay next semester too in Leipzig, where, all things considered, I am extremely comfortable. Would it be possible for you to continue your military service in Leipzig? I would be very happy if you could, because I especially miss you. I do have many acquaintances now, but nobody with whom I have so many past and present things in common. Perhaps I can persuade old Deussen also to come to Leipzig; he wrote recently that he now quite understands that he has done a foolish thing. "Better late than never" is his realization as to what theological studies mean. He wants to leave Tübingen, it is no matter to him which university he chooses, because he has no hope of finding much anywhere for his theology, a yoke he means to bear to the end (not the end of the world, but as far as the first examination). Perhaps he could still now be "converted." Classical philology would be delighted if the long-lost son, who has feasted on the husks of theology, should return, and especially comparative philology would kill the fatted calf for him.

Our Classical Society is flourishing: it was recently photographed, and honored Ritschl with a picture, to his great joy. Rohde is now a full member, a very clever but obstinate and self-willed mind. When new members are to be admitted, I try to insure that the greatest strictness is exercised in the choice. Herr von Voigt did not have the honor to be admitted.

The last few weeks in Leipzig were very interesting. The Riedel Society gave a concert for the war-wounded in the Nicolaikirche. All the church doors were as crowded as at the theater when Hedwig Raabe is playing. We took in more than a thousand talers. Half an hour before the concert began, the telegram with the text of the royal speech arrived; no other act of the king has delighted me more than this uncompromising, unambiguous speech. The old party positions—that is, the extremist standpoints—are now in complete disarray. Men like Treitschke and Roggenbach have suddenly become representatives of public opinion. A large part of the so-called conservatives—for example Pinder in Naumburg—is swimming gaily in the new current. For me it is also—frankly—a rare and quite new joy to feel for once entirely at one with the existing government. Of course one must leave various dead to their dead; moreover, one must be clear that Bismarck's game was a most audacious one, that a policy which dares to call *va banque* can be just as much cursed as worshiped, according to how well it succeeds. But the success is there this time; what has been attained is grandiose. I try, for a moment now and then, to stand aside from the consciousness of the time, from the subjectively natural sympathies for Prussia, and then I see a great puppet play, of the kind of stuff which, after all, does constitute history

—certainly not moral stuff, but fairly beautiful and edifying for the beholder.

You will have read, I expect, Treitschke's work on the future of the central states. I acquired it with great difficulty in Leipzig, where it was prohibited, as everywhere in Saxony—*proh pudor*. On the other side, people who think as we do—the Freitags, Biedermanns, and so on—have obtained a vote of the Saxon national-liberal party demanding unconditional annexation.[21] This would also serve my own personal interests best. I hope King Johann is pigheaded enough to force Prussia into annexing Saxony.

Finally, Schopenhauer must be mentioned, for whom I still have every sympathy. What we possess in him was recently made quite clear to me by another work, which is excellent of its kind and very instructive: F. A. Lange's *History of Materialism and Critique of Its Meaning in the Present* (1866). Here we have an extremely enlightened Kantian and natural scientist. His conclusions are summed up in the following three propositions.

1. The world of the senses is the product of our organization.

2. Our visible (physical) organs are, like all other parts of the phenomenal world, only images of an unknown object.

3. Our real organization is therefore as much unknown to us as real external things are. We continually have before us nothing but the product of both.

Thus the true essence of things—the thing-in-itself—is not only unknown to us; the concept of it is neither more nor less than the final product of an antithesis which is determined by our organization, an antithesis of which we do not know whether it has any meaning outside our experience or not. Consequently, Lange thinks, one should give the philosophers a free hand as long as they edify us in this sense. Art is free, also in the domain of concepts. Who would refute a phrase by Beethoven, and who would find error in Raphael's *Madonna*?

You see, even with this strictly critical standpoint our Schopenhauer stands firm; he becomes even almost more important to us. If philosophy is art, then even Haym should submit himself to Schopenhauer; if philosophy should edify, I know no more edifying philosopher than our Schopenhauer.[22]

With that, goodbye for today, dear friend. Think whether or not you can come to Leipzig. But in any case, let me know when and where we can meet. For I am all too eager to see you again, which I could not do in Leipzig

21. Freitag was editor of *Der Grenzbote;* Biedermann, editor of the *Deutsche Allgemeine Zeitung.* Both were opponents of Bismarck.

22. Rudolf Haym (1821–1901), the literary historian, was the author of epoch-making books on Herder and on the German romantics.

since you left the area again so soon. Yet I have heard your regiment's music, somewhat unclassical and a great deal of the African about it.

I have not been to Pforta yet. Volkmann is happily married. I will loyally convey your greetings. My relatives send you their best wishes and assure you of their sympathy. Adieu, dear friend.

Your F. W. Nietzsche

6 · *To Carl von Gersdorff*   Leipzig, Wednesday
[January 16, 1867]

My dear friend:

It was also in the first days of January that I stood in Naumburg beside a deathbed, that of a close relative who, next to my mother and sister, had the most claim to my love and esteem, who had faithfully taken an interest in my life, and with whom a great part of my past and especially my childhood has passed away.[23] And yet, when I received your letter, dear, poor, afflicted friend, a much stronger grief took hold of me: the two deaths are indeed so different. In the one case, a life had been completed, used up in good works, carried through into old age with a frail body: we all felt that the powers of body and mind had been consumed and that death came too soon only for our love. But what departed from us with your brother, whom I too always admired and esteemed?

What left us was one of those rare, noble, Roman natures, of which Rome in her best times would have been proud, of whom you as a brother have much more right to be proud. For how seldom does our pitiable time produce such heroic figures! But you know of course how the ancients think of these things: "Whom the gods love, die young."

What might such a power have done? What strength and comfort might it not have been for thousands in the midst of life's confusion, as a model of authentic, praiseworthy aspiration, as an example of resolute character, lucid, unconcerned with the world and its opinions. Well do I know that this *vir bonus* in the most beautiful sense was more to you, that he was the ideal, as you often told me, for which you strive, your trusted lodestar in the changing and by no means comfortable ways of life. Perhaps this death was the greatest pain that you could ever suffer.

23. N's aunt Rosalie had recently died. Gersdorff's brother Ernst (b. 1840) also died in January.

Now, dear friend, you have experienced at first hand—I notice this from the tone of your letter—why our Schopenhauer exalts suffering and sorrows as a glorious fate, as the δεύτερος πλοῦς to the negation of the will. You have experienced and felt also the purifying, inwardly tranquilizing and strengthening power of grief. This is a time in which you can test for yourself what truth there is in Schopenhauer's doctrine. If the fourth book of his chief work makes on you now an ugly, dark, burdensome impression, if it does *not* have the power to raise you up and lead you through and beyond the outward violent grief, to that sad but happy mood which takes hold of us too when we hear noble music, to that mood in which one sees the earthly veils pull away from oneself—then I too want to have nothing more to do with this philosophy. He alone who is himself filled with grief can decide on such things: we others in the midst of the stream of things and of life, merely longing for that negation of the will as an isle of the blessed, cannot judge whether the solace of such philosophy is enough also for times of deep mourning.

I find it difficult to pass on to other things, for I do not know if, in your mood, you will not find accounts of my life and doings tiresome. Yet you will like to hear that Einsiedel and I, since we share this sorrow, have often come together and are wondering how we can do something to bring you a little joy and refreshment.[24] In Einsiedel you have an altogether sympathetic friend; just now I read him your beautiful, long, and heartfelt letter. We both want nothing more than to see you and speak with you again.

I am well. There is much work to be done, but it is rewarding and therefore pleasing. I value more and more, as the days pass, continuous concentrated work. At the moment I am testing my capacities on a university prize-essay subject: *De fontibus Diogenis Laertii*; it is gratifying to feel that I did not come to this theme through the lure of honor and money but set it for myself. Ritschl knew this and was kind enough to suggest it, later on, as a prize-essay subject. I have a few challengers, if I am rightly informed; yet I have no little self-confidence in this matter, because until now I have had nothing but good results. At bottom it is only a question of advancing knowledge: if someone else has made even more discoveries, this will not hurt my feelings much.

I heard from Deussen at the New Year. He is once more a classical philologist—bravo!—and feels, as he himself says, the firm ground under his feet again. He is studying in Bonn, and seems gradually to be getting into his stride. He sent me his translation of a French book, *Theodore Parker's Biography*, which has earned him some money.

24. Graf Haubold Einsiedel-Milkel was a student friend of N's in Leipzig; he died in 1868.

Finally, dear friend, I ask you one thing of you: do not burden yourself with writing letters. Soon I shall write again, a good long letter, which it is impossible for me to write today. Einsiedel asks me to tell you the same. I end with a warm farewell and a saying from Aristotle:

τί γάρ ἐστιν ἄνθρωπος; ἀσθηνείας ὑπόδειγμα,
καιροῦ λάφυρον, τύχης παίγνιον, μεταπτώσεως
εἰκών, φθόνου καὶ συμφορᾶς πλάστιγξ.[25]

Your loyal friend who shares your grief

Friedrich Nietzsche

7. *To Carl von Gersdorff*   Naumburg, April 6 [1867]

My dear friend:

Why I have been silent for so long, God alone knows. For nothing makes me feel more grateful and happy than the arrival of letters from you, telling me truly your experiences and moods. There is very often a chance to speak of you, and I never let the chance go by. Even more often my thoughts run to you just when I am surrounded by books and should be thinking all kinds of learned things, which you would rightly find somewhat tasteless. And yet I still do not write. Sometimes it makes me wonder at myself. It has just occurred to me why this may be. The hand which writes all day, the eye which sees all day white paper turning black, asks for a change or a rest. But today Suidas and Laertius had to wait the whole afternoon, because I had a visitor; therefore they will have to wait this evening too. Why do they give away their authority over me? If the disadvantage is now theirs, I at least have the advantage—I can converse with my friend in a letter and do not need to supervise the two old boys, whose follies usually keep me occupied.

This vacation I want to get my work on the Laertius sources down on paper; at the moment I am still pretty much in the early stages. For your amusement I will confess what has given me the most trouble and worry: my German style (not to mention Latin; once I have come to grips with the mother tongue, foreign languages will be next in turn). The scales are falling from my eyes: I lived all too long in a state of stylistic innocence. The cate-

---

25. *Aristoteles Pseudepigraphus*, Leipzig, 1863, p. 610 (ed. Valentin Rose). The attribution to Aristotle is doubtful. The passage means: "What is man? Exemplum of weakness, booty of the moment, plaything of fortune, image of mutability, balance weighing the gods' displeasure and disaster."

gorical imperative, "Thou shalt and must write," has aroused me. I tried something that I had never tried except at school: to write well, and suddenly the pen froze in my hand. I could not do it, and was annoyed. And all the while Lessing's and Lichtenberg's and Schopenhauer's stylistic precepts were buzzing in my ears. It was always my solace that these three authorities unanimously agree that it is difficult to write well, that no man has a good style by nature, that one must work at the uphill job of acquiring one. I honestly do not want to write again so woodenly and drily, in such a logical corset, as I did, for example, in my Theognis essay, at whose cradle no Graces sat (rather there was a distant thundering, as if from Königsgrätz). It would be a very sad state of affairs not to be able to write better and yet warmly to want to do so. Above all, a few gay spirits in my own style must once more be unchained; I must learn to play on them as on a keyboard, but not only pieces I have learned by heart—no—but also free fantasias, as free as possible, yet still always logical and beautiful.

Second, another wish disquieted me. One of my oldest friends, Wilhelm Pinder of Naumburg, is on the verge of his first law examination; we too know the well-known fears of such times. But what appeals to me, and what goads me to imitation, is not the examination but the preparation for it. How useful, how elevating even, it must be in roughly one semester to have all the disciplines of one's field of knowledge march past one and thus for once really to have a total view of them! Is it not as when an officer, always accustomed only to drilling his company, suddenly has in battle a definite idea of what great fruits his small efforts can produce? For we would not deny that most philologists lack that elevating total view of antiquity, because they stand too close to the picture and investigate a patch of paint, instead of gazing at the big, bold brushstrokes of the whole painting and—what is more—enjoying them. When, I ask, do we ever have that pure enjoyment of our studies in antiquity, of which we unfortunately speak often enough?

Third, our whole way of working is quite horrible. The hundred books on the table in front of me are so many tongs which pinch out the nerve of independent thought. I believe, dear friend, that you have chosen, with a daring grasp, the best lot of all.[26] That is, an effective contrast, a turned-about way of looking, an opposite attitude to life, to human beings, to work, to duty. This does not honestly mean that I applaud your present profession as such, but only insofar as it is the negation of your previous life, aspiration, thought. With such contrasts, soul and body stay healthy and do not bring forth those necessary diseases which the preponderance of scholar-

26. Gersdorff had received his commission in the Prussian army in the latter part of 1866.

ly activity produces and the excessive predominance of physical ones no less, and from which the scholar suffers just as much as the country bumpkin. Except that these diseases have other symptoms in the former than in the latter. The Greeks were no scholars, but they were also not mindless athletes. Must we then so necessarily choose one side or the other? Has perhaps Christianity here produced in human nature a split, of which the people of harmony knew nothing? Should not the image of a Sophocles put to shame the scholar who could dance so elegantly and knock a ball about and yet still showed some intellectual accomplishment?

But it is for us in such matters as it is in life as a whole: we recognize that things are in a bad state, yet still do not lift a finger to change things. And here I could really begin a fourth Lamento, which I will restrain, in the presence of my military friend. For such complaints must be even more offensive to a warrior than to a stay-at-home such as I now am.

This reminds me of a story I recently heard, which is an illustration, to be sure, of the scholarly forms of disease, and should not be bruited about, but which might amuse you, because it seems to translate into real life Schopenhauer's essay "On the Professors of Philosophy."

There is a city, in which a young man, with exceptional powers of thought, and especially competent in philosophical speculation, conceives a plan to acquire a doctorate. To this end he puts together his system, "On the Basic Patterns of Representation," which he has been laboriously working out for years and is happy and proud to have done so. With feelings such as these, he submits it to the philosophical faculty of the place, in which there happens to be a university. Two professors of philosophy put in their reports: one says the work shows intelligence but advances views which are not taught here; the other declares that the assertions do not concur with common sense and are paradoxical. Therewith the work is rejected, and the candidate does not get his doctoral hat. Fortunately the injured party is not humble enough to hear the voice of wisdom in this judgment; he is even reckless enough to maintain that a certain philosophical faculty lacks the faculty for philosophy.

In brief, my friend, one cannot go one's own way independently enough. Truth seldom dwells where people have built temples for it and have ordained priests. We ourselves have to suffer for the good or foolish things we do, not those who give us the good or the foolish advice. Let us at least be allowed the pleasure of committing follies on our own initiative. There is no general recipe for how each man is to be helped. One must be one's own physician but at the same time gather the medical experiences at one's own cost. We really think too little about our own well-being; our egoism is not clever enough, our intellect not egoistic enough.

With that, dear friend, enough for today. Unfortunately I have nothing "solid" or "real" to tell you, or whatever the current slogans of the shopkeepers are, but you will not be asking for such things. It goes without saying that I rejoice with you when you discover someone who thinks as we do and who is, moreover, such a competent and lovable person as Krüger.[27] Our freemasonry is increasing and expanding, though without badges, mysteries, and denominations.

It is late at night, and the wind is howling outside. You know that I shall be staying in Leipzig next summer too. My wishes carry me, the philologist, to the Imperial Library in Paris, to which I shall go perhaps next year if the volcano has not erupted by then. My thoughts, though, carry me, the human being, often enough and thus tonight to you, whom I now warmly wish goodnight.

Friedrich Nietzsche
in loyal friendship

Naumburg, April 6: which place I shall leave on April 30. My new Leipzig address: Weststrasse 59, 2d floor.

8 · *To Erwin Rohde*[28]   Naumburg, November 3, 1867[29]

My dear friend:

Yesterday I received a letter from our Wilhelm Roscher in Leipzig, with news which should, with your permission, form the opening of this letter. First, the glad announcement that Father Ritschl's health and serenity are in an excellent state, which does surprise me, because the behavior of the Berlin people has opened a few of his wounds.[30] Then also the Classical Society, which has adopted a solemn official stamp, seems to be advancing into a fine future. The reading circle has twenty-eight members: Roscher intends to make Zaspel's café into a sort of philological stock exchange. A cupboard has been bought, in which the periodicals are kept. Friday meetings probably have not yet taken place; at least, Wilhelm says nothing about them. Also various members have not yet arrived, for example Koch who

27. Paul Krüger was a jurist and former Schulpforta student.

28. The friendship between Rohde and N had begun in Leipzig, and lasted for many years. Rohde is best known for his book *Psyche*, a pioneering study of Greek literature, religion, and mythology (1894).

29. N had been drafted into a mounted artillery regiment in October, 1867.

30. The Berlin Academy of Sciences had refused to elect Ritschl a member.

is unfortunately prevented by serious illness. Likewise the excellent Kohl, who, curious to relate, wants to spend several weeks with a friend in the country, and so has pushed away somewhat the hazardous scenery of the examination. Finally, I will not conceal from you that Roscher's letter brought me the pleasant news that my Laertius work on October 31 in the aula won a victory in competition with Herr Outis [Mr. Nobody]; which I tell you above all because I remember your friendly efforts which helped to launch the said *opusculum*. It may be a long time before something of this gets into print: I have withdrawn all previous plans, and retained only one, to deal with this field in a larger framework together with friend Volkmann. But since we both have much else to do, our pretty fables about the learnedness of Laertius and Suidas may continue to enjoy life for a while yet. The only person who must be told somewhat more quickly about the probable state of affairs is Curt Wachsmuth, who wishes to hear about it in person and by word of mouth, and who will do so, now that I have met him in Halle at the meeting of the Philological Association. He really has a touch of the artist, above all a powerful, banditlike ugliness, which he carries with panache and pride.[31]

Those days in Halle are for me the merry finale, or let us say the coda, of my philological overture. Such troops of teachers make a better showing than I would ever have thought. Perhaps the old spiders were staying in their webs: briefly, people were well and fashionably dressed and mustaches are very popular. True, old Bernhardy presided as badly as he could have done, and Bergk was boring, with an unintelligible three-hour lecture. But most things were well done, above all, the dinner (at which someone stole old Steinhart's gold watch—that will give you an idea of the mood which prevailed) and an evening meeting in the Schützengraben. Here I also met Magister Sauppe of Göttingen, with that clever look of his; he interests me, as protagonist of the Naumburg philologists. His lecture on some new Attic inscriptions was the most piquant thing we heard; that is, if I except Tischendorf's talk on paleography, which let go with the whole works, that is, with the Homer girl, the Simonides forgeries, the Menander and Euripides fragments, and so on; also he acted generously as a go-between and finally announced his paleographic opus, with naïve details of the price—value approximately five thousand talers.[32] The meeting was extraordinarily well attended, and there were plenty of acquaintances. At the dinner we formed a Leipzig corner, consisting of Windisch, Angermann, Clemm, Fleischer, and so forth. I was very glad to find in Clemm an especially friendly person, whereas I had hardly met him in Leipzig and, be-

31. Curt Wachsmuth (1837–1905) was a classical scholar and Ritschl's son-in-law.

32. Volumes 5 and 6 of *Monumenta sacra inedita* appeared in Leipzig in 1869–70.

cause of my accursed Bonn habits, had even felt an aversion to him and used to look at him askance in the way that a fraternity brother pleases to size up the "gentlemen of the choir." Naturally he heartily agreed to participate in the Leipzig "symbolic lectures."[33] Only he found the date fixed was too early, and I am almost inclined to concur in his judgment. Every day—even every hour—in Halle we were waiting for the arrival of Father Ritschl, who had announced his coming and unfortunately had to comply with the bad weather. We were hungering for his presence, I especially, who owe him so many debts of gratitude. It is due to his mediation that I now possess a complete series of the *Rheinisches Museum*, without doing anything about it myself, with a certain prospect too of being able to do nothing with that index for a long time.[34] I did not waste the first few weeks after our journey on this drudgery, but put together my *Democritea* in the merriest way; they are intended *in honorem Ritscheli*.[35] So at least the main thing is done; although on a carefully reasoned grounding of my follies and on a robust combining of all the elements, only too much remains to be done, much too much for a man who "is heavily occupied elsewhere."

Now, you will ask, if he does not smoke and gamble, if he is not manufacturing an index and not piecing Democritea together, and is disrespectful to *Laertius et Suidas*, what then is he doing?

He is doing military training.

Yes, my dear friend, if some *daimon* were ever to lead you early one morning between, let us say, five and six o'clock to Naumburg and were to have the kindness to intend guiding your steps into my vicinity, then do not stop in your tracks and stare at the spectacle which offers itself to your senses. Suddenly you breathe the atmosphere of the stable. In the lanterns' half-light, figures loom up. Around you there are sounds of scraping, whinnying, brushing, knocking. And in the midst of it all, in the garb of a groom, making violent attempts to carry away in his bare hands something unspeakable, unsightly, or to belabor the horse with a comb—I shudder when I see his face—it is, by the Dog, none other than myself.[36] A few hours

33. Original: "symbolis" (refers to papers read to the Classical Society). I take this to be a play on terms from Freemasonry, where *symbolum* is a symbolic lecture or discourse on the symbols of the order, as contrasted with a "historical lecture," which deals with the external vicissitudes of the same.

34. *Rheinisches Museum* was a long-established journal of classical studies; N had undertaken to write the index for volumes 1–24 of the new series. The index appeared in 1871.

35. N's work on the Democritus fragments, parts of which are extant, was intended for a Ritschl *Festschrift*, containing essays by nine members of the Classical Society, which never appeared.

36. N was doing his artillery training in Naumburg. The original here is adapted from Heine's poem "Der Doppelgänger": "Mir graut es wenn ich sein Antlitz sehe, / Der Mond zeigt mir meine eigne Gestalt." This scene reminds one of the beginning of Kafka's

later you see two horses racing around the paddock, not without riders, of whom one is very like your friend. He is riding his fiery, zestful Balduin,[37] and hopes to be able to ride well one day, although, or rather because, now he still rides on the blanket, with spurs and thighs, but without a whip. Also he had to forget in a hurry everything he had heard at the Leipzig paddock and, above all, to acquire, with great effort, a safe and statutory seat.

At other times of the day he stands, industrious and attentive, by the horse-drawn cannons and pulls shells out of the limber or cleans the bore with the cloth or takes aim according to inches and degrees, and so on. But most of all he has a lot to learn.

I assure you, by the aforementioned Dog, my philosophy now has the chance to be of practical use to me. Until now I have not felt a moment's depression, but have very often smiled as at something fairytale-like. Sometimes hidden under the horse's belly I murmur, "Schopenhauer, help!"; and if I come home exhausted and covered with sweat, then a glance at the picture on my desk soothes me;[38] or I open the *Parerga*,[39] which, with Byron, I find more congenial than ever before.

Now at last the point has been reached at which I can say the things with which you would have expected the letter to begin. My dear friend, you now know why my letter has been so unduly slow in reaching you. I have, in the strictest sense, had no time. But also I have often not been in the right mood. One does not write letters to friends whom one loves, as I love you, in any mood. Just as little does one write, in stolen moments, one line today and another tomorrow, but one longs for a full and expansive hour and mood. Today the friendliest of autumn days is looking through the window. Today I have the afternoon free at least until six-thirty, which time summons me to the stables for the evening fodder and drink. Today I am celebrating Sunday in my way, by remembering my distant friend and our common past in Leipzig and in the Bohemian woods and in Nirvana. Fate has with a sudden wrench torn the Leipzig page out of my life, and what I see next in this sibylline book is covered from top to bottom with an inkblot. Then was a life of free self-determination, in the epicurean pleasure of knowledge and the arts, among people with aspirations like one's own, close to a lovable teacher and—greatest of all that remains for me to say of those Leipzig days—in the constant company of a friend who is not only a comrade in

---

"Ein Landarzt" (see also the remark in No. 7, about being one's own physician). Cf. the remark in No. 188, about music as "nourishment," a motif in Kafka's *Die Verwandlung* and *Untersuchungen eines Hundes*. Kafka's interest in N around 1901–3 is authenticated in K. Wagenbach, *F. K.*, Hamburg: Rowohlt, 1964, p. 40.

37. The name of N's horse.

38. Rohde had given N a picture of Schopenhauer.

39. Miscellaneous writings of Schopenhauer.

studies or linked to me by common experiences, but who takes life seriously to a degree which equals that of my own mind as to the matter, whose estimation of things and people obeys approximately the same laws as my own, whose whole being, finally, has on me a strengthening and steeling influence. So now I miss nothing more than just that company; and I venture even to believe that, if we were condemned to pull under this yoke together, we would carry our burden serenely and with dignity, whereas at the moment I am only thrown back on the solace of remembering. At first I was almost surprised not to find that you were sharing the same fate with me; and sometimes, when out riding I look round for the other volunteers—it is as if I saw you sitting on horseback.

I am fairly lonely in Naumburg; I have neither a philologist nor a friend of Schopenhauer among my acquaintances; and even these are seldom together with me, because my duties claim much of my time. Thus I often need to chew over the past and to make the present digestible by adding that spice to it. When this morning I walked through the black, cold, wet darkness, and the wind blew restlessly round the dark masses of the houses, I sang to myself "Ein Biedermann muss lustig, guter Dinge sein"[40] and thought of our crazy farewell party, of Kleinpaul hopping about—whose existence at the moment is unknown in Naumburg and Leipzig but is therefore not in doubt—of Koch's Dionysian face, of our memorial on the banks of that Leipzig river, which we christened Nirvana, and which bears the solemn words from me, which I have proved victorious: γένοι' οἷος ἐσσί.[41]

If, finally, I apply these words to you, dear friend, let them contain the best that my heart feels for you. Who knows when changeful fate will bring our paths together again: may it be very soon; but whenever it may happen, I shall look back with joy and pride to a time when I gained a friend οἷος ἐσσί.

Friedrich Nietzsche

Artillery private in the 21st battalion of the mounted artillery section of the 4th Field Artillery Regiment.

N.B. The letter has been delayed a few days because I wanted to send you a box of grapes to follow it; the miserable post office finally declared they would not accept the same, because on arrival the grapes would be nothing but juice.

Ignoscas.

40. Quotation from Offenbach's opera *Die schöne Helena*, act 3: "A man of honor must be merry and bright."

41. Quotation from Pindar, *Pythian Odes* 2, 73: "Become the being you are."

9 · *To Carl von Gersdorff*   Naumburg [November 24 and]
                                December 1, 1867

My dear friend:

Curious, one sees to letters about business matters and to people one cares less about far more punctually than to letters to one's intimate friends. How many lines have I written this summer, each with the awareness that there is somebody else who has been waiting a long time and *suo jure* for a long letter from me? How many fragments of letters are lying among my papers, a few comprising whole sides, others only a heading? But nothing was completed, because the quantity of work and events crossed out the unfinished page again, and I did not feel like describing for you obsolete things and moods. Let me now run quickly over that summer, so that I can dwell on the present, a present into which you will feel your way, because you have had experiences similar to my present ones.

This summer, the last I spent in Leipzig—that is, my second one there—I had a great deal to do. You know that I was working on the prize-essay subject, *De fontibus Laertii Diogenis*. It worked out as I wished: with a mass of nice results, in part important ones—important, that is, by our standards—and finally came the hoped-for decision of the faculty. May I show you a few lines from Ritschl's *iudicium*, about which I am very glad, because they encourage me and drive me forward on a path which I am tempted, out of skepticism, to leave. It runs as follows, preceded by my name and my epigraph (γένοι' οἷος ἐσσί): "ita rem egit ut Ordinis expectationi non tantum satis fecerit, verum eam superaverit. Tanta enim in hac commentatione cum doctrinae e fontibus haustae copia tum sani maturique iudicii subtilitas enitet, coniuncta ea cum probabili et disserendi perspecuitate et dicendi genuina simplicitate, ut non modo insigniore laude scriptoris indoles et industria aligna videantur, sed plurimum emolumenti in ipsas litteras, philosophorum potissimum Graecorum historiam et plenius et rectius cognoscendam, ex illius opera redundare existimandum sit"—which judgment was announced to a tightly packed aula.[42] Unfortunately, I could not be there; which grieved me all the more because the Classical Society was to arrange for me, its founder and former president, a symposium at Simmer's, to which Father Ritschl had promised to come. That work occupied me until early in August; as soon as I was free of it, I fled with friend Rohde to the Bohemian woods, to bathe my tired soul in nature,

42. This was Ritschl's own judgment, and differed from the official one slightly. Ritschl's praise of N's scholarship and insight was more high-flown than the measured, but still encomiastic, tone of the official one by Reinhold Klotz.

mountain, and forest. Here I must say something of Rohde, whom you also know from an earlier time. We were together most of this summer, and felt a strange intimacy between us. It goes without saying that over this friendship hovered the genius of the man whose picture Rohde sent me a few weeks ago from Hamburg—Schopenhauer. I think you will be very glad to hear that precisely such robust and good natures as Rohde has, in the best sense, are gripped by that philosophy.

Another week has passed—it is Sunday again, the only day now left to me for writing the letters I owe. But to continue roughly the same line of thought as eight days ago, I shall tell you about another influence of Schopenhauer. In this case two literary works, one scientific and one a novel, have been born under this star. Perhaps you have already heard of a book called Bahnsen's *Essays in Characterology*. This is an attempt to reform characterology into a science; since this is done on a Schopenhauerian basis and with great love for the "master," and since this two-volume work contains, moreover, many good thoughts and observations, I recommend it to you as well as to all initiates of that open and yet hidden wisdom. What satisfies me least is the form: the author hurries his thoughts too much and by this he spoils the line of beauty. The novel, of which I want to speak, is the first product of a literature that is tragic in that almost ascetic sense of Schopenhauer's, a book whose heroes are driven through the red flame of Sansara to that reversing of the will; and this makes it a work full of the highest artistic value, with a great richness of thought, and one written in a most beautiful and amiable style. It is Spielhagen's latest novel, entitled *In Reih und Glied*, about which little can be read, because its author is too proud to join a clique such as that around [Gustav] Freitag [Freytag.] My teacher Ritschl thinks that this latest novel is ten times as valuable as the whole of Freitag.

Third, I will tell you of an event with which Schopenhauer is also remotely connected, even if he is not, as well-paid schoolmasters assert, the cause of it. That is the unfortunate suicide of Kretzschmer in Schulpforta. The reasons are really unknown, or are being well hushed up. There is something enigmatic about the fact that this excellent and conscientious man had beome engaged three months before and so has made a young girl unhappy too. You know that he was a follower of Schopenhauer; and the last time he and I were together in Almrich, we discussed Schopenhauer's attitude to suicide.

But now I'll come back to the narrative of my experiences. The news of that death reached me in Meiningen, where I was spending the last days of my journey in the Bohemian woods.[43] For a grand four-day music festival was being held by the Zukünftler, who were celebrating their strange musical orgies here.[44] Abbé Liszt was presiding. This school has thrown itself passionately into the arms of Schopenhauer. A symphonic poem by Hans von Bülow, *Nirvana*, was based on a collection of Schopenhauer sentences; but the music was frightful. On the other hand, Liszt himself, in a few of his sacred pieces, has hit off the character of that Indian Nirvana excellently, above all, in his *Seligkeiten*, "beati sunt qui" and so on.

After these weeks of relaxation and of merely enjoying nature, a well-meaning *daimon* drove me to get zealously down to a new philological theme, "On the Spurious Writings of Democritus." This work is intended for a collection of essays to be presented next year to Ritschl. I suggested the idea, during my last days in Leipzig, of having his special students in Leipzig—naturally, a select few—honor their teacher in this way. Rohde, Roscher, Windisch, Clemm, and four others, whom you do not know, have been persuaded to collaborate. Thereafter in Halle I was at the meeting of the classical philologists—and then fate intervened.

For I am now an artilleryman, in the 2d mounted section of the 4th Field Artillery Regiment.

It will not be difficult for you to imagine what a surprise this change was, how violently I was alienated from my usual work and my comfortable existence. Yet I am enduring this change with composure, and even feel a certain sense of well-being as a result of this trick of destiny. Only now am I really thankful for our Schopenhauer, now that I have a chance to practice a little ἄσκησις. During the first five weeks I also had to perform stable duties: every morning at five-thirty I was in the stables to clean out the manure and to groom my horse with comb and brush. Now my duties keep me busy on the average from seven to ten-thirty in the morning, and from eleven-thirty to six in the afternoon, most of this time with drilling on the square. Four times a week both of us one-year volunteers have a lecture

43. N's phrasing here is characteristic of the solemn, if not stilted manner which he adopts in his letters to Gersdorff. He writes, "Die Nachricht von jenem Tode ereilte mich . . . ," not "Ich hörte von jenem Tode. . . ." In his letters to Rohde, N was consistently more relaxed. Great stylist though he was to become, N in his younger days had several voices. The solemn and sententious voice persists to some extent even in his last letters.

44. "Zukünftler" was a shortened form of "Zukunftsmusiker," or practitioners of "music of the future" grouped around Liszt and Wagner. The festival in question took place from August 22 to 25, and was organized by the Allgemeiner Deutscher Musik-verein. Works by Liszt, Volkmann, Berlioz, Cornelius, and Schumann were performed. (The composer Volkmann is not to be confused with Dietrich Volkmann, the teacher at Schulpforta, referred to at the end of this letter.)

from a lieutenant as preparation for the territorial officers' examination. You will know that a mounted artilleryman is supposed to learn an amazing number of things. I like the riding lessons best. I have a very good-looking horse, and people say that I have a talent for riding. When I whirl around the exercise area on my Balduin, I am very satisfied with my lot. On the whole, I am treated excellently well. Above all, we have a pleasant captain.

I have told you about my life as a soldier; it is the real reason why I have been so late in sending you news and in replying to your last letter. In the meantime you will probably, I think, have got rid of the military shackles. That is why I am doubtful about addressing my letter to Spandau.

But my time is up already; a business letter to Volkmann and another to Ritschl have stolen our time. Now I must close, in order to get ready to go on parade in full equipment.

So, dear friend, forgive my long neglect and ascribe most of the guilt to the war god.

Truly, your friend
Friedrich Nietzsche
Artilleryman

10 · *To Erwin Rohde*   [Naumburg, October 8, 1868]

My dear friend:

Now as I think back over an extremely various year, a year full of warm emotion and of uneasy emotion, full of ascetic and eudaimonistic experiences, a year begun in the stables, continued in the sick bed,[45] ended in indicificatory slave labor: now as I count up this year's good moments, lovely hopes, quiet hours of thought, I chew again also with the warmest pleasure on the feeling of those lovely days which brought us together in August, and like a contented cow I roll in the sunshine of these memories.

Since our discussions about heaven and earth in those days, hardly anything important has happened to me; I worked on my index on the veranda—"Dort sass ich unter falben Blättern ein frommer Mann."[46] The friendly late summer, with its half-cooled sunshine and its leisure, is now ending, I am expected in Leipzig, and a notice in the daily paper seeks an

45. In early March (?) N had received a severe chest injury while mounting a horse. This confined him to his bed for several months.

46. "There sat I, a pious man, under faded leaves," a quotation which was not identified in *Briefe 2* of the *Historisch-Kritische Gesamtausgabe* and which I have not been able to identify either.

"elegant" bachelor's apartment for a scholar. Our good acquaintances there have all mounted ladders of fame: I, poor *homo litteratus*, must think first of all about getting a degree, so as to avoid being counted among the *pecus* of *Literaten*.[47] Moreover, I am deciding to become more of a society man: in particular, I have my sights on a woman of whom people tell me marvels, the wife of Professor Brockhaus, sister of Richard Wagner, of whose capacities friend Windisch (who has visited me) has an astonishingly high opinion. What pleases me about this is the confirmation of Schopenhauer's theory of heredity; Wagner's other sister (in Dresden, a former actress) is also said to be a remarkable woman. The Brockhauses are almost the only family with whom the Ritschls are friendly.[48]

Recently I also read (for the first time, what is more) Jahn's essays on music, including the ones on Wagner.[49] One needs to have some enthusiasm to do such a person justice, whereas Jahn has an instinctive antipathy to him and hears with his ears half shut. Yet I grant him many points, particularly his maintaining that Wagner is a representative of a modern dilettantism which consumes and digests all varieties of artistic interest; but precisely from this standpoint one cannot be astonished enough at the significance that one single artistic disposition has in this man, a disposition which allies indestructible energy with many-sided artistic gifts, whereas "culture" ["Bildung"], the more various and embracing it is, usually appears with dulled eyes, weak knees, and enfeebled loins.

Moreover, Wagner has a sphere of feeling which is totally hidden from O. Jahn: Jahn remains a frontier hero, a healthy man, to whom the *Tannhäuser* saga and the *Lohengrin* atmosphere are a closed world. In Wagner, as in Schopenhauer, I like the ethical air, the Faustian odor, Cross, Death, Grave, and so on.

The only person whom I visit with a pleasure renewed at every occasion is Wenkel, our tireless investigator of Kant and Schopenhauer, who by this exclusiveness of his studies shows a remarkable strength of will.[50] His constant concern with philosophical thought makes him a wicked critic of our philology; I have often brought something along to show him, in order

47. *"Pecus"* = "crowd"; *"Literaten"* here is loaded with scorn; literally, it means "writers" or *"hommes de lettres."*

48. Refers to Ottilie Brockhaus (b. 1811), wife of Hermann Brockhaus, the Indologist (1806–77), and to Luise, wife of Friedrich Brockhaus of Dresden.

49. Otto Jahn, *Gesammelte Aufsätz über Musik* (Leipzig, 1866).

50. The same (Friedrich August) Wenkel whom N mentions in his letter to Gersdorff of April 7th, 1866. He was chief Protestant minister in Naumburg. This reference is of some interest in the argument that inert "Naumburg" Christianity is what N had in mind when attacking Christianity in general. Also, Wenkel's criticism of the academic classical scholars must have encouraged N in his agitation against them.

to hear his opinion, for example, articles by Bernays and Ritschl. He recognized in Ritschl a certain touch of genius, but laughed at the rhetoric in such trivialities; he did not like Bernays at all. He is quietly thinking also of an academic life, and he too wants first to obtain a doctorate.

Just think, I am still not finally done with military service, and my certain prospect is life in the artillery. My captain has graciously inscribed in my documents the qualification for my becoming a territorial army lieutenant: depending on my doing a month of duty in the spring, in order to obtain the necessary knowledge in gun-hauling exercises. Since a war is inevitable sooner or later, and since there is no prospect of my being completely freed from the military shackles, a promotion to lieutenant is of the highest value.

Finally, dear friend, I have to say a few words about your very successful Pollux essay. I have read it through; the whole complex of combinations I find highly illuminating, though this does not mean that I make a "judgment," for which I lack all competence and, because of lack of books, cannot become more competent. The first chapter has a real propaideutic value, insofar as it combines numerous separate findings into a total picture, yet nowhere presupposes specialist knowledge but tells the tale nicely *ex ovo*. Beyond that, the academic posing of questions is clumsy. (The first *stemma* does not quite agree with the text—for example, it consequently uses Eustathius the Diogenian's Περιεργοπένητες, whereas in the text it uses Hesychius. Also in the *stemma* it is not indicated that Photius used the Περιεργοπένητες directly: though I would not say this was certain. Dionysius made use of the Pamphilea epitome as well as the Περιεργοπένητες.) Do you know M. Schmidt's discussion of the Suidas sources (Fleckeisen, *Jahrbücher* [*für klassische Philologie*], Bd. *I*, 1885)? Westphal's *History of Ancient Music*, page 167, moreover, cites Tryphon as the chief source for the musical section of the fourth Pollux book.

The first two chapters of my Laertius appeared in the last issue of the *Rheinisches Museum*, and you will receive an offprint soon. O how repulsive I find this whole work! *Nonum prematur in annum!*[51] There's nothing more to it! It is all too foolish to publish this just recently concocted wisdom right away, and it means only annoyance for me. So much is actually wrong, even more is impudent stammering, and the whole thing is immaturely expressed. My only excuse is the fact that I shall be of age only on October 15 of this year, on which day I also take off my military coat.

The next batch of Laertian eggs I am brooding I shall keep to myself until a good basketful is ready. Recently I reviewed Val. Rose's *Anacreontea*

---

51. Horace, *Ars Poetica*, 388: "Keep it in the drawer for nine years."

for the *Centralblatt*—with a few remarks on Rose's clumsiness and hedgehog style.[52]

Well, what a useless gossip this has been! But who would write letters straight after a meal, letters to such friends, letters in which one is aware of few thoughts and much digesting. "O Hund, du Hund, du bist nicht gesund" to write such letters.[53]

With this girlish curtsy
I remain your friend
Friedrich Nietzsche
Prussian Artilleryman

Best wishes from my relatives.

11 · *To Erwin Rohde*   [Leipzig, November 9, 1868]

My dear friend:

Today I am going to tell you a succession of gay things; I am going to look happily into the future and conduct myself in such an idyllically snug way that your wicked visitor, that feline fever, will arch its back and trot away in a dudgeon. And in order to avoid any note of discord, I mean to discuss the anticipated *res severa*, which your second letter occasioned, on a special sheet of paper, which you can then read in a special mood and in a special place.

The acts in my comedy are headed: 1. An evening meeting of the society, or The subprofessor; 2. The ejected tailor; 3. A rendezvous with X. The cast includes a few old women.

On Thursday evening Romundt took me to the theater, for which my feelings are growing very cool; we planned to see a play by our future director Heinrich Laube, and sat like enthroned Olympians in the gods, and in judgment on a potboiler called *Graf Essex*. Naturally I grumbled at my abductor, who invoked emotions he had had as a ten-year-old, and I was glad to leave the place in which not even Glaukidion was present, as proved to be the case after a microscopic search in every corner of the theater.[54]

---

52. *Literarisches Centralblatt*, no. 45, October 31, 1868.

53. Quotation from Heine, 'Über die französische Bühne,' in *Vertraute Briefe an August Lewald* (Zweiter Brief): "O hound, you hound, your health is unsound."

54. The name is written in Greek capitals in the original. This was N's name for Suschen Klemm, an actress in the Leipzig Stadttheater company, with whom he was friendly and of whom he owned a photograph. Heinrich Romundt, a philosophy-student at Leipzig, later moved to Basel and had lodgings in the same house as N (April 1874).

At home I found two letters, yours and an invitation from Curtius, whom I am glad to know more closely now.[55] When two friends like ourselves write each other letters, the angels, as is known, rejoice; and rejoice they did as I read your letter—they even giggled.

The next morning I solemnly went to thank Frau Curtius for the invitation, because I, unfortunately, could not accept it. I do not know if you have met this lady; I have grown to like her very much, and there is an irrepressible gaiety in my relations with the couple. In this mood I went to my editor-in-chief Zarncke,[56] was heartily welcomed, put our joint affairs in order—the field of my book reviewing is now, among other things, almost the whole of Greek philosophy, excepting Aristotle, with whom Torstrik copes, and another sector in which my former teacher Heinze (privy councillor and prince's pedagogue in Oldenburg) is active. Incidentally, have you read my notice of Rose's *Symposica Anacreontea?* Soon it will be the turn of my namesake,[57] who has become knight-at-arms to the Endocia—a boring lady, a boring knight!

Arriving home, I found your second letter, was taken aback, and resolved on a villainy.

The first Classical Society lecture of the semester had been arranged for the evening, aud I had been very courteously asked if I would take this on. I, who need opportunities to lay in a stock of academic weapons, had soon prepared myself and had the pleasure to find, on my entering the room at Zaspel's, a black mass of forty listeners. Romundt had been instructed by me to be personally very attentive, so that he could tell me how the theatrical side had been, and how effective—the delivery, voice, style, organization of the material. I spoke quite freely, helped only by notes on a slip of paper, my topic being Varro's satires and the cynic Menippus: and lo and behold, everything was καλὰ λίαν. It will be all right in this academic career!

Here now I must mention that I intend to get through all the business of habilitation by Easter and to finish my doctorate at the same time.[58] This is permitted: I need only a special dispensation, insofar as I do not yet have the usual five-year period behind me. Of course, getting habilitated and lecturing are two different things, but I think it will suit me excellently, once I have my hands free, to go out into the world, for the last time without

55. Georg Curtius (1820-85) was a professor of classics at Leipzig.

56. Friedrich Zarncke was editor of the periodical *Literarisches Centralblatt.*

57. Richard Nietzsche was author of *Quaestionum Eudocianarum capita quatuor* (which N reviewed for Zarncke).

58. The "Habilitationsschrift" follows the doctorate, usually as a piece of substantial research which every would-be German university teacher has to write in order to obtain an appointment.

an official appointment. Ah, dear friend, it will feel like being a bridegroom, joy and vexation mingled, humor, γένος σπουδεγέλοιον, Menippus![59] Conscious of having done a good day's work, I went to bed and thought over the scene which I knew there would have to be with Ritschl and which did take place the following noon.

When I arrived home, I found a note addressed to me, with the few words: "If you want to meet Richard Wagner, come at 3:45 P.M. to the Café Théâtre. Windisch."

This surprise put my mind in somewhat of a whirl, so that I quite forgot—forgive me—the scene itself and was in a state of turmoil.

Naturally I ran out, found our honorable friend Windisch, who gave me more information. Wagner was strictly incognito in Leipzig, staying with his relatives; the press knew nothing, and all Brockhaus's servants had been told was to keep as quiet as liveried graves. Now Wagner's sister, Frau Professor Brockhaus, that intelligent woman whom we know, had introduced her good friend Frau Professor Ritschl to her brother: which gave her a chance, the lucky thing, to show her brother off to her friend and her friend off to her brother. In Frau Ritschl's presence, Wagner plays the *Meisterlied*, which you know too; and the good woman tells him that this song is well known to her, *mea opera* [my doing]. Joy and amazement on Wagner's part; announces his supreme will, to meet me incognito; I am to be invited for Friday evening. But Windisch explains that I shall be prevented by functions, duties, obligations; so Saturday is proposed. Thereupon, Windisch and I went along, found the professor's family but not Richard, who had gone out with an immense hat on his large head. Here then I met the aforementioned excellent family and was kindly invited for Sunday evening.

During these days my mood was like something in a novel; believe me, the preliminaries to this acquaintance, considering how unapproachable this eccentric man is, verged on the realm of fairy tale.

Thinking that many people were invited, I decided to dress very smartly, and was glad that my tailor had promised for this same Sunday an evening suit. It was a terrible day of rain and snow; I shuddered at the thought of going out, and so I was content when Roscher visited me in the afternoon, told me a few things about the Eleatics and about God in philosophy—for, as a doctoral candidate, he is treating the topic, set by Ahrens, "The Development of the Concept of God up to Aristotle," while Romundt is attempting to work out the university prize-essay topic, "On the Will." It was getting dark, the tailor had not come, and Roscher left. I went with

---

59. Menippus was the creator of the philosophical farce, or *spoudegeloion* (σπουδεγέλοιον).

him, visited the tailor in person, and found his slaves hectically occupied with my suit; they promised to send it in three-quarters of an hour. I left contentedly, dropped in at Kintschy's,[60] read *Kladderadatsch*,[61] and found to my pleasure the notice that Wagner was in Switzerland but that a beautiful house was being built for him in Munich; all the time I knew that I would see him that same evening and that he had yesterday received a letter from the little king,[62] bearing the address: To the great German composer Richard Wagner.[63]

At home I found no tailor, read in a leisurely way the dissertation on the Eudocia, and was disturbed now and then by a loud but distant ringing. Finally I grew certain that somebody was waiting at the patriarchal wrought-iron gate; it was locked, and so was the front door of the house. I shouted across the garden to the man and told him to come into the Naundörfchen: it was impossible to make oneself understood through the rain. The whole house was astir; finally the gate was opened, and a little old man with a package came up to my room. It was six-thirty, time to put on my things and get myself ready, for I live very far out. Right, the man has my things, I try them on, they fit. An ominous moment; he presents the bill. I take it politely; he wants to be paid on receipt of the goods. I am amazed, and explain that I will not deal with him, an employee of my tailor, but only with the tailor himself, to whom I gave the order. The man becomes more pressing, the time becomes more pressing; I seize the things and begin to put them on; the man seizes the things, and stops me from putting them on—force on my side, force on his side. Scene: I am fighting in my shirttails, for I am trying to put on the new trousers.

Finally, a show of dignity, solemn threat, cursing my tailor and his assistant, swearing revenge; meanwhile, the little man is moving off with my things. End of second act: I brood on the sofa in my shirttails and consider a black jacket, whether it is good enough for Richard.

Outside the rain is pouring down.

A quarter to eight; at seven-thirty, I have told Windisch, we are to meet in the Café Théâtre. I rush out into the windy, wet night, also a little man in black, without dinner jacket, but feeling intensely that it is all like a fiction; fortune is propitious, even the scene with the tailor has about it something monstrously extraordinary.

60. Kintschy's, like Zaspel's, was a Leipzig café-restaurant frequented by students.

61. Humorous, illustrated magazine of the time.

62. Ludwig II of Bavaria, whose patronage of Wagner had begun in 1864.

63. The word used for "composer" here was "Tondichter" ("tone poet") more solemn than "Komponist" and dating back to the early Romantic period.

We enter the very comfortable drawing room of the Brockhauses; nobody is there apart from the family circle, Richard, and the two of us. I am introduced to Richard, and address to him a few words of respect; he wants to know exact details of how I became familiar with his music, curses all performances of his operas except the famous Munich ones, and makes fun of the conductors who call to their orchestras in a bland voice: "Gentlemen, make it passionate here!" "My good fellows, a little more passionate!" W. likes to imitate the Leipzig dialect.

Now I shall briefly tell you what this evening offered: truly enjoyments of such peculiar piquancy that I am today not quite my old self and can do nothing better than talk to you, my dear friend, and tell you "passing wondrous tales." Before and after dinner Wagner played all the important parts of the *Meistersinger*, imitating each voice and with great exuberance. He is, indeed, a fabulously lively and fiery man who speaks very rapidly, is very witty, and makes a very private party like this one an extremely gay affair. In between, I had a longish conversation with him about Schopenhauer; you will understand how much I enjoyed hearing him speak of Schopenhauer with indescribable warmth, what he owed to him, how he is the only philosopher who has understood the essence of music; then he asked how the academics nowadays regarded him, laughed heartily about the Philosophic Congress in Prague, and spoke of the "vassals of philosophy." Afterward, he read an extract from his biography,[64] which he is now writing, an utterly delightful scene from his Leipzig student days, of which he still cannot think without laughing; he writes too with extraordinary skill and intelligence. Finally, when we were both getting ready to leave, he warmly shook my hand and invited me with great friendliness to visit him, in order to make music and talk philosophy; also, he entrusted to me the task of familiarizing his sister and his kinsmen with his music, which I have now solemnly undertaken to do. You will hear more when I can see this evening somewhat more objectively and from a distance. For today, a warm farewell and best wishes for your health.

F. N.

Res severa! Res severa! Res severa!

My dear friend, I implore you to write direct to Dr. Klette in Bonn and (without further civilities and reasons) ask to have your manuscript back.[65] At least, that is what I would do.

64. N proofread this (called here *"Biographie,"* not *"Selbstbiographie"*) when it was being secretly printed in 1869/70; it was not published until 1911.

65. Concerns Rohde's work on Lucian's *The Ass* (ἡ ὄνος): ΛΟΤΚΙΟΣ Η ΟΝΟΣ *und ihr Verhältniss zu Lucius von Patrae und den Metamorphosen des Apuleius.* Rohde

Ritschl's *tactlessness* is too much: in the interview with him it came out very strongly, so that I spoke with him somewhat coolly, which took him very much aback.

Actually it is true that the *Rheinisches Museum* has too many contributions on hand; the last issue of the year will show you this—it exceeds by four sheets the usual number of pages.

It is obvious that I am personally most annoyed by this matter. For it was I who, with the best intention and friendliest opinion, suggested that you should entrust the manuscript to the *Rheinisches Museum*; I thought by this to do them a really *pleasant* service. It nags me especially to think what the original purpose of the article was.

If you want to take revenge on them, send the manuscript to *Hermes*; for my part, I do not favor such vengeance. In the circumstances, *Philologus* is out of the question, and Fleckeisen's *Jahrbücher* are in the same position as the *Rheinisches Museum*.

So, dear friend, a publisher must be found (and if I may give you the advice, publish the Ὄνος at the same time, the text according to the codices you accept). Naturally you will prefer to look for a publisher in your beloved Hamburg; otherwise, you can trust me to look zealously for a generous bookseller, if you ask me to do so.

In any case, it must be done quickly; the work with its three or four sheets must be printed even within a month.

If haste is not important to you, we can plan something between the two of us: we can do a book together entitled "Contributions to the History of Greek Literature," in which we collect several longer essays (by me, for instance, the one on Democritus' writings, the one on the ἀγών in Homer and Hesiod, the one on the cynic Menippus) as well as a number of miscellaneous pieces.

What do you think of this idea?

In loyal friendship and sympathy
in rebus secundis et adversis
the Leipzig Eidylliker.[66]

---

had heard from the publisher of the *Rheinisches Museum* that Ritschl had preferred another paper on Lucian, by C. F. Ernst Knaut, to his. He felt that Ritschl had been frivolous in his judgment of the differences between the two studies, of which his own was the more detailed (cf. *Werke und Briefe, Briefe 2*, p. 459). N took the work to Dr. Englemann, the Leipzig publisher, and it appeared under his imprint early in 1869.

66. A pun, referring to a comment in Rohde's letter of November 4 about N's cosy and idyllic life and his photograph of Suschen Klemm (εἴδωλον, "eidolon").

12 · *To Erwin Rohde*   Leipzig, Day of Repentance
[November 20, 1868]

My dear friend:

To see again from close at hand the seething brood of the philologists of our time, and every day having to observe all their moleish pullulating, the baggy cheeks and the blind eyes, their joy at capturing worms and their indifference to the true problems, the urgent problems of life—not only the young ones doing it, but also the old, full-grown ones—all this makes me see more and more clearly that the two of us, if this is to be our only means of remaining true to the spirit in us, shall not go our way in life without a variety of offenses and intrigues. When scholar and human being do not completely tally, first the aforementioned brood looks on the miracle with amazement, then it gets annoyed, and finally it scratches, barks, and bites, as you yourself recently found out.[67] For it is obvious to me that the trick played on you is not directed against what you have in particular achieved, but is meant personally; and I am living in the certain hope that I too shall soon have a foretaste of what awaits me in this hellish atmosphere. But, dear friend, what does anyone else's judgment on our personalities have to do with your actual work and mine? Let us think of Schopenhauer and Richard Wagner, of the indestructible energy with which they kept faith in themselves throughout the hullaballooing of the whole "educated" world; and if it is not permissible to invoke any *deos maximos*, we always have the consolation that eccentrics cannot be denied the right to exist (including the little one in the photograph enclosed)[68] and that two eccentrics of one heart and mind are a happy spectacle for the gods.

Ultimately nothing is more to be regretted than that precisely now, just when we are starting to verify our view of life by action, and to touch with our cornucopias all things and matters in turn, people, states, studies, world histories, churches, schools, and so on—that precisely now there should be so many miles separating us, and that each of us must experience alone the half-pleasurable, half-painful feeling of digesting his view of life, just as we once used to digest our bodily meals together at Kintschy's; and so nothing would better refresh us now than to drink an afternoon cup of coffee together and to look back and forward from the midday of our life.

Well, it will not be too late for that when we get to Paris, where there will be the great ἀναγνώρισις[69] in our comedy, on the most beautiful

67. See note 65 to No. 11.
68. Suschen Klemm.
69. *Anagnorisis*, "recognition scene" (Aristotle, *Poetics* 6, 1450a, 34).

stage in the world, what is more, and with the most colorful scenery and with countless brilliant extras in the cast.

Ah, how beautiful it is, this mirage!

Keep your distance, therefore, common reality, infamous and mean empiricism, debit and credit, *Grenzbote* sobriety—may this whole letter be dedicated to my friend "with all my soul as a solemn lofty greeting." (Drinks up the inkbottle.) Chorus of ascetics:

> Happy the loving one,
> He who has passed
> The saddening, healing
> And trialsome test.[70]

13 · *To Erwin Rohde*   [Leipzig, January 10, 1869]

My dear friend:

Before I can get down to all our heartfelt common concerns today, Baalam's ass would like to speak a few words. The beast is wondering very much about the proof sent to Hamburg, but now it has been enlightened by the chief of the Drugulin printers and thinks henceforth like an enlightened printer. For I read the first proof myself; but since it is an empty dream to spoil, by one single attack, the printer's predilection for crazy words and barbaric Greek, the second correction was left to you—who are assisted as author, by a much higher authority (as Richard Wagner would say)—and the third once more to me, which is already done. So let us hope that the newly fledged little creature will soon be leaping about gaily and in good spirits, comparable to Γλαυκίδιον in teenage roles. Heaven grant you and me such good midwives as Dr. Englemann, to whom you have perhaps already written a few lines, especially since he wishes to meet you. And with that the ass speaks no more, and the humans can talk again.

Ah, dear friend, what a lovely Christmas greeting you sent me in Naumburg! It arrived on the first day of the festival, and festal bells were ringing. The whole world has been given presents on this morning, and is therefore a little better than in all the rest of the year. (N.B.) I myself was inhaling my home town's warm temperature with distended nostrils; and look, along came the postman and completed my joy. Whoever has become used to feeling like a hermit, whoever sees with a cold gaze through all the

---

70. The end of this letter parodies Goethe's *Faust*, part I, sc. 1 ("Night"), and the "Chorus of Angels" passages in the last two scenes of part 2.

social and comradely connections and notices the tiny threads which tie people together, threads so strong that a gust of air breaks them; whoever sees in addition that it is not the flame of genius which makes him a hermit, that flame from whose circle of light all things flee away, because it makes them appear so like a dance of death, so mad, so spindly, and so inane; whoever is, on the contrary, lonely because of a caprice of nature, because of a curiously brewed mixture of wishes, gifts, and endeavors of the will, he knows what an "incomprehensibly lofty marvel" a *friend* is; and if he is an idolater, he must first and foremost erect an altar to the "unknown god who created the friend." Here I have an opportunity to observe from close at hand the ingredients of a happy family life; here there is no comparison with the loftiness, the singularity of friendship. Feelings clad in a dressing gown, the most quotidian and trivial things shimmering with this comfortably expansive feeling—that is the joy of family life, which is much too common to be of any great value. But friendships! There are people who despair over their existence. Yes, it is a choice delicacy, allotted only to few people, to those exhausted travelers whose way through life leads through the desert; a friendly spirit consoles them when they lie in the sand, and he moistens their parched lips with the divine nectar of friendship. But in the crevices and caves where, far from the world's noise, they bring sacrifices to their gods, these few sing beautiful hymns to friendship, and there too the old high priest Schopenhauer swings the censer of his philosophy.

At the point where I have written N.B., a message came calling me into the town as soon as I had reached the foot of the page; now returned, I am trembling all over and cannot free myself of it even by pouring out my heart to you. Absit diabolus! Adsit amicissimus Erwinus![71]

14 · *To Carl von Gersdorff*   [Naumburg, April 11, 1869]

My dear friend:

The last moment has come, the last evening I shall spend in my old home; tomorrow morning I go out into the wide, wide world, into a new, unfamiliar profession, into a heavy and oppressive atmosphere of duty and work. Once more I have to say goodbye; the golden time of free untrammeled activity, of the sovereign present, of pleasure taken in art and in

71. The news N received was an invitation from the University of Basel; he was to take up his appointment as professor (*extraordinarius*) of classical philology there in April.

the world as a detached, or at least weakly attached, spectator—this time is irretrievably past; now the stern goddess rules, the daily dutiful task. "Bemooster Bursche zieh ich aus"[72]—you must know the stirring student song. Yes, yes! Now I must be a philistine too. Somewhere that phrase still contains a truth. One does not enter professional work and dignities with impunity—it just depends on whether the bonds are of iron or of thread. And I still have the guts to break out one day and attempt to live this hazardous life somewhere else and in some other way. I still feel no trace of the professor's obligatory hump. As for being a philistine, ἄνθρωπος ἄμουσος—may Zeus and all the muses protect me from that! Also I would hardly know how to set about becoming one, since I am not one. True, I have come near to one kind of philistinism, the "specialist" variety; it is only too natural that the daily burden, the hour-by-hour concentration of thought on a particular field of knowledge and on particular problems, should somewhat dull one's free receptivity and attack the philosophical sense at its root. But I believe that I can approach this danger more calmly and safely than most philologists; my philosophical seriousness is already too deeply rooted, too clearly have the true and essential problems of life and thought been shown to me by the great mystagogue Schopenhauer, for me ever to have to fear that I might despicably defect from the "idea." To permeate my discipline with this new blood, to transmit to my listeners that Schopenhauerian seriousness which is stamped upon the brows of the sublime man, this is my wish, my daring hope; I would like to be something more than a drillmaster for competent philologists—the generation of present-day teachers, the care of the growing younger generation, this is what I have in mind. If we must bring to birth all the life that is in us, let us try to use this life so that others will bless it, for its value, once we have been happily absolved from it.[73]

72. Quotation from a famous student song (words by Gustav Schwab): "Student of long standing, I go forth."

73. The phrasing here is Schopenhauerian ("life-negating"). But Schopenhauer was not the only author whom N read outside his field. His studies in Democritus had included scientific reading, and from his Schulpforta days he had retained a desire for "universal knowledge" (influence, certainly, of Klencke's biography of Alexander von Humboldt, possibly of Humboldt's monumental work *Kosmos*). At Schulpforta, N had also been an avid reader of encyclopedias. The hostility to specialization and professionalized learning has its roots in his early teens. In Leipzig, in addition to Lange's *History of Materialism*, he also read Eugen Dühring and Eduard von Hartmann. A list of twenty-one scientific books "to be read," dated 1868, includes books by Moleschott, Lotze, Helmholtz, Fries, Oken, and Carus. Mittasch also quotes a sentence on Democritean atomism in the light of chemistry which contains the germ of N's "dynamic" natural philosophy: "An eternal rain of diverse corpuscles, which fall in manifold motion, consume themselves in falling, creating a vortex" (A. Mittasch, *Ns Naturbeflissenheit*, Heidelberg, 1950, p. 100).

To you, dear friend, with whom I am of one mind on many basic problems of life, I wish good luck, which you deserve, and to myself I wish your old loyal friendship. Farewell!

Friedrich Nietzsche Dr.

Thank you so much for your very full letter. My πολυπραγμοσύνη is the reason for my replying so late. I am sorry. I have written a letter of thanks to Wieseke.

Note: The following autobiographical fragments, dated 1868/9, are included at this point because they provide a summary retrospect on N's mental history so far, and reveal his doubts as to his real vocation on the threshold of his appointment to Basel. The source is: *Werke in drei Bänden*, vol. 3 (ed. K. Schlechta), pp. 148–52.

What I am afraid of is not the terrible shape behind my chair but its voice; also not the words but the horribly unarticulated and inhuman tone of that shape. Yes, if only it spoke as human beings do.

A chain of events, of endeavors, in which one looks for coincidences of external fate or baroque caprice, later reveals itself to be a way for which the unerring hand of instinct had been groping.

Pforta.[74] The compulsory allocations of time, making everything uniform. Reaction in open neglect of certain areas in artistic studies. Perhaps the sobriety and stiffness of classical philology would have revolted me; but Steinhart was valuable as the image of an all-round live personality enlivening his special philological field. Corssen as natural enemy of all philistinism and yet a most rigorous active scholar.

Our image of a profession is usually abstracted from the persons of those teachers who are closest to us.

From a vague diffuseness in the many directions taken by my talents I was protected by a certain philosophical seriousness, which was never satisfied except when facing the naked truth and did not fear hard and evil consequences but was even partial to them. The feeling that I should never get to the root of things by encyclopedic studies drove me into the arms of a strict scientific discipline.[75]

Then the longing to be done with rapid changes of feeling in my artistic studies by taking refuge in the haven of objectivity.

74. Schulpforta, the famous boarding school where N was a pupil, 1858–64.

75. "... in der Universalität": in an autobiographical fragment written at Schulpforta in 1864, N wrote, "This whole period from my ninth to my fifteenth year is marked by a real passion for "universal knowledge," as I used to call it ..." (*Werke in drei Bänden*, 3: 117).

One is honest about oneself either with a sense of shame or with vanity.

It has always seemed to me worthwhile to consider individual ways in which people come to classical philology nowadays, for I think it is recognized that some other sciences, in their flowering youthfulness and astonishing productive power, have a greater right to the fresh vigor of aspiring talents than our philology, which does indeed still continue robustly on its way but shows here and there the tired features of old age. I discount those natures who come to it in a usual way, in order to earn a living; and others, too, are not very attractive, the ones who are directed by their philological educators into the same profession and put up no resistance. Many are motivated by an innate talent for teaching; but for these also the science is only an affective instrument, not the serious goal of their life's journey, regarded with eyes full of longing. There is a small community which delights in the Greek world of forms and finds artistic gratification therein, an even smaller one for which the thinkers of antiquity still yield new findings and ideas for development. I have no right to include myself in either of these classes exclusively; for the way in which I came to classical philology is as distant from that of practical expertise as it is from that along which enthusiastic love for antiquity carries the torch. To say this is no easy matter, but it is honest.

Perhaps I do not belong at all among the specific philologists on whose brows nature with a stylus of bronze has set the mark, This Is A Philologist, and who go their prescribed way without the least tremor of a doubt, with the naïveté of a child. Here and there one comes across such philological demigods, and then one notices what a fundamental difference there is between all that which instinct and the power of nature create and that which is produced by education, reflection, perhaps even by being resigned.

I do not actually mean that I am in every way one of these resignation philologists; but when I look back and see how I have come from art to philosophy, from philosophy to a science and here again into an increasingly narrow field, then it almost looks like conscious renunciation.

I ought to consider that a man who is twenty-four years old already has behind him the most important things in his life, even if it is only later that he produces work that makes his life valuable. For, up to about this age, the young soul extracts what is typical from all events and experiences of living and thinking, and it will never again relinquish the world of these types. When, later on, the idealizing gaze is extinguished, then we are under the spell of that world of types which is the heritage we receive from our youth.

It is another question whether or not we shall be able, at the age indicated . . . [breaks off].

May I, who have hardly crossed the threshold of that age, now be permitted . . . [breaks off].

The main areas of my education were ones in which I was left to my own devices. My father, a Protestant clergyman in Thuringia, died all too soon; I missed the strict and superior guidance of a male intellect. When, as a boy, I came to Schulpforta, I found only a surrogate for a father's education, the uniformizing discipline of an orderly school. But precisely this almost military compulsion, which, because it has to affect the mass, treats coolly and superficially what is individual, made me fall back on my own resources. I rescued my private inclinations and endeavors from the uniform law; I lived a secret cult of certain arts; I tried to break the rigidity of schedules and timetables laid down by the rules, by indulging an overexcited passion for universal knowledge and enjoyment. The external chances were lacking, or I might at that time have ventured to become a musician. For, since my ninth year, music was what attracted me most of all; in that happy state in which one does not yet know the limits of one's gifts and thinks that all objects of love are attainable, I had written countless compositions and had acquired a more than amateurish knowledge of musical theory. Only then in the last period of my Schulpforta life did I give up, in true cognizance of myself, all my artistic plans; classical philology moved, from that moment on, into the gap thus made.

What I wanted was some counterweight to my changeable and restless inclinations, a science which could be pursued with cool impartiality, with cold logic, with regular work, without its results touching me at all deeply. The conditions for studying this science are immediately available for any Schulpforta pupil. In this institution specifically philological assignments are sometimes given—for instance, critical commentaries on certain Sophoclean or Aeschylean choruses. Moreover, it is a special advantage at Schulpforta, one that suits a future philologist very well, that among the pupils a strenuous and wide reading in Greek and Latin writers is a requisite for good tone. The most fortunate thing was, however, my finding excellent teachers in classical philology, whose personalities shaped my judgment of their science. If at that time I had had teachers of the kind sometimes found in high schools, narrow-minded frog-blooded micrologists, who know nothing of their science except its learned dust, then I would have flung far from me any thought of ever being party to a science served by such wretches. But, as it was, there were living before my eyes philologists like Steinhart, Keil, Corssen, Peter, men with open and energetic minds, who were in part also personally sympathetic. So it came about that in the last

years of my Schulpforta life I was working independently on two philological papers. In one, I aimed to give an account, from the sources (Jor-
danes, Edda, etc.), of the sagas of the East Gothic King Ermanarich, in their
various ramifications; in the other, to sketch a special type of Greek tyrant,
the Megarian. It is the custom in Schulpforta to leave some written memorial behind; this second work was intended as such, and, as I worked on
it, it became a portrait of the Megarian Theognis.

After saying farewell to Schulpforta, which had been an austere but
useful instructress during my six years there, I came to Bonn. Here I
realized with astonishment how well taught but how badly educated such a
student from a princely foundation is when he enters the university. He has
thought much for himself, and now he lacks the skill to express these
thoughts. He has learned nothing of the educative influence of women; he
thinks he knows life from books and traditions, and yet everything now
seems so foreign and unpleasant. That is how it was for me at Bonn; probably not all the means I adopted for altering this sorry state of things were
well chosen, and annoyances, uncongenial company, duties undertaken,
made . . . [breaks off].

II

1869-76

*First
Years
at
Basel;
Wagner
and the
Break
with
Wagner*

II. *1869–76: First Years at Basel; Wagner and the Break with Wagner*

1869

April: becomes Swiss citizen. May: first visit to Richard Wagner and Cosima von Bülow at Tribschen, near Lucerne. May 28: inaugural lecture on Homer. Summer semester lectures: on Aeschylus, *Choephorae*, and Greek Lyric Poets. Frequent visits to Tribschen during the summer. Winter semester lectures: Latin Grammar. Christmas vacation at Tribschen.

1870

Early spring: public lectures on Ancient Music Drama and Socrates and Tragedy. April 9: promotion to full professorship. Summer semester lectures: on Sophocles, *Oedipus Rex*. August–September: medical orderly in Franco-Prussian War. Severe dysentery and diphtheria. Hereafter, N is almost continuously unwell, often severely, with digestive disorders and migraine. His sight is also poor. Return to Basel: reading Wagner's essay on Beethoven; beginning of friendship with Franz Overbeck, professor of theology, critic of Protestantism. Winter semester lectures: Metric; Hesiod's *Works and Days*.

1871

January: applies for Chair of Philosophy at Basel. March: in Lugano, writing *Die Geburt der Tragödie*. Contemplates (with Rohde) leaving academic life: "A completely radical institution for truth is not possible here" (1870). Summer semester lectures: Introduction to the Study of Classical Philology. Winter semester: Introduction to the Study of the Platonic Dialogues; Introduction to Latin Epigraphy. November/December: printing of *Die Geburt der Tragödie*.

1872

Advance copies of *Die Geburt der Tragödie* arrive at the New Year. January–March: public lectures, *Die Zukunft unserer Bildungsanstalten*. End of April: the Wagners move from Tribschen to Bayreuth. May 22: laying of foundation stone at the Wagner theater in Bayreuth. N meets Malwida von Meysenbug there. Summer semester lectures: Pre-Platonic Philosophy;

Aeschylus, *Choephorae*. Summer: preparing Rohde's pamphlet defending *Die Geburt der Tragödie* against criticism of Ulrich von Wilamowitz-Moellendorf. N travels to Splügen: abortive trip to Bergamo and back to Splügen. No students of Classics enroll for his winter semester lectures (only two non-Classics students) on Greek and Latin Rhetoric.

1873

"Die Philosophie im tragischen Zeitalter der Griechen": unfinished, large project to be entitled "The Philosopher as Physician of Culture." March: reading Rudjer Boscovitch. Summer semester lectures: Pre-Platonic Philosophy. May: meets Paul Rée in Basel, visit of Carl von Gersdorff. *David Strauss, der Bekenner und Schriftsteller* (first of the *Unzeitgemässe Betrachtungen*). Writing: *Vom Nutzen und Nachteil der Historie für das Leben* (second of the *Unzeitgemässe Betrachtungen*, published 1874). Threat of closure of Fritzsch's Wagnerite publishing house. Financial problems at Bayreuth: Wagner's pressure on N as propagandist. Winter semester lectures: Plato's Life and Works.

1874

Schopenhauer als Erzieher. Second edition of *Die Geburt der Tragödie*. Summer semester lectures: Aeschylus, *Choephorae*. Karl Hillebrand invites N to contribute to his periodical *Italia*. Summer: composes "Hymnus an die Freundschaft" at Schaffhausen. June: hears music by Brahms in Basel. August 4 to 15: in Bayreuth. Renewed reading in Emerson. Winter semester lectures: History of Greek Literature, and Aristotle, *Rhetoric*. October: visits from Rohde and Gersdorff. November: hears Berlioz's "Carneval Romain." Christmas vacation in Naumburg.

1875

Richard Wagner in Bayreuth. February: Romundt's threatened conversion. Gersdorff stays with N in Basel. Summer: Elisabeth Nietzsche comes to Basel to stay with N. His health very poor: "Every two or three weeks, I spend 36 hours in bed in real torment." Winter semester lectures: Antiquities of Greek Religion; History of Greek Literature. Heinrich Köselitz (Peter Gast) comes to Basel to attend N's lectures. December: reading the Buddhist text *Sutta Nipáta*. Severe illness from December until February 1876.

1876

Convalescence at Veytaux, near Montreux and Chillon. April: mood of exaltation on Lac Leman. Proposal of marriage (by letter) to Mathilde

Trampedach, who declines. Summer semester lectures: On the Pre-Platonic Philosophers; On Plato's Life and Teaching. Rohde announces his engagement. N's poem on the lonely traveler. July–August: two brief stays in Bayreuth for the first Wagner music festival, flight, amid splitting headaches, to Klingenbrunn. Begins there writing *Menschliches, Allzumenschliches*. Has obtained sick-leave from Basel: October—via Bex, Geneva, and Genoa to Sorrento (Malwida von Meysenbug) with Rée and Brenner. November: last meeting with Wagner in Sorrento. Tacit rupture with Wagner. Reading: Voltaire and other eighteenth-century French moralists.

15 · *To Richard Wagner*   [Basel, May 22, 1869][1]

Sehr verehrter Herr:[2]

How long have I intended to express unreservedly the degree to which I feel grateful to you; because indeed the best and loftiest moments of my life are associated with your name, and I know of only one other man, your great spiritual brother Arthur Schopenhauer, whom I regard with equal reverence, even *religione quadam*. I am happy to confess this to you on a festive day, and I do this not without a feeling of pride. For, if it is the lot of genius to be for a while the possession of only *paucorum hominum*, then certainly these *pauci* may feel themselves especially fortunate and privileged, because it is granted to them to see the light and to warm themselves by it, while the mass is still standing and freezing in the cold fog. Also to enjoy the genius does not come easily to these few; rather they have to contend with omnipotent prejudices and their own opposite inclinations, so that, if the struggle's outcome is a happy one, they have a sort of conqueror's right to the genius.

1. N had arrived in Basel on April 19. The date of the letter was Wagner's fifty-sixth birthday. Much later (April 7, 1884), when N was beginning to receive adulatory letters of this kind himself, he wrote to Overbeck that it was Wagner who had "introduced this adulatory style among the German youth." Here it is hard to tell where N's own solemnity and the Wagnerian "adulatory style" can be distinguished. The *Schwärmerei* of this and other letters to Wagner (also to Gersdorff) does show what N had to recognize and combat in himself and in the sluggish idolatrousness of the German intelligentsia: this turgid manner—sanctimoniousness and unction—is the background against which his doctrine of energy and critical independence was formed. It consorts, within the nine-teenth-century "Spiesser-Ideologie," with the chauvinism and anti-Semitism of which N is also not free during this period (see his letter to Gersdorff, July 21, 1871, first paragraph). Cf. Hermann Glaser, *Spiesser-Ideologie: Von der Zerstörung des deutschen Geistes im 19. und 20. Jahrhundert* (Freiburg, 1964).

2. Hereafter, certain forms of address will be left untranslated, since their English equivalents are so badly dated as to sound ridiculous; e.g., "Very (or Highly) esteemed sir."

I have ventured to count myself among these few, after realizing how incapable almost the whole world with which one is concerned has shown itself to be when it comes to grasping your personality as a whole, to feeling the undivided, deeply ethical current that passes through your life, writings, and music—in brief, to be aware of the ambiance of a more serious and spiritual world view such as we poor Germans have simply lost, through all kinds of political *misère*, through philosophical mischief and importunate Jewry. My thanks are due to you and to Schopenhauer if I have till now held fast to the Germanic seriousness, to a deepened view of this so enigmatic and questionable life.

How many purely scientific[3] problems have been gradually clarified for me by contemplating your personality, so solitary and of such remarkable presence; this I would rather tell you one day in person, just as I would also wish not to have had to *write* all that I have just written. How I would have liked to appear today in your lake and mountain solitude, had not the tiresome chain of my profession kept me in my kennel in Basel.[4]

Finally, I ask that you give my best wishes to Baroness von Bülow, and that I may have the honor to remain your most devoted and obedient adherent and admirer.

                                        Dr. Nietzsche, Professor, Basel

16. *To Elisabeth Nietzsche*   [Basel, May 29, 1869]

Dear Lisbeth:

Later than I would have liked, I now have time and opportunity to thank you for your letter and tell you in more detail about my experiences here. First of all, I was glad to hear that you feel comfortable in Leipzig and that you will perhaps find it as useful and pleasant as you had hoped. Certainly it is a stimulating change, and one that will offer you new ideas, compared with the slow rhythm of life in Naumburg. You will have no trouble, it seems, in getting used to the Biedermann house and intimate family life; I always kept my distance, so that the moods and occasional

---

3. N uses the words "Wissenschaft" and "wissenschaftlich" with reference to classical studies, a field to which the words "science" and "scientific" can hardly be applied today. In most instances, his terms are translated as "scholarship" or "scholarly"; but here, at least, the emphasis seems to require the other term.

4. N had been invited to spend the day at Tribschen, near Lucerne, where Wagner was now living. He spent much time there subsequently.

depressions of individual members of the family did not affect me.[5] Incidentally, I gave the maid two talers at Christmas and three talers when I left. This does not put any obligation on you.

Please do me the pleasure of writing fully about what is going on in Leipzig, also about particular people with whom I am concerned, and give my regards to everyone to whom you may like to mention it. Tell Frau Brockhaus that I visited her brother on Whit Monday and spent a very pleasant noon and afternoon with him and Frau von Bülow. Tribschen is a perfectly charming country house on the Vierwaldstätter See, half an hour from Lucerne. Last Friday I received an invitation to spend his birthday (May 22) there, and to stay the night, but could not do so because of my professorial duties and so on.

Well, I have been since the beginning of May very busy at the university and the Pädagogium,[6] but only yesterday gave my inaugural lecture, "On the Personality of Homer," in the main aula of the museum to a full audience. I have arranged my lectures for the hour between seven and eight every weekday, and find this kind of work satisfying; also one gets used to the drawback of having a class of eight students, considering that is the total number of classics students, and there is even one theologian. At the school, I am pleased to have an intelligent class, and flatter myself that, though I am not a born schoolmaster, at least I am not a bad one.

We have lunch—three colleagues, that is—at Recher's at the Central Station; an acquaintance of Biedermann's, a former Weimar officer and editor, Heinrich von Göckel, also lunches with us. Many invitations, of course; for example, on Sunday, Tuesday, Wednesday, and Thursday of next week. A very pleasant German family of the director of all the insurance companies, Gerkrat; then the family of Councillor Vischer.[7] With the latter I have a standing invitation for the family Tuesday evenings, which you know about. Recently we had a big garden- and magic-party there and ended up playing Schwarzer Peter and writing games—the public, all professors, and a quantity of ladies. Also General von Hardegg's wife (her husband is commandant to the king of Württemberg), who brought me warm greetings from Frau von Grimmenstein. I have rented a splendid and (cheap) grand piano. The person I see a great deal of is Jakob Burckhardt, well-

5. Karl Biedermann (1812–1901) was a political historian and professor at Leipzig. Elisabeth was staying *en famille* while studying at Leipzig.

6. N's appointment at the University of Basel included duties at the Pädagogium, a Basel public school.

7. Wilhelm Vischer-Bilfinger (1808–74) was ordinarius for classical philology at the university; as a high official at the university and president of the Institute of Education, he had the title of councillor.

known esthetician and art historian and an intelligent man—ask Biedermann. With greetings and best wishes,

Your brother

17· *To Gustav Krug*   [Pilatus, August 4, 1869]
                                   As from tomorrow, I shall be
                                   back in Basel

My dear Gustav:[8]

As proof that even at an altitude of six thousand feet above sea level my
friendship and affection for you are not frozen, in spite of the blanket
of ice-cold cloud, I sit down with a bad pen and numb fingers, with which
this unfriendly and somber Pilatus provides me, to write and tell you at once
about my recent experiences, which are such as to interest you more than
any of my friends. Once more I have spent the last few days with my revered
friend Richard Wagner, who has most kindly given me unlimited rights to
visit him and is angry with me if I fail to make use of these rights at least
once every four weeks. You will understand what I have gained by this
permission; for this man, on whom as yet *no* judgment has been pronounced
which would characterize him completely, shows in all his qualities such an
absolute immaculate greatness, such an ideality in his thought and will, such
an unattainably noble and warm-hearted humanity, such a depth of seriousness that I always feel I am in the presence of one of the century's elect. He
has recently been so happy too over finishing the third act of his *Siegfried*
and proceeding in an abundant sense of his power to the composition of
Götterdämmerung. Everything that I now know of *Siegfried*, from the first
draft, is grandly conceived—for example, Siegfried's fight with the dragon,
the song of the forest bird, and so on. On Sunday morning in my charming
room, with its free outlook over the Vierwaldstätter See and the Rigi, I
looked through a quantity of manuscripts which Wagner had given me to
read, strange novellas from his first Paris period, philosophical essays, and
sketches for dramas, but, above all, a profound exposé addressed to his
"young friend," the Bavarian king, for the latter's enlightenment as to
Wagner's views in *State and Religion.* Never has a king been spoken to more
beautifully, nobly, and profoundly; a pity that the young man has, it seems,
learned so little from it. Wagner's whole life is patriarchal; his intelligent
and noble Frau von Bülow fits perfectly into this whole atmosphere; to her,

8. N had known Gustav Krug (1843–1902) since boyhood in Naumburg. He
later became an eminent Rhineland civil servant and founded the Wagner Society in
Cologne.

Wagner dictated his autobiography. And the place is seething with small Bülows, Elsa, Isolde, Senta, Siegfried, and so on, who also collectively form a biography of Wagner. On Saturday evening a Herr Sérov came, a Russian minister of state and author of a series of articles on Berlioz in the *Gazette de St. Petersbourg*, which I strongly recommend to you, because, for all the severity and cruelty of their judgment, they express completely Wagner's opinion of Berlioz. I was invited for Wagner's birthday, but could not come because of work, and so I missed making the acquaintance of the foremost quartet of France and, according to Wagner, of the entire world.[9] In addition, an intelligent man from Alsace was invited, who has written a very important and detailed article on Wagner (in the April issue of the *Revue des deux mondes*), and is very well suited to be the *propagateur* of the Wagnerian spirit in France.[10] Thanks to Pasdeloup's efforts, *Lohengrin* is being prepared for performance in Paris, and Wagner intends to make an exception and take over the chief rehearsals, perhaps the performance itself. Normally he stays in the background, above all, as far as the *Rheingold* performance in Munich was concerned, which is a concession to the young king, basically a contradiction of the overall idea of the *Nibelungen* trilogy.

Yet what use are all these disconnected details? If only I could spend a few hours on end giving you an idea of the wonderful character of this man of genius.

These days spent at Tribschen during the summer are quite the most valuable result of my professorship at Basel.

How much I would wish you to put into effect, during the course of the year, the idea you mentioned at Easter of a journey with Wilhelm [Pinder] to Switzerland.[11] You will be certain to find me here, for from to-morrow till September 15 I shall be in Basel in any case, kept here by my rigorous and laborious professional work.

Give my most affectionate best wishes to Wilhelm and my regards to your respected relatives. I like to think of Naumburg, especially of the last week I spent in my fatherland, as a boundary between past and future, which had something of the fascination of the vague, hopeful happiness of being a freshman. Now "Life is earnest," but, as you see and hear, "Art is cheerful."[12] In loyal friendship,

Fritz Nietzsche

Dr.

Professor, Basel

9. The Morin-Chevillard Quartet.

10. Edouard Schuré.

11. Wilhelm Pinder (1844–1928) was another boyhood friend of N's.

12. Quotation from the prologue to Schiller's play *Wallensteins Lager* (last line).

18 · *To Carl von Gersdorff*   Basel, September 28, 1869

(From October 7 to 17 I shall be in *Naumburg*)

My dear friend:

Now you shall hear the effect of your last letter; I too no longer belong, since receiving it, to the "sarcophagi." I recalled how once in Leipzig itself I made a shy attempt, after reading Shelley,[13] to explain to you the paradox of vegetarianism, with its consequences; unfortunately, in an inappropriate place, at Mahan's [restaurant], with the familiar cutlets and all sorts of other things in front of us. Forgive the vulgar detail of memory, at which I am myself astonished, but the contrast between your nature and the vegetarian world view seemed to me then so strong that even those details stamped themselves on my mind.

After this first confession, the second: I am indeed once more convinced that the whole thing is a fad, and, what is more, a highly questionable one. But I doubt if I have at hand at present all the reasons against it which have occurred to me in the meantime. For, as I often do now, I spent again a few days with a man who for years used to practice this same abstinence and who has the right to talk of it: I mean Richard Wagner. And he has explained to me, not without the warmest temperamental concern and with the strongest eloquence, the inner errors of that theory and practice. The most important thing for me is that here is another tangible case of that optimism which keeps cropping up, in the strangest forms, now as socialism, now as cremation—as opposed to burial—now as vegetarian doctrine, and in countless forms; just as if the removal of a sinfully unnatural phenomenon could mean the establishment of happiness and harmony. Whereas our sublime philosophy teaches that wherever we reach out our hands we grasp total ruin, the pure will to life, and here all palliatives are meaningless. Certainly respect for animals is a state of mind which graces the noble human being; but the goddess Nature, so cruel and immoral, has with tremendous instinct forced those of us who inhabit this part of the world to be carnivorous, while in the warm parts, where the monkeys have a vegetarian diet, the human beings too are content with that, following the same tremendous instinct. Among us also, in the case of especially strong people, who are

13. In N's library there was a copy of Adolf Strodtmann's translation of Shelley: *Ausgewählte Dichtungen*. He wrote some notes, "Anmerkungen zur Königin Mab VIII" (*Hist.-Krit. Gesamtausgabe* 1: 133-47).

active in a very physical way, a purely vegetarian diet is possible, but only through a powerful revolt against nature, who takes revenge in her own way, as Wagner personally knows from the most searing experience. One of his friends even became a victim of the experiment, and he himself has thought for a long time that he would not be alive now if he had continued with that diet. The rule which experience in this field offers is this: intellectually productive and emotionally intense natures *must* have meat. The other mode of living should be reserved for bakers and bumpkins, who are nothing but digesting machines. The other viewpoint is just as important: such an abnormal mode of life, which causes struggle on every side, consumes an unbelievable amount of mental strength and energy, these being thus withdrawn from nobler and generally useful aspirations. The man who has the courage to stand up actively for something unheard of should make certain that that thing also has dignity and greatness but is not a theory concerned with the nourishment of matter. And even if one might grant that some individuals are martyrs to such things, I would not want to be one of them so long as we still have some banner to be kept aloft in the domain of the spirit. I can well see, dearest friend, that your nature contains a heroic quality which would like to create for itself a world full of struggle and endeavor, but I fear that wholly insignificant blockheads are trying to abuse this noble inclination of yours by insinuating such a principle into it. At least, I regard those widely circulated literary products as infamous fabrications, dictated, it is true, by an honestly stupid fanaticism. Let us fight, and, if possible, not for windmills. Let us bear in mind the struggle and the asceticism of truly great men, Schopenhauer, Schiller, Wagner. Answer me, dear friend.

F. N.

I am starting another page, because it really worries me that I cannot agree with you on this. All the same, to show you my well-meaning energy, I have kept to the same way of life till now and shall continue doing so until *you yourself* give me permission to live otherwise. Yet why must one take moderation to an extreme? Obviously because it is easier to maintain an extreme standpoint than to follow without error the golden mean.

I do agree that in restaurants one is made accustomed to "overfeeding"; that is why I no longer like to eat in them. Also it is clear that occasional abstention from meat, for dietetic reasons, is extremely useful. But why, to quote Goethe, make a "religion" of it? But then that is inevitably entailed in all such eccentricities, and anyone who is ripe for vegetarianism is generally also ripe for socialist "stew."

On this point too Schopenhauer said and did the right thing, with the unerring sureness of his great instinct. You know the passage in question.[14]

But I do not want to continue on this point. Certainly, however, on everything concerning our master—whose picture, by the way, I still have not received. I really do stand now at a center from which Schopenhauerian threads reach out into all parts of the world. When we meet again, I shall tell you about Wenkel's Schopenhauerianism,[15] also about that of Wagner, who is thoroughly saturated and initiated in this philosophy. I shall read you the most remarkable and intelligent letters of my friends Dr. Rohde (in Florence) and Dr. Romundt (Leipzig), which are all most deeply and decisively permeated by that philosophy. As for myself, finally, that to me most deeply sympathetic world view permeates my thinking more and more every day, also my scholarly thinking; as you will perhaps notice when I send you, soon, my Basel inaugural lecture. It is about "The Personality of Homer"; one has to have assimilated a great deal of Schopenhauer to sense how much of it all is subject to the decisive spell of his peculiar mode of thinking.

Next winter I shall have the opportunity to be useful on *our* behalf, as I have announced a course in the "History of Philosophy before Plato" and lectures on Homer and Hesiod. I shall also be giving two public lectures, "On the Esthetics of the Greek Tragic Poets"—that is, "On the Ancient Music Drama"—and Wagner will come from Tribschen to attend them.

I have already written telling you how invaluable this genius of a man is to me, as a flesh-and-blood illustration of what Schopenhauer calls a genius.

With my academic activity, the first semester of which I have just successfully concluded, I can be fairly well satisfied. At least I notice among my students a lively interest and a real liking for me, which expresses itself in their often coming to me for advice.

But it is a strenuous life, believe me.

Ah, if I hadn't had to write all these words! All warmth, immediacy, and energy of feeling are gone the moment the *word*, veiled in Alizarin ink, stands on the page. And yet I expect something from this letter. Or is that not allowed?

In any case, an answer soon?

> With affection and in loyal friendship
> also with best wishes to your good friends
> Friedr. Nietzsche

14. To be found in Bd. 3 of Deussen's edition of Schopenhauer: *Sämtliche Werke*, 3: 715 ff.: "Grundlage der Moral," cap. 19, 7.

15. See note 50, letter No. 10.

19. *To Erwin Rohde*   [Basel, end of January and
February 15, 1870]

My dear friend:

I was worried recently, thinking how you might be getting on in Rome, and how cut off from the world and how lonely you might be there. You might even be ill and without proper attention or friendly care. Remove my worries and take from me my pessimistic fancies. Rome with its council seems to be so gruesomely poisonous—no, I won't write any more, for the privacy of a letter is not secure enough for me against all things ecclesiastical and Jesuitical; people might want to know what was in the letter and make you suffer for it. You are studying antiquity and living in the Middle Ages.

But one urgent thing I will say. Consider living with *me* for a while on your return journey—you know, it might be the last chance for a long time. It is incredible how much I miss you; so bring me the comfort of your presence and make sure that it is not too brief. It really is a new feeling for me to have *absolutely* nobody on the spot to whom one can speak about the best and most difficult things of life. And not even a really understanding colleague either. My friendship is assuming, under such hermetic conditions, in such young and hard years, a veritably pathological character. I implore you, as a sick man might: "Come to Basel!"

My true refuge here, one I cannot overpraise, remains Tribschen near Lucerne—except, however, that I can seldom visit it. I spent the Christmas vacation there: most beautiful and elevating memory! It is most necessary that you should be initiated into this magic. If you become my first guest, then we can travel to friend Wagner together. Can you write me anything about Franz Liszt? If you could perhaps return via Lake Como, it would be a wonderful chance for you to delight us all. Us—that is, we Tribschen people—have an eye on a lakeside villa near Fiume latte, called villa Capuana—two houses. Can you inspect this villa and give us your critical opinion of it?

You will have read about Wackernagel's death. It is on the books that Scherer in Vienna will succeed him.[16] A new theologian is also on the way—Overbeck from Jena.[17] Romundt is an assistant to Professor Czermak and is well situated, thanks to Ritschl. Roscher, who has written to me of his warmest admiration for you, is an "important" pedagogue in Bautzen.

16. In fact, Wackernagel's Chair of German Literature at Basel was inherited by Moritz Heyne.

17. Franz Overbeck was to become one of N's closest friends. See note 99 to letter No. 45.

Bücheler is supposed to have been offered an appointment at Bonn. The *Rheinisches Museum* now has Latin type. I have given a lecture to a mixed audience on "The Ancient Music Drama," and am giving a second on February 1 on "Socrates and Tragedy." I love the Greeks more and more; there is no better approach to them than the tireless education and cultivation of one's own small person. The stage I have now reached is the most shameful confession of my ignorance. The philologist's existence, with some critical pretensions but a thousand miles away from the Greeks, seems to me more and more anomalous. Also I doubt if I could ever become a true philologist; unless I become one by the way, as if by accident, there is no hope for it. My misfortune is this: that I have no model and am in danger of making a fool of myself all on my own. My immediate plan is to work for four years at making myself a cultured being, then to travel for a year—perhaps with you. We really do live a very difficult life, sweet ignorance guided by teachers and traditions was such bliss—it was safe.

Incidentally, you are wise not to choose just a small university to live in. One gets lonely even in one's field of knowledge. What would I not give for us to be able to live together! I am forgetting the very use of speech. The most irksome thing of all is that I am always having to impersonate someone—the teacher, the philologist, the human being, and that I first have to prove myself to everyone with whom I have dealings. But I am so bad at doing this, and I keep forgetting how. I say nothing or only just so much as a polite man of the world usually says. In brief, I am more dissatisfied with myself than with the world, and therefore all the more devoted to my dearest friend.

Middle of February. Now I am extremely worried because your letters are not reaching me and mine are not reaching you. I have heard nothing from you since November. My esteemed friend Cosima[18] advised me to inquire about you through her father (Franz Liszt). And I shall be doing this very soon; today I shall try it once more with a letter to you. We are well informed about the council through the "Roman" letters in the *Augsburger* [*Allgemeine Zeitung*]. Do you know their author?[19] If so, don't let anyone notice it—people are out to get him. I gave a lecture here on "Socrates and Tragedy," which excited terror and incomprehension. On the other hand, it has strengthened the ties with my Tribschen friends even more. I shall yet become a Walking Hope; Richard Wagner too has most touchingly indicated the aim he sees mapped out for me. This is all very frightening. You know what Ritschl has said about me. But I refuse to be tempted: I

18. Baroness von Bülow.

19. "Römische Briefe über das Konzil von Quirinus"; the author was Ignaz von Döllinger. These letters began to appear on December 27, 1869.

have really no literary ambition at all; I do not need to conform to a ruling stereotype in the search for distinguished and illustrious positions. But when the time comes, I shall express myself with as much seriousness and freedom of mind as possible. Knowledge, art, and philosophy are now growing into one another so much in me that I shall in any case give birth to a centaur one day.

My old comrade Deussen has gone over to Schopenhauer with heart and soul, as the last and oldest of my friends.[20] Windisch is spending a year in England, in the service of the East-Indian-Office [*sic*], in order to compare Sanskrit manuscripts. Romundt has founded a Schopenhauer Society. A scandalous piece against Ritschl has just been published (against his *Plautus* critique and the final D) by Bergk, a disgrace to German scholarship.[21]

Once more, warmest and friendliest greetings. I am looking forward to the spring, because it will bring you to Basel. Only do tell me when that will be. I am spending the Easter holidays with my relatives on Lac Leman.

Farewell! Farewell!

20 ·　*To Paul Deussen*　　　　Basel, Schützengraben 45
　　　　　　　　　　　　　　　　　[February, 1870]

My dear friend:

Your last letter differed unbelievably from all the previous ones. Now at last a long estrangement between us has vanished; we both speak the same language and do not feel different things when using the same words. Perhaps, if we had always remained together, the somewhat laborious and not altogether even and direct path to the present high level of your education would have been spared you and would have been a more natural and more gentle one instead. At least you are, of all my friends, the last to find the way to wisdom. Now at last I have for you altogether the highest hopes: you will be able to see clearly much that was cloudy. Of course, you will then feel more lonely than ever, as I do. Also many illustrious and striking positions in life cease to be attainable for us, and not worth striving for, either. To be hermits of intellect, having occasional converse with like-minded people, that is our lot; more than other beings, we need the solaces of art. Also

20. Deussen was at this time in Minden, having obtained his doctorate at Marburg in January, 1869.

21. F. Ritschl, *Neue Plautinische Excurse: sprachgeschichtliche Untersuchungen. Erstes Heft: Auslautendes d im alten Latien* (Leipzig, 1869). Theodor Bergk, *Auslautendes D im alten Latein: Beiträge zur lateinischen Grammatik, erstes Heft* (Halle, 1870).

we do not wish to convert others to our way of thinking, because we feel the gulf between them and ourselves to be one established by nature. Pity becomes truly a familiar feeling to us. We grow more and more silent—there are days on which I do not speak at all except in the service of my work. Certainly I have the invaluable good fortune to possess as a real friend Schopenhauer's true spiritual brother, who is related to him as Schiller to Kant, a genius, to whom has been given the same terribly sublime lot of coming a century before he can be understood . . . I therefore see deeper into the abysses of that idealistic view of life; also I observe how my philosophical, moral, and scientific endeavors strive toward a single goal, and that I may perhaps become the first philologist ever to achieve wholeness.[22] How marvelously new and changed history looks to me, especially the Greek world! I would like soon to send you my most recent lectures, of which the latter ("Socrates and Tragedy") has been understood here as a chain of paradoxes and has aroused hatred and anger in some quarters. Offense must come. I have, in the main, cast caution aside; to the individual human being, let us be compassionate and yielding, in the expression of our view of life as rigorous as the virtue of ancient Romans.

Now I expect you will write more often; for to you also there must come a longing to pour out to someone your new experience of things. Also you will be unlikely to find someone who has seen so many conversions as I, and has loved so often in others the enthusiasm of the neophyte.[23]

Most loyally
F. W. Nietzsche

21 ·   *To Carl von Gersdorff*   [Basel, March 11, 1870]

My dear friend:

I would have written long ago if I had not been living in a strange belief: that I did not know your address or even where you are living. I was

22. N's interest in scientific writings continued at Basel. It is on record that he borrowed the following works from the university library between 1870 and 1874: Boscovitch, *Philosophia naturalis* (1763) [three times]; Cantor, *Mathematische Beiträge;* Funke, *Lehrbuch der Physiologie*, 2 vols.; Helmholtz, *Die Lehre von den Tonempfindungen* (1863); Kopp, *Geschichte der Chemie*, vol. 2; Ladenburg, *Entwicklung der Chemie;* Moedler, *Das Wunderbare des Weltalls;* Mohr, *Allgemeine Theorie der Bewegung und Kraft* (1869); Pouillet, *Physik*, 2 vols. [twice]; Zöllner, *Natur der Kometen* [three times]; Zöllner, *Enzyklopädie der Physik*, vol. 9. Details from Mittasch, *Ns Naturbeflissenheit.*

23. In addition to becoming one of the foremost Indologists of his time, Deussen also became an authority on Schopenhauer and edited a new edition of his writings.

supposing that your new profession as a jurist had changed everything for you, and I was on the point of applying to the Berlin Koberstein Committee for information about you. Then you wrote me two letters in quick succession, and both have made a strong impression on me and aroused a longing to see you again. What do you think about coming to Switzerland this summer, perhaps in July?

That we are now agreed about Richard Wagner is for me an invaluable proof of our belonging together. For it is not an easy matter, and it demands a robust, manly spirit not to become confused in the terrible hullabaloo. Also one sometimes finds very fine and intelligent people in the enemy party. Schopenhauer must raise us theoretically above this conflict, just as Wagner does, in practice, as an artist. I always keep two things in mind. The incredible seriousness and the German depth in Wagner's view of life and art, which well up in every note he writes, are for most people in our present age a horror like Schopenhauer's asceticism and negation of the will. Our "Jews"—and you know how embracing that concept is—particularly hate Wagner's idealistic cast of mind, which is what relates him most closely to Schiller: this glowing high-hearted struggle for the dawning of the "day when men shall be noble,"[24] in brief, the knightly character which is utterly opposed to our plebeian political daily fuss. Ultimately I find even in excellent people often an *indolent* view of things, as if an independent effort, a serious and thorough study, for the sake of understanding such an artist and such works of art, were not necessary at all. How glad I was to hear that you are so opportunely studying *Opera and Drama!*[25] I immediately told my Tribschen friends of this. My friends are in no way strangers to you; and if you want to write a detailed letter to R. W. after the first *Meistersinger* performance,[26] this will be a great joy to them, and they will be already well informed about the writer of the letter. Also it goes without saying that, if you ever visit me, we shall travel to Tribschen. It is an infinite enrichment of one's life to know such a genius really closely. For me, all that is best and most beautiful is associated with the names Schopenhauer and Wagner, and I am proud and happy to share this feeling with my closest friends. Do you know *Art and Politics?*[27] I can also announce to you the publication of a little work by R. W., entitled *On Conducting*, which can be best compared with Schopenhauer's essay on "The Professors of Philosophy."[28]

24. Refers to Goethe's poem "Epilog zu Schillers Glocke." N misquotes; the line actually reads, "May the day dawn for the man who is noble."

25. By Wagner.

26. The first Berlin performance of *Die Meistersinger* was on April 1, 1870.

27. By Wagner.

28. The actual title is "Über die Universitäts-Philosophie" ("On Philosophy as Practiced in the Universities").

I was much saddened by the fate of your good brother.[29] We met not infrequently in Leipzig, even after you had left, and I always thought highly of him. I hope that everything will turn out well. But our life is such misery: ruination and terror gape on every side. It takes much to keep a courageous mind. Ah, and how much one needs to know that there are *true friends!* Sometimes the solitude is all too comfortless.

Loyally

Your F. N.

22 · *To Richard Wagner*   Basel, May 21, 1870

Pater seraphice:

Just as I was not destined last year to witness your birthday celebrations, so now again an unfavorable constellation prevents me; today my pen thrusts itself reluctantly into my hand, whereas I had hoped to make a Maytime journey to visit you.

Permit me to outline the compass of my wishes for you today as closely and personally as possible. Others may venture to congratulate you in the name of holy art, in the name of the highest German hopes, in the name of your own most intimate wishes; let me be satisfied with the most subjective of all wishes: that you may remain what you have been to me this last year, my mystagogue in the secret doctrines of art and life. Though I may seem at times somewhat distant from you, through the gray mist of philology, I am never far, my thoughts always circle around you. If it is true, as you once wrote, to my pride, that music is my conductor, then you are at all events the conductor of this music of mine; and you have told me yourself that even something middling, if *well* conducted, can make a satisfying impression. In this sense I bring you the strangest of all wishes: let it remain so, let the moment stay—it is so beautiful.[30] I ask only this of the coming year, that I may prove myself to be not unworthy of your inestimable interest and your firm encouragement. Accept this wish among the others with which you begin your life's new year!

One of the *selige Knaben*[31]

29. Gersdorff's brother Theodor had been committed to an insane asylum.

30. Allusion to the scene near the end of *Faust, part 2*, in which Faust recalls the terms of his pact with Mephistopheles, which forbade him to dwell in the perfect moment.

31. Allusion to the end of *Faust, part 2*, where a chorus of "selige Knaben" sings Faust into heaven. I have refrained from translating this phrase as "blissful boys," for obvious reasons. It means something nearer to Verlaine's "voix d'enfants chantant dans la coupole." The address *Pater seraphice* is also borrowed from the last scenes of *Faust*.

23 · *To Erwin Rohde* [Basel, July 19, 1870]

At last, dear friend, I too can write again. Imagine, I have in the meantime spent several weeks in bed because of a sprained ankle, evidently because I did not sacrifice a cock to Asclepios but eat the chickens (remember Köbi!)[32] always myself (remember Goethe).[33]

After these learned quotations I feel compelled to quote verbatim a passage from one of the latest Bülow letters.[34] "We have a pleasant memory of these days; the master is quite delighted with your friend; his manly seriousness, his acute interest, and the real friendliness which from time to time lit up his austere features, were extremely to his liking. If he goes to Freiburg, the two of you must visit Tribschen together, for 'two in one is best for man,'[35] as our authority says."

At this moment a terrible thunderclap: the Franco-German war is declared, and our whole threadbare culture plunges at the frightful demon's breast. What things we shall see! Friend, dearest friend, we saw each other once again in the sunset of peace. How grateful to you I am! If your life becomes bearable to you again, come back to me. What are all our goals!

We may be already at the beginning of the end! What desolations! We shall need monasteries again. And we shall be the first *fratres*.

Your loyal Swiss[36]

24 · *To Franziska Nietzsche* Sulz, near Weissenburg, in the vicinity of Wörth [August 29, 1870]

Warmest greetings!

We are five days' journey out of Erlangen;[37] the going is unthinkably slow, although we have every means of speeding it up, and entered France,

32. Köbi was the nickname of Jakob Burckhardt. N, Rohde, and Burckhardt had gone for a walk together to the village of Muttens, near Basel, on June 8, 1870. "Cock to Asclepios": allusion to the last words of Socrates.

33. Allusion to Goethe's poem "Diné zu Coblenz im Sommer 1774."

34. Letters from Cosima von Bülow.

35. Quotation from *Die Meistersinger*, Act 2: Sachs and Beckmesser.

36. N had had to become a Swiss citizen on his appointment at Basel.

37. N had been permitted by the authorities at Basel to join the Prussian forces as a medical orderly (other military service was out of the question, since he was officially

for example, sitting on the brakes in an endless supply convoy. Yesterday we had an eleven-hour march to carry out our missions in Gersdorf and Langensulzbach and on the battlefield at Wörth. A memory of the terribly devastated battlefield, scattered all over with countless mournful remains and reeking with corpses, comes with this letter. Today we go to Hagenau, tomorrow to Nancy, and so forth, following the Southern Army. Mosengel and I travel alone; not until Pont à Mousson shall we meet up with our Erlangen colleague Ziemsen.

For the next few weeks your letters cannot reach me, for we are continuously on the move and the mail travels extremely slowly. One hears nothing now of military advances here—no newspapers are being printed. The enemy populations here seem to be getting used to the new state of affairs. But then they are threatened with the death penalty for the least offense.

In all the villages we pass through there is hospital after hospital. You will hear from me again soon; do not worry about me.

Your Fritz

Perhaps you could send this letter to Lisbeth; one cannot write often or in any comfort.

25. *To Richard Wagner*   Erlangen, Sunday
                                 [September 11, 1870]

Lieber und verehrter Meister:

So then your house is completed and firmly established in the midst of the storm. Far away though I was, I kept thinking of this event and wishing blessings upon you, and it makes me very happy to see, from the lines written me by your wife, whom I dearly love, that it was finally possible to celebrate these festivities,[38] sooner than we suspected when we were last together.[39]

You know what stream it was that tore me away from you and made me unable to witness such holy and longed-for observances. My work as an

---

a Swiss citizen). He arrived at Erlangen on August 13 and took a ten-day course for medical orderlies. By September 7 he was back in Erlangen, suffering from diphtheria, and left for a period of convalescence in Naumburg on September 14.

38. On August 25, Wagner had legally married Cosima von Bülow following her divorce from Hans von Bülow. The baptism of their son Siegfried took place on September 4.

39. Mid-July, at Tribschen.

auxiliary has come provisionally to an end, unfortunately through sickness. My many missions and duties brought me close to Metz; it was possible for me and my—very trusted—friend Mosengel to accomplish most of our work with success. In Ars sur Moselle we took charge of casualties and returned with them to Germany. These three days and nights spent together with serious casualties were the climax of our efforts. I had a miserable cattle truck in which there were six bad cases; I tended them, bandaged them, nursed them during the whole journey alone—all with shattered bones, several with four wounds—moreover, I diagnosed in two cases gangrene. That I survived in those pestilential vapors, and could even sleep and eat, now seems a marvel. But I had hardly delivered my transport at a Karlsruhe hospital when I showed serious signs of illness myself. I reached Erlangen with difficulty, to give various reports to my group. Then I went to bed and am still there. A good doctor diagnosed my trouble as, first, a severe dysentery and, then, diphtheria. But we took strong measures against both infectious maladies, and today the outlook is hopeful. So I have made the acquaintance of two of those ill-famed epidemics at once; they weakened and enervated me so rapidly that I must for a start give up all my plans for working as a medical auxiliary and am obliged to think only of my health. Thus after a short run of four weeks, trying to work on the world at large, I have been thrown back once more upon myself—what a miserable state of affairs!

I prefer not to say a word about the German victories: these are the letters of fire on the wall, intelligible to *all* peoples.

I am not allowed to write any more; my next letter will be to your respected wife, at whose feet I lay my heartiest felicitations. A cheery greeting to the baptismal child! Greetings to the whole Tribschen household.

Your loyal Friedr. Nietzsche

26 · *To Erwin Rohde*   Basel, Wednesday, about November 27 [November 23, 1870]

Absolution! My dear friend, such years do not happen so soon again, and so my long deathly silence about myself will not happen again so soon. I am alive once more—true, I have not escaped the coils of dysentery and diphtheria, and they have sufficiently ruined me, but on the whole I am once more a man among men. I would prefer not to tell you about my experiences in the war—why were *you* not there with me? Incidentally, I did not see a single line of any of your letters—they all vanished "on the field of action."

I had a very valiant traveling companion, to whom I told a few things about you, in the hope that he may come to know you. Try to make this possible; you will be glad of it. His name is Mosengel, he is a painter and lives in Hamburg, Katharinenstrasse 41. He is one of the best people I have met, and is a landscape artist who does my heart good. He has done much for me and, finally, he even looked after me when I was sick.

Now I am very active again and am giving two courses, *Hesiod* and *Metric*, plus a seminar on scholarly method and *Agamemnon* at the Pädagogium. How are you getting on? Are you already under the academic yoke? If so, then good luck for the merry hunt,[40] and for your travels with Diogenes' lantern!

I shall tell you briefly the several joyful things that have come my way. Firstly there is a long essay by Wagner on Beethoven, which contains a philosophy in Schopenhauer's spirit and with Wagner's energy. It will soon be in print. Frau Wagner asked me in a letter whether you were on active service and how you were. Second joy: Jakob Burckhardt is giving a weekly lecture on the study of history—in the spirit of Schopenhauer—a lovely but rare refrain. I am attending his lectures. Third joy: on my birthday I had the best philological brain wave that I have ever had—well, I confess, that does not sound proud, and it should not do so! I am working on it now. If you are willing to believe me, then I can tell you that there exists a new metric, which I have discovered, and in contrast with which the whole recent development of metric from G. Hermann to Westphal or Schmidt is an aberration.[41] Laugh or mock as you will—to me the thing is very astounding. There is a lot of work to do, but I eat dust and enjoy it,[42] because this time I have the highest confidence and can keep on deepening the basic idea. In the summer I wrote, for my own benefit, a long essay, "On the Dionysian View of Life," so as to keep myself calm as the storm brewed.

Now you know how I am getting on. Add to this the fact that I am greatly worried about the future (in which I fancy I see a Middle Ages in disguise),[43] also that my health is bad—except when I receive letters from

40. Allusion to a song by Friedrich de la Motte Fouqué, "Kriegslied für die freiwilligen Jäger."

41. N is referring to his theory that the principal law of Greek metric was the variability of the time quantities with retention of word accents. Cf. his "Zur Theorie der quantitierenden Rhythmik und rhythmische Untersuchungen"; also the letters to Carl Fuchs, winter, 1884–85, and August 26, 1888.

42. Allusion to *Faust*, part 1, Prologue in Heaven, in which Mephistopheles says of Faust, "Staub soll er fressen und mit Lust."

43. Cf. the letter (No. 23) of July 19, 1870, to Rohde. On November 7, 1870, N had written to Carl von Gersdorff: "I am greatly worried about the immediate cultural future. . . . Confidentially, I regard Prussia now as a power which is highly dangerous to

friends or such fine essays as yours in the *Rheinisches Museum*.[44] It occurs to me that Vischer expressed great interest in you and also gratitude.

You have been of such great service to my ἀγών too; my warmest thanks for your help.[45] Ritschl maintains that you are no proofreader; I have never assumed to regard myself as one. So at least we are both equally damned. See if you cannot escape from that fatal anticultural Prussia, where the slaves and the priests sprout like mushrooms and will soon darken all Germany for us with their vapors. We agree, do we not? Well? And you do not look askance at me? God knows, that would be a pity.

Adieu, dear friend.   F. N.

In sending you my festive birthday greeting, I wish you good health, a professorship and, *si placet*—a wife.

27· To Carl von Gersdorff   Basel, December 12 [1870]

My dear friend:

How happy I shall be if you have survived the big attacks of these last weeks without suffering any harm![46] One should give no thought to these terrible things if one wants to keep one's spirit up.

---

culture. The organization of schools I shall expose later in public; let someone else try exposing the religious machinations now developing from Berlin in favor of Roman Catholic ecclesiastical power. Sometimes it is very difficult, but we must be philosophers enough to keep lucid in the general frenzy—so that the thief may not break in and steal or diminish that which, to my way of thinking, stands in no conceivable relation to the biggest military events, or even to feelings of national exaltation." N's fear of the rise of the Prussian power state under Bismarck was shared, but only by a minority of the German intelligentsia. (See Hans Kohn, *The Mind of Germany*, New York, Harper Torchbooks, 1965, pp. 207–21.) Wagner's fanatical and chauvinistic Germanophilism, combined with his theatrical religiosity, underlay the later break between N and him. At this stage, N is still fascinated by the allures of his "depth," and "seriousness," and "inwardness" (cf. letter of June 21, 1871, to Gersdorff)—qualities that he finds admirable in things German.

44. Rohde's essay "Unedirte Lucianscholien, die attischen Thesmophorien und Haloen betreffend," *Rheinisches Museum*, 25, 1870, pp. 548 ff.

45. Refers to Rohde's proofreading of N's treatise *Certamen quod dicitur Homeri et Hesiodi* . . . , Leipzig, 1871.

46. Refers to the attempts of the French 2d Army under General Ducrot to break through on the Brie-Villiers-Champigny front between November 30 and December 4. Gersdorff was a lieutenant in the 4th Guards Regiment of the 1st Prussian Infantry Division.

But now I want to write you a letter in the hope, even on the assumption, that you have escaped even these terrible dangers, with courage and luck, as a darling of the war god—but without loving him in return.

When will this letter ever reach you? Perhaps on your *birthday;* and if you celebrate it this time safe and sound, be like Polycrates and make sacrifice to the demons.

I am sending you Wagner's latest work, on Beethoven, as a symbol of the inmost community of our endeavors and thoughts under *one* flag, the one to which Wagner points in this work as the only one leading to the goal. I read it in a mood of elation and reverence. There are deep secrets in it, beautiful and terrible, as are the profoundest revelations of music itself.

From Tribschen I have Wagner's photograph to send you, with warm greetings. Frau Wagner wrote me: "Here is the promised photograph for the soldier-philosopher; Wagner can think of no better recipient than the man who valiantly does his duty, while not disdaining to ponder the essence of things."

Now another pleasant matter. You were so kind as to tell me in your letter from the field about a publication which guarantees the spreading of Schopenhauer's ideas in France also.[47] It was with a feeling of triumph that I recently found in the reports of the Vienna Academy of Sciences an article by Professor Czermak on Schopenhauer's theory of colors.[48] This confirms that Schopenhauer discovered independently and originally what is now known as the Young-Helmholtz theory of colors: the latter and the Schopenhauerian theory correspond in a most marvelous way, down to the very infinitesimals. It is claimed that the whole point of departure, color as primarily a physiological product of the eye, was first established by Schopenhauer. Czermak regrets that Schopenhauer was unable to free himself from the "scientifically untenable" theorem of Goethe and from Goethe's *furor Anti-Newtonianus.* Moreover, Czermak calls Schopenhauer (he is *not* an adherent of our philosopher) the "most powerful philosopher since Kant." And that ought to satisfy us well enough.

This treatise and Wagner's assent to the Schopenhauerian doctrine are also in their way contributions to the Hegel memorial.[49] Actually polemical articles are hardly necessary any more. Even the fact that Hart-

47. Alexandre de Balche, *Renan et Schopenhauer* (Odessa, 1870).

48. Johannes N. Czermak, *Über Schopenhauers Theorie der Farbe: ein Beitrag zur Geschichte der Farbenlehre* (Vienna, 1870).

49. The bronze bust of Hegel by Bläser was eventually unveiled in Berlin in 1872. The Hegelian school had perpetuated the old fight between Hegel and Schopenhauer (which had formerly resulted in the latter's fortunate failure ever to obtain an academic appointment).

mann's *Philosophy of the Unconscious* is already in a second edition—a book in which the problems at least are posed in a Schopenhauerian way—deserves to be cited as another sign of the general change of attitude.[50] Give me a few more years and you will notice a new influence in the study of antiquity too, and with it, I hope, a new spirit in the scientific and ethical *education* of our nation.

But what enemies of our faith are now growing out of the bloody soil of this war! I am prepared for the worst and at the same time confident that here and there in the mass of suffering and of terror the nocturnal flower of knowledge will bloom. Our struggle is still to come—therefore we must live! Therefore I also trust that you are immune; the bullets that are intended for us are not shot from rifles and cannon! And so farewell, dear friend!

Loyally as ever,   Your Friedrich Nietzsche

In the meantime I have received your lines and am heartily glad that my assumption was correct. May the *daimon* continue to bring you good fortune! The post office will not allow me to send the Beethoven essay now. You will not receive it until January.

28 · *To Erwin Rohde*   [Basel, December 15, 1870]

My dear friend:

Not a minute has passed since reading your letter, and already I am writing to you. For I wanted to say that I entirely share your feelings, and think it a disgrace if we do not by a drastic action extricate ourselves from this craving and languishment. Now listen to what I keep turning over in my mind. Let us drag on in this university existence for a few more years; let us take it as a *sorrowful lesson* which must be tolerated with seriousness and astonishment. This should be, among other things, a period of instruction for teaching, for which it is my task to train myself—only I have set my aim somewhat higher.

For, in the long run, I also realize what Schopenhauer's doctrine of university wisdom is all about. A completely radical institution for *truth* is not *possible* here. Above all, from here nothing really revolutionary can come.

50. N had already moved away from Schopenhauer by the time that the latter's allure began to spread during the 1870's, in conjunction with political indifference and economic stability among the German middle class.

Afterward we can become real teachers by levering ourselves with all possible means out of the atmosphere of these times and by becoming not only wiser but also better human beings. Here too I feel the need to be *true*. And that is another reason why I cannot go on breathing the academic atmosphere much longer.

So one day we shall cast off this yoke—for *me* that is certain. And then we shall create a new Greek academy. Romundt will certainly join us. From your Tribschen visit you will know of *Wagner's* Bayreuth plan. I have been quietly considering if we too should not likewise break with philology as practiced till now and with its educational perspective. I am preparing a big *adhortatio* for all who have not yet been utterly suffocated and swallowed up by the present age. How regrettable it is, though, that I must write to you about this, and that every idea has not already been *discussed* by us together! And because you do not know the whole present apparatus, my plan may seem to you like an eccentric whim. That is not the case—it is an urgent inner need.

A recent book of Wagner's on Beethoven will give you a good idea of what I desire of the future. Read it—it is a revelation of the spirit in which *we*—we!—shall come to live.

Even if we do not find many people to share our views, I still believe that we can fairly—not without losses, of course—pull ourselves up out of this stream and that we shall reach an island on which we shall not need to stop our ears with wax any more. Then we shall be teachers to each other; our books will be merely fishhooks for catching people into our monastic and artistic community. We shall love, work, enjoy for each other—perhaps this is the only way in which we can work for the *whole*.

To show you how seriously I mean this, I have already begun to limit my needs, in order to save a little capital. Also we should try our luck in *lotteries;* when we write books, I shall demand during the coming period the highest fees. In brief, every permitted means is to be used, so that it will be physically possible to found our monastery. Thus we have our task for the next few years too.

Above all, I hope that this plan will seem to you worth considering! Your most moving letter, just received, testifies that it is time, above all, to present it to you.

Surely we should be able to bring a new kind of academy into being:

> And should I not, by force of sheer desire,
> Draw into life the form most singular?

as Faust says of Helena.

Of this project *nobody* knows a thing, and it must be up to you whether or not we now give Romundt some advance notice of it.

Our school for philosophers is certainly not a historical reminiscence or an arbitrary whim—is it not an urgent inner need which sets us on this course? It seems that our plan we made as students, our journey together, is coming back again in a new, symbolically larger form. I shall not be the one to leave you in the lurch as I did before; that still nags me.[51]

With the highest hopes, your loyal *Frater Fredericus*

From December 23 to January 1 I shall be at Tribschen, near Lucerne. I have had no news of Romundt.

29. *To Wilhelm Vischer-Bilfinger* [Basel, probably January, 1871]

Verehrtester Herr Ratsherr:

For the scheme which follows I need to a special degree your considerate advice and the *true* concern which you have already often shown me. You will see that I have kept the welfare of the university in view with all seriousness, and that its real interest constrains me to put forward the following somewhat detailed argument.

My doctors will have told you of the extent to which I am once more in a poor state of health, and that this intolerable circumstance is due to overstrain. Now I have repeatedly asked myself how this overstrained condition, which occurs in the middle of practically every semester, can be explained; and I even had to consider whether I should not give up my university work completely, as a mode of life unsuited to my nature. Finally, however, I came in this regard to another conclusion, which I would now like to present to you.

I live here in a peculiar conflict, and it is this which so exhausts me and even grates on me physically. Urged most intensely by my nature to make thorough philosophical inquiry into a homogeneous field of thought, and to dwell undisturbed and with sustained reflection on one problem, I feel myself always thrown hither and thither, and driven off my course, by my daily variegated professional work and by the way it is disposed. This juxtaposition of Pädagogium and university I cannot in the long run tolerate, because I feel that my real task, to which I must if necessary *sacrifice any*

51. N is referring to their earlier plans to go to Paris; his appointment to Basel had prevented this.

profession, my philosophical task, is being made to suffer by it, and is even being reduced to an activity on the side. I believe that this description outlines most precisely what it is that so grates upon me here and prevents me from fulfilling my professional task with regularity and serenity, and which, on the other hand, exhausts my body and grows into such sufferings as I am undergoing now—which, if they should recur often, would quite physically force me to give up the profession of classical scholar altogether.

On these grounds I take leave to apply to you for the chair of philosophy vacated by Teichmüller's departure.

As regards my personal right to aspire to the chair of philosophy, I must of course write my own testimonial, in the belief that I possess the capacity and learning for it, and even feel myself to be better qualified for that office than for a purely philological one.[52] People who know me from my years at school and university have never had any doubt about the dominance of my philosophical inclinations; and even in my philological studies I was most attracted by those aspects which seemed important to the history of philosophy or to ethical and esthetic problems. This being so, I entirely agree with your judgment and apply it to myself, that, in the present somewhat difficult state of university philosophical studies, and considering how few applicants are really suitable, that person has a somewhat greater right who can exhibit a solid training in classical philology and can stimulate among the students an interest in the careful interpretation of Aristotle and Plato. I would remind you that I have already announced two courses which would be philosophical in this sense: "The Pre-Platonic Philosophers, with Interpretation of Selected Fragments,"[53] and "On the Platonic Question."[54] As long as I have been studying philology, I have spared no efforts to keep in close contact with philosophy; indeed, my chief interest lay always in philosophical questions, as many can vouch who have

52. N certainly understood by "philosophy" something like an integrator of all fields of knowledge, as agreed by the young Adrian Leverkühn and Serenus Zeitblom in Thomas Mann's *Doktor Faustus:* "Among them [the sciences], we had affirmed, [philosophy] took a place like that of the organ among instruments: she afforded a survey, she combined them intellectually, she ordered and refined the issues of all the fields of research into a universal picture, an overriding and decisive synthesis comprehending the meaning of life, a scrutinizing determination of man's place in the cosmos." (*Doctor Faustus*, translated by H. T. Lowe-Porter, New York: Knopf, 1948, pp. 80–81.) The first essay to dispute this view of philosophy in N's case as a clearing house for the findings of the other disciplines seems to have been Alfred Werner's "N als Philosoph und die Philosophie unserer Tage," *Archiv für Gesichchte der Philosophie* (Berlin, 1916).

53. N had announced this course for the winter semester 1869–70, but he did not give it until the summer of 1872.

54. N never gave a course with this title; during the winter semester 1871–72 he gave a course entitled "Introduction to the Study of the Platonic Dialogues."

known me. Of colleagues here, Overbeck, for example, could give you information on this; of others elsewhere, none could be better informed than my friend Dr. Rohde, *Privatdozent* at Kiel. It is, as a matter of fact, a mere accident that I did not plan for philosophy from the start of my university work, the accident which denied me a distinguished and truly stimulating philosophy teacher, which certainly need surprise no one, considering the present constellation of conditions for philosophy at universities. But in this, certainly, one of my warmest wishes would be fulfilled, if here too I might follow the voice of my nature; and I hope and trust that, once the conflict I mentioned has been removed, my physical state will also be far more regular. I shall be able, soon enough, to show publicly my competence for an appointment in philosophy: my published works on Laertius Diogenes are in any case also to be taken into account with regard to my aspirations in the history of philosophy. I have always been interested in educational questions and inquiries; to be allowed to lecture on these would be a particular joy to me. Of more recent philosophers, I have studied Kant and Schopenhauer with especial predilection. You will certainly have gained from the last two years of good faith that I know how to avoid anything inept and offensive, and that I can distinguish between what is appropriate for a lecture to students and what is not.[55]

If I may present my project to you in its entirety, I would have thought that you would find in Rohde a completely suitable successor for my professorship in classical philology and for my position at the Pädagogium. Rohde, whom I have known very closely for four years, is the most competent of all the younger philologists I have known, and a true adornment for any university that acquires him; moreover, he is still actually available, although I hear that Kiel is negotiating to keep him permanently by establishing a new Extraordinary Professorship in classical philology. I cannot express how profoundly my life here in Basel would be alleviated by the nearness of my best friend. The whole change-about could begin at once with the beginning of the summer semester, so that there would be no hiatus in the filling of the positions. For my part, I would be prepared at once to give you details of my lectures in philosophy and would commence my new appointment at the start of the summer with a regular inaugural lecture.

55. Academics at this time were highly dubious about Schopenhauer's credentials as a philosopher—owing, not least, to the respectability credited to Hegel. One cannot have much difficulty in picturing the incredulous faces of the officials as N's project was laid before them (if it ever was); yet, if the letter seems to display a great and even bewitching naïveté, Basel would have been a great and bewitching university, with N as philosopher, Rohde in classical civilization, and Burckhardt as historian.

Do not be fearful, *verehrtester Herr Ratsherr*, at the unusual nature of my proposition, and grant it a consideration.

Asking the favor of your indulgence, your advice, and your interest, I remain your most obedient servant

Dr. F. Nietzsche, Professor Ordinarius in
Classical Philology

30 · *To Erwin Rohde*   Lugano, Hotel du Parc (but leaving
                             here at the end of the week)
                             [March 29, 1871]

Yes, my dear friend, to break the spell! That is difficult for me and at present quite impossible. For I have no idea how the matter is developing—none at all. Vischer has written to me once here (in Lugano), but his letter contained not a word about our common concern. On the other hand, before leaving Basel and after I had written to you, I found some indication that the "philosopher" Steffensen was not favorable toward our project. Think how much I am in their clutches if they can invoke my liking for Schopenhauer, of which I have never made a secret. Moreover, I must prove and legitimize myself as a philosopher somewhat; to that end I have finished, except for a few touches, a short work, "The Origin and Aim of Tragedy." It means, I think, that we shall have to wait a little at least—until Michaelmas, when, if all goes well, a decision will come in our favor. The sad state of unrest and dissatisfaction, as our *perpetuum mobile*, will of course be drawn out for quite a while, and we have plenty of time in which to test our philosophical cold-bloodedness on a none too hopeful expectation! So that is the reverse side of my brain wave; if it worked out quickly and unexpectedly, glory be! If it means delay, misery! We have chosen the longer share, which is this time the shorter one also.

I am still not in the best of health; one night in every two I cannot sleep. Although I am much brighter and calmer and feel all right on the whole, I may not think of traveling yet; I snatch the hem of Italy and soon let it drop again. I have not yet seen even Lake Como and the Langensee, and have been in Lugano more than six whole weeks. The weather is not very Italian, on the whole; I have felt as yet nothing of a spring that should be more springlike than our German one—even the lower mountains round about still have snow on them, and until two weeks ago it was still in the hotel garden—a good hotel, by the way. Abnormal! people say, cold comfort, to which I have grown accustomed since I came to Switzerland.

In addition to many depressed moods and half moods, I have also had a few quite elated ones and have given some sign of this in the small work I mentioned. From philology I feel exuberantly remote in a way which is quite disgraceful. Praise and blame on that side of things, even all the highest glories, make me shudder. Thus I am gradually habituating myself to being a philosopher, and already I believe in myself, I would even be prepared for it if I were to become a poet. I have no orientation at all vis-à-vis the kind of knowledge for which I am destined; and yet, when I sum things up, everything seems to fit together, as if I had till now been following a benevolent daimon. I never thought that anyone so uncertain of his aims and completely lacking in the highest ambition as regards tenure in the profession could feel as lucid and calm as I do feel on the whole. What a wonderful sense it gives to see one's own world, a pretty ball, growing round and full before one's eyes! Sometimes I see some metaphysic growing, sometimes a new esthetic; then at other times I ponder a new principle of education, rejecting entirely our high schools and universities. Everything that I learn now finds a good place in some corner of what I have learned already. And most of all I feel the growth of this world of my own when I contemplate, not coolly, but calmly, the so-called world history of the past ten months, and use that as a means for my good ends, without any exaggerated reverence for the means. The words "pride" and "craziness" are really too weak to describe my intellectual "insomnia." This state makes it possible for me to look upon the whole university situation as something incidental, often as a mere nuisance even, and that chair of philosophy itself attracts me, as a matter of fact, only for your sake, since I regard that too as being merely provisional.

Ah, how I long for good health! One has only to plan something that will last longer than oneself—then one is thankful for every good night spent, for every warm ray of sun, even for an orderly digestive system! But with me certain abdominal organs are disturbed. Hence nerves and sleeplessness, hemorrhoids and the taste of blood, and so on. Kindly do not ascribe the condition of mind described above to the condition of my ganglia too! Or I might fear for my immortality, for I have never heard of flatulence inspiring a philosophical state.

With this—this state[56]—I commend myself to you and beg you not to give up hope entirely; I know how glad Vischer will be to see to the matter. My remissness in writing I prefer not to excuse; but you know that

56. A joke—the word for "flatulence" ("Blähungen") and the words for "philosophical state" ("philosophische Zustände") set up an ambiguity in "this" (in original, "Mit diesen," plural), to which "this state" (in original, "mit diesen Zuständen") calls attention while canceling it.

the more one needs friends, the less one usually writes. It is as it should be—but it is not right, all the same. So you will get a letter from me again shortly. Meanwhile be thinking of me as I am always thinking of you, dear friend.

F. N.

31 · *To Carl von Gersdorff*   Basel, June 21, 1871

My dear, dear friend:

So you have returned home safely and *integer* from the monstrous perils.[57] At last you can think again of peaceful occupations and tasks, and regard that terrible episode of war as an earnest but vanished dream in your life. Now new duties beckon; and if in peace there is one thing remaining for us from that savage game of war, it is the heroic and at the same time reflective spirit which, to my surprise, like a beautiful unexpected discovery, I found fresh and vigorous in our army, full of old Germanic health. We can build on that: we may still have hope! Our *German* mission is not yet past! I am in better heart than ever, for not everything has been ruined by French-Jewish superficiality and "elegance" and by the greedy turmoil of the present age. There is still courage—and German courage—between which and the élan of our poor neighbors there is an inward difference.

Over and above the struggle between nations the object of our terror was that international hydra-head, suddenly and so terrifyingly appearing as a sign of quite different struggles to come.[58] If we could discuss this together, we would agree that precisely in that phenomenon does our modern life, actually the whole of old Christian Europe and its state, but, above all, the "Romanic" civilization which is now everywhere predominant, show the enormous degree to which our world has been damaged, and that, with

57. N uses the Latin word: "glücklich erhalten und 'integer' . . . heimgekehrt" (= "whole," or "intact").

58. See Hans Kohn, *The Mind of Germany*, for a study of Germanophile pro-"Kultur" and anti-liberal, anti-"Western" ideology, including anti-internationalism in Germany, at this time. In this letter there is for the first time a slight shift in N's attitude, even if he is still far from being the Francophile of later years. The first paragraph, with its laboring solemnity, shows how strongly he clung to the idea of German "health" and "depth"—with, probably, the *arrière pensée* that these were properties of a transforming, rather than purely destructive, barbarism out of which might come a cultural regeneration (cf. *The Birth of Tragedy* [written in 1871], chap. 24: "The German spirit is still alive . . . like a knight who . . . dreams far underground. . . . One day the knight will awaken. . . . He will slay dragons, destroy the cunning dwarfs. . . ." [Translated by Francis Golffing. New York: Doubleday Anchor Books, 1956, p. 144.]).

all our past behind us, we are all of us responsible for such terror coming to light, so that we must make sure we do not ascribe to those unfortunates alone the crime of fighting against culture. I know what it means, the fight against culture. When I heard of the fires in Paris,[59] I felt for several days annihilated and was overwhelmed by fears and doubts; the entire scholarly, scientific, philosophical, and artistic existence seemed an absurdity, if a single day could wipe out the most glorious works of art, even whole periods of art; I clung with earnest conviction to the metaphysical value of art, which cannot exist for the sake of poor human beings but which has higher missions to fulfill. But even when the pain was at its worst, I could not cast a stone against those blasphemers, who were to me only carriers of the general guilt, which gives much food for thought.

I enclose a treatise which shows more of my philosophical doings than the title suggests.[60] Read it charitably; I have many things in the making, and am getting ready for a struggle in which, I know, my friends will take great interest. How much we could talk about together, my dear friend! And when can I hope you will visit me?

Of Wagner you have heard much, and I think, only good things, in the *Norddeutsche Allgemeine* [*Zeitung*], also of the big plans for Bayreuth. Everything is going extremely well. You are remembered kindly at Tribschen; I told them that you have promised a visit in the summer.

This summer my health has improved. Yet the weather is extremely changeable. Today it is cloudy and there is a cold rain. During the summer I shall be from July 15 to August 13 in Grimmelwald, near Mürren, in the Bernese Oberland, together with my sister. We have already booked rooms there in a small, wonderfully situated pension. Did you witness the march into Berlin?

Once more, dear friend, I am happy to think of your coming visit. Councillor Vischer (who used to visit your father's house in Weimar often as a student) is also looking forward to your arrival. For all my acquaintances know of your doings.[61]

Fare well and fare better and better: you have deserved it.

Please give my best regards to your respected parents from, as ever, your loyal friend,

Friedrich Nietzsche

59. The Tuileries had been destroyed by fire on May 24, 1871, during the Commune rising; it was also reported at the time that the Louvre had been destroyed.

60. *Socrates and Greek Tragedy.*

61. The original says "von Deinen Schicksalen," which is considerably more heroic in tone.

32 · *To Carl von Gersdorff*   [Basel, November 18, 1871]

Forgive me, my dear friend, for not thanking you earlier for your letters, of which each one reminds me of the vigorous cultural life you lead, as if you were basically still a soldier and were now seeking to show your military cast of mind in the realm of philosophy and art. And that is as it should be; only as fighters have we in our time a right to exist, as vanguard fighters for a coming *saeculum*, whose formation we can roughly presage from our own selves—that is, from our best moments; for these best moments do obviously estrange us from the spirit of our *own* time, but they must have a home somewhere; therefore I believe that we have in these moments a sort of obscure presentiment of what is to come. Have we not also retained from our last common Leipzig recollection the memory of such estranged moments which belong in another *saeculum?* Well then—that is how it is—and let us live for wholeness, fullness and beauty! But that takes a vigorous resolve and is not for anyone.[62]

Today I was strongly reminded of our life in Leipzig and in a certain sense I can say: now I join to the happy end the happy beginning, as the gay song says.[63] For today, only today, the excellent publisher Fritzsch replied to my Leipzig visit; that is why I must give you news of it today of all days. For it was you and Rohde, you two, who brought me morally and physically to the excellent Fritzsch: something that I still must celebrate. He could not help it that his answer took so long. He had sent the manuscript at once to a specialist for his judgment, and the latter had shillyshallied until November 16. You will know that my song "Dear Friend, This Greeting as a Birthday Gift" was intended for November 16, that is, for Krug's birthday. On this same day the good Fritzsch wrote, "that annoyance may nag and flay me not,"[64] and he promises to have the book ready as soon as Christmas. Well then, the design is settled—to be modeled on Wagner's *The Object of Opera*—rejoice with me! This means that there will be a glorious place for a nice vignette; tell this to your artist-friend, and give him my most amicable regards as well.[65] Take out the Wagner pamphlet, open the title

---

62. The phrase "let us live . . . beauty" is a quotation from Goethe's ballad "Der Schatzgräber."

63. Allusion to a song by August von Kotzebue, "Gesellschaftslied."

64. Both phrases are quotations from N's song composed for his friend Gustav Krug (the composition is discussed in N's letter of November 13 to Krug, not translated).

65. Leopold Rau, of Berlin.

page, and calculate the size which we can give the graphic work. It depends only on the title:

The
Birth of Tragedy
from the Spirit of Music
by
Dr. Friedrich Nietzsche
Professor of Classical Philology
Leipzig Fritzsch

I have at present still the greatest confidence that the book will have tremendous sales and the gentleman who does the vignette can prepare himself for a modicum of immortality.

Now some more news. Imagine, my dear friend, how strangely those warming days of reunion[66] during my vacation came at once to fruition in me, in the form of a longish composition for two pianos, in which everything echoes a beautiful autumn, warm with the sun. Because it connects with a youthful memory, the opus is called "Echo of a New Year's Eve: With Processional Song, Peasant Dance, and Midnight Bell." That is a jolly title; one might well have expected even too much: "With Punchbowl and Wishes for the New Year." Overbeck and I play the piece—it is now our *pièce de résistance*—with which we outdo all four-handed people. At Christmas this music will be a present and a surprise for Frau Wagner. You, my dear friends, are the unwitting *dei ex machina* to the comp. [*sic:* composition] also; I had composed nothing for six years, and *this* autumn stimulated me again. When properly performed, the music lasts twenty minutes.

Beyond this, I am back at being a philologist. Work: I am lecturing on "Introduction to the Study of Plato" and "Latin Epigraphy," and am preparing, for after the New Year, six public lectures, "On the Future of our Educational Institutions."

Next Tuesday our new philosopher is giving his inaugural lecture, on the "obvious" subject: "Aristotle's Meaning for the Present."[67]

You are kindly remembered here. I celebrated the daimon rites with Jakob Burckhardt in his room; he joined my ritual act and we poured a good two beer glasses of Rhone wine down on the street below.[68] In earlier centuries we would have been suspected of witchcraft. When I got home

66. N had spent October in Naumburg and Leipzig, where he had met Gersdorff and Rohde again.

67. Rudolf Eucken had been appointed to the chair of philosophy at Basel. He left in 1874.

68. This was to commemorate the meeting with Gersdorff and Rohde in Leipzig.

at eleven-thirty that night, feeling rather demonic, I found to my surprise friend Deussen there, and walked the streets with him until about two in the morning. He left by the first train in the early morning. I have an almost ghostly memory of him, as I saw him only in the pale lamplight and moon-light.

Write again soon, my brave and valued friend! You now know that the vignette is needed in a hurry. Cordial greetings from your

Friedr. N.

33. *To Erwin Rohde* [Basel, after December 21, 1871]

My dear, dear friend:

First of all, my heartiest best wishes for Christmas.

I was hoping to be able to send you my book, but there have been some delays, not through any fault of mine, so that my Christmas present will arrive a little late this time. The vignette for the title page has caused a few interruptions; the drawing, by Gersdorff's friend Rau, has our highest praise, but the "trusty" woodcut artist whom Fritzsch found has done a botched job, so that his block is altogether unusable and incorrigible, and we have had to hand the work over to one of the best woodcut artists, the academic Vogel in Berlin. Gersdorff has been standing by me and has been signally helpful in every way (have you dropped him a line? I think that would please him very much. He is on the management committee of the Berlin Wagner Society; why not ask him for a ticket? Alexandrinenstrasse 121, 2d floor).

The type is considerably more compact than in *The Object of Opera*, so that the book is not long, about 140 pages. Eight sheets are done, page for page, and I have only a little more to correct, and the introduction. The whole last part, which you do not know, will certainly astonish you; I have been very daring, and can exclaim to myself in an altogether huge sense, *Animam salvavi!* for which reason I am very pleased with the book and am not disturbed by the chance that it may cause as much offense as may be and that from some quarters there may be raised a "cry of outrage" when it is published.

Moreover, I feel wonderfully assured in my knowledge of music and convinced of its rightness—as a result of what I have experienced in Mann-heim this week together with Wagner. Ah, my friend, if only you had been there! What are all the other artistic memories and experiences compared with this latest one! I felt like a man whose presentiments have at last come true. For that precisely is music, and nothing else is. But I consider that if only a few hundred people of the next generation will have from music what I have from it, then I anticipate an entirely new culture! Everything that is left over and cannot be grasped in terms of musical relations does of course sometimes disgust and horrify me. And when I returned from the Mannheim concert, I actually had an oddly intensified, weary dread of daily reality, because it seemed no longer real to me but ghostly.[69]

I am spending this Christmas alone in Basel and have declined the cordial invitations from Tribschen. I need time and solitude to think out my six lectures ("Future of Educational Institutions") and to collect myself. To Frau Wagner, whose birthday is on December 25 (and to whom I would write if I were you!), I have dedicated my "New Year's Eve," and am excited as to what I shall hear about my musical work from there, for I have *never* heard a competent judgment. When I play it to you one day, I am sure you will detect the warm, contemplative, and happy tone which sounds through the whole work and which denotes for me a transfigured memory of the joy I felt during the autumn vacation.

I have spent some good days with Jakob Burckhardt, and we have many discussions about Greek matters. I think that one could learn a great deal about such matters in Basel at present. He has read your Pythagoras essay with great interest and has copied out parts of it for his own use; what you say about the whole development of the Pythagoras image is certainly the best that has so far been said on this very serious subject.[70] In the meantime, I have had a number of fundamental insights into Plato, and I think that we two might one day well and truly warm up and illuminate from inside the hitherto so shabby and mummified history of Greek philosophers. Only do not give the damned philological journals everything of a general nature that you have to say; just wait a little for the *Bayreuther Blätter.*[71] I am very glad you have agreed to write a piece for Zarncke, and am of course very grateful.[72] My dear friend, we have still a large piece of life to measure out together. Let us be loyal to each other.

F. N.

69. The program, arranged by Wagner for the Mannheim Wagner Society, consisted of the following: Wagner, *Kaisermarsch;* Mozart, Overture to *The Magic Flute;* Beethoven, Symphony in A major; Wagner, Prelude to *Lohengrin;* Wagner, Prelude to *Die Meistersinger;* Wagner, Prelude and conclusion to *Tristan und Isolde.*

70. E. Rohde, "Die Quellen des Iamblichus in seiner Biographie des Pythagoras," *Rheinisches Museum,* 26: pp. 554 ff.; 27: pp. 23 ff.

71. This journal did not begin to appear until 1878.

72. Rohde's (highly partisan) review of *The Birth of Tragedy,* written for Zarncke's journal *Literarisches Centralblatt,* was rejected by the editor. It differs from the later review in the *Norddeutsche Allgemeine Zeitung.* The text is published in Nietzsche, *Werke und Briefe: Briefe 3,* pp. 451–56.

34 · *To Franziska and Elisabeth Nietzsche*

Basel, Saturday [December 23, 1871]

My dear mother and sister:

With all my heart I wish that my small Christmas presents may bring you some joy. I shall begin my explanation of them with the one which is dedicated to you both: the composition entitled "Echo of a New Year's Eve" you must soon get someone to play to you; and I recommend for this the willing help of Gustav Krug, to whom I shall make the request in a letter. It was written a short while after my return from last vacation, and is for me a sign of how warming and beneficent that vacation must have been for me. For after an interruption of six years it is my first attempt of this kind—and, if I am not mistaken, a successful attempt. I have had a nice copy made for you, and would like the cost of the trouble it took to make the copy to be counted among my presents to you. I must hear from you soon how you like this music. You will have some feeling for it, for this time my dedication is not so nonsensical as was the case with my earlier compositions, of which the "Hungarian Cavalry March" was dedicated to Uncle Theobald and the "Love Song" to Aunt Rosalie.

For you now, dear Mother, the curtains are meant; their effect should delight us both when I come to Naumburg again. Then someone told me that you would like the carved salad servers. Do please, I ask you, accept the presents kindly.

To you, dear Lisbeth, I give Lübke's *History of Art*, from which you can learn much, and will have learned much when I ask you questions on it one day. It is an entirely new edition. You will be more satisfied with this book than with the Springer one that you wanted (how can you expect me to order a book from a scandalous Jewish antiquarian bookseller!). Also, our dear mother will have given you, at my request, a good album. You will like the little Hebel too.[73]

So much for my presents. The reason why my book on tragedy is not among them is simply that it is not ready yet. But in the New Year, and perhaps even with the New Year, you will receive it. They have dawdled a

73. Johann Peter Hebel (1760–1826) was a native of Basel who is best known for two works: the dialect poems *Alemannische Gedichte* (1803), and the collection of masterly short tales and anecdotes *Schatzkästlein des rheinisches Hausfreundes* (1811). It is not known which of these N gave to Elisabeth. Possibly it was the edition of the former, published in Leipzig in 1850, with the poems translated from dialect by R. Reinick and with illustrations by Ludwig Richter.

bit over the printing. Actually it was to be my Christmas present to Richard Wagner, but now it will be too late.

I am not celebrating Christmas this time at Tribschen, in spite of the most cordial invitations, because I need time to work out my lectures, which begin in the New Year—the lectures on the future of our schools. But I have had my Christmas with the Wagners in advance, by spending last week in Mannheim with them and having the indescribable pleasure of attending a Wagner concert right beside them. We had the first floor in the Europäischer Hof, and the many honors shown to W. included some that fell upon me too as his closest confidant. The whole journey, by the way, cost me relatively little, though I was away from Monday to Thursday. A letter is no place in which to tell of my artistic experiences there—the greatest in my life; in a certain sense, the fulfillment of a deep presentiment.

Farewell now, my dears, and think of me at this Christmas time.

Your Fritz
Loving as always

N.B. Frau W. has her birthday on December 25. It will be good of you, dear Lisbeth, to write to her. Do not forget.

35· *To Franziska and Elisabeth Nietzsche*

[Basel, December 27, 1871]

My dear mother and sister:

At last—that is, since an hour ago—I have your glorious Christmas presents, and at once I feel an urge to thank you most heartily for them. How long did the post take? Today is Wednesday. Your letter sent in advance had given me some inkling, but really not much, for as I unpacked I was altogether taken by surprise. The house decorator helped me and, without suffering a single knock, the wonderful picture in its splendid frame emerged, after some effort on our part, for it was very thoroughly packed and nailed up. Also, as always happens with me, once more we had removed the wrong side of the box first. Also I was surprised how expensive the postal delivery was, I think they asked for eighteen francs. It is certainly very expensive, living so far apart. This afternoon the pictures will be hung in my room: naturally the *Madonna* will be over the sofa; over the piano there will be a picture by Holbein, the big Erasmus, which the young Vischers gave me at their Christmas Eve celebration. From which you will have learned where I spent that evening; today I am invited to the celebration at the Bachofens and for New Year's Eve to the old Vischers, so that I shall have seen three Christmas trees. For Friday lunch old Stähelin has invited me to go to Liestal.

That is my program for the festivities—now to continue admiring your presents. The *Madonna della Sedia* is a glorious picture: my room becomes more and more large and exalted. I am already doubtful whether my small, monotonous student pictures are worthy of such a room. These are now grouped, with Papa Ritschl and Schopenhauer, above the book table beside the stove. Anyway, the picture affected me strongly and I thank you most heartily, dear Lisbeth. Also it seems as if such a picture were drawing me involuntarily toward Italy—and I almost believe you sent it to me in order to lure me there. The only answer I can give to this Apollonian effect is through my Dionysian one—that is, the New Year's Eve music—and after that, through the Apollonian-Dionysian double effect of my book, which will be published at the New Year and which you will receive direct from Fritzsch in Leipzig. He has had instructions since three days ago.

Now I proceed and tell of the impression made on me by the beautiful pink package, from my dear mother. When I saw the beautiful Russian leather, I thought you were really spoiling me—where would such aristocratic tendencies land me! Such a writing case was certainly something I needed, and the first letter I write on it is for you, my dear mother. Equally useful and delightful were the good comb, the hairbrush, the clothesbrush (except it is somewhat too soft), the nice socks, and the large quantity of delicious gingerbread—all of them beautifully and festively packed. Not forgetting the suspenders! Fate struck only yesterday, and both the old suspenders finally tore, so that I had to go out without wearing them. So the new ones come at the right moment; "When the need is greatest, the suspenders are closest," I thought as I unpacked them. For all these things, my heartiest thanks; I was very delighted and still am, when the fragrance of my blotting pad comes to my nostrils. Nothing could remind one more strongly of a present than this smell: thus how often shall I be reminded!

Well, so now we have reached the limit of the year. I think of the past year with reassurance and leave it with gratitude. You will be seeing how it has been, in a certain sense, an epoch-making one for me. My book will soon appear; with it I shall begin the new year, and now people will know what I want, what I aspire to with all my strength—my time of activity begins. Good moments they were in which this book was written; it was a good year, despite its doubtful beginning. Soon health returned; and what lovely warm times in Lugano and Basel and Naumburg and Leipzig I now see in my mind's eye!

To all who think kindly of me—and who more than you? I give hearty thanks at this limit of the year and wish you and myself a happy New Year, vigorous as ever, loving as ever, my dear mother, dear sister.

Your Fritz

36 · *To Gustav Krug*   [Basel, December 31, 1871]

My dear friend:

I owe you my warmest thanks not only for your detailed and kind letter but also for your sending a fragment of a very attractive composition. To begin with the latter, I liked the sure touch of the counterpoint in this experiment in canon: that is our modern way of introducing *scherzoso* the most tremendous feats, somewhat as Wagner does in the "Prügelszene."[74] On the other hand, your *scherzo* has for my feeling a somber, melancholy aftertaste; when I think also of the sound of the strings, I have the impression of feverish excitement: rapid, wild resolutions in amazingly quick succession, and we look longingly for a saving middle movement:

> Conducted by joy we pass through the gate,
> The clouds are shining, the flowers separate,
> And an image appears to us, image divine—

as we sang in Goethe's "Ergo bibamus." Well then, dear friend, a divine image. Sadness is not made for man but for the animals, says Sancho Panza. But if man is addicted to sadness overmuch, it makes him an animal. I avoid nowadays, as far as possible, this "animal" quality in music. Even pain must be surrounded by such a halo of dithyrambic ecstasy that it drowns in it, to some extent; this I feel about the greatest example of all, the third act of *Tristan*. Laugh as much as you like about my absurd advice and wish, I wish and advise for you *more* joy—in music too, and let that be my New Year's wish for you.

Ah, we both know, my dear friend, how foolish such a wish is, this inner, quietly blessed joy which streams out of art is not in our power, does not obey our wishes—but may fall unexpectedly here and there from heaven into our laps. May this "here and there" be yours often in the new year! And may the whole quartet be *in specie* an echo of such moments, without any "animal" aftertaste, or with just such a delicate and noble dose of it as your original fragment contains. When I am in Naumburg again I

---

74. The last scene of Act 2 in *Die Meistersinger.*

shall count it among my first pleasures actually to *hear* your quartet; between then and now you will probably have succeeded in collecting a quartet society. One learns too from the performance of one's own compositions by others what "conducting" means. The personal experience alone shows one how many mistakes can be made in the performance of the simplest music. To that extent it is very instructive, but also very embarrassing and painful, as I have recently often found with my composition for two pianos, which nobody can play to my satisfaction.

All the more do I hope that precisely you, my dear friend, as the only person really initiated into my musical development, will be able to understand fully the composition which you will probably come to know during the coming few days. For I would like to ask you to give my mother and sister, to whom I dedicated it at Christmas, an idea of the piece, and do not think that I ask you this in vain. Do understand that this music makes no pretensions; they were beautiful days on which I wrote it—for me, but I do not know how beautiful they were for others. Or rather, I do know, from reactions here. But it is not much to my glory to speak of that. It is odd how difficult it is to transmit one's own feelings, and what one can perceive in this music *without* my feelings, God alone knows. It must be something strange, and I am utterly incapable of imagining it.

My book is being published by Fritzsch in the new year. It will of course be sent to you, as a regular melomaniac. Oh! It is naughty and offensive. Read it secretly, closeted in your room.

I am thinking with every interest and sympathy of our dear friend Wilhelm [Pinder] and expect to hear soon the cry of victory over a freshly demolished examination. Meanwhile, take heart and courage! And keep well! And a strong sword and steed for such perils!

Give my best New Year's greetings to your respected parents and be assured of the old loyalty of your

friend Friedrich Nietzsche

37. *To Richard Wagner (draft)*

[Basel, probably January 2, 1872]

In your presence, my esteemed friend and master, I will at least refrain from confessing that everything I have to say here about the birth of tragedy has already been said more beautifully clearly and convincingly by you: for

that is why I would like to compare my task with that which the unwritten dogmas of Plato

for here is your domain. On the other hand, I feel just as clearly that you are the only person to whom I must excuse the existence of this book, to many

if you were ever to have descended to this historicizing. For to you I must excuse the existence of this book   for what concerning this area of esthetic inquiry could I possibly have to tell you, who would have guessed it long ago? While, on the other hand, I fear that you find me groping uncertainly and going wrong, where you yourself have the decisive information ready with a single word.

38 · *To Richard Wagner*   Basel, January 2, 1872

Verehrtester Meister:

At last my New Year's greeting and my Christmas present come to you: certainly very late, but through no fault of Fritzsch's or of mine. But the sometimes unpredictable post belongs among the "powers of fate," with which no eternal bond can be woven.[75] The package left Leipzig on December 29, and I have been waiting hourly for its arrival, in order to be able to send you my greetings and good wishes together with it.

May my book be at least in some degree adequate to the interest which you have till now shown in its genesis—an interest which really puts me to shame. And if I myself think that, in the fundamentals, I am right, then that means only that *you* with *your art* must be eternally right. On every page you will find that I am only trying to thank you for everything you have given me; only doubt overcomes me as to whether I have always correctly received what you gave. Later, perhaps, I shall be able to do some things better; and by "later," I mean here the time of "fulfillment," the Bayreuth cultural period. Meanwhile I feel proud that I have now marked myself out and that people will now always link my name with yours. God have mercy on my philologists if they persist in learning nothing now!

I shall be happy, *verehrtester Meister*, if you will accept this book, at the beginning of the new year, as a good and friendly token.

I shall shortly be sending you and your wife bound copies.

With good wishes for you and your household, and with the warmest thanks for your love, I am, as I have been and shall be,

Your loyal Friedrich Nietzsche

75. Quotation from Schiller's "Das Lied von der Glocke," lines 144–45.

39·. *To Erwin Rohde*   Basel, Sunday, January [28], 72

My dear good friend:

Recently I received through Susemihl a tentative inquiry whether I would accept a professorship at Greifswald, but I declined at once in your favor, recommending you. Has the matter gone any further? I referred to Ribbeck. People here got to know of it, and it aroused great sympathy for me among the good Basel people. Though I protested that it was not an offer but only a tentative inquiry, the students decided to stage a torchlight procession for me, with a view to expressing how much they value and respect my activities till now in Basel. Anyway, I declined the procession. I am lecturing here now on "The Future of our Educational Institutions" and have created almost a "sensation," rousing even enthusiasm here and there. Why don't we live together? For what I now have in mind and am preparing for the future cannot be touched on in letters at all. I have made an alliance with Wagner. You cannot imagine how close we are now and how our plans coincide. The things I have heard said about my book are quite incredible: for which reason I shall not write about it either. What do you think of it? A tremendous seriousness overcomes me every time I hear it spoken of, because I detect in such voices the future of what I intend. This life will become very difficult.

They say that there is bitterness everywhere in Leipzig. Nobody writes me a word from there. Not even Ritschl. My good friend, sometime we must live together again; it is a sacred necessity. For some time now there has been a great flow of life around me: almost every day something astonishing happens; likewise, my aims and intentions become higher. I am telling you in secret, and asking you to keep it a secret, that I am preparing, among other things, a memorandum on Strasbourg University, as an appeal to the Imperial Council, for the attention of Bismarck, in which I mean to show how disgraceful it is that a great moment has been missed for founding a truly German educational institution, which would regenerate the German spirit and destroy "culture," till now so called. War to the knife! Or into the cannon's mouth!

The Mounted Gunner with the Heaviest Gun

40 · *To Friedrich Ritschl* Basel, January 30, 1872

Verehrtester Herr Geheimrat:

You will not grudge me my astonishment that I have not heard a word from you about my recently published book, and I hope you will also not grudge me my frankness in expressing this astonishment to you. For this book surely is by way of being a manifesto, and surely it challenges one least of all to keep silence. Perhaps you, my respected teacher, will be surprised if I tell you what I anticipated your impression would be: I thought that if ever you had met with anything promising in your life, it might be this book, promising for our classical studies, promising for what Germany means, even if a number of individuals might be ruined by it. For I at least will not fail to carry out the practical consequences of my views, and you will divine something of these if I tell you that I am lecturing here on "The Future of Our Educational Institutions." From personal intentions and precautions, I feel—you will believe me—pretty free, and because I seek nothing for myself, I hope to achieve something for others. My first concern is to win over the younger generation of classical philologists, and I would think it shameful if I did not succeed in doing so. Now your silence disturbs me somewhat. Not that I have ever doubted your interest in me for a moment—of that I am wholly convinced—but I might conclude that you are personally worried about me, precisely because of your interest. To dispel this, I am writing to you.[76]

I received the index to the *Rheinisches Museum.* Have you perhaps sent a copy to my sister?

To an inquiry, whether I would consider accepting an offer from Greifswald, I have given my refusal without a moment's hesitation.

I hope that I may remain assured, *mein vereherter Herr Geheimrat,* of your good will and of your wife's, and I send you cordial greetings.

Friedrich Nietzsche

76. Ritschl wrote in his journal on December 31, 1871: "N's book *Birth of Tragedy* (=intelligent rakish dissoluteness)"; and on February 2, 1872: "Amazing letter from N (=megalomania)"; and on February 15, 1872: "To N about his *Birth of Tragedy:* conceived by Mamma."

41 · *To Erwin Rohde*   [Basel, mid-February, 1872]

Quickly, my dear loyal friend, I want to write you a few lines. The *Augs-bürgerin*[77] is no good; we do not want to have anything to do with this paper, because it has infamous anti-Wagner tales on its conscience. The *Norddeutsche* [*Allgemeine Zeitung*] would help us, but does that not seem laughable to you? It does to me. Realize too that I disagree with you as to the tactics for reviewing my book, to the extent that I would like to keep clear of everything metaphysical, everything deductive; for precisely this, crowded inside a convex mirror, is no attraction at all to the reader—quite the reverse. Do you not think that a reader of Zarncke's paper, when he reads your review and knows nothing else about the book, would rightly feel relieved of the burden of reading it, while precisely the reverse would have the successful result of making everyone concerned with antiquity *have* to read it, as a matter of duty. We do not want to make it so easy for the good philologists by chasing them away—they should recognize them-selves in the book.[78] Moreover, it is not at all necessary that this book should have a purely metaphysical and to some extent "transmundane" effect; in this I see Jakob Burckhardt as a living proof. He, who keeps energetically at arm's length everything philosophical and, above all, every-thing to do with philosophy of art—thus my philosophy of art too—is so fascinated by what the book's discoveries bring to the understanding of what Greece means that he thinks about it day and night and in a thousand details gives me an example of the most fruitful historical application of it; so that I shall have much to learn during his summer course on the history of Greek culture, all the more because I know how familiar and intimate is the ground on which this course has grown. You and he—you two together—are really the ideal reader; while you speak of a "cosmodicy," he tells me that he only now correctly understands Athenaeus, and so on. Now since, as Burckhardt says, a book must have a degree of "notoriety" before it is taken serious-ly, the tactics of a review are worth thinking over. By the way, Wagner finds your review "excellent"; Frau Wagner too finds it much, much too good for the *Augsbürgerin*, but would like you to have drawn attention more to the act than to the work. I do not quite agree with that, for the nature of the act is not so easy to express without greatly offending the reading public, and an act should be assessed by its successes—perhaps these are

77. *Augsburger Allgemeine Zeitung.*

78. Alludes to the criticism in the book of post-Socratic "Alexandrian" culture, with its pusillanimous bookishness and objectless, superficial fact collecting.

here very slight; perhaps it will peter out after one stroke of lightning—
in brief, I do not like people to talk about me. This means that when "acts"
are to be assessed, one must be able to speak with authority.[79]

So, my dear friend, I tell you my feelings quite frankly. I thank you
for your noble efforts and will send your review to friends, but let us not
think that we can achieve anything new with such reviews as this. The desired "notoriety" will perhaps be achieved by scandalous judgments and
attacks; I recommend that you write *nothing* on my behalf, just as I certainly
expect nothing either from Wagner or from Burckhardt. Let us all wait and
be glad or vexed *privatim*.[80]

Just this moment I was surprised to hear from Ritschl, and in the
main quite pleasantly surprised: he has lost none of his friendly gentleness
toward me and writes without any irritation, which I put very much to his
credit. I am sending you his letter, with the same request as before—to return the documents to me safely sometime. The letter will also tell you
something about Dorpats.

Here I am intensely active thinking out the future of our educational
institutions, and day by day the matter is being "organized" and "re-
generated," only in my head of course, but with the most definite practical
"tendency." I am expressing myself infamously today; attribute my
stylistic failing to a streaming cold and general discomfort from κατάρρους
with βρόγχος. Did you write to Tribschen? I shall end by telling you about
May 22, Wagner's birthday: the laying of the foundation stone of the Bayreuth theater, likewise of the Wagner's house, and, finally, a classic performance of the Ninth Symphony—so, "Let's all go to Konnewitz!"[81] In
fact, we are all going to Bayreuth for the Whitsun week. Dear friend, it is
almost a necessity for you to be there too. I mean this as seriously as may be,
and believe that it will seem just such a serious matter to you as well. Fifty
years later we would think it unforgivable, think it mad, not to have been
there; so, let us overcome the known discomforts—Basel and Kiel will have

79. In the last chapters of *The Birth of Tragedy*, Wagner is celebrated as the in-
augurator of a new tragic and mythic musical art. It would seem from N's statements here
that he did not want to have himself judged as a Wagnerite propagandist but to have his
book judged on its merits as a study of the cultural and psychological roots of tragedy and
music and as a critique of the false and mythless culture of the times. Cosima's remark
about Rohde's review (which Zarncke had rejected) shows where her interests lay (and
presumably Wagner's also).

80. Nevertheless, Rohde did write another review, the one published in the *Norddeutsche Allgemeine Zeitung* on May 26, 1872.

81. Allusion to an oft-repeated advertisement in the *Leipziger Tageblatt;* the joke
means, "Let's all go to Bayreuth!"

their *center* in Bayreuth.[82] I entreat you really by our holiest of holies, art—come! We must share this experience, and likewise next year the "Theater Festival." Write soon, my dear loyal good friend, and think of me as one who calls you with an immense megaphone, Bayreuth!!

F. N.

42 · *To Erwin Rohde*   [Basel, July 16, 1872]

Here, my dear good friend, is the title, discovered amid rejoicing and shrieks of derision by my fellow lodger Professor Overbeck.

Dr. U. Wilamowitz-Moellendorf's
Afterphilologie
Open Letter
to Richard Wagner
by a Philologist[83]

You can then put your own name under the letter, at the end (but in full and with all titles!) In the conclusion you can placidly address Wilamowitz as an "Afterphilolog." For us he represents a "false" philology, and the success of your piece will be to show him as such to others. I shall write a very serious and forceful letter to Ritschl, asking him to give up the incomprehensible idea that we intend it as an attack on classical studies (or on *historiography*). I had written to him that you intended to dispose of the impudent fellow in a simple philological manner. But now Wagner's letter has so frightened him that he is scared of every one of us. And there is his solicitude about "Teubnerian philology"! I recommend this to you as a shibboleth.

As regards Wil.'s contention about Aristarchus and Titans, I can find nothing to which he might be referring. On the pre-Homeric character of the war of the Titans, Welcker has given us most information: Mythologie 1, 262. If only people would stop this soft talk of the Homeric world

---

82. Rohde was teaching at Kiel University.

83. Ulrich von Wilamowitz-Moellendorf (b. 1848), a young Turk of the Berlin school of classical philology, had published his pamphlet against N's *Birth of Tragedy* in late May: *Zukunftsphilologie! Eine Erwiderung auf Friedrich Nietzsches Geburt der Tragödie* (Berlin, 1872). During June, N and Rohde were planning a counterattack. The following letter deals with some scholarly points and answers certain questions asked by Rohde in a letter of July 12. "Afterphilologie" is a pun: "After-" corresponds to English "sub-" or "sham"; hence, *Afterblatt* ("stipule"), *Afterlehre* ("false doctrine"), and the cognate *Aberglaube* ("superstition"). The substantive "After" means, however, "anus" or "backside." In some words too, "After-" as prefix has the same meaning as English "after": hence *Aftergeburt* ("afterbirth"), *Afterkind* ("posthumous child"). Overbeck's invention thus also puns against Wilamowitz's title *Zukunftsphilologie* ("Philology of the Future"), which had ridiculed N's Wagnerite pretensions, since Wagner's music was currently called *Zukunftsmusik*.

as a youthful one, the springtime of the Greeks, and so on. In the sense in which it is maintained, the idea is false. That a tremendous, wild conflict, emerging from dark crudity and cruelty, precedes the Homeric era, that Homer stands as victor at the end of this long comfortless period—this is one of my most certain convictions. The Greeks are much older than people think. One can speak of spring as long as one has a winter to precede it, but this world of purity and beauty did not drop from the sky.

My theory about the satyrs is of great importance to me in this field of inquiry, and is something essentially new, isn't it? It is very offensive that I should have called the satyrs, in the oldest form, goat-legged, but it is exceedingly stupid to invoke evidence against this from archaeology and so on. For archaeology knows only the ennobled type from the satyr play; before that is the idea of the goats as servants of Dionysus and of the goatish leapings of his worshipers. The goat legs are the true characteristic of the oldest idea; and without any archaeological proof, I would maintain that Hesiod's οὐτιδανοὶ καὶ ἀμηχανόεργοι were goat-legged, thus *capripedes*, as Horace says, Odes 2, 2,[84] and other poets (Greeks also).[85] σάτυροι I explain, like τίτυροι, as a reduplication of the root τερ (as in the relation of Σίσυφος to σοφός); τορός = "penetratingly bright"; σατύροι = "those uttering penetrating shrieks," as epithet for the goats, just as μηκάδες is the epithet for the she-goat. I think that is a splendid equation τορός/τίτυρος = σοφός/σίσυφος. If you like it, include it. Of course I am not guilty of confusing satyrs and Pan figures, as Wil. says. I say on page 8, "Apollo, who could hold up the Medusa head against no more perilous power"; Wil. says for this "brandish," pages 9 and 18, where he even misquotes me between quotation marks. I still cannot see what W. is objecting to, assuming that he knows what the *aegis* is. That I am only picturing a fictitious scene, as, say, for the Apollo Belvedere, is quite obvious. For Archilocus, consult especially Westphal's *History of Ancient and Medieval Music*, pages 115 ff.—the fellow has no idea of this. On the note on page 26, naturally the oracular verse reads Σοφοκλῆς σοφός, σοφώτερος δ'Εὐριπίδης. "The eternally serene kindliness of Sophocles," as a sweeping predicate, amused me greatly. Page 29, the top of the page, gives a heavenly example of the thoughtless flatness of Wil's reading. The whole page is a laugh. Page 18, the scandalous dirty jokes in the middle of the page deserve to be punished; would you see what I have actually said on page 19? The motto too is horribly vulgar. The con-

84. Actually 2, 19, 4.

85. The archaeological evidence adduced by Pickard-Cambridge (*Dithyramb: Tragedy and Comedy*, London: Cambridge University Press, 1927, p. 174) suggests that N was forcing this point: on sixth-century Greek pottery the satyrs are equine, not capriform—not goat figures at all, but horse demons, wearing horse tails. Pickard-Cambridge maintains that the capriform satyr was a relatively late (fifth-century) invention.

fusing of elegiac and lyric poetry is also nice. The αὐλητὴς Mimnermus
would also be delighted by what appears on page 17. That Aeschylus marks
the climax of ancient music, beside Simonides, Pindar, Phrynicos Pratinas—
here we simply have to take Aristoxenus' word for it. (Wil., p. 21). To his
general feeling, I also accede with regard to the later dithyrambic poets.
On "stimulant music," Aristophanes speaks quiet clearly; as regards
mimesis, I can, unfortunately, think of no further references. I do not "be-
little." For the spirit of the new nomen- and dithyramb-music, we have to use
Euripides, whose σκηνικὴ μουσικὴ was internally related to that of music, and
the Aristophanic parody too. On the attitude of Socrates to tragic art, there
is an extremely remarkable passage in Aristophanes, Ran. [Frogs] 1491
χαρίεν οὖν μὴ Σωκράτει │παρακαθήμενον λαλεῖν │ἀποβαλόντα μουσικὴν │τὰ
τε μέγιστα παραλιπόντα τῆς τραγῳδικῆς τέχνης. . . . You know that for the
"muses with Dionysus in their midst," I had in mind Genelli's water-
color which Wagner had at Tribschen. Tell the philogists that my Socrates
is all of a piece; I feel so strongly the contrast between my description and
the others, which all seem so dead and moldy. Moira as eternal justice meted
out by Zeus is the essential Aeschylean idea. The penultimate page in
Wilamowitz is very crude, with interpolations and so on. Aristophanes too
indicates Aeschylus' relation to the mysteries. My dear friend, have no
doubts and do not be vexed; you have a grim work on your hands, and when
I think how exposed you are in this I am ashamed and painfully regret having accepted from you such a sacrifice. I recommend to you some derisive
laughter and a few diabolic joys to spice your existence. When we have a
quiet moment, you will then hear from me some things about *Tristan* and
about a huge undertaking for Bayreuth which I engendered in Munich and
which involves a great responsibility.[86] I am always close to you, dear
fr[iend].

F. N.

43 · *To Malwida von Meysenbug*[87]

Schützengraben 45 [Basel, August 27, 1872]

Gnädigstes Frl. von Meysenbug:
So everything is arranged for Saturday; you will send me an imperative
word, and I shall run to the station. Perhaps I can also be of some service

86. N had proposed the reorganization of all Wagner societies and a public appeal
to be sent to persons of importance.

87. Malwida von Meysenbug (b. 1816) is first mentioned by N in a letter to
Rohde, dated about April 11, 1872, as having written a "kind" letter about *The Birth of*

to you during the afternoon. Give me sometime, I ask you, a chance to be useful—useful in the most literal and real sense!

And I can show you my sister, can I? At least she begs me to do this and would also like to meet Frl. Olga.[88] Just the other day I first got to see Herr Gabriel Monod's book, about which I have heard much spoken. I will be very glad to see personally such an impartially minded man, who, moreover, has the advantage of being so highly commended as the fiancé of Frl. Herzen.[89]

That you are the translator of Herzen's memoirs was quite new to me; I am sorry not to have expressed to you my feelings about the merits of this translation before I was aware of this.[90] I was astonished at the aptness and vigor of expression, and, tending to assume that Herzen possessed every distinctive talent, I had tacitly supposed that he had translated his memoirs from Russian into German himself. I have drawn my friends' attention to this work; from it I have learned to think about a number of negative tendencies much more sympathetically than I could until now—and I would not even call them negative. For such a nobly fiery and persistent soul could not nourish itself on negation and hatred alone.

Of many other matters I hope to speak with you very soon; therefore today I permit myself to be brief and once more to commend myself to your kindly interest.

Your devoted servant
Friedr. Nietzsche

Tragedy. At this time she was living in Florence. N was also pleased that the Italian periodical *Rivista Europea* published the first review of his book. He first met her at Bayreuth on May 20, 1872. This remarkable lady was a prominent member of the international liberal set of the time, which included several Russian *émigrés*—, Herzen and Ogareff. See E. H. Carr, *The Romantic Exiles*, Boston: Beacon Press, 1961, pp. 144 ff. She had first met Wagner in 1860, in Paris. Her correspondence with N continued until shortly before his breakdown. She was indirectly responsible for the spread of N's influence in France. Romain Rolland visited her much later in Italy, and there was a lengthy correspondence between him and her.

88. Olga Herzen, daughter of Alexander Herzen.

89. Gabriel Monod, a Frenchman, was the author of *Allemands et Français: Souvenir de campagne* (Paris, 1872).

90. Alexander Herzen, *Aus den Memoiren eines Russen* (1st–4th series, Hamburg, 1855–59). Herzen's memoirs might well have had some formative influence on N's ideas at this time—e.g., the tempering of his Wagnerite Germanophile chauvinism and scorn of liberal democratic ideas.

44 · *To Franziska Nietzsche*   [Splügen, October 1, 1872]

My dear good mother:

You will laugh this time, for here comes a long letter, with travel description and all kinds of jollities. Half-reluctantly, I decided to leave for Italy; it was heavy on my conscience that I had already sent a letter of acceptance to you.[91] But who would resist the moodily and suddenly changed, most beautiful and pure autumn hiking weather! Or, to be even more accurate: I felt the most burning urge to be for once *quite alone* with my thoughts for a short time. How successful I have been you can guess perhaps from the hotel address printed above.[92]

Our kind Lisbeth can tell you what a curious departure from Basel it was: I had this time half a minute to spare, as you every Sunday had half a minute too little, and I just caught the train, thanks to this half minute. First I traveled with a married couple from Basel, whom I did not know, though I had to seem to know them—familiar situation, but not without its dangers. From Baden (Switzerland) I telegraphed to Lisbeth; because there was no stop, a gentleman who was getting out (Herr Haller from Bern) had the great kindness to see to the telegram. Just before Zürich I discover that the other person in the compartment is a musician of whom I know well and who has been even better recommended to me, Goetz (a pupil of von Bülow's); he tells me of his musical activities in Zürich, much increased since Kirchner left; but, most of all, he was excited by the likely prospect of having his opera accepted by the Hanover theater and performed there for the first time.[93] From Zürich onward, despite the good and modest company, I felt so shivery and exhausted in the compartment that I lost the courage to proceed to Chur. With an effort—my head aching—I reached Weesen on the Wallensee;[94] it was now dark night. I find the carriage of the Hotel Schwert and take it; thus I arrived at a nice, comfortable, but quite empty hotel. My head aching, I got up the next morning. My window looked out on the Wallensee, which you can picture as resembling the Vierwald-

91. In a letter from Splügen to Carl von Gersdorff, dated October 5, N wrote that he might continue to Brescia, where he wanted to study paintings by the Venetian Moretto. He did continue his journey into Italy, reached Bergamo, but returned quickly to Splügen (see letter No. 47).

92. The manuscript has the letterhead of Hotel Bodenhaus, Splügen.

93. The only finished opera by Hermann Goetz, *Der Widerspenstigen Zähmung*, was first performed in Mannheim on October 11, 1874.

94. This is a lake which extends a few miles eastward after the larger Lake of Zürich.

stättersee, only more simple and without the latter's sublimity. Then I travel to Chur, with unfortunately increasing discomfort, which meant passing Ragaz and so on in a state of almost complete listlessness: I was glad to be able to get out in Chur, declined the offers of the postal-carriage officials to give me a lift—though that had been my plan—and I go quickly to bed as soon as I reach the Hotel Lukmanier.[95] It was ten in the morning. I slept well until two, felt better, and ate a little. An efficient and knowledgeable waiter recommends to me the walk to Pasugg, which I could recall from a picture in the illustrated paper. It is a peaceful Sunday in Chur, in an afternoon mood. Feeling quite at ease, I mount the road into the country; everything is spread out before me, as on the previous day, in a goldish autumn glow. Glorious views when I look back, the views on either side continuously changing and more spacious. After half an hour a little side path, which brings me into lovely shadow—for till now it has been quite warm. Now I came into the gorge through which the Rabiusa roars, a place I cannot marvel at enough. I walk on, over bridges and on small paths leading along the cliffside, for about half an hour, and now find, marked by a flag, the springs of Pasugg. At first it disappointed me, for I was expecting a pension, and found only a modest inn, though it was full of Sunday visitors from Chur, of families comfortably feasting and quaffing a lot of coffee. At first I drink three glasses at the saline soda spring; then soon my changed head permits me to add to that a bottle of Asti spumante—you remember?—and some very soft goat cheese. A man with Chinese eyes, who is also sitting at my table, has some of the Asti too; he thanks me and drinks, feeling himself flattered. Then the innkeeper's wife hands me a whole mass of analyses of the waters and so on; finally, the owner of the springs, Sprecher, an excited man, conducts me around all his property, whose unbelievably fantastic location I have to acknowledge. I drink again, and in good quantities, from the three quite different springs; the owner promises other chief springs besides, and offers me, noticing my interest, the chance to become shareholder in a new hotel—the mockery of it! The valley is entirely charming, for a geologist it has an inexhaustible variety, even capriciousness. There were veins of graphite as well as quartz with ocher, and the owner even had stories to tell of gold deposits. The various rock layers and rock species are curved, deflected, cracked, somewhat as at the Axenstein on the Vierwaldstättersee, only much smaller and wilder. Late, toward sundown, I walk back, very delighted with the afternoon, although my thoughts were often of my arrival—or non-arrival—in Naumburg. A little child with pale-colored hair is looking for hazelnuts, and is funny. Eventually an old

95. The post bus is still one of the chief means of rural transport in Switzerland.

couple catch up with me, father and daughter, speaking to me, and so I make reply. He, an ancient graybeard, master carpenter, was in Naumburg fifty-two years ago during his apprentice travels, and he remembers a very hot day. His son is a missionary in India, has been there since 1858, and is expected in Chur next year, to see his father again. The daughter had been in Egypt several times and spoke of Basel as an unpleasantly hot and stuffy town. I accompany the good people a little way, as they hobble along. Then I dine in my hotel, where I already find a few companions for the Splügen trip the next day: they include, unfortunately, a Jew.[96] On Monday I get up at four in the morning; the post coach left at five. Before leaving, we had to wait in an evil-smelling waiting room, among peasants from Graubünden and the Tessin; altogether at this hour man is a repulsive creature. The departure saved me, for I had made an agreement with the conductor that I could use his seat high up on the coach. There I was alone: it was the most lovely post-coach journey I have ever made. I shall write nothing of the tremendous grandeurs of the Via Mala;[97] I feel as if I have never yet come to know Switzerland. This is *my* nature; and as we approached Splügen, I was overcome by the desire to stay here. I found a good hotel and a touchingly simple little room. It has a balcony outside it, with the loveliest view. This valley in the high Alps (about 5,000 feet) is sheer delight to me: here there are pure, vigorous breezes, hills and rock formations of all shapes and sizes, huge snow mountains all around. But most of all I like the glorious country roads, along which I walk for hours, sometimes toward the San Bernhardino Pass, sometimes to the Splügen Pass, without having to think of the way; but whenever I look around, there is certain to be something grand and undreamed-of to see. Tomorrow it will probably snow, to which I am greatly looking forward. I eat at noon, when the post coaches arrive, together with the visitors. I do not need to speak a word; nobody knows me—I am wholly alone and could stay here and walk around for weeks on end. In my little room I work with new vigor—that is, I make notes and collect thoughts for my main subject at present, "The Future of Educational Institutions."

You cannot believe how much I like it here. Since I have found this place, Switzerland has acquired for me quite a new fascination; now I really know a corner where I can live so as to regather my forces and work vigor-

96. N is still conventionally anti-Semitic here. In a letter to Rohde, of December 7, 1872, his attitude is shifting somewhat, for reasons of vanity: he complains that Jacob Bernays had said that N had used and amplified ideas of his (Bernays') in *The Birth of Tragedy*, but adds: "This is an amusing sign that the 'Schlauen im Lande' [shrewd but quiet people] are getting wind of something. The Jews are in the vanguard everywhere—here too—while Usener . . . stays put in the fog."

97. Mountain road in the Swiss Alps, famous for its scenic splendors.

ously but without having any company around. People here seem like shadows.

Well, I have described everything to you; the days to come will pass like the first. There is, thank God, none of that accursed distraction and doing-things-for-a-change. Here I am, and here also are pen, ink, and paper —we all send you the warmest greetings.

Your loyal son
Friedrich Nietzsche

45 · *To Erwin Rohde*   Basel, October 25, 1872

At last, dear friend, the first excitement is over—which almost gave me an attack of indigestion; it would have been a pity if I had choked to death on this glorious grape, don't you think?[98] Now I am sitting in my warm room feeling very comfortable and postprandial and am happy as a child at your present, snuffling and nibbling at it over and over again. What you have done for me is beyond words; I would be quite incapable of doing it for myself, and I know of no other person from whom I could hope for such a gift of friendship. The sacrifices you must have made, poor dear friend, to spend so long a time dealing with that fellow! How disgusting and awkward that attack was I realize in retrospect more strongly when I feel how much you yourself suffered from it. But now your book streams into open waters, hauling the fellow, drowned, behind it. The results to be expected from this you can gather from the following communications I have received—without my ever having (honestly!) asked for them. *One* person in Leipzig has pronounced on my book: the good Usener in Bonn, whom I greatly respect, has divulged to his students, who asked him, what that pronouncement means: that my book is sheer nonsense, quite useless, that anyone writing like that is dead to scholarship. It is as if I had committed a crime; people have kept quiet now for ten months, because all actually think they are beyond and above my book, that it is not worth talking about. That is the impression from Leipzig, which Overbeck has described to me.[99] All parties are agreed in this; but to provide the requisite baroque

98. Allusion to the story that Sophocles died from choking on an unripe grape. N had just received a copy of Rohde's pamphlet in defense of *The Birth of Tragedy* (Leipzig, 1872).

99. Franz Overbeck (1837–1905) had come to Basel as a professor of theology in 1870. N's correspondence with him began in 1877 and lasted until his breakdown. For several years they had lodgings in the same house in Basel. I have adapted the following details

exception, a grannyish letter from E. Leutsch arrived yesterday, which betrays *sympathies!* The whole affair has something batty about it! (Incidentally, the old boy sent a bulky volume, perhaps ten or fifteen articles, programs, and so on—all his Theognis reports in a fancy old-fashioned binding! Utterly ridiculous!) People half think I am off my head, for that is the consolation of our "healthy" types, if no other consolation is available.

Now your book, with all its big-heartedness and brave comradeship-in-arms, falling into the midst of this cackling tribe—what a spectacle! Romundt and Overbeck, the only people to whom I have been able to read it so far, are beside themselves with joy at your complete success! They are continually praising and stressing particulars in it and its general lines; they say that its polemic is "like Lessing"—and, well, you know what good Germans mean by this predicate. What I like best is hearing always, under all else, the deep booming basic tone, like a strong waterfall, which alone consecrates any polemic and gives the sense of grandeur to it, that basic tone in which love, trust, courage, vigor, pain, *victory*, and hope collectively sound. Dear friend, I was quite overcome when you spoke of the "friends"; I could not continue reading for a long time. What wonderful experiences I have had this past year! And how all troubles crashing upon me from elsewhere have simply dispersed when they met against them! From Wagner's heart and soul too, I am proud and happy—for your book marks a notable turning point in his position vis-à-vis German scholarly and scientific circles. I am told that the *Nationalzeitung* recently had the cheek to count me among "Wagner's literary lackeys"; what a surprise for them when you take up his cause as well! Surely that is somewhat more important than your

---

about Overbeck from C. A. Bernoulli, *Overbeck und Nietzsche*, vol. 1. The cosmopolitan pattern of his external life predisposed him to being the type of man whom N called the "good European"—the coming supersession of the man of national culture by the man of international culture. His grandfather, a businessman with an old Low German bourgeois surname, emigrated from the Frankfurt of Goethe's time to England and was marooned there because of the Napoleonic decree which stopped reimmigration to the Continent. His son kept his British nationality and emigrated to Russia. The grandson, N's friend, even as an adult, used to travel for a time on an English passport. Franz Overbeck's mother was a Frenchwoman and a Catholic. He was born in St. Petersburg on November 16, 1837. Later he was sent to live with maternal relatives in Paris, went to a boarding school there, wore a blue dress suit with yellow stockings, and sang the *Marseillaise* in the school choir at the outbreak of the February revolution in 1848. Not until he was twelve did the family move to Dresden, where he joined his parents and learned German (his other languages being, already, English, Russian, and French). In 1857 he met Treitschke, later the great (and deaf) Prussian historian, in Dresden; the two men became friends. At Leipzig University, Overbeck was especially interested in history, although his main field was theology. There is a considerable correspondence between Treitschke and Overbeck (1863–71), which gives a good picture of the latter's independence of mind around his thirtieth year, when he was teaching at Jena University.

coming to my support, is it not, old friend? And that—precisely that—makes this day the happiest I have had for a long time; I see what you have *done for Wagner* by your act of friendship toward me. When Gersdorff reads your book I am convinced he will stand on his head two or three times for sheer joy! And how well and grandly has Fritzsch once again done his job! If only he could now manage the distribution just as well as the production— and somewhat more quickly; during these past few days I was almost at my wits' end and was on the verge of writing to him. You know W.'s latest book, *On Actors and Singers*, don't you? It uncovers an entirely new area of esthetics! And what a fruitful turn it gives to some of the thoughts in *The Birth of Tragedy*. I converse with this new book as if I were together with W., whose proximity I do now miss, have missed for quite a time.[100]

Let us have courage, my dear, dear friend! I believe now that things will only improve, that *we* shall improve, in the growth of our good intentions, good means, in our race toward ever more noble and distant goals! O, we shall reach them, and after every victory the goal is marked further off, and we shall run more courageously onward. Should it trouble us that there are not many spectators, that there are indeed very few who have eyes to see the race we are running? Does this trouble us, as long as we know that these few spectators also are for us the only judges of the contest? For my part I would forgo, for one such spectator as Wagner, all the garlands that the present could afford; and to gratify him stimulates me more and raises me higher than any other power does. For it is *difficult*—and he always makes it quite clear whether he likes it or not, and is for me like a good conscience, punishing and rewarding.

Now may all good spirits be with us, dearest friend! Now we walk together, with *one* faith and *one* hope. Whatever happens to you happens to me, and there is nothing more that could affect us separately, nothing good and right!

I thank you, my friend, I thank you.

Your Friedrich

100. The Wagners had moved from Tribschen to Bayreuth at the end of April, 1872. N had helped with the packing for the move, and had visited them at Bayreuth for the laying of the foundation stone, on May 22, of the opera house there and for the festive performance of Beethoven's Ninth Symphony. Gersdorff and Rohde had both been there, and it was on this occasion that N had met Malwida von Meysenbug.

46. *To Hans von Bülow (draft)*

[Basel, October 29, 1872, or just before]

Well, thank God, that is what you have to tell me, and precisely that.[101] I know quite well what an uncomfortable moment I have given you, and to compensate for it let me tell you how useful you have been to me. Just think, since my music is self-taught, I have gradually lost all discipline in it; I have never had the judgment of a musician on it; and I am truly happy to be enlightened in such a simple way as to the character of my latest period of composition. For unfortunately, I must admit, I have been writing home-made music since childhood, know musical theory from studying Albrecht-berger, have written fugues *en masse*, and can compose in the pure style, with a certain degree of purity. Yet sometimes I have been overcome by such a barbarically excessive urge [to compose], compounded of defiance and irony, that I have as much difficulty as you in perceiving sharply what is serious, what is caricature, and what is derisive mockery in my latest music.[102] I treated my next-door fellow lodgers (O, the good fellows)[103] to it as a pamphlet on program music. And the spontaneous characterization of the mood was *cannibalido.* This has unfortunately made it quite clear to me now that the whole piece, together with this mixture of pathos and malice, did correspond absolutely to a real mood, and that I experienced pleasure as never before in writing it. So it is a sad outlook for my music and even more for my moods. How does one characterize a state of mind in which delight, scorn, exuberance, and sublimity are all jumbled together? Here and there I end up in this dangerous, moonstruck region. At the same time, I am infinitely far—you will believe me—from judging or admiring Wagner's music from the viewpoint of this half-psychiatric musical excitement.[104] Of

101. N had received, probably toward the end of July, Hans von Bülow's opinion on his *Manfred Meditation*, a composition for two pianos, which he mentions first (not with the title) in a letter to Gustav Krug, dated May 2, 1872. He had played it to Rohde at Bayreuth later in May. Hans von Bülow (1830–94) was Cosima Wagner's first husband, a prominent conductor, and close friend of Franz Liszt, Cosima's father.

102. Kurt Leidecker, in *Nietzsche: Unpublished Letters*, translates the phrase "in der letzten Musik" as "in the most recent modern music"; I read this phrase as referring only to N's own composition.

103. N uses Latin here ("O die *boni*"), which seems to connote, for him, "men of goodwill." His fellow lodgers were Overbeck and Romundt. The subsequent "it" (*es*) must refer not to Bülow's judgment (*Urteil*, n.) but to N's composition.

104. N is using the epithet *psychiatrisch* here (for the first time) to denote nervous and emotional states of overexcitement which can be discharged in music—hence, music

my music, I know only one thing: that it enables me to master a mood which, if it is not gratified, is perhaps a more dangerous one. In honoring Wagner's music, I honor precisely this highest necessity—and where I do not grasp it, being an inadequate musician, I presuppose it by an act of faith. But what gave me most pleasure in the latest piece was precisely, in the midst of the wildest exuberance, a certain caricature of that necessity. And precisely this desperately split counterpoint must have so confused my feelings that I lost all judgment.[105] And in this exigency I myself sometimes thought better of this music—a highly regrettable circumstance, from which you have now rescued me. Thank you! So that is not music at all? This makes me quite happy; I need no longer concern myself with this kind of *otium cum odio*, with this altogether odious way of passing my time. What I want is the truth; you know that it is more pleasant to hear it than to speak it. So I am doubly indebted to you. But I ask only one thing of you—do not make *Tristan* responsible for my sin. *After* hearing *Tristan* I would certainly never again have written any such music—*Tristan* will cure me of my music for a long time. If only I could hear it again![106]

I shall try, then, to take a musical cure; and perhaps I shall remain, if I study Beethoven sonatas in your edition, under your tutelage and guidance. The whole thing, as a matter of fact, is a highly instructive experience for me; the educational problem, which occupies me in other areas, has now been posed for me in the domain of art, with particular cogency. To what frightful aberrations is the solitary individual nowadays exposed!

47. *To Malwida von Meysenbug*   Basel, November 7, 1872

Verehrtestes Fräulein:

At last my little bundle is ready for you, and at last you hear from me again, after it must have seemed I had sunk into a dead silence. Just think,

---

as catharsis. Later he did turn against Wagner's music for its *Rausch* effects: its pathological and histrionic, rather than therapeutic, allures; see book 4 of *Morgenröte* (1881), section 255, "Dialogue on Music."

105. *Verzweifelte Kontrapunktik;* N exploits the sense of the German word "verzweifelt" ("split in two"), which the English "desperate" lacks. The element of musical self-parody which N noticed here is of some interest; Thomas Mann, in *Doktor Faustus*, attended closely to the parodic element in Adrian Leverkühn's music (though N's *self*-parody appears to have a different basis).

106. *Tristan* had been performed in Munich on June 20 and 22.

in the meantime I have been once quite close to where you were—in Bergamo, and only a complete and sudden revulsion against Italy (especially paintings!) quickly drove me back again. Otherwise we would have met for a fourth time this year and could have celebrated a reunion like that of the Council of Basel, which I recall with warm memories and with gratitude to you and the dear engaged couple.[107] For the fourth time! Perhaps more than is good, according to the old proverb which says that all good things come in threes—briefly, the *daimon* drove me back again and set me upon the Splügen Pass, where I lived tranquilly and thoughtfully, altogether remote from people and society, in vigorous, even keen air (whereas the Italian atmosphere had on me the effect of bathroom steam—horrible and flabby!).

By the way, friend Gersdorff will be crossing the Alps next year and has already asked me if he could hope to meet you in Florence. He is very happy, because now his dice have been well and truly shaken up—so well that he can give up his law career in December. He will travel somewhat now, and then study agriculture, with the necessary scientific prerequisites. Next summer he is thinking of spending in Basel, studying chemistry and "culture," as he writes—which surely should mean not agriculture but real human culture.

For the third week in November, and for eight days, a glorious visit has been announced—here in Basel! The "visit in itself"—Wagner and wife.[108] They are on the grand tour, intending to touch on every main theater in Germany, on this occasion including the famous Basel "Dentist," to whom I owe a debt of thanks.[109] Do you know Wagner's latest book, *On Actors and Singers?* You will certainly not yet know the apologia by Professor Rohde of Kiel, which he has written with sword as well as pen, and with great superiority over his opponents. You see, my *Birth of Tragedy* has made of me the most offensive philologist of the present day, to defend whom could be a true marvel of courage, for everyone is of a mind to condemn me. Apart from the polemics, with which I would not burden you, Rohde's book contains many good things about the philological foundations of my book, which may make it of interest to you. If only I did not have to fear that Rohde's generous move will take him into a regular hornets' nest of disfavor and malice! Now we are both on the index together!

107. They had met at the Bayreuth celebration on May 20, at the *Tristan* performances in Munich, and in Basel on August 31. *Council:* N uses the word "Konzil"— meaning "Council of Churches"—in a jocular sense.

108. "Besuch an sich": a play on the Kantian *"Ding an sich"* ("thing-in-itself"), meaning thus the "visit of visits."

109. N's dentist was James van Marter.

At root there is a mix-up. I did not write for the classical scholars, although these—if only they *could*—might be able to learn even some purely philological matters from my book. Now they turn on me bitterly, and seem to think I have committed a crime, because I did not first think of them and their understanding. Rohde's act too will have no outcome, for nothing can bridge the enormous gap. Now I proceed calmly on my way, and am careful not to feel the disgust for which one otherwise might everywhere find occasion.

Dearest Frl. von Meysenbug, you have known worse but similar things, and who knows how much like your life mine may come to be? For till now I have only just begun to speak my mind somewhat; I still need confidence and strong friendship—above all, good and noble *examples*, so as not to run out of breath in mid-speech. Yes, good examples! And here I think of you and am heartily glad to have met with you, dearest Frl. von Meysenbug, who are a lonely fighter for the right. Believe me, once and for all, when I say that I have absolute trust in you, such as I can feel only, in this world of distrust, among my closest friends, and that this has been my attitude toward you from the moment we met. Likewise Frl. Olga can be assured that she can count on me whatever happens in her life. I heartily like you both and hope that I may have opportunities to show it.

Now there comes your friendly letter from Florence and reminds me first and foremost that my awful silence really must seem quite different from what I could assure you of in my letter, which I left unfinished. Why on earth did I not write for such a long time? That is what I ask myself in amazement, without finding good reasons or even excuses. But I have often found it most difficult to decide on writing to those of whom I am thinking most. Yet I do not understand it. Only interpret it as kindly as you can and then forget it. There is so much that is irrational, and only forgetting can help one against it.

With this dark saying I will conclude for today. You will receive with this letter the photograph, Rohde's book, and my five lectures on our educational institutions.[110] Read the last picturing a quite definite audience—the Basel audience; I would at present think it impossible to have this kind of thing printed, for it does not go deep enough and is disguised as a farce, of pretty poor invention.

Cordially, your loyal Dr. Friedrich Nietzsche

My sister has asked me to send you her warmest best wishes; she is no longer here, but intends to visit me again in the summer.

110. Malwida von Meysenbug had asked N to send a photograph of Basel showing the view of the Rhine bridge and the Minster.

48 · *To Richard Wagner*   [Basel, mid-November, 1872]

Geliebter Meister:

After everything that has recently happened to me, I truly have the least
right to be in any way despondent, for I live really in the midst of a solar
system of loving friendship, consoling encouragement, and enlivening
hopes. But there is one point which troubles me greatly at present: our
winter semester has begun, and I have no students at all! Our philologists
have not appeared! This actually is a *pudendum* and should be fearfully
concealed from the world. To you, beloved master, I tell it because you
should know all. The fact is, indeed, so easy to explain—I have suddenly acquired such a bad name in my field that our small university suffers
from it! This agonizes me, because I am really very devoted and grateful to
it, and want least of all to do it any harm; but now my philological colleagues—even Councillor Vischer—are celebrating something he has never
in all his career experienced. Until last semester the number of students in
classical philology was constantly growing—now, suddenly, they are all
blown away! Yet this tallies with what I hear from other university cities.
Leipzig naturally blossoms forth again with envy and arrogance; everyone
condemns me, and even those "who know me" cannot get beyond com-
miserating with me for this "absurdity." A professor of classical philology
at Bonn, whom I highly regard, has simply told his students that my book is
"sheer nonsense" and is quite useless: a person who writes such things is
dead to scholarship. Thus too I have been told of a student who wanted to
come to Basel, but was then kept back at Bonn and recently wrote to a relative in Basel that he thanks God he has not gone to a university where I am
teaching. Do you then think that Rohde's noble action can do anything but
redouble the hatred and ill will and direct them against us? That is, at least,
what Rohde and I expect with complete certainty. That might possibly be
borne, but the damage done by me to a small university, one that has placed
a great deal of trust in me, pains me very much and could in the long run
force me to make decisions which have occurred to me from time to time
for other reasons. Of course I can make good use of this winter semester,
because my only assignment now as a simple schoolmaster is the Pädagogium.

Well, that was the "dark spot," and otherwise all is light and hope.
I would have to be a very morose mole not to leap for joy on receiving such
letters as yours. So, you are coming! I celebrate my good luck and the
dentist, for such a surprise is beyond my wildest dreams. Would you like to
try staying at the Drei Könige this time? I find it better than Euler; this

summer I ate there with my sister and also spent a very pleasant day there with Frl. von Meysenbug and the Herzen-Monod couple.

Your glorious book on actors and singers aroused afresh in me the wish that someone should sum up your esthetic inquiries and findings, in order to show that the whole concept of art has in the meantime been so changed, deepened, and defined that there is at root nothing left of traditional "esthetics." At Splügen I had been thinking also of the way in which the choreography defined Greek tragedy,[111] of the connection between sculpture and the miming and grouping of actors; I thought I had grasped precisely how much Aeschylus himself had set that *example* of which you speak, so that even in our texts symmetries of motion can be detected in strange numerical symmetries;[112] and with your tragedies I linked the high hope that from them may derive measure, aim, and rule for a German dynamic style,[113] a style of plastic reality. These thoughts prepared me for your book, which I then read as a revelation.

Then came Rohde's book; I had a right to maintain, don't you think, after the pamphlet had appeared, that I am correct, even in the smallest incidental points? It is always nice to have a second person corroborate this. For sometimes one begins to distrust oneself if all one's fellow specialists are unanimously hostile in opposition. But what my poor friend has had to suffer in his long tussle with such a "baggage boy"![114] If he lasted it out, it was the thought of you, dear master, which gave him courage and strength. We are both so happy now to have *one* example—and how enviable my position is, don't you think, having a friend like Rohde?

As a curiosity I would like to tell you that I was recently asked by a musician for advice on a libretto, the actual reason being that he wanted me to write it myself.[115] I wrote him a wise epistle, advising him against the idea; I suggested he should write a good cantata, using Goethe's *Walpurgisnacht*, only *doing it better than Mendelssohn!* Will he take my advice? Yet the whole thing is very amusing.

In the hope that, during your wanderings through dear villainous Germany, you are having your old and tested Bayreuth luck, and with the

111. Original: "die choreographische Bestimmtheit der griechischen Tragödie."

112. In *The Birth of Tragedy* N's tendency had been to regard the texts of Greek tragedies (Aeschylus and Sophocles), as librettos for which the music and choreographic arrangement had been lost, as prototypes of the Wagnerian *Gesamtkunstwerk*.

113. Original: "für einen deutschen Stil der Bewegung."

114. Original: "Trossbube" (N's quotation marks); this also connotes "camp-follower"—N regarded Wilamowitz an ultra-conventionalist of the Berlin school of classical philology.

115. Hugo von Senger.

wish that I may soon be instructed as to what accommodation should be prepared for you here, I now say a most cordial farewell and *auf Wiedersehen.*

Loyally as ever, your   F. N.

49 · *To Malwida von Meysenbug*   Basel, December 20, 1872

Verehrtestes Fräulein:

Your letter and photograph brought me great joy, for which I would have thanked you there and then if it had not been necessary to enclose a photograph of myself. But there was none available, and, as you see, now there is only the kind which makes me look like a pirate, and so I am forced to make the metaphysical supposition that what always appears in photographs of me is my "intelligible" character; for my intellectual character is so slight that I was doubtful about offering you this replica of my worse half. What I mean to say is, briefly, that there was, first of all, one delay because I had no photograph, and then another delay because I did have one—but one like this. I make a point of explaining this because I think the photograph of yourself is amazingly good; likewise, my sister has every reason to express both her gratitude and her delight over the photograph of Frl. Olga. I am going now to Naumburg for two weeks, to celebrate Christmas there; during that time I will persuade my sister to have herself photographically executed—at least, this way of putting it expresses my feelings when the one-eyed Cyclops stands before me as *deus ex machina.* I try, each time, to prevent the disaster, but the inevitable always occurs— and out I come, eternalized anew as a pirate or a prominent tenor or a boyar *et hoc genus omne.*

By now you will have read the lectures and have been startled that the story should break off suddenly, after such a long prelude, with the thirst for real new thoughts and proposals tending more and more to end up in mere *negativis* and prolixities. One gets parched while reading them, and then there is nothing to drink at the finish! What I had in mind for the last lecture—a very droll and colorful scene of nocturnal illuminations— was not exactly suitable for my Basel public, and it was certainly a good thing that the words stuck in my throat.[116] As a matter of fact, the continuation troubles me greatly, but since I am putting off for a while my reflections on the whole

116. Refers to the sixth of the lectures on educational institutions (*Die Zukunft unserer Bildungsanstalten*).

subject, for four months or so—which is done easily enough at my age—the last lecture will certainly never be worked out. The whole Rhineland scenery, as well as everything apparently biographical, is terribly fabricated. I shall be cautious about regaling—or not regaling—the people of Basel with truths about my life; yet I have a suspiciously vague memory even of the region around Rolandseck. However, Frau Wagner writes that while traveling along the Rhine she remembered my description.

Our meeting took place, and most happy it was, though not here in Basel, but in *Strasbourg;* after a long exchange of signals by telegram between here and several South German towns, it was realized that their stopping in Basel would be impossible, and so one Friday I went to Strasbourg, where we spent two and a half days together, with no other business to be done, just talking and going for walks and making plans and all of us together happy to belong to one another so intimately.[117] Wagner was very satisfied with his journey; he has found capable supporters and people, and was in a serene mood, ready for any eventuality.[118] The whole winter will be spent traveling, for after Christmas they will be in northeast Germany, especially Berlin, where they will stop for about three weeks. It is not certain, but possible, that he may go to Milan for the performance at La Scala.[119]

Gersdorff will be arriving here in the first half of January, and then traveling on at once to Florence and Rome. He is at present, as is his father, doubly in need of this long-planned journey, because recently his only brother died after three years of suffering in an insane asylum (Illenau). He is now the only hope of his family; his parents are all bereft and alone, because his last and youngest sister, who used to live with them, was recently married to a Count Rothkirch-Trach. Gersdorff recently wrote to me a very enthusiastic letter about your memoirs and those of Herzen—from which you will see, at least, that in making preparations for Italy he is preparing himself especially well for Florence.[120]

117. Original: "der herzlichsten Zueinandergehörigkeit uns gemeinsam erfreuend."

118. Original: "zu allem Unvermeidlichen gerüstet." This phrase, the one quoted in the note preceding, and the word "Gemeinsamkeiten" ("common concerns and meetings") at the end of this letter are typical of the *abstracta* which flourish in N's letters of this period. It is difficult not to translate them into tortuous English because of the concrete tendency of English vocabulary.

119. Wagner visited Dresden, Berlin, Hamburg, Schwerin, and Berlin again on his travels between January 12 and February 6, 1873. The performance of *Lohengrin* at La Scala was a flop.

120. Gersdorff must have read the (anonymous) French version of Malwida's book *Mémoires d'une idéaliste* (1869); the German version did not begin to appear until 1875 (see note 208 to letter No. 65, of April 14, 1876, to Malwida).

By the way, what sort of philological questions, dear Frl. von Meysenbug, do you have (as you say in your letter) on your mind?[121] You can try me out, unless Wilamowitz has shaken your faith in my philology. If he has, I am still at your service, for I could then refer the matter to friend Rohde, of whose philology I permit no one to have any doubt.

What have you decided to do next summer, after your painful separation from Frl. Olga? And when is the wedding to take place? And will it be in Paris? Or with you in Florence?

Herr Monod's book on Gregory of Tours has been highly praised in the German learned journals, and has been described, precisely from the standpoint of the strict historical school, as the best and most valuable work to have yet been written on Gregory.[122]

I leave this evening. Heartiest Christmas greetings to you and Frl. Olga. Long live this year, for many other reasons, but especially because it has brought such beautiful and hopeful common concerns and meetings

121. The original phrasing calls for a longish note, since it is symptomatic of N's epistolary style at this stage. He wrote: "Was sind denn das für philologische Fragen, verehrtestes Fräulein, die Sie wie Sie schreiben auf dem Herzen haben?" The word order, though not particlarly complicated in German, as well as the vocabulary, which is not unusual, create difficulties in English. I settled for "dear," rather than "most respected," tor "verehrtestes Fräulein"; for "auf dem Herzen," I settled for "on your mind," rather than "on your heart." Both "dear" and "mind" recreate the respectful but affectionate tone in a truer way than "respected" and "heart" would. As for the word order, the following disasters were possible: (1) "What sort of philological questions do you have, dear Frl. von M., on your mind as you write?" (2) "What philological questions are they, dear Frl. von M., that you have, as you write, on your mind?" (In both phrases, the temporal "as" confuses the issue.) (3) "What sort of philological questions do you have on your mind, dear Frl. von M., of which you write?" ("Wie Sie schreiben" does not mean that she wrote "of" them, only that she said she had questions.) (4) "Of what kind are those philological questions that you have, as you write in your letter, dear Frl. von M., on your mind?" And so on. The syntax in N's letters, at points labyrinthine, at points archly ophidian, must be treated with tact because it is this which establishes his tone but frequently conspires to conceal, rather than reveal, his feeling and thought. (Cf. especially the letter to his sister, of May 20, 1885: "The feeling that there is about me something very remote and alien, that my words have other colors than the same words for other people. . . .") Podach (Ns Zusammenbruch, Heidelberg: Niels Kampmann, 1930, p. 67) quotes Overbeck on N's reticence even in conversation.

What Malwida wanted to ask for was N's view on the learning of several foreign languages at the same time by children. His reply (end of February, 1873) was that for a German child it might be good to learn at an early age a "strenge Cultursprache"—Latin or French, in order to develop a feeling for style, which might then help the child with his own somewhat barbaric language. Schopenhauer, N. wrote, spent much of his youth speaking French, English, or Spanish—hence his good style; also S himself said that he had studied and imitated Seneca. N concluded by saying that too many books (twelve thousand published in 1872) spoil the broth.

122. Gabriel Monod, Etudes critiques sur les sources de l'histoire mérovingiennes, 2 vols. (Paris, 1872–85), vol. 1, Introduction: Grégoire de Tours, Marius d'Avenches.

into being! Everything is moving along a single course, and to the person who has courage, good and bad must be equally welcome.[123]

With respects, your loyal Fr. Nietzsche

50 · *To Erwin Rohde*   Basel, mid-March—no! about March 22 [1873]

Beloved friend:

Yesterday this semester too, the eighth in my experience, went to the devil or wherever you like, and today there is a chance to breathe somewhat again. But nothing will come of the breathing unless I first make peace with my friends, for these will be reproving me for writing so seldom and being so ungrateful for their letter-writing love. Recently I received, during the carnival days, in a deep depression, your lines, beloved friend, and once more I cursed the demon who separates us, or—to speak directly—the stupid behavior of the Freiburg people, who could have you or—even more directly—the placid perfidy of my "friend" Ritschl, who prevented them from having you.[124] So we sit on our little chairs and do not come together! One would like to start every letter with a curse, and finish—yes, I recommend it to you for *our* use—with the new expression "I lettercurse, thou lettercursest," and so on.

Yet I am, I do feel, much better off than you. Overbeck and Romundt, my friends at table, at home, and in thought, are the best company in the world, so that from this point of view I have put aside all the complaining. Yesterday Romundt finished his first semester as a teacher and has gained from this first attempt a great rostral *furor*.[125] He has really excited the students' interest and will certainly be in his element if he remains an academic. Overbeck is the most serious, open-minded, and personally kind and simple man and scholar whom one could wish to have for a friend. Also he is radical, and I am now beyond having to do with people who are less than that. During the Easter vacation he will be putting this radicalism on record,

123. Original: "das Gute und das Schlimme"; not "Gut und Böse," the later formulation.

124. There had been a possibility of Rohde's receiving an appointment at the University of Freiburg, which is close to Basel.

125. Original: "Kathedralen *furor*." "Katheder," "lecturer's rostrum"; "*furor*," "a sensation." Romundt did not move into the house at Schützengraben 45 until March 31, 1874.

in an open letter to Paul de Lagarde.[126] The quantity of important and penetrating matters that we discuss during any one year is very large, and this always makes me feel what we miss in your not being here. Our lives must spin themselves out long enough to make sure that many of our wishes become deeds; but for us two it will be sometime a *necessitas* to live together, precisely for the sake of these deeds.

I hope that I shall soon be able to send you, for perusal, a large part of my slowly evolving book on Greek philosophy. The title is not certain; but if it were to be "The Philosopher as Physician of Culture," you would see that I am concerned with a fine general problem, not merely one of historical interest.[127] The matter of the printer in Leipzig is not settled yet; hence a long delay over the second edition.[128] I have read Wilamowitz's second piece; it was sent to me here, and I found it jolly enough and completely self-negating.[129] Gersdorff has seen the joker in Rome; I am sending you his joyous letter, so that you can share in the rollicking cavalier's joy.

Frl. Olga Herzen and Herr Monod from Paris were married not long ago. I was in evidence with a wedding composition, for two pianos, with the following title, which should be interpreted as a symbol of a good marriage: "A Monody for Two."

Frl. von Meysenbug is deeply unhappy, and deserves every sympathy; she asked me to come to Florence at Easter, in order to console her a little. Unfortunately I have practically no vacation, thanks to the honorable Pädagogium. R. W[agner] has sent me his book *State and Religion*, written in 1864 and not published until now, intended originally for the king of Bavaria—I am deeply edified. There is no man living who can write in this way on religion and the state, least of all for kings. Incidentally, to what scandal is Wilamowitz alluding in his remark about the *Philological Advertiser*, about page 3 of his pamphlet?[130] Surely old Leutsch isn't two-faced as well?

I keep forgetting to send you my essay on the *Certamen*, which is now stored well away but none the better for it. Please accept it, said the child to its father on his birthday, dropping the cake on the floor.

126. Author of the recent book *Das Verhältnis des deutschen Staates zu Theologie, Kirche und Religion* (Göttingen, 1873).

127. N was working on such a book (his *Philosophenbuch*) in 1872–73 and 1875; his results were published in vol. 10 of the *Grossoktavausgabe* (1894, f.).

128. Of *The Birth of Tragedy*.

129. *Zukunftsphilologie: Eine Erwiderung auf die Rettungsversuche für F. Ns "Geburt der Tragödie"* (Berlin, 1873).

130. The passage in question reads: "A fourth escapade, a renewed advertisement for *The Birth of Tragedy*, in the *Philological Advertiser*, foundered, as I am told, against the refusal of the editor to accept the same."

If only we had learned another art, dearest friend, so that we might travel the world together! For it is really no honest trade, being a conjecture-hunting dachshund.[131] It would be better playing the barrel organ. This last semester I managed to get two students, one a Germanist, the other a law student; I lectured to both on rhetoric! It seems so unbelievably perverse, especially when I consider that one is a personal enthusiast of mine and would be just as happy polishing my boots as listening to my lectures on rhetoric! Next semester it will be a little better—the Pädagogium is spawning a few good philologists, with whom one can get along.

The *Abundantia* pictures arrived today, and I remember our happy days in Leipzig and Naumburg.[132] We shall do our best to repeat the occasion this year, shall we not, dearest friend? My sister is visiting me this summer. But in October I shall be traveling in your direction, to good old Thuringia. Or shall we meet in Dresden? At all events, not in that God-damned Leipzig again!

I wish you a clear sky, serene mind, and recommend to you, as my own means of fortifying myself, Marcus Antoninus; reading him makes one feel so tranquil.

Loyally and always thinking of you

Fridericus

In Gersdorff's letter there is something very touching—you will find it— to do with my lectures. What a friend he is![133]

51 · *To Richard Wagner*[134]   Basel, April 18, 1873

Verehrtester Meister:

Memories of the Bayreuth days are with me always, and the many new things that I learned and experienced in so short a time keep unfolding

131. Original: "Konjekturen-Dachshund." The dachshund was originally bred for hunting badgers underground.

132. *Abundantia* was a painting by Hans Makart, which N and Rohde had admired while it was being shown in Leipzig during their days there in autumn, 1871.

133. Gersdorff, in Florence, had copied out N's lectures on "The Future of our Educational Institutions" from the manuscript in Malwida von Meysenbug's possession.

134. On April 5, N had written to Gersdorff that he hoped to repair, by going the next day to Bayreuth for a week, the damage done to his relations with Wagner by his having had to decline an invitation to see him at Christmas time. The present letter shows that the visit had not had the desired effect.

before me in ever greater abundance. If you seemed not satisfied with me when I was present, I understand it only too well; but I cannot help it, for I learn and perceive very slowly and, every moment when I am with you, I realize something of which I have never thought, something that I wish to impress upon my mind. I know very well, dearest master, that such a visit cannot be a time of leisure for you, and must sometimes even be unbearable. I wished so often to give at least the appearance of greater freedom and independence, but in vain. Enough—I ask that you take me simply as a pupil, if possible with my pen in my hand and my notebook before me, as a pupil too with a very slow and not at all versatile mind. It is true that I grow more melancholy every day when I feel so strongly how much I would like to help you somehow, to be of use to you, and how completely incapable of doing so I am, so that I cannot even contribute somewhat to diverting and amusing you.

Or perhaps I can, when I have finished what I am now writing, a piece which attacks the famous writer David Strauss.[135] I have now read his *Old and New Faith*, and have been amazed at his obtuseness and vulgarity as an author and as a thinker too. A fine collection of examples of his most appalling style should show the public once and for all what this supposed "classic" actually is.

While I was away, my fellow lodger Overbeck added considerably to the book he is writing, "On the Christianity of Our Theology"; it is so aggressive against all parties, and, moreover, so incontrovertible and honest, that he too will be outlawed, once it is published, as a man who, to quote Professor Brockhaus, has "ruined his career." Basel is gradually becoming thoroughly offensive.

Friend Rohde and I parted at Lichtenfels (where your bust stands in the railway station). On Easter Sunday we went for one more morning walk together, to Vierzehnheiligen, an hour away from Lichtenfels. I do have excellent friends, don't you think?

To your most deeply respected wife I am sending Renan's *Paul* today; I shall send the promised book by Paul de Lagarde[136] together with Overbeck's when the latter is ready.

I am so sorry that we did not see the dean at all.[137]

Farewell! Farewell, dearest master, to you and all your family.

Your loyal Friedrich Nietzsche

135. This became "David Strauss, der Bekenner und Schriftsteller," the first of N's *Thoughts out of Season* (written 1873-76).

136. See note 126 to No. 50.

137. An ecclesiastic in Bayreuth named Dittmar.

52 · *To Erwin Rohde*   On the Swiss Frontier [Basel]
October 18, 1873

Dearest friend:

The above hotel advertisement means only that I was at Splügen last year and that I have no other paper at the moment. But the person who is writing this letter and has such bad handwriting is called Romundt.[138]

Since you left,[139] I have just about managed to survive, had to stay in bed one day out of every four, and was incapable of celebrating your birthday properly by a letter and libations. As far as my own is concerned, I have decided to celebrate hereafter only the passing of another year, and to see with resignation the approach of the future. If the gods are very merciful, may they grant me in the new year what I had in the old—that is, my friends and the desire to do something properly and well.[140]

For everything that is new is terrible, as I came to realize during the first days of this new year. New, for example, is the request which arrived today that I should write, for the benefit of the Bayreuth project and on behalf of the council of patrons, an appeal to the German People (to put it chastely). This request is also terrible, for once I tried to write something similar of my own accord without success. Therefore I beg you, dear friend, with all urgency, to help me with this, in order to see if we can perhaps manage the monster together. The gist of the proclamation, which I beg you to draft for me, is that all people great and small, as far as the German tongue resounds,[141] should give money to their music dealers; the following motivation might spur them to such action (details seemingly from Wagner via Heckel).[142] 1. Importance of the project, importance of its initiator. 2. Disgrace that the nation in which such a project—each participant in which is making personal sacrifices for no selfish gain—can be represented and attacked as the project of a charlatan. 3. Comparison with other nations; if in France, England, or Italy, a man who had given the theaters, against all the forces of public opinion, five works which are performed and applauded from

138. The original is written on notepaper with the Hotel Bodenhaus Splügen letterhead. At this time, because of his deteriorating eyesight, N was beginning to dictate letters whenever possible.

139. Rohde had visited N in early October.

140. N's birthday was October 15; the "new year" here refers to the year beginning for him on that day.

141. Allusion to E. M. Arndt's poem "Des Deutschen Vaterland."

142. Emil Heckel, of the Wagner circle, had written such a proclamation himself, but Wagner had told him to ask N to do it.

one end of the country to the other, if such a man exclaimed: "The existing theaters do not correspond at all to the spirit of the nation; as public art, they are a disgrace. Help me to build a shrine to the national spirit"—would not everyone come to his aid, even if only out of a sense of self-respect? And so on.[143] At the end it should be indicated that every German book dealer, art dealer, and music dealer has a subscription list and will provide any information needed. Do not be annoyed, dearest friend, and go to work on it; I will work on it also, but cannot guarantee anything because of the greyish state of my heart and stomach. The matter is urgent too. So can I count on having from you soon a page in Napoleonic style?[144]

Meanwhile another thing has waxed gigantic and really beyond our control. Even in letters we are not allowed to speak out clearly about it—only to murmur. There exists, as Overbeck and I are most firmly convinced, a dreadful plot to amalgamate the – – – –[145] Leipzig publishers with the International Publishers.[146] F[ritzsch] is, as we fear, already compromised and has probably received money by now. Our hopes and concerns will be destroyed the moment this becomes a matter of public discussion. Actually I wanted to leave for Leipzig this evening and intervene personally. An unexpected university commitment prevents me, and so I shall only go to Leipzig from Bayreuth.[147] The acute critic E[rwin] R[ohde] has no access to the whole *apparatus criticus* (letters and statements from the female phantom R[osalie] N[ielsen]). From what we do know, even less experienced crytycs[148] can draw a frightfully definite conclusion, especially when they avail themselves of R[omundt]'s famous speculative classroom void.[149] Please tell us too if F[ritzsch] came to mention that testament of his own

143. The five works in question were: *Der fliegende Holländer, Tannhäuser, Lohengrin, Tristan und Isolde, Die Meistersinger.*

144. Rohde refused, in a letter dated October 23.

145. Dashes in original: *Briefe 4*, No. 737.

146. Fritzsch was the (Leipzig) publisher of Wagner's writings and of Nietzsche's, which made him subsequently the publisher for the Bayreuth circle. Charles Andler, *Nietzsche, sa vie et sa pensée* (Paris, 1920), 2: 396, ff., gives details of the supposed "Communist" plot against the Wagner-Bayreuth establishment; see also the Gersdorff letters to N.

147. N was in Bayreuth from October 30 to November 2, for a meeting of delegates from Wagner societies. In a letter to Gersdorff dated November 7, he describes the meeting, at which his appeal was rejected by the delegates, though Wagner approved of it and wanted to use it if an "optimistic appeal" were to fail (*Briefe 4*, No. 742).

148. Original: "Krütüker" (for "Kritiker").

149. Rohde designated Romundt jocularly, in his letter to N of October 23, a "Sälenentleerer" ("classroom emptier"). The phrase must have caught on, as the result of some tendency of Romundt's to empty classrooms by becoming speculative in his philosophy lectures.

accord, in what tone he mentioned the phantom, and if he happened to speak of his health.[150] Incidentally, it is earnestly requested by the dictator and writer of this letter that you burn it *at once.*

Is your strong manly heart beating against your ribs?

After such events I no longer dare to put my name to this letter. We are living Samarow—thinking only in terms of bombs and counter-bombs, we sign only pseudonymous names and wear false beards.[151]

> Hooi, hooi! How the wind howls!
> In the name of our fellow conspirators
>
> Hugo with the growly ghost voice

Warmest greetings also from

The Writer

Everything is in danger; even Overbeck has the bellyache; he feels he has been poisoned; he sends his best wishes.

53 · *To Malwida von Meysenbug*　　Basel, February 11, 1874

Verehrte Freundin:

I did not know where my thoughts might find you; only I heard from Gersdorff that your life in Bayreuth has come to an end; now I hear where you are, lonely and unwell, and I would have liked to come to you at once, if only it had somehow been compatible with my university post and with my duties.[152] But I do promise to visit you in Rome. Or would you consider whether Geneva or Lugano might improve your health? From time to time I have thought of suggesting Basel to you, for till now we have had a mild and sunny winter, and only since yesterday has there been snow and really cold weather. At least I do know that there is a great difference between our

150. In a letter of October 14, Rohde had written that Rosalie Nielsen (International Publishers) had wanted to make her will in favor of Fritzsch.

151. Gregor Samarow was the pen name of Oskar Meding, author of a novel entitled *Europäische Minen und Gegenminen* (*European Bombs and Counterbombs*), the second part of his *Um Szepter und Kronen* (Stuttgart, 1873). Perhaps it was Overbeck, not N, who had read this book.

152. She had planned to settle in Bayreuth, but contracted an ear infection which obliged her to go south. She spent some time in San Remo undergoing treatment (N's letter was addressed to her there), went from there to Ischia, and from Ischia to Rome, which remained thereafter her main place of residence.

climate here and that of Bayreuth and that the trees here come into leaf four weeks earlier. This suggestion is meant only to express my most heartfelt wish to be closer to you once more, for we share one suffering which other people would hardly feel so strongly—our suffering about Bayreuth. For, oh, our hopes were too high! At first I tried not to think any more about the distressing state of affairs there, and, since this was not possible, I have for the past weeks thought about it as much as I can and have scrutinized sharply all the reasons why the project has come to a standstill, why it will perhaps even fail completely.[153] Perhaps I shall tell you later some of my thoughts; but first, in about two weeks' time you will receive something else from me, the expected No. 2 with the title "On the Use and Disadvantage of History to Life." The number "2" reminds me that David Strauss was buried yesterday in Ludwigsburg.[154]

And what is Frau Monod doing? Is it true that she has given birth to a boy?

You see that till now I was dictating this letter—I am having trouble with my eyes. Yet not so much as hitherto. Ah, if only I could help you! Or be somehow of use to you! I think of you, poor lady, with sympathy, and I admire your ability to endure life. Compared with you, I am a lucky prince, and ought to be ashamed.[155] My wishes are all for you.

Your Friedrich Nietzsche

54 · *To Erwin Rohde*   Basel, March 19, 1874

My semester is also nearly over; it ends tomorrow—although only at the university of course; the Pädagogium, in its mean way, throws me only one and a half weeks of Easter vacation—no more. In this you are better off, dearest friend, but only in this, for as brothers we still deplore, singly and together, your other circumstances. I have made another fine plan, for later, which should bring us permanently together—but we still have to wait a few years. Yet the meeting in the autumn, the *consilium Rhaeticum*—that is

153. Adolf Stern's optimistic appeal had had no results at all.

154. The essay is the second of N's *Thoughts out of Season*, the first of which had been the essay attacking David Friedrich Strauss. On February 11 also N wrote Gersdorff a letter in which he expressed the hope that his essay had not made the end of Strauss's life miserable and that Strauss had died without hearing of him. "It affects me somewhat," he wrote.

155. N uses the word "Glücksprinz," which seems to be a personal (?) variant on the conventional word "Glückspilz" (lucky fellow).

definite, isn't it? Now about Bayreuth! From Frau Wagner we know—and it is meant to be a secret among Wagner's friends—that the king of Bavaria is supporting the project in the form of subsidies up to 100,000 talers, which means that operations (machines, decorating) will be vigorously speeded up. Wagner himself writes that the deadline is 1876; he is in good spirits, and believes that the undertaking is now in the clear. God grant it may be! This fearful waiting is hard to recover from; sometimes I really had quite given up hope.

I keep expecting you to announce that you have been appointed a full professor. People certainly are terribly stupid as far as academic tenure is concerned; I was recently in Freiburg, and heard them complaining about that insupportable pedant and grouser Keller.[156] Serves you right! I thought, just keep complaining; I also found out that Ritschl was the cause of his being appointed there. The latter does not write to me, and I take delight in thinking how little he will understand when he reads my "History."[157] This nonunderstanding protects him from being annoyed, and that is the best of it.

Professor Plüss of Schulpforta,[158] whom I do not know, has roused my home town, Naumburg, by giving an enthusiastic speech on *The Birth of Tragedy* and the first *Thought out of Season*. Herr Bruno Meier [*sic*] has written a long, difficult essay refuting Dräseke's contribution to the Wagner question (of belly-laughing memory), in which essay I am solemnly denounced as an "enemy of culture" and presented, moreover, as a wily impostor among dupes. He sent me his essay personally, including even his private address; I am going to send him Wilamops' two pamphlets.[159] That's what Christians call being kind to one's enemies. For the joy that this good Meier will receive from Wilamops is beyond expression.

Dr. Fuchs has praised me sickeningly again in the *Wochenblatt*—I have had enough of him.[160] But why am I telling you of praise and blame! Here our friendship protects us fairly well from whims and annoyances; and since I am once more about to produce, praise and blame are no matter

156. Otto Keller was a professor of classical philology at Freiburg from 1872 to 1876. N had hoped, in 1872, that Rohde would get the appointment.

157. The second of the *Thoughts out of Season*.

158. The school of which N was an alumnus.

159. Bruno Meyer, "Beiträge zur Wagnerfrage," *Deutsche Warte*, 5: 641–43. Johannes Dräseke, "Beiträge zur Wagnerfrage," *Musikalisches Wochenblatt*, vol. 4, 1873. Wilamops ("Mops" = "pug-dog") was their nickname for Wilamowitz-Moellendorf.

160. Carl Fuchs, "Gedanken aus und zu Grillparzers *Aesthetischen Studien*," *Musikalisches Wochenblatt*, vol. 5, 1874 (esp. p. 131). Later, N was on better terms with Fuchs.

to me. I know that I set about my effusions in a rather dilettantishly immature way, but my whole concern is first to get rid of all the polemical, negative stuff in me; I want to sing assiduously the whole scale of my hostile feelings, up and down, really outrageously, so that "the vault resounds."[161] Later—five years later—I shall chuck all the polemics and think of a good work. But now my heart is downright congested with aversion and oppression; so I must expectorate, decently or indecently, but once and for all. I still have eleven fine tunes to sing.[162] Our Overbeck also I have brought to the point, to my great secret joy, of fighting again in the open, to the tune of his essay in polemics and peacemaking No. 1.[163] So, you see, things are spirited here,—we are hitting out. Onward, with rapiers drawn and ready! Only our excellent friend Romundt worries us somewhat; he is becoming a miserable mystic. Clarity was never his strong point, nor was worldly experience; now he is developing a peculiar hatred of everything to do with culture—well, as I said, we (Overbeck and I) are a little worried. He keeps weirdly pondering the inception of sentience, synthetic unity of apperception—the Lord Jesus Christ preserve us!

I have had good letters from all over. Burckhardt, my colleague, who was impressed by the "History," wrote me a very good and characteristic one. Old Vischer is extremely unwell; he has asked to be relieved of most of his work, and looks very miserably greenish-whitish-yellow.

They are busy printing *The Birth of Tragedy*—at last.[164]

When can you come to us in the autumn? I would like to know precise details now, so that our friends can make their plans for the summer.

Farewell, my dearest hermit and romantic of the north with regard to the south.

Curious fellows we are, the lot of us; I get more and more astonisheder.[165]

Your F. N.

161. Allusion to Goethe's *Faust*, part 1, "Auerbachs Keller": "Only when the vault resounds / Does one feel the profound power of the bass."

162. N planned to write thirteen *Thoughts out of Season*.

163. Overbeck's book *On the Christianity of Our Present Theology* was subtitled *eine Streit- und Friedensschrift* (a *Pamphlet of Polemics and Peace*).

164. The second printing. N had hoped that the reprinting would begin during the previous winter.

165. Original: "ich wundere mich sehr und immer sehrer" (the last two words are grammatical horseplay).

55 · *To Carl von Gersdorff*   Basel, April 1, 1874

Dear, loyal friend:

If only your opinion of me were not much too good! I almost think that you will be somewhat disillusioned about me one day; and I will begin the process myself by declaring, on the basis of my best self-knowledge, that I deserve *none* of your praises. If only you knew how despondent and melancholy my thoughts are at root, when I consider myself as a productive person. I am only looking for a little freedom, a little of the real breath of life, and I defend myself and revolt against the quantity—the unspeakable quantity—of unfreedom which clings to me. There can be no talk of real productivity as long as one is still to a large extent confined in unfreedom, in the suffering and burdensome feeling of constraint—shall I ever be really productive? Doubt after doubt. The goal is too far away, and even if one ever reaches it, most often one's powers have been used up in the long search and the struggle; when one reaches freedom, one is as exhausted as an ephemeral fly when evening comes. I am so much afraid of that. It is a misfortune to be conscious of one's struggle so early in life! I cannot set any actual deeds against it, as the artist or the ascetic can. How miserable and sickening I often find it, this bittern-like complaining! At the moment I have more than my fill of it.

My health, by the way, is excellent; do not worry about that. But I am very dissatisfied with Nature, who should have given me more understanding, and a fuller heart besides—I am always deficient in the best things. To know this is the worst agony for a man.

Regular professional work is as good as it is because it brings a certain stupor, so that one suffers less.

In the autumn, then—ah, you do understand the "then," don't you? We *must* see each other at the *consilium subalpinum sive Rhaeticum.*[166] When we are all together, a fellow emerges who is all of a piece, who has no reason for gloom. Collectively and together, we are a being who can drink of joy—at the breasts of Nature.[167] Send me exact details of when you will be allowed to come, will you? Rohde said in his last letter that he was definitely coming. Overbeck and Romundt (since yesterday our fellow lodger) also. I, who have the shortest vacation, plan to be available in the first half of October. Can you give us this time? Dear, dear friend!

166. Refers to the meeting in Basel, for which N was hoping. Rohde and Gersdorff did visit him—but separately—in October.

167. Allusion to Schiller's "Ode to Joy," line 25 ff.

Have you heard, by any chance, that Professor Plüss of Schulpforta, Volkmann's successor, has given an enthusiastic lecture in the Naumburg "Litteraria" [Club] about The Birth of Trag and the Straussiad? Very funny and incredible, don't you think? Dr. Fuchs, in the *Musikalisches Wochenblatt*, is very cheeky and has displeased Overbeck and me—by his importunate attitude in general too. Dear Frl. Meysenbug sent me beautiful fresh flowers, messengers of spring from the Mediterranean.

I enclose a letter from Rohde which is fine and which you will find instructive; return it sometime.

Glorious letters from the Bayreuth people.

Thanks for the misprints—but you missed the most important one, Höderlin for Hölderlin. It looks wonderful, though, don't you think? But not a swine will understand.[168]

My writings are said to be obscure and unintelligible! I thought that, when one speaks of distress, people in distress would understand. That is also certainly true—but where are the people who are in distress?

Do not expect any literary work from me now. I have much to prepare for my summer lectures, and like doing it (on rhetoric). Since Christmas I have thought out and through a great deal, as a matter of fact.

Warmest greetings to your respected parents also.

Yes, if one had no friends! Could one endure it, have endured it? *Dubito.*

Fridericus

56. *To Carl von Gersdorff*   [Basel], July 4, 1874

Now, dearest good friend, I have a few things that I want to tell you, despite the heat of the summer sun. First, there is a longing to find a cool place. Second, there is a lot being done on the *Thought out of Season*.[169] I hope to be finished by the vacation, but cannot, because my body gets in the way and needs a little cheering up. On the other hand, everything is fitting nicely

168. "Hode"="testicle." "Höderlin" might be read as a double diminutive agent, "little testicler." The last phrase in this paragraph is not altogether clear: "Aber es versteht kein Schwein." Possibly N infers that you would have to be a "Schwein" to see the accidental meaning made by this misprint (the poet Friedrich Hölderlin as a "seminal" mind) but that, even then, no "Schwein" would get the point.

169. Refers to the third of the *Thoughts out of Season*, "Schopenhauer as Educator," which was originally to be called "Schopenhauer among the Germans." N was negotiating with Ernst Schmeitzner of Leipzig, who published it in October. Fritzsch had closed his business in the summer.

into place; it would be a pity if I spoiled or forgot it. Probably I shall go to the Engadin for a while with my sister.[170] As for Bayreuth, I got no further than having good intentions; for it seems to me that their household and life there are in a restive state, and that just now our visit would be inconvenient. They are not upset about my condition; you have all been looking too much on the dark side. Finally, all I can think about now is finishing No. 3 and making it *good*. By the way, dear friend, how did you hit upon the droll idea of trying to force me, by a threat, to visit Bayreuth?[171] It almost looks as if I did not want to go of my own free will; and still I met the Bayreuth people twice last year and twice the year before, traveling from *Basel*, what is more, and with my pitifully short vacations! We both know that Wagner's nature tends to make him *suspicious*, but I did not think that it would be a good thing to stir up his suspiciousness.[172] And last but not least, consider that I have obligations toward myself, which are very hard to fulfill, with my health in such a fragile state. Really, nobody should try forcing me to do anything.

Take all this in a friendly and human way!

Just think, old Vischer took to his deathbed a few days ago, and his family is gathered around him. You know what I am losing in him.

I have just been told of the death of Judge Krug, the father of my friend.[173] My friend Pinder and Gustav Krug too are getting married in the autumn—and the generations go on flowering.

For our meeting I have something very fine—but please bring something yourself as well. Perhaps the Italian translations![174]

But only if you have the time and the leisure, dear loyal friend.

[no signature]

170. In fact, N spent the second half of July at Bergün in the Engadin with Romundt.

171. Gersdorff had written to N that he would not come to Switzerland in the autumn if N did not go to Bayreuth.

172. Meaning that Gersdorff's "threat" might have had this effect, if Wagner had got wind of it.

173. Gustav Krug's father.

174. Gersdorff was translating Machiavelli's *Life of Castruccio Castracani* (1281–1328), who led the Ghibelline faction in Lucca. An account of Castruccio's exploits is given in Machiavelli's *History of Florence*, chap. 6.

57. *To Malwida von Meysenbug*   Basel, October 25, 1874

At last, *verehrtestes Fräulein*, I can once more give you some news of myself, by sending you something new that I have written; from the contents of this latest book you will be able to see what thoughts have been occupying my mind in the meantime.[175] Also you will see that I was sometimes during the year in a far worse and more dubious state than the book shows. *In summa*, however, things are going on all right, going *forward*, only I am lacking the sunshine of life; in all other ways I would have to say that things could not be better for me than they are. For it is certainly a great good fortune to proceed with one's task step by step—and now I have finished three of the thirteen *Thoughts* and the fourth is haunting my mind.[176] How shall I feel when I have got out of me all the negative and rebellious ideas that are in me? And yet I can hope to be near this glorious goal in about five years' time. Already I can feel, with a true sense of gratitude, how I am learning to see with greater clarity and sharpness—intellectually (unfortunately not physically!) and how I can express myself more and more definitely and intelligibly. Unless something happens to put me on the wrong track entirely, or unless I flag, something *must* come of all this. Imagine a series of fifty books like my four to date, all of them *forced* into the light of day out of inner experience—they would have to make an effect, for one would certainly have loosened many tongues, and things enough would have been expressed in language, things that people could not quickly forget, things that do now seem forgotten, nonexistent. And what could happen to put me on the wrong track? Even hostile counteractions I now find useful and beneficial, for they enlighten me often more quickly than friendly actions; and I desire nothing more than to be enlightened about the whole highly complicated system of antagonisms which constitutes the "modern world." Luckily I have no political and social ambition at all; so I need fear no dangers from that quarter, no distractions, no pressure to make transactions and to be circumspect; in brief, I may say outright what I think, and I mean to test how far our fellow beings, proud of their freedom of thought, can tolerate free thoughts. I do not ask too much of life—I ask nothing excessive of it; so during the next few years we shall come to see a thing or two that

175. Original: "was ich inzwischen in mir erlebt habe" ("what I have experienced in myself"), a normal locution for "what I have been thinking." In the context of this and other letters, the phrase does emphasize the telescoping of cogitation and experience to which N was given. He was sending her "Schopenhauer as Educator."

176. At this time, the essay N planned as the fourth was "We Philologists," not "Richard Wagner in Bayreuth."

may make our predecessors and posterity envy us. I have also been vouch-safed excellent friends, beyond my deserts; now, confidentially, I wish soon to find a good wife, and then I shall consider my wishes for life fulfilled—everything else then will be up to me.

I have talked enough about myself, *verehrteste Freundin,* and have still given you no idea of the warm concern with which I think of you and your difficult life. Gauge by the tone of absolute trust in which I speak to you about myself how near to you I have always felt and how much I have wished to console you a little now and then and to entertain you. But you live so terribly far away. Perhaps I really shall set out around next Easter and visit you in Italy, as long as I know where you are to be found there. Meanwhile my warmest best wishes for your health and the old request that your friendliness toward me may continue.

Loyally, your humble servant Friedrich Nietzsche

58 · *To Hans von Bülow*   [Naumburg], January 2, 1875

Hochverehrter Herr:

I felt much too delighted and honored by your letter not to consider ten times over your suggestion about Leopardi.[177] I know his prose writings only very slightly of course; one of my friends, who shares lodgings with me in Basel, has often translated parts of them and read them to me, and each time I was greatly surprised and full of admiration; we have the latest Livorno edition. (A French work on Leopardi has recently appeared, by the way, published by Didier in Paris; I forget the author's name at the moment—Boulé?)[178] I know the poems in Hamerling's translation. The fact is I do not know Italian well enough and, despite being a philologist, am unfortunately no linguist (the German language gives me trouble enough).

But the worst thing is that I have no time at all. I have put aside the next five years for working out the remaining ten *Thoughts out of Season* and thus for clearing my soul of as much impassioned polemical mess as possible. But in truth I can hardly see how I shall find the time for this, for I am not only an academic teacher but also teach Greek at the Basel Pädagogium. My written productions (I would prefer not to say "books" and also not "pamphlets") I have virtually tricked out of myself during rare

177. Bülow himself had been translating Leopardi for some time; he had asked N if he would translate Leopardi's poems.

178. Bouché-Leclercq, *Giacomo Leopardi, sa vie et ses œuvres* (Paris, 1874).

vacations and times of sickness; I even had to dictate the Straussiad, because at that time I could neither read nor write.[179] But since I am now in a good physical state, with no prospect of sickness, and my daily cold baths offer no likelihood of my ever being sick again, my future as a writer is almost hopeless—unless my literary endeavors can be realized some day on a country estate.[180]

Such a modest possibility, *verehrter Herr*, is naturally nothing for you to rely on; therefore I must ask you to exclude me from your plans. But that you should have thought of me at all is a form of sympathy which could not gladden me more, even if I must recognize that there are persons who are more worthy and suited to the office of mediating between Italy and Germany.

Assuring you of my continued respect and esteem

I remain, Sir, your servant

Friedrich Nietzsche

59. *To Erwin Rohde* [Basel, February 28, 1875]

How much I would like to hear, dearest friend, if only by a single tiny word, that things are well with you! I was recently troubled by a dream—if it was a dream. From Bayreuth also I have been asked to give news of you; you know—and yet can hardly know clearly enough—how cordially and warmly people there remember you and how worried they are. At present my sister is in Bayreuth and will be staying there for a few weeks. I shall also tell you at once of Frau Wagner's request that you apply, as soon as possible, and somewhat tempestuously, to the burgomaster of Bayreuth for a lodging there this summer; it will be very difficult to find places there for all the visitors; and we must press the burgomaster hard, because things are still in a very bad way as far as accommodation is concerned. You certainly should not ask for a "modest lodging." My sister is trying to find something for herself and me, so far without success.

179. "Written productions" = "schriftartige Erzeugnisse" (literally, "writing-like productions"). N was generally reluctant to have his writings classified as literary works or "books"; cf. letter of April 6, 1883, to Peter Gast: ". . . now nobody can save me from being cast among the writers of 'belles lettres.' Hell!" He most often uses the word *Schrift* for his productions—"a writing." Owing to the exigencies of English, I must, however, translate this as "book," except when the plural occurs.

180. That is, "I have time to write only when I am sick; now that I am not sick, my academic work will take up all my time, unless I give it up and retire into the country."

The semester is nearly at an end—there are three more weeks at the university, five more at the Pädagogium. There is much excitement here, for the city council is deliberating the new Basel constitution; all parties are bitterly at odds, and then in the spring the people will decide. (Today a passage on state omnipotence from No. 3 was used in the political struggle—which amused me.)[181] At Easter our Pädagogium will be losing old Gerlach, who is finally being retired; but who can guess what will happen then? I have been asked if I would take over four hours of Latin next semester for the highest grade, but I refused because of my eyes.

On the whole, things are going fairly well with me; I feel as if I am turning into a feudal baron, my way of life is becoming gradually so entrenched and inwardly independent.

No. 4 should be finished by Easter. Did I tell you that the French translation of No. 3 is finished and provided with a letter of dedication to me?[182] Gersdorff is coming here for a while on March 12—you know about that also.

But now something you do not know and have a right to know, as my most intimate and sympathetic friend. We also—Overbeck and I—have a domestic problem, a household ghost; do not fall off your chair when you hear that Romundt has plans to enter the Roman Catholic Church and wants to become a priest in Germany. This transpired recently, but is a thought, as we later heard to our great alarm, which he has had for some time, but which is nearer to fruition now than ever before. This wounds me inwardly somewhat, and sometimes I feel it is the most wicked thing that anyone could do to me. Of course Romundt does not mean it wickedly; until now he has thought of nothing but himself, and the accursed accent he places on the "Save your own soul" idea makes him quite indifferent to everything else, including friendship. It has gradually become a mystery to Overbeck and me that R. should have nothing more in common with us and was annoyed or bored by everything that inspired or stirred us; especially, he has bouts of peevish silence, which have worried us for some time past. Eventually there came confessions and now, almost every three days, come clerical explosions. The poor fellow is in a desperate state and beyond help—that is, he is so drawn by obscure intentions that to us he seems like a walking velleity. Our good, pure, Protestant atmosphere! Never till now have I felt so strongly my inmost dependence on the spirit of Luther; and does the unhappy fellow mean to turn his back now on all these liberating influences?[183]

181. From "Schopenhauer as Educator."

182. The French translation was by Marie Baumgartner, wife of an industralist, mother of Adolf Baumgartner, who was one of N's students at Basel.

183. "Influence"—N uses the word "Genien" here, in the older sense of "daimonic influences."

I wonder if he is in his right mind and if he should not undergo medical treatment with cold baths. I find it so incomprehensible that, right beside me, after eight years of intimacy, this ghost should have risen up. And ultimately it will be me to whom the stain of this conversion will attach. God knows, I say this not out of egoistic anxiety; but I too believe that I represent something holy and am deeply ashamed when it is suspected of me that I have had anything to do with this utterly odious Catholic business. Figure this awful story out according to your friendship for me and send me a few comforting words. I have been wounded precisely in a matter of friendship, and hate the dishonest, sneaking character of many friendships more than ever, and shall have to be more careful. R. himself will feel content in some institution or other—there is no question of that—but among *us* he suffers constantly, as it now seems. Ah, dearest friend! Gersdorff is right when he often says, "There's nothing crazier than what goes on in the world." In grief

      Your friend Friedrich N., also in Overbeck's name—burn this letter if you think fit.[184]

60 · *To Richard Wagner*   Basel, May 24, 1875

My wishes come limping and late; you must forgive me, beloved master. I mean by this the uncertainty and weakness of my physical state, and admire the robustness with which you have fought your way during the last years through the chaos of new tasks, hardships, annoyances, fatigue; so that even I have no right to wish you anything in this regard. (If only I could, rather, learn something from you!) When I think of your life, I always have the feeling that its course is *dramatic*, as if you were so much of a dramatist that you yourself could live only in this form and could die, in any case, only at the end of the fifth act. Where everything is pressing and rushing toward a goal, chance vanishes, is afraid—so it seems. Everything becomes as necessary and unbreakable as brass, because of the intensity of

---

184. In a letter to Gersdorff, of April, 17, 1875, N described Romundt's departure from Basel. Overbeck and N took him to the railway station and put him in the train, after much weeping and pleading for forgiveness on Romundt's part. The train doors were then closed by the porters, and Romundt began trying to lower the window of his compartment, in order to say something; but, despite the most arduous efforts, the window would not budge, and the train slowly moved out of the station. N was so upset by this departure that he had to spend the next day in bed with a headache lasting for thirty hours, and frequent vomiting. Romundt did not enter the Roman Catholic Church in the end; he soon became a relatively contented schoolmaster in Oldenburg.

movement—just as I find it in your expression on the beautiful medallion which was recently given to me. We other people flicker somewhat, and thus not even health has anything steady about it.

Now I would tell you only that I have found a remarkably fine prophecy, which I would have liked to send you for your birthday. It runs as follows:

> O holy heart of the peoples, O fatherland!
> Enduring all things like the silent mother Earth.
> Ignored by all, though from your profundities
> Foreigners draw their best possessions.
>> They harvest thought, gather from you the Spirit,
>> Gladly they pluck the grape, yet do they mock
>> The shapeless vine, wherefore your tread
>> Across the ground is wild and random.
> Land of the high, more earnest Genius!
> Land of love! As I am yours for sure,
>> Often I raged, weeping, that always you
>> Stupidly hide and deny your own soul.
> Still you delay, are silent, brooding a joyous work,
>> Your own testimony, brooding *a new image,*
>> *One unique, as yourself, an image*
>> *Born of love, and good as you are.*
> Where is your Delos, where your Olympia,
> That we may meet, all, at the sublimest feast?
>> How can your son fathom, goddess immortal,
>> What you have long in store for your people?[185]

It was poor Hölderlin who said all this, who had a harder time than I, and who had only a presentiment of what we trust in and shall see.

Truly, beloved master, to write to you for your birthday means only one thing: to wish us luck, to wish us health, so that we can properly share in your life. For I am inclined to think that it is being unwell, and the egoism that lurks in sickness, which compels people always to think of themselves, whereas the genius, in the fullness of his health, always thinks only of the others, involuntarily blessing and healing wherever he may place his hand. Every sick man is a rascal, I recently read; and what a host of sicknesses men have! On your travels through Germany you will have heard of some of them, for example, the very widespread sickness of "Hartmannianism."[186]

185. Hölderlin, "Gesang des Deutschen," lines 1–12 and 53–60. Italics and lay-out are N's. For N, the Delos and Olympia references would have applied to Bayreuth.

186. Eduard von Hartmann, *Die Philosophie des Unbewussten*. N had read this book in Leipzig. He had criticized Hartmann in section 9 of "The Use and Disadvantage of History for Life," calling him "the first-ever philosophical parodist" and charging him

Farewell, *verehrter Meister*, and keep the health that we lack.[187]

Loyally, your servant Friedrich Nietzsche

61 · *To Carl von Gersdorff*   Basel, September 26, 1875

My beloved friend:

Yesterday the semester ended—my thirteenth semester—and from today there are two weeks of vacation. I would have liked to go on a short walking tour, because in the autumn I always have a desire to see the Pilatus once more before winter comes; the longer I stay in Switzerland, the more personal and dear to me this mountain becomes, but, outside, it is horribly wet and like early November, and I shall have to *wait* or *forgo*—as so often in life.[188] One does notice it, when one is out of one's twenties. A certain kind of disillusionment, but a kind that spurs me to actions of my own, like the fresh air of autumn, accompanies me almost from one day to the next.

Meanwhile I have set up house, with the aid of my sister, and it has turned out *well*.[189] So I am again at last, for the first time since I was thirteen,[190] in more intimate surroundings; and the more one has exiled oneself from everything that other people enjoy, the more important it becomes for people like us to have a stronghold of one's own, from which one can look out and where one does not feel so pestered by life. For me, things have

---

with adopting an unconsciously ironic conciliatory attitude to the historical status quo. He had an exchange of letters with Mathilde Meier of the Bayreuth circle during March, 1874; she had welcomed N's critique of Hartmann.

187. N certainly idealized Wagner's health; the latter had had interminable digestive troubles and chronic constipation during earlier years. In June, 1875, N was in fact himself extremely unwell, with headaches lasting for several days and vomitings for several hours (cf. letter to Gersdorff, dated June, 1875: *Briefe 4*, No. 868). During July and August, he spent several weeks at Steinabad undergoing a cure, under the distinguished physician and dietitian Josef Wiel, for what had been diagnosed as chronic gastric catarrh with considerable dilation of the stomach. The dilation was accompanied by hyperemia, which disturbed the flow of blood to the head (letter to Gersdorff, dated July 19, 1875). In a letter to Malwida von Meysenbug, from Steinabad, dated August 11, he wrote: "People like us—I mean you and I—never suffer just physically—it is all deeply entwined with spiritual crises—so I have no idea how medicine and kitchens can ever make me well again." *Briefe 4*, No. 895.

188. The Pilatus is the mountain near Lucerne which overlooks Tribschen.

189. Elisabeth had kept house for N during June also. His new lodging was at Spalentorweg 48 (old spelling, Spalenthorweg).

190. *I.e.*, since he had left home to go to Schulpforta.

turned out perhaps better than for very many others, through my sister's happy nature, which suits my temperament excellently; the Nietzsche character, which I have found to my joy even in all my father's brothers and sisters, takes joy only in being by itself; it understands how to keep itself occupied and gives to people rather than demanding much of them.[191] This makes it perfectly tolerable to live as a thinker and teacher—and one is condemned, after all, to being that.

To this praise of the domesticity I have begun, I join the praise of your decision, or rather the cordial expression of my joy at seeing you confident and decided about making a *good* marriage. But do settle the whole matter this autumn by going to Berlin. I advise you only in the wish that you may not suffer too long from what is the most terrible element in life— uncertainty.

Can I trust that you will bring me happy news, when you visit me before your semester begins?[192] If not, I imagine that a new Berlin winter season could seriously endanger your project.[193] But I have little understanding of such matters.

Our friend Rohde, who usually puts his hand into life's unlucky-dip and pulls out something unpleasant, was here on a visit, and said just before he left that it was the only place on earth where he still felt at home. I would prefer not to say in a letter what a dreadful situation he was in; a letter from the lady's father had hit him in a particularly vulnerable spot, and he was extremely upset. From here he went to Munich and heard a performance of *Tristan*, which he found quite shattering. For the next few days he will probably be in Rostock to attend the conference of classical philologists and read a paper on "the Novella in Greek Literature."[194] I got more from being with Rohde this time than from any previous meeting; he was unusually confiding and affectionate, so that it did me a world of good to mean something to him in his absurd situation, now that his life revolves around a young girl—heaven protect you and me from such a fate!

Our Baumgartner will soon be coming back too; he is to occupy my previous lodging. He returns home much reproved and instructed; he has had several strokes of bad luck—for instance, he recently had a very danger-

191. Considering later developments between N and Elisabeth, this was a somewhat partial appraisal of the "Nietzsche character."

192. Gersdorff visited N for about a week in mid-October.

193. Gersdorff was at this time studying agriculture at the Agricultural Academy at Hohenheim; his *fidanzata* was in Berlin.

194. "Über griechische Novellendichtung und ihren Zusammennang mit dem Orient," *Verhandlungen der XXX Philologen-Versammlung zu Rostock 1875* (Leipzig, 1876); reprinted in the 2d ed. of Rohde's *Der griechische Roman und seine Vorläufer* (Leipzig, 1900).

ous fall with his beloved horse, was himself unhurt, but had to shoot the horse at once.

J. Burckhardt is as well as ever. Yesterday I heard that he had spoken very favorably about me with an intimate old friend at Lörrach— I was not told precisely in what way. I heard only one thing—he had said that Basel would never again get such a teacher as me.

They are changing the times of our summer vacation again. If the worst comes to the worst, it is possible that the Bayreuth festivals may not see me next year and the following years; the most I could get would be a few days' leave of absence. But things might get better than they are now— if, that is, the whole month of August is allowed for vacations. Whatever happens, I mean to see that I am not cheated of Bayreuth as I was this year.

I have good hopes for my health as long as I continue the new mode of life, which I have devised on Dr. Wiel's advice since the vacation. I eat every four hours: at eight in the morning, an egg, cocoa, and biscuits; at noon, a beefsteak or some other meat; at four in the afternoon, soup, meat, and some vegetables; at eight at night, cold roast and tea. To be recommended for everyone! It brings a balance which saves one from suffering with digestive fevers after the usual evening dinner.

Yet I do have recurrences of my gastric trouble, and I must have a great deal of good will in order to get well.[195]

Thank you very much for seeing to the letters which I sent to Bayreuth; both reached their destination, and I have received replies to both.

Very good news from Romundt! How glad I am! A letter came, with a complete change of attitude, as from a man recovering from a sickness. He has more to do and more drudgery than ever before, but he feels that it is doing him good and says himself that something inside him must have turned around. He is teaching in Oldenburg; he has had until now complete charge of Greek for the upper grades, and from now on will teach German to the highest grade.[196] And it works! His address is c/o Frau Oberjustizrat Mencke, Peterstrasse 17, Oldenburg im Grossherzogtum.

So Miaskowski will be going to Hohenheim at Easter, the thing is settled, after being a long time in the balance.[197]

195. A letter to Gersdorff, of January 18, 1876, describes a serious relapse that N had on December 25, 1875, so severe that he thought some brain damage was at the root of his troubles. His anxiety was increased by the thought that his father had died of a stroke at the age of thirty-six. Not until February, 1876, did he begin to feel better again.

196. Original: "hat bis jetzt den ganzen griechischen Unterricht in Unter- und Obersecunda gegeben und bekommt von jetzt ab das Deutsch für Prima." Briefe 4, No. 901. The classes correspond to the two top grades in the United States (and the two top forms in England).

197. August von Miaskowski (b. 1838), a professor of economics at Basel, moved in 1876 to the Hohenheim Agricultural Academy. N mentions visits to his Basel home in

My address is: Spalenthorweg 48.

Dearest friend, I am not a man of letters;[198] my horror of publishing grows from day to day. But when you come I shall read you something you will enjoy, something out of the unpublished fourth *Thought out of Season*, with the title "Richard Wagner in Bayreuth." Your silence on this is requested.

Farewell, my most loyal and beloved friend,

Your F. N.

Best regards also from my sister.

Please give my best wishes to your most respected parents. Be in good spirits. You have every right to be.

62 · *To Erwin Rohde*   Basel, December 8, 1875

Ah, beloved friend, I did not know what to say to you; I was silent; I feared for you and worried for you; I could not even ask you how things stood; but how often, how often my most sympathetic thoughts ran to you! Now things are as bad as they could be, only one thing could be worse: if the matter were not so terribly clear as it now is. Definitely the most unbearable thing is doubt, with its ghostly half reality; and at least you are relieved of this condition, under which you suffered so horribly while you were here. What shall we do now? I rack my brains for some way in which you might be helped. I fancied for a long time that a change of place might be made possible, which is very important, and that you might get an appointment at Freiburg im Breisgau. But subsequently it seems to me that you were not even considered for one. Then of course the publication of your writings remains the most salutary thing; something of that kind is not without its joys, and in any case it concentrates the mind, and such work is steady-going and might help you through this terrible winter. I shall tell you how things are with me. As far as my health is concerned, not as I really anticipated when I completely changed my way of life here. Every two or three weeks I spend about thirty-six hours in bed, in real torment, the way you know. Perhaps I am gradually improving, but this winter is the worst there has been, I keep thinking. It is such a strain getting through the day that, by evening, there is no pleasure left in life and I really am surprised how diffi-

---

two letters dated during the autumn of 1874; Gersdorff had asked N to inquire if Mia-skowski would move to Hohenheim if invited. He stayed there only one year.

198. Original: "Litteratur mache ich nicht."

cult living is. It does not seem to be worth it, all this torment; one's use to others or to oneself is nullified by the distress one causes for others and oneself. This is the opinion of a man who is not racked by the passions— and of course experiences no pleasure from them either. When I am resting my eyes, my sister reads to me, almost always Walter Scott, whom I would call, as Schopenhauer does, an "immortal"; so much do I like his artistic tranquility, his *andante*, that I would like to recommend him to you; yet what strikes a chord for me does not always affect you; because you think more sharply and quickly than I do; and I do not want to talk about the way in which novels treat our sensibility, especially since you must need help yourself by working on your own "Novel."[199] But perhaps you will now read *Don Quixote* again—not because it is the gayest book I know but because it is the most stringent; I took it out during the summer vacation, and all my personal sufferings came to seem so much smaller—they even seemed to be worth a good laugh, with no accompanying grimaces. All seriousness and all passion and everything which goes to the human heart are Quixotic; it is good to know this in some cases; in others it is usually better not to know it.

Gersdorff means to set about getting engaged during the Christmas vacation. Our friend Krug has become the father of a little boy; Dr. Fuchs has been invited to use my sister's patron's ticket for a cycle of Bayreuth performances next year. Two good young musicians and composers are studying here this winter, in order to attend my lectures; they are friends of Schmeitzner's.[200] I am trying to get a publisher and an orientalist interested in an edition of the Buddhist Tripitaka. Dr. Deussen is giving inspiring lectures this winter on Schopenhauer—three a week, at Aachen, with an enrollment of more than three hundred students. Baumgartner is studying classical philology here under my supervision. In my philological seminar I have thirteen students, some of them talented people. My student Brenner is unwell and has had to go to Catania; I sent with him greetings to Frl. von Meysenbug. Dr. Rée, very devoted to me, has anonymously published an excellent little book, *Psychological Observations;* he's an extremely acute "moralist," a gift most rare among Germans.[201] I have found Arnim's book

199. Refers to Rohde's work on the Greek novel.

200. Schmeitzner was N's publisher. The two musicians were Paul Heinrich Widemann and Heinrich Köselitz. Köselitz later adopted the name Peter Gast (1854–1918) and became one of N's closest friends and most industrious correspondents.

201. Berlin, 1875. N's reply to Paul Rée, on receiving the book, is dated October 22, 1875. He had first met Rée, a friend of Romundt's, in May, 1873, when both Gersdorff and Rée were visiting Basel and heard N lecture on the pre-Platonic philosophers. Rée soon became an habitué of Bayreuth; and it was he who introduced N to Lou Salomé in Rome in March, 1882.

Pro Nihilo very instructive.[202] The Wagners are staying in Vienna until the end of January. I live in complete seclusion, with my sister, and am as satisfied as a hermit who has no further wishes, except that it would be really good if everything were over and done with.

So farewell, live tolerably, most beloved friend, think that we here always think of you in such a way as to make you *feel* our friendship. But since that cannot be, content yourself with these poor lines. My sister and Overbeck send you their most sympathetic greetings, and I remain your

Friend F. N.

63 · *To Carl von Gersdorff*   [Basel, December 13, 1875]

Yesterday, my beloved friend, your letter came, and this morning, aptly, at the start of a heavy working week, your books: surely one should keep in good heart when one has such sympathetic, kind friends![203] Really, I marvel at the fine instinct of your friendship—I hope the expression does not sound too animal for you—which caused you to hit on precisely these *Indian* proverbs, while it has been precisely during the past two months that I have been looking out for Indian things with a growing thirst. I borrowed from Schmeitzner's friend Herr Widemann the English translation of the Sutta Nipáta, from the sacred books of the Buddhists; and I have already adopted for home use one of the firm concluding words of a sutta—"So wander alone like the rhinoceros."[204] The conviction that life is valueless and that all goals are illusory impresses itself on me so strongly, especially when I am sick in bed, that I need to hear more about it, but not mixed with Judeo-Christian phraseology, a surfeit of which, at some time or another, has so disgusted me with it that I have to guard against being unjust toward it. How life now is you can see by the enclosed letter from our friend Rohde, who is suffering unspeakably; one should not hang one's heart on life—that is clear—and yet what can make it endurable if one *wills* nothing more! In my

202. *Pro Nihilo: Vorgeschichte des Arnim Prozesses* was first published in French, in Switzerland, in 1875; the author was reputed to be Graf Harry von Arnim.

203. Gersdorff had sent him *Indische Sprüche*, ed. by Otto Böhtling, with Sanskrit and German texts, St. Petersburg 1870–73 (2 vols.).

204. "Let one wander alone like a rhinoceros" is the translation in the English version by V. Faustböll, *Sacred Books of the East*, vol. 10, part 2 (Oxford, 1881), pp. 6–11. N probably read the translation by Coomára Swámy: *Sutta Nipáta* (London, 1874). Karl Eugen Neumann's translation (*Die Reden Gotamo Buddho's aus der Sammlung der Bruchstücke Suttanipato des Pali-Kanons*) did not appear until 1905.

opinion, the *will to knowledge* may remain as the ultimate region of the will to live, as a region between willing and ceasing to will: a bit of purgatory, as long as we are dissatisfied with life and look back in scorn; and a bit of Nirvana, as long as the soul thereby approaches a state of pure contemplation. I am training myself to get rid of the habit of *haste* in willing to know; all scholars suffer from that, and it is what deprives them of the glorious calm which comes from all insight gained. It happens I am still yoked too rigidly between the various demands of my professional work, so that I have been *forced*, too often, and against my will, into being hasty; I mean to put everything right gradually. Then my health too will become more reliable: a state I shall not reach until I *deserve* it, until I have found the state of soul which is, as it were, my promised land, the state of health in which the soul has retained only one impulse—the will to knowledge—and has become free from all other impulses and desires. A simple household, a completely regulated daily routine, no irritating appetite for honors or for society, the life together with my sister (which makes everything around me so *Nietzschean* and strangely tranquil), the awareness of having most excellent and kind friends, the possession of forty good books from all ages and peoples (and of several more which are not exactly bad), the constant joy of having found in Schopenhauer and Wagner educators and in the Greeks the daily objects of my work, the faith that from now on I shall no longer lack good students—this is what makes my life at present. Unfortunately there is added to this my chronic misery, which seizes me for almost two whole days every two weeks, and sometimes for longer periods—well, that ought to come to an end one day.

Later, when you have established your house firmly and carefully, you can also count on my being your guest for longish periods in vacations; it does me good to think of your later life and that I can be useful to you in your sons as well. So far, loyal old friend Gersdorff, we have shared a fair portion of our youth, experience, education, predilections, hatreds, aspirations, and hopes; we know that we are deeply happy even just to sit beside one another; we need make no mutual promises or vows, because we have a *very good* faith in one another. You help me where you can—I know this from experience—and whenever I am glad about anything, I think, "How glad this will make Gersdorff!" For you possess, let me tell you, the glorious power of *sharing joy;* I think that this is even more rare and noble than the power of sharing someone's suffering.

Farewell now, and enter the new year of your life the same person as you were in the old—I can think of no more I could wish for you. As such you have gained your friends; and if there are sensible women still in the world, then you will not much longer "wander alone like the rhinoceros."

Loyally, your Friedrich Nietzsche

Warmest greetings and birthday wishes from my sister. My regards to your respected father.

I sent you Rütimeyer's program; hope you received it.

64. *To Mathilde Trampedach*   [Geneva, April 11, 1876][205]

Mein Fräulein:

You are writing out something for me this evening; I want also to write something for you.[206]

Muster all the courage of your heart, so as not to be afraid of the question I am going to ask you: Will you be my wife? I love you and feel that you already belong to me. Not a word about the suddenness of my feelings! At least they are innocent; so there is nothing that needs to be forgiven. But I would like to know if you feel as I do—that we have never been strangers at all, not for a moment! Do you not also think that in our association each of us would be better and more free than either could be alone— and so *excelsior?* Will you dare to come with me, as with one who is striving with all his heart to become better and more free? On all the paths of life and thought?

Be candid and keep nothing back. Nobody knows about this letter, and my inquiry, except our mutual friend Herr von Senger. I return to Basel at eleven tomorrow morning by the express—I have to return; I enclose my Basel address. If you can answer yes! to my question, I shall write immediately to your mother, for whose address I shall then ask you. If you can manage to decide quickly, with a yes or a no, your letter will reach me then by tomorrow morning at 10 in the Hotel garni de la Poste.[207]

Wishing you all good things and blessings for always

Friedrich Nietzsche

205. N had been extremely unwell at Christmas, 1875; recovery was slow, but he was able to travel to western Switzerland in early March for convalescence at Veytaux, near Geneva. Gersdorff traveled and stayed with him there until March 29. Early in April he went to Geneva and spent a few days staying with Hugo von Senger, a conductor with whom his association had begun in Bayreuth. At Senger's house he met Fräulein von Trampedach, a young Livonian lady. It was Senger who eventually married her.

206. She was copying for him Longfellow's poem "Excelsior."

207. Mathilde Trampedach declined; N replied on April 15 from Basel, expressing gratitude for her having treated his "cruel, violent procedure" so tolerantly. On May 26, he wrote to Gersdorff: "I am not getting married. In the last analysis I hate limitation and being tied into the whole 'civilized' order of things so much that there can hardly be a woman who would be of generous enough mind to follow me" (*Briefe 4*, No. 942).

65 · *To Malwida von Meysenbug*

Good Friday, April 14, 1876, Basel

Hochverehrtes Fräulein:

About two weeks ago there was a Sunday which I spent alone by Lac Leman and very close to you, from early until the moonlit evening; with restored senses I read your book to the end and kept telling myself that I had never spent a more consecrated Sunday; the mood of purity and love did not leave me, and nature on this day was a mirror of this mood.[208] You walked before me as a higher self, as a *much* higher self—but encouraging rather than shaming me; thus you soared in my imagination, and I measured my life against your example and asked myself about the many qualities I lack. I thank you for so much more than a book. I was sick, and doubted my powers and aims; after Christmas I thought I would have to give everything up, and feared above all the weariness of life that oppresses like a monstrous burden once higher aims have been abandoned. I am now more healthy and more free, and the tasks to be done stand before me without tormenting me. How often I have wished to have you near me, in order to ask you a question which can be answered only by a higher morality and being than I am! Now from your book I receive answers to very definite questions which concern me; I think that I have no right to be satisfied with my attitude to life until I have your assent. But your book is to me a more severe judge than perhaps you yourself would be. What must a man do, with the image of your life before him, if he is to escape accusing himself of unmanliness?—this is what I often ask myself. He must do all that you did, and absolutely nothing more! But most probably he will not be able to do so; he lacks the safely guiding instinct of love that is always ready to help.[209] One of the highest themes, of which you have first given

208. Malwida von Meysenbug's *Memoiren einer Idealistin* were published in 1875 (2 vols.) and 1876 (vol. 3). This was an enlarged German version of the original *Mémoires d'une idéaliste* (1869).

209. The self-criticism implied here need not be read in application to N personally alone. A broader context is provided by his remarks (reminiscent of Pascal's *Le Moi est haissable*) on sanctity and love, hatred and pessimism, in "Schopenhauer as Educator." Here, having defined the "fundamental idea of culture" as being "to further the production of the philosopher, of the artist, and of the saint within us and outside us, and thereby to work at the consummation of nature" (reiterating Schopenhauer's thoughts), he continued: "There are moments and, as it were, sparks of the brightest fire of love in the light of which we no longer understand the word "I"; beyond our being there lies something which in these moments becomes a here-and-now, and therefore we desire from the bottom of our hearts to bridge this distance. In our usual state we can admittedly

me an inkling, is the theme of motherly love without the physical bond of mother and child; it is one of the most glorious revelations of *caritas*. Give me something of this love, *meine hochverehrte Freundin*, and look upon me as one who, as a son, needs such a mother, needs her so much!

We must have long talks in Bayreuth, for now I can hope again to be able to go there, whereas for several months I had to abandon even the idea of it. If only I could do something for you, now that I am better! And why do I not live near to you!

Farewell, I am and remain yours in truth

Friedrich Nietzsche

I am very grateful for the Mazzini letter.[210]

66 · *To Erwin Rohde* Basel, May 23, 1876

So let us heartily rejoice together that your work is finished, my beloved friend; I was always worried about it, for I guessed that it would become a μέγα βιβλίον, and knew that it had been till now in some ways a μέγα κακόν.[211] Now it is there, swathed moreover in a beautiful little hide and it shines and delights me. It disillusioned me at once in a very agreeable way, for I had been a little afraid of it, as if my small philological wisdom would turn out to be utter foolishness in this abstruse region. Now I see enough already to realize that I shall profit greatly from your results (the general

---

contribute nothing to the production of the redeeming man; therefore we hate ourselves in this state. This hatred is the root of that pessimism which Schopenhauer had to re-teach our age but which is as old as the longing for culture itself. Hatred is the root but not its flower [. . .]: for at some time or other we must learn to hate something more general than our individuality with its miserable limitations and restless flux. In that heightened state we shall also love somewhat differently than we do now. Only when we, in our present and coming incarnation, are ourselves taken into that exalted order of philosophers, artists and saints will a new goal of our love and hate be set before us" (translated by James W. Hillesheim and Malcolm R. Simpson), Chicago (Gateway Editions), 1965, pp. 56–58. If such thoughts as these, on transcending the ego, were in N's mind on Sunday, April 2, as he strolled on the shores of Lac Leman, by a remarkable coincidence they resemble those of Amiel two months earlier and not far away (in Geneva); see Amiel's *Journal intime*, February 1, 1876 (English edition: London, 1901, pp. 227–28). N also writes of "nature" as the "mirror of this mood"; it was Amiel who had coined the phrase "paysage d'âme." The two men did not know of one another.

210. She had sent N a letter written to her by Mazzini.

211. Refers to Rohde's book on the Greek novel: *Der griechische Roman und seine Vorläufer*. μέγα βιβλίον = "big book"; μέγα κακόν = "big evil"—a reference to Callimachus, Fr. 359 (Schneider ed.).

ones as well as particular details), and that I too have thought about the Greeks in this connection enough to make this book indispensable to me. It will be the same for J. Burckhardt, whom I have told about it. (I am with him every day now; our relations are most intimate.) From what I have read so far, I shall point out a few things which poured into me immediately, as smoothly as olive oil—for example, the way in which novel and novella stand in mutual contrast. Then there are pages 56 ff. on the characterological studies of the Peripatetics; then page 18 (with the *morale di solitari*);[212] a very instructive section on pages 4–22 ff.; then page 67 on female readers; page 121 on the kind of real popularity of the Alexandrian poets; then page 142 (with footnote), very fine on the art of elegiac narrative. It struck me that you said very little about pederasty; yet the idealization of eros and the most pure and wistful feeling for the passion of love among the Greeks first grew upon this ground, and, it seems to me, was only transferred from there to sexual love, whereas earlier it actually hindered the more delicate and higher development of sexual love. That the Greeks of the older period should have founded male education on the former passion, and, as long as they had this older education, should have thought unfavorably of sexual love, is odd enough in itself but seems to me to be true. On pages 70 and 71, I thought, you would have to draw attention to these things. Eros, as πάθος of the καλῶς σχολάζοντες,[213] in the best period, is pederastic love; the view of eros which you call "somewhat high-flown," according to which the Aphrodite aspect of eros is not essential but only occasional and accidental, the main thing being φιλία, does not seem to be so un-Greek to me. But it strikes me that you have intentionally avoided the whole area; J. Burckhardt also never speaks of it in his lectures. Perhaps as I read on I shall find some hints on this too; I have not got far yet—my eyes are so bad. You have attended very carefully to the presenting of the material; but, through it, I would like to hear more of you, the real Rohde, even if that meant less polish in the style; just as I enjoy personally Overbeck's style, despite all the "althoughs." There is something *difficult*, incidentally, in your frequent use of long adjectives combined with [adverbs and adverbial] participles—for example, "brimmingly fertile talent," "artistically communicating procedure," "frivolously versatile work," "laboriously careful procedure" (p. 127).

But I should keep my mouth shut on such matters. Yet I must unburden myself of a great and open-mouthed admiration—what a curious person you are! In these last years, as they have unfortunately been for you,

---

212. Rohde had referred here to Vico's calling Stoic and Epicurean morality "una morale di solitari" ("a morality for solitary men").

213. "Passion of those who study well."

to work out precisely this book—it is quite beyond my comprehension! (Incidentally, beyond my talent also, at any time; I could not do such a thing as this, even if I wanted to be able to.) You have the demon of philology so much in your bones that I sometimes really shudder at his raging (in acumen and in immense learning). I know of nobody whom I would credit with such capacity; and that this arch-philologist should also be an arch-man, and moreover my arch-friend, that is truly an αἴνιγμα δύσλυτον,[214] but, quite apart from that, "a good gift of God"!

> Farewell, my loyal friend

We shall try to work it out another way with the musician Köselitz. Overbeck will be writing in the next few days.

67. *To Erwin Rohde*   [Basel, July 18, 1876]

May it be for the best, dear loyal friend, the news you have sent me, really for the best: I wish you this with all the fullness of my heart.[215] So you will be building your nest, then, in the year of grace 1876, like our Overbeck, and I think that I shall not lose you through your becoming happier. I shall even be able to think of you with greater assurance, even if I should perhaps not follow you in taking this step. For you *needed* so badly a completely trusting soul, and you have found her and have found therewith *yourself* on a higher level. For me it is different, heaven knows, or does not know. It does not seem to be all that necessary, except on rare days.

Perhaps I have here a bad gap in myself. My desire and my need are different—I hardly know how to say it or explain it.

Last night it occurred to me to make a poem out of this; I am no poet, but you will understand me.[216]

> A traveler wanders through the night,
> His step is firm;
> And curling valley, long hill
> He takes with him.
> The night is beautiful—
> On he walks, and does not stop,
> Does not know where his road leads.

---

214. "An enigma that is hard to solve."
215. Rohde had announced his engagement.
216. The original has frequent rhyme.

> And then a bird sings through the night.
> "Ah bird what is it you have done?
> Why detain my thought and foot,
> Pouring sweet chagrin of the heart
> Upon me, so that I must stop,
> Must listen, to interpret well
> Your song and salutation?"
> The bird stops singing and it speaks:
> "No, traveler, no! It is not you
> My song salutes.
> I sing because the night is beautiful:
> But *you* must always travel on
> And never understand my song!
> So get you gone,
> And only when your step sounds far
> Shall I begin my song again
> As best I can.
> Now fare thee well, poor traveling man."

That is what I was saying to myself, in the night after your letter arrived.[217]

F. N.

With heartiest congratulations from my sister.

68 · *To Elisabeth Nietzsche*   [Bayreuth, August 1, 1876]

My dear sister:

Things are not right with me, I can see that! Continuous headache, though not of the worst kind, and lassitude. Yesterday I was able to listen to *Die Walküre*, but only in a dark room—to use my eyes is impossible![218] I long to get away; it is too senseless to stay. I dread every one of these long artistic evenings; yet I go to them.

Things being distressing as they are, I suggest that you have a talk with the Baumgartners. Offer mother and son eight tickets for the second cycle of performances, all for a hundred talers (I can have my tickets for the third series transferred to Baumgartner for the second). You can all stay

217. The elliptical original "So geredet zu mir" could also mean "This is what a voice said to me."

218. The first full rehearsal of the opera was on July 31. A few days before this, N had arrived in Bayreuth, leaving Elisabeth in Basel to clear their apartment; he had obtained a leave of absence from Basel, and planned to travel in October to Sorrento.

together in the Giessel's house; for the rent we are paying, it is the cheapest lodging in Bayreuth. You should hear what the other prices are!

This time you will have to hear and see the performances in my place.

It will be easy to arrange with the Baumgartners about the lodging (for their share of the costs).

I have had enough of it all!

I do not even want to be at the first performance—but somewhere else, anywhere but here, where it is nothing but torment for me.

Perhaps you could write a few words to Schmeitzner as well, and offer him my seat for the first performance—or someone else, whomever you like, Frau Bachofen, for example.[219]

Forgive me for giving you all the trouble again! I want to get away into the Fichtelgebirge or some other place.[220]

Your Fritz

Don't forget to telegraph your arrival to Frl. von Meysenbug.
Naturally, you can attend the dress rehearsal—that is arranged.

69 · *To Richard Wagner*   Basel, September 27, 1876

Hochverehrter Freund:

It was a pleasure to do you the small service which you asked of me; it reminded me of the times at Tribschen.[221] I now have time to think of things past, far and near, since I sit much in a darkened room for the atropine treatment of my eyes—it was found to be necessary when I returned home. The autumn, after *this* summer, is for me, and probably not only for me, *more* autumn than any previous one. Behind the great events

---

219. Wife of J. J. Bachofen, the polymath and mythologist, whom N occasionally visited in Basel.

220. When Elisabeth arrived on August 5, N had already gone to Klingenbrunn, in the Bayrischer Wald, where he began to write the first notes for *Menschliches, Allzumenschliches* (1878). He returned to Bayreuth on August 12, the day before the first performance of *Das Rheingold*. He returned to Basel on August 27, three days before the end of the festival. His headaches continued to torment him in Basel, despite a course of atropine treatment.

221. Wagner had asked N to send him some underwear from the Basel firm of C. C. Rumpf.

there lies a streak of blackest melancholy, from which certainly no escape can come soon enough—to Italy or into productive work, or both. When I think of you in Italy, I recall that you had your first inspiration for the *Rheingold* music there. May it remain for you a land of beginnings! So, then, you will be rid of the Germans for a while, and that seems to be necessary now and then, so that one can really do something for them.[222]

Perhaps you know that I myself am going to Italy next month, into a land, I think, not of beginnings but of the end of my sufferings. These have once more reached a climax; it is really high time. The authorities know what they are doing in giving me leave of absence for a whole year, although this is a disproportionately big sacrifice for such a small community; they would lose me in one way or another, if they did not give me this way out; during the recent years, thanks to the patience of my temperament, I have put up with torment after torment, as if I were born for that and for nothing else. To the philosophy which teaches approximately this, I have amply paid practical tribute. This neuralgia goes to work so thoroughly, so scientifically, that it literally probes me to find how much pain I can endure, and each of its investigations lasts for thirty hours. I have to count on this study's recurring every four to seven days—you see, it is a scholar's sickness; but now I have had enough of it, and I want to live in a state of good health or not at all. Complete quiet, mild air, walks, darkened rooms—that is what I expect from Italy; I dread having to see or hear anything there. Do not think that I am morose; not sicknesses—only people—can put me in a bad mood, and I always have friends around me who are most ready to help and most considerate. First, after my return, the moral philosopher Dr. Rée; now the musician Köselitz, who is writing this letter; also I would name Frau Baumgartner among the good friends; perhaps you will be glad to hear that this lady's French translation of my latest book (*Richard Wagner in Bayreuth*) will be published next month.

If the "spirit" were to come over me, I would write a poem to bless your journey; but recently this stork has not built his nest on me, which is forgivable. So accept, instead, my warmest best wishes and may they follow you as good companions: you and your respected wife, my "most noble friend," if I may steal from the Jew Bernays one of his most impermissible Germanisms!

Loyally as always, your Friedrich Nietzsche

222. The Wagners were also going to Italy; see Letter No. 71.

70 · *To Franziska and Elisabeth Nietzsche*

[Genoa, October 22, 1876][223]

A bad time leaving Bex; somewhat better in Geneva—had lunch in the Hotel Post. Brenner met us there. Night journey through Mont Cenis; the next day arrival in Genoa with splitting headache—to bed at once, vomiting, and this state lasting forty-four hours. Today, Sunday, better; just back from a trip around the harbor and out to sea. Most beautiful evening tranquility and color. Tomorrow (Monday) evening departure by steamer to Naples; we three friends have decided on the sea journey. Warmest greetings to you.

[no signature]

71 · *To Franziska and Elisabeth Nietzsche*

[Sorrento], October 28, [1876]

Here we are, in Sorrento! The whole journey to here from Bex took eight days. In Genoa I was ill; from there we took about three days for the sea journey, and—look!—we were not seasick; I also prefer this way of traveling to train journeys, which are quite terrible for me. We found Frl. von M[eysenbug] in a hotel in Naples, and traveled together yesterday to our new home, the Villa Rubinacci, Sorrento, near Naples. I have a very big high room, with a terrace outside it. I have just got back from my first swim—the water was warmer, according to Rée, than the North Sea in July. Yesterday evening we were with the Wagners, who are in the Hotel Victoria, five minutes away, and will be staying through November.[224]

223. N had met Rée in Montreux and spent two weeks with him in Bex. On October 20 they left Bex for Genoa (via Geneva, where they collected Albert Brenner, a student of N's, who also wrote stories, and who died in 1878). The three left Genoa for Naples on October 23, and arrived on October 26. From Naples they traveled with Malwida von Meysenbug, in a horse-drawn carriage, to Sorrento.

224. The Wagners stayed in Sorrento from October 5 to November 5, and then went to Rome. On the evening of November 4, N and Wagner met for the last time. See the version of this meeting given by Elisabeth: *The Nietzsche-Wagner Correspondence*, edited by Elizabeth Förster-Nietzsche, pp. 293–96. What appalled N at this meeting with Wagner was the religious tone of Wagner's talk. Worst of all, he thought that he was simulating religiosity in an opportunistic way; hence his later hostile comments on *Parsifal* and Wagner's histrionics (cf. No. 79, 1878, and No. 137, 1886). The shock to N can be gauged from his remarks (No. 59, 1875) on Romundt's threatened conversion,

Sorrento and Naples are beautiful—people have not been exaggerating. The air here is a mixture of mountain and sea air. It is very soothing for my eyes; from my terrace I look down first on a big green tree garden (which stays green in winter), beyond that the very dark sea, beyond that Vesuvius.

Let's hope.

Love and devotion,

Your F.

---

for example, "this utterly odious Catholic business." At Sorrento too, Wagner was frequently in a bad mood; the last Bayreuth festival had incurred a huge deficit (something like 160,000 marks is the figure which Elisabeth gave).

III

1877-82

*End
of the
Professorship;
Lou
Salomé ;
Genoa*

III · 1877–82: End of the Professorship; Lou Salomé; Genoa

1877

In Sorrento till early May. Contemplates marrying: "a good but rich woman." Health not improved. Rohde's marriage. May: via Lugano to Ragaz (Bad Pfäfers?), thence to Rosenlauibad in the Bernese Oberland for the summer. Quest of "Höhenluft." July: letter to Carl Fuchs on Wagner's rhythms. September: return to Basel. Elisabeth shares his apartment and keeps house; Peter Gast also moves in, as occasional amanuensis. Winter semester lectures: Religious Antiquities of the Greeks. December: break with Gersdorff. Resigns from Pädagogium, because of ill health. Publication of Rée's *Der Ursprung der moralischen Empfindungen*.

1878

January: receives from Wagner the score of *Parsifal*. March: treatment at Baden-Baden. May: sends Wagner *Menschliches, Allzumenschliches*, vol. 1; open rupture with Wagner and Wagnerites. Burckhardt salutes the new book as "the sovereign book." End of June: dissolution of the Basel household; Elisabeth returns to Naumburg. July: at Interlaken, letter to Mathilde Maier on his break with Wagner and alienation from friends. August: Wagner attacks N with his article "Publicum und Popularität" (*Bayreuther Blätter*). Winter semester: N moves into an apartment on the outskirts of Basel. Lectures: Greek Lyric Poets; Introduction to the Study of Plato. Still mostly unwell: "Half dead with pain and exhaustion." Close friendship with Overbeck and his wife.

1879

June: resignation from Basel accepted. Leaves Basel, travels via Bremgarten and Zürich to St. Moritz. Writes "Der Wanderer und sein Schatten" (part 2 of vol. 2 of *Menschliches, Allzumenschliches*). Continuous struggle against illness. October: to Naumburg (until early 1880). Reading: Janssen, *Geschichte des deutschen Volkes*, vol. 2; sees through "falsified Protestant view of history," outburst against Luther ("L's hideous, arrogant, peevishly envious abusiveness"); also Gogol, Lermontov, Twain, Poe. One hundred and eighteen days of bad migraine attacks during this year.

1880

Rée visits N in Naumburg. February: in Riva on Lago di Garda, where he meets up with Gast. March–June: with Gast in Venice. Reading: Stifter's *Der Nachsommer.* July–August: at Marienbad, reading Mérimée and Sainte-Beuve. "I often dream of Wagner, as things were when we were intimate." September: in Naumburg. October: visits Dr. Otto Eiser in Frankfurt and Overbeck in Basel. Travels to Stresa on Lago Maggiore: very ill here. November: arrives in Genoa. First Genoa winter: "Help me to hold on to this hiddenness, tell people that I am not living in Genoa. . . . I also want to have no more to do with the aspirations of contemporary 'Idealism,' least of all German Idealism." Writing: *Morgenröte.*

1881

Very cold winter; unheated room. Almost constant violent headache. End of April–May: with Gast in Recoaro; discovers Gast as composer. Reads Keller, *Der grüne Heinrich.* Gast leaves on May 31. Early July: via St. Moritz to Sils Maria (Oberengadin) for the first time. Discovers Spinoza. First half of August: vision of 'eternal recurrence.' First sketches of *Zarathustra I.* "I really shall have to live a few more years." Estrangement from friends. Likens Sils Maria to "the high plateaus of Mexico." Publication of *Morgenröte.* "I am desperate. Pain is vanquishing my life and will. . . . Five times I have called for Doctor Death." Beginning of October: return to Genoa. November: hears Bizet's *Carmen* for the first time. Receives Gast's copy of Robert Mayer's *Mechanics of Heat* (March 1882: clings to Boscovitch and theory of non-material atoms).

1882

Writing: *Die fröhliche Wissenschaft* ("Sanctus Januarius"—"crossing of a tropic"—written during some clear January days). Refuses sister's request that he should go to Bayreuth in the summer: "Has not this nerve-shattering music ruined my health?" Resumption of correspondence with Malwida von Meysenbug. March 29: takes ship to Messina (Sicily), writes 'Idyllen aus Messina.' Thence to Rome. Meets Lou Salomé with Rée at Malwida von Meysenbug's. Travels with Lou, Rée, and Lou's mother to Orta. Sancta Rosa sunset walk alone with Lou. May 8–13: in Basel with the Overbecks; sees Burckhardt also. May 13–16: in Lucerne with Rée and Lou, they visit Tribschen and are photographed (N and Rée yoked to a small cart, in which Lou sits, toying with a small whip). N proposes marriage to Lou; she declines. July–August: in Tautenburg: "What is *Geist* to me? I value nothing but impulses." Lou comes to Tautenburg from Bayreuth with Elisabeth

(August 7–26). August: publication of *Die fröhliche Wissenschaft*. September: in Naumburg, sets Lou's poem "An den Schmerz" for piano. Elisabeth stays in Tautenburg. Breaks with her and mother, goes to Leipzig. Contemplates a winter of study there, or in Vienna, or in Paris, with Lou and Rée. Rupture with Lou and Rée. Meets Heinrich von Stein. Adopts Polish ancestry. November: via Basel to Genoa. November 23: arrives in Santa Margherita/Rapallo. December 24: breaks off correspondence with mother. To Overbeck: "Unless I can discover the alchemical trick of turning this— muck into gold, I am lost."

72 · *To Franziska Nietzsche*   [Sorrento], January 27, 1877

My warmest best wishes, first of all, beloved mother; let us both wish that the coming year of your life will be spared more sorrow, loss, and worry than the past year has been.[1]

I cannot write a proper letter; it affects me so badly that I always have to pay for it for a few days (as recently when I finally had to write to poor Frau Ritschl).[2] There have been more bad days and bad moments; but *in summa* I think I am progressing, but nobody should think that things will come all right at once. The weather is cool and windy now too. My head still seems to be short of blood; I have done too much thinking, over the past ten years (which, as is well known, has worse effects than just "doing too much work"—although I have done that also).[3]

Where has the French translation of my book about Wagner got to? I am having *Lorenzo Benoni* read to me now, and we are all enjoying it.[4]

1. N was writing to his mother for her birthday on February 2; her mother, Wilhelmine Oehler, had died on November 3, 1876.

2. Ritschl had died toward the end of 1876. In January, N had written his wife a letter of condolence.

3. Between November, 1876, and March, 1877, Paul Rée wrote five letters to N's sister and one to his mother, giving detailed accounts of N's physical state and his treatment (which entailed a snuff cure as well as walks in the mountains): *Briefe 4*, pp. 455–461.

4. By Giovanni Ruffini (1807–81), a boyhood friend of Mazzini's. Malwida's reading circle at the Villa Rubinacci was very active. In her memoirs she mentions the following authors and works as having been read and discussed: the manuscript of Burckhardt's lectures on Greek culture, Herodotus, Thucydides, French moralists (e.g., Voltaire), Kalidasa's *Sakuntala;* Goethe's ballad "Die Braut von Korinth" and his play *Die natürliche Tochter*, and *Don Quixote* (*Der Lebensabend einer Idealistin*, Berlin, 1918, pp. 239–50; *Briefe 4*, p. 463).

Dr. Rée has sent his manuscript "On the Origins of Moral Sentiment" to Schmeitzner. Brenner has written some nice novellas;[5] Frl. von Meysenbug is working on a novel.[6] It is possible that Prince Lichtenstein will join our little community. Later, Seydlitz and his wife will pay us a visit, already arranged, also a few Roman ladies.[7]

I shall teach you later how to cook risotto—I know now.

Last of all, my warmest thanks for your long, entertaining letter.

Your Fritz

73 · *To Elisabeth Nietzsche*   Sorrento, April 25 [1877]

Nothing more cheerful than your letter, dearest sister, which hit the nail on the head in every possible way. I was so unwell! Out of fourteen days, I spent six in bed with six major attacks, the last one quite desperate. I got up, and then Frl. von Meysenbug was down for three days with rheumatism. In the very depths of our misery we had a good laugh together when I read her a few selected passages from your letter. The plan which Frl. von Meysenbug says must be kept firmly in view, and in the execution of which you must help, is this: We convince ourselves that, in the long run, my Basel University existence cannot continue, that to carry it through at best would mean abandoning all my important projects and still sacrificing my health completely. Naturally I shall have to spend next winter there, with no change in my circumstances, but Easter, 1878, should be the end of it, should the other move succeed—that is, marriage with a suitable but necessarily affluent woman. "Good *but* rich," as Frl. von M. said, this "but" making us laugh aloud. With this wife I would then live for the next few years in Rome, which place is suitable for reasons alike of health, society, and my studies. This summer the plan should be carried out, in Switzerland, so that I would return to Basel in the autumn a married man. Various "persons" are invited to come to Switzerland, among them several names unknown to you—for example, Elise Bülow from Berlin, Elsbeth Brandes from Hanover. As far as intellectual qualities are concerned, I still find Nat[alie] Herzen the most suitable.[8] You did very well with the idealiza-

5. One of these was published in *Die neue Rundschau*, 3, Heft 10, July, 1877, under the pseudonym Albert Nilson.

6. Her three-volume novel *Phaedra* (1885).

7. Reinhart and Irene Seydlitz. He was a writer and painter, also a Wagnerite. N had a considerable correspondence with him.

8. Daughter of Alexander Herzen, she was the same age as N and died in 1936.

tion of the little Köckert woman in Geneva! All praise and honor to you! But it is doubtful; and money?—

Rohde must have the bust of Wagner[9]—I cannot think of anything else, I am so *stupid*. So will you see to that, with a little letter to Rohde?

I have been invited to lecture on Wagner in Frankfurt. Frau Baumgartner's translation has been found *not* good by competent people. This in confidence.

Fraternally, as ever, your   Fritz

in future (if I am living still a year from now) a Roman.

You have been spared the trouble in Bayreuth; on which I congratulate you, for the responsibility is too great. Lulu and the governess are managing the whole household. Poor Loldi has been taken to an orthopaedic institution in Altenburg.[10]

74· *To Malwida von Meysenbug*

Lugano, Sunday morning [May 13, 1877]

Verehrteste Freundin:

It has occurred to me, on thinking it over, that a postcard, though lighter than a letter, travels no faster than a letter; so it is a longish letter that you must receive from me now, on the subject of my Odyssean wanderings up to the present.

Human misery during a sea journey is terrible, and yet actually laughable, which is how my headaches sometimes seem to me when my physical condition may be excellent—in brief, I am today once more in the mood of serene crippledom, whereas on the ship I had only the blackest thoughts, my only doubts about suicide concerned where the sea might be deepest, so that one would not be immediately fished out again and have to pay a debt of gratitude to one's rescuers in a terrible mass of gold. As a matter of fact, I knew very precisely what the worst part of sea sickness was like, from the time when I had been tormented by violent stomach pains in league with headache—it was a memory of half-vanished times. Only there was the added discomfort of having to change my position three to eight times every minute, day and night, in close proximity, moreover, to the smells and

9. As a wedding present.

10. Lulu was Daniela von Bülow; Loldi was Isolde von Bülow; both were the daughters of Cosima Wagner by her previous marriage.

conversations of a group of people feasting, which is something infinitely nauseous. It was nighttime in the port of Leghorn and it was raining; nevertheless, I wanted to go ashore, but the captain's cold-blooded promises kept me back. Everything on board was rolling about with a great deal of noise, the crockery leaped about and came to life, the children shrieked, the wind howled; "eternal sleeplessness was my fate," as the poet might say. The disembarkation brought new torments; full to the brim with my splitting headache, I was wearing my strongest glasses and mistrusted everyone. The customs boat came laboriously by, but I had forgotten the most important thing, which was to register my luggage for the railway journey. Then began a journey to the fabulous Hotel Nationale, with two rogues on the coach box, who wanted to force me to get off at a miserable *trattoria;* my luggage was continually in alien hands, and there was always a man gasping under my suitcase ahead of me. Several times I got angry and intimidated the driver, and the other fellow cleared off. Do *you* know how I reached the Hotel de Londres? I don't, but, briefly, it was a good one—except that the arrival was awful and a whole retinue of hoodlums wanted to be paid off. There I went straight to bed, feeling very unwell! On Friday, with the weather dark and rainy, I summoned my strength at noon and went to the Palazzo Brignole art gallery; and, astonishingly, it was the sight of these family portraits which raised me up and inspired me anew; a Brignole on horseback, and all the pride of this family shown in the eye of this powerful war-horse—that was something for my depressed humanity! For myself, I think more highly of Van Dyck and Rubens than of any other painters in the world. The other pictures left me cold, except for a dying Cleopatra by Guercino.

So I came to life again and spent the rest of the day sitting in my hotel, *quiet* and in *good spirits.* The next day I had another gladdening experience. I traveled all the way from Genoa to Milan with a very pleasant young ballerina from a Milan theater; *Camilla era molto simpatico*—O, you should have heard my Italian! If I had been a pasha, I would have taken her to Pfäfers with me, where, whenever intellectual occupations failed, she would have been able to dance for me.[11] I am still sometimes rather angry at myself for not having stayed at least a few days in Milan for her sake. Now I was approaching Switzerland and traveled along the first stretch of the Gotthard railway, which is now finished, from Como to Lugano. How did I get to Lugano? I did not really want to go there, but that is where I am. As

11. Probably Bad Pfäfers, about two miles south of Ragaz (in east Switzerland), which the 1883 *Baedeker* describes as a spa in one of the most remarkable spots in Switzerland, with its baths built into walls of nummulitic limestone.

I crossed the Swiss frontier, in a downpour of rain, there was a single flash of lightning, followed by loud thunder. I took it as a good omen; also I shall not conceal from you the fact that the closer I came to the mountains the better I felt. In Chiasso my luggage was split up and left in two different trains; there was hopeless confusion, and, what is more, I had to go through the customs. Even the two umbrellas obeyed opposing impulses. Then a kind porter helped me—he spoke the first Swiss-German I had heard; just think, I was moved to hear it, and I suddenly realized that I preferred to live among German-Swiss people rather than among Germans. The man looked after me so well, and ran about so paternally—all fathers are rather clumsy—that finally everything was brought together again and I traveled on to Lugano. The coach from the Hotel du Parc was waiting for me, and here a real shout of joy rose up in me—everything is so good—I mean, it is the best hotel in the world. I have got involved somewhat with country gentry from Mecklenburg, who are the kind of Germans that suit me; in the evening I watched an improvised dance of the most harmless sort—everyone English, everything so funny. Later I slept, for the first time deeply and well; and this morning I see all my beloved mountains before me, all mountains of memory. It has been raining here for a week. This afternoon I shall ask at the post office what the conditions are like on the Alpine passes.

Suddenly I have been thinking that it is years since I wrote such a long letter, also that you will not read it at all.

So just take the *fact* of this letter as a sign that I am feeling better. I do hope that you can decipher the end of the letter![12]

I think of you with warmest love several times every hour; so much motherliness has been given to me that I shall never forget it.

My best wishes to kind Trina.[13]

I am trusting more than ever in Pfäfers and the high mountains.

Farewell! Remain for me what you have been, for I feel much more protected and sheltered; sometimes such a feeling of emptiness comes over me that I want to scream.

Your grateful and devoted   Friedrich Nietzsche

Third report from Odysseus.

How nicely the Seydlitz's brought me to the ship! I felt like a piece of ideal luggage from a better world.

12. N was by now so shortsighted that when he was writing his eyes would be only about two inches from the pag —often making his script difficult to read.

13. Malwida's maidservant, who had looked after N in Sorrento.

75.   *To Malwida von Meysenbug*

Rosenlauibad, Sunday, July 1, 1877[14]
four thousand feet above sea level,
but how sheltered, mild, good for
the eyes! (six francs a day pension—very good)

Hochverehrte Freundin:

It was depressing to hear that my detailed itinerary concerning Splügen
arrived in Florence too late, probably only one day too late. I did not
think that you would be leaving there so soon. (This ink is terrible, and I
sent for it especially! But they have not given me the real thing; there is no
genuine food in the whole world, and ink is food for us).[15]

Ah, now it's better!

I am very sorry that your journey made you unwell; that really
should stop, and the many people who love you should take the trouble to
make the Alpine crossing themselves.[16]

Aeschi, I think, will suit you: the climate is like that of Sorrento,
of course somewhat more Alpine; but a similar mixture of good mountain-,
forest-, and sea-air. For my needs it is—as long as the hot season lasts—
not nearly high enough; so I can come there only later. High mountain
altitudes have always had a beneficent influence on me. I do lie sick in bed
here as in Sorrento and drag myself around in pain, day after day; the thinner
the air is, the more easily I endure it. I have now begun a treatment with
St. Moritz waters, which will keep me busy for several weeks. I was strongly urged to go to a place at a high altitude *after* the Ragaz treatment and to
drink *this* water, as a medicine against deeply rooted neuroses, combined
with precisely the Ragaz treatment. Until the autumn I now have the enjoyable task of winning a wife. May the gods make me nimble enough for
this task! I have had a whole year for thinking it over and have let it pass
unused. I am determined to go back to Basel in October and resume my
former activity. I cannot carry on without feeling *useful*, and the Basel
people are the only ones who let me know that I am. My very problematic

14. A small mountain resort between Meiringen and Grosse Scheidegg in the
Bernese Oberland.

15. The German for food here, "Lebensmittel," has the sense of "means of life"
—hence the point of the pun.

16. Refers to Malwida's annual journeys north to Bayreuth.

thinking and writing have[17] till now always made me ill; as long as I was really a scholar, I was healthy too; but then came music, to shatter my nerves, and metaphysical philosophy and worry about a thousand things which do not concern me at all. So I want to be a teacher again; if I cannot stand it, I shall perish at my trade. I told you how Plato sees these things. My best wishes and greetings to the indefatigable Bayreuth people (I admire their courage three times a day). Please send me quieting news of the overall results of London; I have heard very bad things.[18] How much I would like to talk with Frau Wagner—it has always been one of my greatest pleasures and for years I have been deprived of it!

Your motherly kindness gives you the mournful privilege of receiving also letters of woe!

Overbeck was far from advising me to go to Basel. But my sister did, and she has far more good sense than I have.

Several postcards (from me to you) must have gone astray.

Farewell, fare very well,

Your cordially devoted Friedrich Nietzsche

76 · *To Carl Fuchs*[19]   [Rosenlauibad], end of July, 1877

Dear Dr. Fuchs:

I was away from Rosenlauibad for a few weeks; on my return I found you had treated me so generously that I had to let two or three days pass in order to bring the whole treasure to light. Everything you wrote went straight to my heart and senses; thank you especially for the description of the "evening" and the preparations for it; I even think it made me weep— and I tell you this only to prove that my position is not far from yours, whatever happens and whatever is said. Altogether, it seems that some good has come of my having earlier given vent to my feelings in such unpleasant and hard terms, for I now feel quite clearly that my attitude to you has changed into a hopeful and happy one. (A skeptic would say: so one sees how useful a few grains of injustice can be in tipping the scales.) Everything else can wait until we meet personally, which I hope will be not far

17. The original has a singular verb here.

18. Wagner had been in England in May, 1877. On May 17 he was received by Queen Victoria at Windsor Castle.

19. Fuchs was a pianist, organist, and writer on music. N had been irritated by his importunacy not so long before. The present letter shows a complete change of attitude. Cf. also the letters of winter 1884–85 and August 26, 1888 (Nos. 129 and 174).

off. When I come to Basel (at the beginning of September, I think), I shall write to Volkland myself too.[20] There *was* some doubt whether I should return: even during the spring I had seriously to consider giving up my position at Basel; even now the thought of next winter and my activities then worries me—it will be a venture, a last attempt. From October to May I was in Sorrento with three friends and—my headaches. I shall tell you who the dear friend was who looked after me there: she is the author of the anonymous *Memoirs of an Idealist* (please *read* this really excellent book and make a present of it to your wife!).

Your counting of rhythmical beats is an important find, real gold, out of which you will be able to mint some good coin. It reminded me that while studying ancient metric in 1870 I had been hunting for five- and seven-beat phrases and had counted through *Die Meistersinger* and *Tristan*—which told me a few things about Wagner's rhythms. He is so averse to anything mathematical and strictly symmetrical (as is shown on a small scale in his use of triplets—I mean the excessive use of them) that he prefers to prolong four-beat phrases into five-beat ones, six-beat ones into seven-beat ones (in *Die Meistersinger*, Act 3, there is a waltz; check to see if it is not governed by seven-beat phrases). Sometimes—but perhaps this is a crime of *lèse-majesté*—it reminds me of Bernini's manner; he can no longer tolerate simple columns but makes them, as he thinks, come alive with volutes all the way up. Among the dangerous after-effects of Wagner, it seems to me that one of the worst is wanting to make things come alive at any price, for in an instant that can become a mannerism, a trick.

I have always wanted some competent person simply to describe Wagner's various methods in the context of his art as a whole, to make an historical and plain statement as to how he does it here and how he does it there. Now the scheme drawn up in your letter raises all my hopes; the description would have to be simply factual in just this way.

Other people who write about Wagner do not really say anything except that they have been greatly pleased and mean to be grateful for that; one learns nothing from them. Wolzogen does not seem to be a good enough musician for the job; and as a writer he is laughable, with his muddling of the languages of artist and psychologist.[21] Could one not, by the way, say "symbol" instead of using the unclear word "motif"? That is what it is, after all. When writing your "Musical Letters," use the terms of Schopenhauer's metaphysics as little as possible, for I think—forgive me!—I think I *know* that his metaphysics are wrong and that all writings which bear its stamp will be one day unintelligible. More of that later, and not in writing.

20. Alfred Volkland was a conductor in Basel.

21. Hans von Wolzogen, a music critic who edited the *Bayreuther Blätter*.

I would like to talk to you also about some of my Bayreuth impressions, concerning fundamental esthetic problems, partly in order to have you put my mind at rest. I am so hungry for your "Letters" that I cannot even decide whether I would prefer to have your discussion of Beethoven's style, rhythm, dynamics, and so on first or your instructive guide to the Distress of the Nibelungen (for all that is Nibelungish brings distress).[22] Best of all, I would like to have both at once, and then I would gladly lie down in the sun, like the boa constrictor, and spend a quiet month digesting.

But now my eyes tell me to stop. Can you do without your notes for a while yet? Or would it be better if I sent them at once? I shall be staying in Rosenlaui for another four weeks.

More than hitherto

Your F. Nietzsche

77. *To Erwin Rohde*   [Rosenlauibad, August 28, 1877]

Dear, dear friend:

How shall I put it into words? Whenever I think of you, emotion comes over me; and when I was recently writing to somebody that "Rohde's young wife is an extremely charming person, whose noble soul shines forth in every feature," I even shed tears—I know no tenable reason why. Let us ask the psychologists one day; they will explain in the end that it is envy that makes me grudge you your happiness, or annoyance that someone has taken my friend away and is now keeping him hidden—God knows where in the world, on the Rhine or in Paris—and refuses to give him up again! Recently I was singing over in my mind my "Hymn to Loneliness," and I suddenly felt that you did not like my music at all and were asking firmly for a "Song of Twosomeness"; and the next evening I played one, to the best of my ability, and it worked out, so that all the angels could have listened with pleasure, especially the human angels. But it was in a dark room, and nobody was listening, so I have to swallow down all my happiness and tears and everything.

Should I tell you about myself? How I am always on the road, two hours before the sun comes over the mountains, and especially in the long

22. Refers to Wagner's *Der Ring des Nibelungen*, first performed at the Bayreuth Festival, August 13–17, 1876. The phrase "der Nibelungen Not" ("Not" = "distress") goes back to the early medieval epic. The pun is another indication of N's aversion to the Wagner establishment, which certainly grew more intense at the 1876 festival; *Der Ring* had been performed amid great pomp, in the presence of several monarchs and numerous other eminences, quite the reverse of the popular festivals planned earlier at Tribschen.

shadows of the afternoon and the evening? How I have thought about many things and feel so rich in myself, now that this year has at last allowed me to lift away the old moss of daily *compulsion* to teach and think? Given the way in which I am living here, I can endure it even with all the pain—which has of course followed me even into these altitudes—but between times there are so many happy exaltations of thought and feeling.

Very recently I spent a veritable day of consecration reading *Prometheus Unbound*. If the poet is not a real genius, I do not know what a genius is; it is all wonderful, and I feel as if I have confronted in it myself, but myself made supreme and celestial. I bow down to the man who could experience and express such things.[23]

In three days I return to Basel. My sister is already busy there getting everything ready.

The faithful musician P. Gast is moving in and will take over the duties of a helpful secretary-friend.

I am rather afraid of the coming winter; things *must* change. A person who has only a little time every day for his own principal affairs, and has to spend almost all his time and strength on duties which others can do as well as he can—such a person is not harmonious; he is at odds with himself and eventually he must fall ill. If I have any influence on young people, I owe it to my writings; and my writings I owe to my stolen moments, the interim times seized by illness, between profession and profession. Well, things will change—*Si male nunc, non olim sic erit.*[24] Meanwhile, may the happiness of my friends grow and blossom—it always does my heart good to think of you, my beloved friend (I see you now, beside a lake, surrounded by roses, and a beautiful white swan swimming toward you)!

In brotherly love,

Your F.

78 · *To Malwida von Meysenbug*

Basel, Monday, September 3, 1877
Gellertstrasse 22

Verehrte, liebe Freundin:

How glad we are that we shall see you here; how sorry that the Monods will only be honoring Basel on the way through! Whatever happens, we want to be at the station—at what time? Probably five o'clock?

23. See note 13 to No. 18.

24. "Things may be bad now, but one day they will not be so."

Well, here I am. The last days in Rosenlauibad were, without exception, dreadful; I left the place with a violent headache at four in the early morning, alone, in darkness.

The apartment, the neighborhood, and my good sister—everything *around me* I find charming, stimulating, steadying, but *in* me there are still worms of anxiety moving around.

I had two nights of sleep—so good, so good!

There were pleasant letters waiting for me too from Overbeck, Frau Ott, and Dr. Eiser, who, as my doctor, demands that I come to Frankfurt soon for a fresh consultation.[25]

The things you say about Sorrento! Not long ago in Rosenlaui I spent a sleepless night reveling in delicious images of nature and wondering if I might not somehow live up on Anacapri. I always sigh when I realize that Italy discourages me, takes my strength away (*what* a person you must have found me to be this spring! I am ashamed; I have never been like that before!). In Switzerland I am more *myself*, and since I base ethics on the sharpest possible definition of self, and not on its vaporization, then . . .

In the Alps I am unassailable, especially when I am alone and have no enemy except myself.

I have taken up my studies in Greek literature again—who knows what will come of it?[26]

Farewell. Have you found the fairy princess who shall free me from the pillar to which I am chained?

With warmest and best wishes to you on your way here.

F. N.

79 · *To Reinhart von Seydlitz*　　　Basel, January 4, 1878

You are so kind, dear, dear friend, with your wishes and promises, and I am so poor. Each letter of yours is some of the joy of life for me, but I can give you nothing in return—nothing. During the Christmas holidays I again had

25. Louise Ott was the wife of the sculptor Paul Ott. She and her husband lived in Paris. N had made friends with her at Bayreuth in July and August, 1876. Otto Eiser, the family doctor, had visited N at Rosenlauibad.

26. During the winter semester N lectured on "Religious Antiquities of the Greeks," for which six students enrolled. During the following summer (1878) he lectured on Hesiod's *Works and Days* (thirteen students) and on Plato's *Apology* (six students); during the winter semester 1878/79 he lectured on "The Greek Lyric Poets" (thirteen students) and "Introduction to the Study of Plato" (eight students).

bad, bad days, even weeks;[27] we shall see now what the new year can do. Will it bring us together? I firmly hope it will.

Yesterday *Parsifal* reached me, sent by Wagner. First impression: more Liszt that Wagner, spirit of the Counter-Reformation; for me, all too accustomed as I am to Greek things, to what is human in a generally valid way, it is all too Christian, time-bound, limited; sheer fantastic psychology; no flesh and much too much blood (especially too much blood at the Holy Communion); also, I do not like the hysterical women; much that is tolerable to the inner eye will be almost insupportable in performance—think of our actors praying, trembling, and with ecstatic throats. Also the interior of the Grail castle *cannot* be effective on the stage, likewise the wounded swan. All these fine inventions belong in the sphere of epic, and are, as I said, for the inner eye. The language sounds like a translation from a foreign tongue. But the situations and their sequence—is not this the highest poetry? Is it not an ultimate challenge to music?

That will be enough for today. Devoted best wishes to yourself and your dear wife.

Your friend Nietzsche

P.S. Lipiner is a good Wagnerian, to judge from his letter to me; one almost wishes, I might add, that he would write the *Parsifal* text over again.[28]

80 · *To Peter Gast*   Basel, May 31, 1878

Dear friend:

On Voltaire's Day two things came for me; both moved and excited me: your letter, and the anonymous gift, from Paris, of a bust of Voltaire, with a card which read, "The soul of Voltaire pays respects to Friedrich Nietzsche."

If I add to you the other two persons who have shown themselves to be really delighted with my book—Rée and Burckhardt (who repeatedly calls it the "sovereign book")—then I have some indication as to what people must be like if my book is to have a rapid effect.[29] But it will not and

27. Toward the end of December, 1877, N had been so unwell that he had asked to be relieved of his work at the Pädagogium. During the same wretched period came his break with Gersdorff.

28. Siegfried Lipiner was a Viennese writer.

29. *Menschliches, Allzumenschliches*, vol. 1, which Schmeitzner published in May, 1878.

cannot have such an effect, sorry as I am for that excellent man Schmeitzner. It has been practically banned by Bayreuth; what is more, the grand excommunication seems to have been pronounced against its author too. They are only trying to retain my *friends* while losing me—and so I get to hear various things that are happening and being planned behind my back. Wagner has failed to use a great opportunity for showing greatness of character. I must not let that disconcert me in my opinion either of him or of myself.

Certainly, if one devoted to such a production so much serious consideration and so much time as you in your kindness have done, something might well come of it—new thoughts, that is, and new feelings and a stronger mood, just as if one had emerged in the lighter mountain air. Rée says that he has only once before experienced a similar mood of productive enjoyment—the other occasion was Eckermann's *Conversations* [*with Goethe*]—he has already filled whole notebooks with reflections.

That is the most I had hoped for, that it would stimulate others to be productive and "increase the amount of independence in the world" (as J. Burckhardt said).

My health is improving; as a walker and solitary ruminant, I am indefatigable. I am enjoying the spring and am tranquil, in the way people are when they cannot so easily be put off course. If only I could go on living in such a way to the end!

That is all about me, because you wish to hear something of me. There are many things that I would prefer not to talk of—Brenner's death and the last tormented months of his life, the peculiar estrangement of many acquaintances and friends.[30]

Be kindly disposed to me, but keep your freedom. How well I understand your "unstable and ephemeral"—how like me you are in this! May you keep growing and growing! In this hope, I am always

Your friend F. N.

81 · *To Mathilde Maier* Interlaken, July 15, 1878

Verehrtestes Fräulein:

It cannot be helped—I must bring distress to all my friends by declaring at last how I myself have got *over* distress. That metaphysical befogging

---

30. Albert Brenner had been a student of N's and had stayed in the Villa Rubinacci.

of all that is true and simple, the pitting of reason *against* reason, which sees every particular as a marvel and an absurdity; this matched by a baroque art of overexcitement and glorified extravagance—I mean the art of Wagner; both these things finally made me more and more ill, and practically alienated me from my good temperament and my own aptitude. I wish that you could now feel as I do, how it is to live, as I do now, in such pure *mountain air*, in such a gentle mood vis-à-vis people still inhabiting the haze of the valleys, more than ever dedicated, as I am, to all that is good and robust, so much closer to the Greeks than ever before; how I now *live* my aspiration to wisdom, down to the smallest detail, whereas earlier I only revered and idolized the wise—briefly, if you could only know how it feels to have known this change and this crisis, then you could not avoid wishing to have such an experience yourself.

I became fully aware of this at Bayreuth that summer [1876]. I fled, after the first performances which I attended, fled into the mountains, and there, in a small woodland village, I wrote the first draft, about one-third of my book, then entitled "The Plowshare."[31] Then I returned to Bayreuth, on my sister's wishes, and had enough inner composure to endure the almost unendurable—in silence too, telling nothing to anyone. Now I have shaken off what is extraneous to me: people, friends and enemies, habits, comforts, books; I live in solitude—years of it, if needs be—until once more, ripened and complete as a philosopher of *life*, I may associate with people (and then probably be obliged to do so).[32]

Can you remain, in spite of everything, as kindly disposed to me as you were—or, rather, will you be able to do so? You can see that I have become so candid that I can endure only human relationships which are absolutely genuine. I avoid half-friendships and especially partisan associations; I want no adherents. May every man (and woman) be his own adherent only.

Your cordially devoted and grateful   F. N.

82 · *To Peter Gast*   [Naumburg, October 5, 1879][33]

Yesterday morning, dear friend, my postcard was sent to you, and three hours later I had new proofs once more of your untiring kindness toward me.

31. Refers to *Menschliches, Allzumenschliches*, begun at Klingenbrunn after N's flight from Bayreuth in August, 1876.

32. N had given up his Gellertstrasse apartment at the end of June; Elisabeth had returned to Naumburg. She continued trying to win him back to the Bayreuth circle.

33. *Werke in drei Bänden*, vol. 3, includes only six letters for the whole period between September, 1878 and September, 1879. None adds significantly to the picture of

If only I could now answer your wishes! But "thoughts are too far away," as Tieck sings. You would not believe with what fidelity I have carried out the program of thoughtlessness so far; I have reasons for fidelity here, for "behind thought stands the devil" of a tormenting attack of pain. The manuscript which you received from St. Moritz was written at such a high and hard price that perhaps nobody would have written it if he could possibly have avoided doing so. Often I shudder to read it, especially the longer parts, because of the ugly memories it brings. All of it—except for a few lines—was thought out on walks, and it was sketched in pencil in six small notebooks; the fair copy made me ill almost every time I set about writing it. I had to omit about twenty *longish* thought sequences, unfortunately quite essential ones, because I could not find the time to extract them from my frightful pencil scribblings; the same was true last summer. In the interim the connections between the thoughts escape my memory; I have to steal the minutes and quarter-hours of "brain energy," as you call it, steal them away from a suffering brain. Sometimes I think that I shall never do it again. I am reading the copy you made, and find it so difficult to understand myself—my head is *that* tired.

The Sorrento manuscript has gone to the devil; my move and the eventual departure from Basel have done away completely with several things—a blessing for me, for such old manuscripts eye me like creditors.[34]

Dear friend, as for Luther, I have for a long time been incapable of saying honestly anything respectful about him: the after-effect of a huge collection of material about him, to which Jakob Burckhardt drew my attention. I am referring to Janssen, *Geschichte des deutschen Volkes*, vol. 2, which appeared only this year (I have a copy). Here, for once, it is not a question of the falsified Protestant construction of history that we have been taught to believe in. At the moment it seems to me merely a matter of *national* taste in the north and the south which makes us prefer Luther, as a human being,

---

the post-Wagner N sketched in the 1878 letters here translated. Biographical details for that period of N's life are the following. For the winter semester 1878–79, N rented an apartment on the outskirts of Basel; he saw much of the Overbecks, and was extremely ill again during the first months of 1879. On May 2 he offered his resignation, and the university formally accepted it on June 4. He was given a retirement pension, from three different sources, of three thousand Swiss francs a year for six years (it was later extended). In June he left Basel, going first to Bremgarten with his sister, then to see Overbeck's mother-in-law in Zürich; at the end of June he went to the Oberengadin for the first time (the promised land, he then called it). He was continuously unwell during this time. In September, 1879, he left for Chur with his sister; thence he traveled to Naumburg. Here he finished "The Wanderer and His Shadow," of which he had completed a draft at St. Moritz in the Oberengadin during September. It is of this work that he writes in the present letter.

34. I do not know if this manuscript has been identified; at the time, N was working on *Menschliches, Allzumenschliches*, vol. 1.

to Ignatius Loyola. Luther's hideous, arrogant, peevishly envious abusiveness—he felt out of sorts unless he was wrathfully spitting on someone—has quite disgusted me. Certainly you are right about the "promotion of European democratization" coming through Luther; but certainly too this raging enemy of the peasants (who had them beaten to death like mad dogs and expressly told the princes that they could now acquire the kingdom of heaven by slaughtering the brute peasant rabble) was one of the most unintentional promoters of it. I grant that *you* have the more charitable attitude toward him. Give me time! For your other suggestions as to gaps in my thinking, I am also grateful, but quite powerlessly so! Ah, I find myself thinking again of my "wishes of wishes." No, I recently thought that my friend Gast was not really a writer—there are so *many* ways of testifying to one's inner condition, one's becoming healthy and ripe. Especially for you, as artist! After Aeschylus came Sophocles! I do not want to give any clearer indication of my hopes.[35] And by the way, a sincere word about you as mind and heart: what a start you have on me, allowing for the difference of years and for what the years bring! Once more sincerely: I believe you to be better and more gifted than I am, and consequently also under a greater obligation. At your age I was investigating with great zeal the genesis of an eleventh-century lexicon and the sources of Diogenes Laertius, and had no idea of my having any right to possess and declare general ideas of my own. Even now I have the feeling that I am a most miserable beginner; my solitude and my illness have accustomed me somewhat to the impudence of my writings. But *others* must do *everything* better, my *life* as well as my *thought*. This needs no answer.

> With truly devoted love,   Your friend, who has hopes for you,
>
> N.

83 · *To Malwida von Meysenbug*

Naumburg, January 14, 1880

Although writing is for me one of the most forbidden fruits, yet I must write a letter to you, whom I love and respect like an elder sister—and it will

35. N had high hopes for Gast as a composer. The analogy here is Aeschylus/Sophocles = Wagner/Gast. The new anti-Wagner and anti-Luther N is a far cry from the Wagnerite crypto-Protestant of Letter No. 59.

probably be the last. For my life's terrible and almost unremitting martyrdom makes me thirst for the end, and there have been some signs which allow me to hope that the stroke which will liberate me is not too distant. As regards torment and self-denial, my life during these past years can match that of any ascetic of any time; nevertheless, I have wrung from these years much in the way of purification and burnishing of the soul—and I no longer need religion or art as a means to that end. (You will notice that I am proud of this; in fact, complete isolation alone enabled me to discover my own resources of self-help). I think that I have done my life's work, though of course like a person who had no time. But I know that I have poured out a drop of good oil for many, and that I have given to many an indication of how to rise above themselves, how to attain equanimity and a right mind. I write this as an afterthought; really it should only be said on the completion of my "humanity." No pain has been, or should be, able to make me bear false witness about life *as I know it to be.*

To whom might I say this, if not to you? I believe—but is it immodest to say so?—that our characters have much in common. For example, we both have courage, and neither distress nor disparagement can make us stray from the course which we know to be the right one. Also, we have both experienced much, inside and outside ourselves, the radiance of which has been seen by few men of the present age—we have *hopes* for humanity, and offer ourselves as modest sacrifices, do we not?

Have you good news about the Wagners? It is three years since I heard from them—*they* have also abandoned me, and I knew long ago that Wagner would cease to stand by me the moment he saw the rift between our aspirations. I have been told that he was writing something against me. I hope he completes it—the truth must come to light by every possible means! I always think of him with gratitude, because to him I am indebted for some of the strongest incitements to intellectual independence. Frau Wagner, as you know, is the most congenial woman I have ever met. But I am not fitted for associating with them, let alone for a resumption of friendly relations. It is too late.

Greetings to you, my dear, sisterly, and respected friend, from a young old man, who has no grievance against life, though he must still want it to end.

Friedrich Nietzsche

84 · *To Peter Gast*   Marienbad, July 18, 1880[36]

My dear friend:

I still think several times a day of how pleasantly I was spoiled in Venice and of my even more pleasant spoiler, and I say only that one should not be *allowed* to have it so good for long, and that it suits me to be a hermit again and, as such, to go walking for ten hours a day, to drink the irksome waters and await their effects. Meanwhile I go on digging zealously in my moral mine, and sometimes seem to myself wholly subterranean—I feel that I may now have found the main gallery and the way out; yet that is a belief which one can have and reject a hundred times.[37] Now and then I catch an echo of Chopin in my mind, and you have seen to it that when this happens, I always think of you and lose myself in thinking of possible things. My confidence has become very strong—you are much more robust than I supposed, and, apart from the damaging influence that Herr Nietzsche has occasionally had on you, your conditioning is fair all around. *Ceterum censeo:* mountains and forests are better than cities, and Paris better than Vienna. But that does not matter.

On the way here I got into conversation with an important ecclesiastic, who seemed to be one of the foremost advocates of old Catholic music; he had answers to the most detailed questions. I found that he was very interested in Wagner's work on Palestrina; he said that the dramatic recitative (in the liturgy) was the seed of sacred music, and, accordingly, he insisted that it should be sung as dramatically as possible. Regensburg, he said, was now the only city on earth where one could study the old music, above all, hear it performed (especially around Easter).

Did you hear about the fire in Mommsen's house? And that his notes were destroyed, perhaps the most huge collection of preparatory work ever made by a living scholar?[38] It is said that he kept on rushing back into the flames and, eventually, covered with burns, had to be held back by force.

---

36. N had left Naumburg on February 12. He traveled via Bozen to Riva on Lago di Garda, where he met Peter Gast. On March 12 Gast and he went to Venice and stayed there until the end of June. It was there that N read Stifter's novel *Der Nachsommer*. He spent July and August at Marienbad, a spa with numerous literary associations.

37. Presumably a reference to his work on *Morgenröte: Gedanken über die moralischen Vorurteile* (1881).

38. Theodor Mommsen (1817–1903), author of *Römische Geschichte*, was one of the great historians of the nineteenth century. He became rector of Berlin University in 1874; during the 1860's he had sided with Treitschke in supporting Bismarck. In the 1880's he turned against Bismarck and attacked Treitschke, the militant pro-Prussian historian, as "the true representative of that moral brutalization which threatens our civilization." (See Hans Kohn, *The Mind of Germany*, pp. 183–88.)

Such undertakings as M's must be very rare, because there is seldom a combination, or rather cooperation, between such a colossal memory and such critical acumen and capacity for ordering such materials. The story made my heart twist around in my body, and I still suffer physically when I think of it. Is that sympathy? But what does Mommsen matter to me? I am not fond of him.

Since yesterday there has been great distress here in this lonely woodland "Eremitage," whose hermit I am; I do not know exactly what has happened, but the house has the shadow of a crime hanging over it. Somebody buried something, others discovered it, there was a terrible outcry, many policemen arrived, there was a house search, and in the night I heard someone sighing agonizedly in the room next to mine, so that sleep fled from me. Also in the dead of night there was more digging in the forest, but there came a surprise, and then more tears and shouts. An official told me it was a "question of banknotes"—I am not inquisitive enough to know as much as everyone around me probably knows. Anyway, the forest solitude is eerie.

I have been reading a story by Mérimée, in which Henri Beyle's character is said to be portrayed—*The Etruscan Vase;* if what they say is right, it would be the character called St. Clair.[39] The story as a whole is sarcastic, grand, and deeply melancholy.

Lastly, a reflection: one ceases to love oneself *aright* when one *ceases* to give oneself exercise in loving others, wherefore the latter (the ceasing) is to be strongly advised against (from my own experience).

Farewell, my dear and *very* much valued friend! May you thrive by day and by night.

Loyally, your F. N.

In your conduct toward the deserter, Schopenhauer would find proof of the immutability of character—and he would be wrong, as he nearly always is.

85 · *To Franz Overbeck*   [Genoa, November, 1880][40]

You will be deep in your work, dear friend, but a few words from me will not disturb you. It always does me good to think of you at your work; it is as

---

39. Henri Beyle was Stendhal, whose books N greatly admired. At this time he was also reading Sainte-Beuve's *Portraits littéraires* (eighteenth-century).

40. N had gone from Marienbad to Naumburg in September. Early in October he traveled, via Frankfurt, Heidelberg, Basel (visiting Overbeck), and Locarno, to Stresa

if a healthy natural force were *blindly* working through you, and yet it is a force of *reason* which operates in the subtlest and most tricky material, and which we have to tolerate whenever it behaves impatiently and doubtfully and sometimes to our despair. I am so deeply indebted to you, dear friend, for letting me watch the spectacle of your life from so close at hand—indeed, Basel has made me the gift of *your* image and of Jakob Burckhardt's; I think that it is not only with regard to knowledge that these two images have been very useful to me. The *dignity* and the *grace* of an original and essentially solitary way of living and of knowing—this is the spectacle which was "delivered to my door" by favor of my destiny, a favor which I cannot overestimate—and consequently I left that house a different person from the one who entered it.

Now my whole endeavor is to realize an ideal attic dweller's solitude, which will do justice to all those necessary and most elementary demands of my nature, as many many torments have taught me to know them. And perhaps I shall succeed. The daily struggle against my head trouble and the laughable complexity of my distresses demand so much attention that I am in danger of becoming *petty* in this regard—well, that is the counterweight to very general, very lofty impulses which have such control over me that without the counterweight I would make a fool of myself. I have just come round from a very grueling attack, and, having hardly shaken off the distress of the past two days, I find my foolery already pursuing quite incredible things, from the moment I wake up, and I think that no other attic dweller can have had the dawn shine upon more lovely and more desirable things. Help me to hold on to this hiddenness—tell people that I am not living in Genoa; for a good long time I must live without people and live in a city where I do not know the language—I *must*, I repeat; have no fears on my account! I live as if the centuries were nothing, and I pursue my thoughts without thinking of the date and of the newspapers.

I want also to have no more to do with the aspirations of contemporary "idealism," least of all, German idealism. Let us all do our work; posterity may decide, or may not decide, how we should be placed— all I want is to feel free and not to have to say yes or no, for instance, to the kind of authentically idealistic little book that I am sending you.[41] It is the last of my dealings with the contemporary "German mind"—equally touching, arrogant, and in unspeakably bad taste: but read it just once, together with

---

on Lago Maggiore. In Stresa he was again very unwell indeed. The winter 1880-81 was the first of several he spent in Genoa.

41. Schlechta suggests that this book may have been Eduard von Hartmann's *Phänomenologie des sittlichen Bewusstseins* (Berlin, 1879).

your wife, of course! And then burn it and read, in order to purge yourself of this German bombast, Plutarch's lives of Brutus and Dion. Farewell, dear friend! Did I wish you a happy birthday? No. But I have wished myself happy on your birthday. Lovingly, yours

[no signature]

Genova, poste restante

86 · *To Erwin Rohde*   Genoa, March 24, 1881

So life passes on and away, and the best friends hear and see nothing of each other! Yes, it is quite an accomplishment—to live and keep one's spirits up. How often do I find myself in a state in which I would like to raise a loan from my old, robust, healthy and brave friend Rohde, in which I am deeply in need of a "transfusion" of strength, not of lamb's blood but of lion's blood!—but there he is in Tübingen, among books and married, in every way for me *unattainable*. Ah, my friend, so I have to go on living off "my own fat," or, as everyone knows who has really tried this, drink my own blood. It is important then not to lose the thirst for oneself, and just as important not to drink oneself dry.

But on the whole I am amazed, I confess, by how many sources a man can set flowing in himself. Even a man like me, who is not one of the richest of people. I think that if I had the qualities in which you surpass me, I would be presumptuous and intolerable. Even now there are moments when I walk about on the heights above Genoa having glimpses and feelings such as Columbus once, perhaps from the very same place, sent out across the sea and into the future.

Well, with these moments of courage and perhaps also of foolishness I must try again to correct the balance of my life's ship. For you would not believe *how many days* and how many *hours* even on tolerable days have just to be *endured*, to say the least. As far as it is possible to alleviate and mitigate a difficult state of health with the "wisdom" of one's way of life, I am probably doing everything that can be done in my case—in this I am neither thoughtless nor uninventive—but I wish upon nobody the fate to which I am beginning to grow accustomed, because I am beginning to realize that I am equal to it.

But you, my dear, dear friend, are not in such a fix that you have to make yourself thin in order to wriggle through; nor is Overbeck; you both do your fine work and, without talking much of it, perhaps without giving it much thought, you have the best that the noon of life can give—plus a little sweat, I expect. How much I would like to hear something of your plans, big plans—for, with a mind and heart like yours, one always carries around with one, behind all the daily and perhaps petty work, some embracing and *very large* project! How it would enliven me if you found me not unworthy to be told! Such friends as you must help me to keep alive my belief in myself; and you do that if you continue to confide to me your best aims and hopes. Should there be behind these words a request for a letter, well then, dearest friend, I would gladly have from you something *very, very* personal, so that I may keep in my heart my feeling not only for my former friend Rohde but also for my present friend and, what is more, for my friend who is coming to be and willing to be—yes, *becoming* and *willing!*

Cordially   Yours.

Say something to your wife in my favor; she must not be angry that she still does not know me; sometime I shall make it all up.

Address: Genova (Italy)
poste restante

87. *To Franz Overbeck*   [Postmarked Genoa April 28, 1881]

Dear, dear friend:

On Sunday I am leaving Genoa for a few months and going to Recoaro (near Vicenza), an Italian summer resort, where Herr Köselitz will also be staying. Would you send me the new edition of *Der grüne Heinrich* there?[42] It is certainly not dissipation to read a good book each year (last year we read *Der Nachsommer*). Rohde wrote a long letter about himself, but two things in it almost hurt me: (1) the kind of thoughtlessness as regards the *direction* of his life—and from such a person! and (2) the quantity of bad taste in his vocabulary and phrasing (perhaps in German universities it is called "wit"—Heaven preserve us from it!). I wish you and your dear and respected wife a good summer and good weather (for me almost everything depends on the sky, so just now things were *not* good!).

[no signature]

42. The novel by Gottfried Keller (1855) had just appeared in a revised edition.

88 · *To Elisabeth Nietzsche*   Recoaro, June 19, 1881

Ah, my dear, good sister, so you think it is all a matter of a *book?* Do even *you* still think of me as a writer? My moment has come. I would like to save you so much trouble; you cannot carry my burden (it is bad enough a fate for you to be such a close relative). I would like you to be able to say with a clear conscience, "I do not know my brother's latest views." (People will certainly tell you that these views are immoral and "shameless"). In the meantime, be cheerful and brave, everyone for himself, and love as always.

My address: St. Moritz in Graubünden (Switzerland) *poste restante.*[43] This is another *last* attempt. Since February I have suffered extraordinarily, and only very few places suit me. Thank you very much for your services regarding R. the painter.

89 · *To Franz Overbeck*   [Postmarked Sils Engd., July 30, 1881]

I am really amazed, really delighted! I have a precursor, and *what* a precursor! I hardly knew Spinoza: what brought me to him now was the guidance of instinct. Not only is his whole tendency like my own—to make knowledge the most *powerful passion*—but also in five main points of his doctrine I find myself; this most abnormal and lonely thinker is closest to me in these points precisely: he denies free will, purposes, the moral world order, the nonegoistical, evil; of course the differences are enormous, but they are differences more of period, culture, field of knowledge. *In summa:* my solitariness which, as on very high mountains, has often, often made me gasp for breath and lose blood, is now at least a solitude for two. Strange!

Beyond that, my health is not as I had hoped. Exceptional weather here too. Continuous change of atmospheric conditions—it will force me to leave Europe. I must have a *clear* sky for months on end, or I shall never make any progress. Six bad attacks already, lasting two or three days! Cordially,

Your friend.

43. Having left Genoa in April, N spent the last days of April and the summer months till early July in Recoaro, near Vicenza. From July 4 to October 1 he stayed for the first time in Sils Maria, where he had his vision of "Eternal Recurrence." He returned to Genoa in early October. The tone of this present letter supports Schlechta's view that the letters to Elisabeth of November 29, 1881, and of January 22, 1882, are not authentic. In them, there is a wholly confiding note.

90 · *To Peter Gast*   Sils Maria, August 14, 1881

Well, my dear good friend! The August sun is overhead, the year passes on, the mountains and the forests become more quiet and peaceful. On my horizon, thoughts have arisen such as I have never seen before—I will not speak of them, but will keep my unshakable peace. I really shall have to live a few more years! Ah, my friend, sometimes the idea runs through my head that I am living an extremely dangerous life, for I am one of those machines which can explode. The intensities of my feeling make me shudder and laugh; several times I could not leave my room for the ridiculous reason that my eyes were inflamed—from what? Each time, I had wept too much on my previous day's walk, not sentimental tears but tears of joy; I sang and talked nonsense, filled with a glimpse of things which put me in advance of all other men.

Ultimately, if I were unable to gather my strength from myself, if I had had to wait for exhortations, encouragements, consolations from outside, where would I be? What would I be? There were truly moments and whole periods in my life (for example, the year 1878) in which I would have felt a strengthening word of approval, an assenting handshake, to be the last word in restoratives—and precisely then everyone left me in the lurch, everyone on whom I thought I could rely and who could have done me the favor. Now I expect it no longer, and have only a certain gloomy sense of surprise when I think, for example, of the letters I now receive; all are so insignificant, nobody has come to experience anything because of me, nobody has had a thought about me—what people say is respectable and benevolent, but it is remote, remote, remote. Even our dear Jakob Burckhardt wrote me such a subdued, despondent little letter.

My compensation I take from the fact that this year has shown me two things which belong to me and are intimately close to me: *your* music, and this *landscape*. This is not Switzerland, not Recoaro, but something quite different, at least much more southern—I would have to go to the high plateaus of Mexico overlooking the Pacific to find anything similar (for example, Oaxaca), and the vegetation there would of course be tropical. Well, I shall try to keep this Sils Maria for myself. And I feel the same about your music; only I do not know how to get hold of it! I have had to delete the reading of scores and piano playing from my activities once and for all. I am thinking of acquiring a typewriter, and am in touch with its inventor, a Dane from Copenhagen.

What are you doing next winter? I presume you will be in Vienna. But for the winter following we must plan a meeting, if only a short one, for I know quite well that I am not suited to companionship with you and that you feel more free and productive when I have left you. On the other hand, my concern is, more than I can say, that your life of feeling should become more and more free, that you should acquire an intimate and proud sense of belonging somewhere—in sum, that your creative life and your maturing should proceed in the most fortunate possible way, so I shall easily adapt myself to any conditions that follow naturally from your needs. I *never* have any ugly feelings toward you, believe me, dear friend!

Tell me, by the way, how German paper money is now selling in Italy (for Italian paper money)—I mean, what is the rate of exchange?

I have forgotten Frl. von Meysenbug's address; at the moment she is probably somewhere together with the Monods; I think that Herr Schmeitzner can send the copy to Paris.[44] Everything has been settled with Herr Schmeitzner in the most considerate way; I have undertaken not to make him suffer from my jumping to conclusions in expecting from him more than his nature permits.

In cordial friendship and with gratitude   Your F. N.

I have been frequently unwell.

91 · *To Franz Overbeck*   [Postmarked Sils Engd.
September 18, 1881]

Thank your dear wife for her kind and precise information. No, a saucepan of that kind does *not* suit my household—which must be transitory and transportable, like myself (the typewriter I mentioned is also unsuitable). Forget about the journals! The essays I am looking for appear in Liebmann's *Analysis*. [*What follows is in Latin in the original*] And now, these matters settled, I shall say what I wanted not to say but cannot withhold. I am desperate. Pain is vanquishing my life and my will. What months, what a summer I have had! My physical agonies were as many and various as the changes I have seen in the sky. In every cloud there is some form of electric charge which grips me suddenly and reduces me to complete misery. Five times I have called for Doctor Death, and yesterday I hoped it was the end—in vain. Where is there on earth that perpetually serene sky, which is my sky? Farewell, friend.

[no signature]

44. Gast was giving Schmeitzner details of persons to whom copies of *Morgenröte*, just published, should be sent.

92 · *To Peter Gast*   Genoa, December 5, 1881

Dear, good friend:

From time to time (why is it?) I have an urgent need to hear something general and unconditional about Wagner, and preferably from you! To have similar feelings about Chamfort should also be a matter of honor for us both; he was a man of Mirabeau's stature, in character, heart and breadth of mind—that is how Mirabeau himself judged his friend.

It came as a great shock to hear that Bizet was dead. I heard *Carmen* for a second time—and had once more the impression of a first-rate novella, like one by Mérimée. Such a passionate and such a graceful soul! For me this work is worth a journey to Spain—an extremely *southern* work! Do not laugh at this, old friend, my taste is not so easily led astray.

In cordial gratitude   N.

Have been very ill meanwhile, but well as a result of *Carmen*—

93 · *To Elisabeth Nietzsche*   Genoa, February 3, 1882

Just a few lines, my beloved sister, to thank you for your good words about Wagner and Bayreuth. Certainly those were the best days of my life, the ones I spent with him at Tribschen and through him in Bayreuth (1872, not 1876). But the omnipotence of our tasks drove us apart, and now we cannot rejoin one another—we have become too estranged.

I was indescribably happy in those days, when I discovered Wagner! I had sought for so long a man who was superior to me and who actually looked beyond me. I thought I had found such a man in Wagner. I was wrong. Now I cannot even compare myself with him—I belong to a different world.

My Wagner mania certainly cost me dear. Has not this nerve-shattering music ruined my health? And the disillusionment and leaving Wagner—was not that putting my very life in danger? Have I not needed almost six years to recover from that pain? No, Bayreuth is for me out of the question. It was only a joke, what I wrote you the other day.[45] But you must go to Bayreuth, all the same. That is of great importance to me.

Loyally, your brother

94· *To Peter Gast*   Genoa, March 20, 1882

My dear friend:

May everything be as you would want me to think it is—ugh! that could be put better in Latin, and in seven words. Consider again whether you will not sell to me and two of my friends the score of your *Matrimonio*.[46] I offer you 6,000 francs, payable in quarterly installments of 1,500 francs. The matter can be kept secret if you wish. You can tell your father that a publisher offered you this sum. Then consider too how one could appeal to Italian feeling by counteracting "impiety" toward their classic Cimarosa. You could commend and dedicate the work to Queen Margherita and profit from the political situation. An act of German *politesse* vis-à-vis Italy—that is how it would have to look. To this end the first performance would have to be in Rome; the dedication to the queen might considerably interest and please Herr von Keudell. On the assumption that this idea appeals to you, I advise, finally, that you win over Frl. Emma *Nevada* for the performance of the work—she has just conquered Rome. Italians are very nice to all famous singers. But I have only once seen them impassioned about one.

The Viennese Operetta Society is here—so we have some German theater. This has given me a very good idea of how your Scapine must be. When it comes to feminine frolicsomeness and grace, the Viennese women seem to be really ingenious. You need for this work, because of its lack of action, nothing but the best leading singers. I dread to think of an idealistically decorous and mediocre performance—well! That's talking like a theater director! I beg your pardon!

I have read in Robert Mayer's book. Friend, he's a great specialist— and nothing more. I am amazed to find how coarse and naïve he is when it

45. Elisabeth had suggested to N that he should go to Bayreuth for the 1882 festival. On January 30 he replied, "But I—forgive me!—will come only on the condition that Wagner personally invites me and treats me as the most honored guest at the festival."

46. N had made this offer in order to help Gast financially. His opera was an arrangement of Cimarosa's *Matrimonio Segreto*. The "two friends" were Gersdorff and Rée. Gast declined the offer.

comes to more general constructions. He always thinks he is being wonderfully logical, but in fact he is just being obstinate. If something has been well and truly disproved, he says it is due to the "material" prejudice—even if the disproving comes not from an idealist but from a mathematician—Boscovitch.[47] Boscovitch and Copernicus are the two greatest opponents of optical observation. With effect from him [Boscovitch] there is no "matter" any more—except as a source of popular relief. He has thought the atomistic doctrine through to the end. *Gravity* is certainly not a "property of matter," simply because there *is* no matter. The *force of gravity* is, like the *vis inertiae*, certainly a manifestation of force, simply because force is all there is! Now the *logical* relation between these phenomena and others—for example, heat—is still not at all clear. But if one goes along with Mayer in still believing in matter and in solid corporeal atoms,[48] then one cannot decree that there is only *one* force. The kinetic theory must attribute to atoms, besides motional energy, the two forces of cohesion and gravity. And this is what *all* materialist physicists and chemists do!—and Mayer's bes

47. Toward the end of 1881, Gast had sent N his own copy of Robert Mayer's *Mechanics of Heat*, bound with an article by Mayer, "Über Auslösung" ("On Energy Discharge"). N had first studied Boscovitch in March, 1873, when he borrowed the *Philosophia naturalis* (2 vols.) from the Basel University Library. Ruggiero Boscovitch (1711–87) was a Jesuit mathematician, born in Ragusa (now Dubrovnik). His theory of the atom as an immaterial center of force was taken up in the nineteenth century by the French physicists Ampère and Cauchy, but it bears no real relation to modern atomic theory, which began in the year 1897 with the discovery of the negatively electrified corpuscle common to all elements and its identification with the electron (Sir William Cecil Dampier, *History of Science*, 4th ed., Cambridge: At the University Press, 1948, p. 389). On N's relation to Mayer, see Alwin Mittasch, "F. N. Verhältnis zu Robert Mayer," *Blätter für deutsche Philosophie* 16 (Berlin, 1942): 139–61. A footnote to No. 136 (1885) shows the application of N's Boscovitchian ideas to his theory of "Eternal Recurrence." His present thinking (1882) on the subject is shown in *Die fröhliche Wissenschaft*, bk. 3, para. 109: ". . . matter is an error, like the God of the Eleatic philosophers." This was developed during the later 1880's (cf. *Werke in drei Bänden*, 3: 777–78): "One translation of this world of effect into a visible world—a world for the eye—is the concept 'motion.' Here it is always assumed that *something* is moved—which means that a *thing* is envisaged, whether in the fiction of a molecule atom ["Klümpchen-Atom"] or even of its abstract version, the dynamic atom: a thing which causes effects—that is, we have not freed ourselves from the habits imposed by the senses and by language. Subject, object, a doer to do what is done, the doing itself and what it does—these are considered in separation; let us not forget that this is mere semeiotics and does not designate anything real. Mechanics as a doctrine of motion is already a translation into the sense language of men. . . . The mechanistic world is imagined in terms of a world as presented to eye and touch (as a world 'in motion'), in such a way that it can be calculated, in such a way that causating units are supposed ['fingiert'], 'things,' 'atoms,' whose effect remains constant (the false concept of the subject carried across into the concept of the atom). . . . If we eliminate all these trimmings, no things remain but dynamic quanta, in a relation of tension to other dynamic quanta, whose essence consists in their being related to all other quanta, in their 'effect' on these."

48. Original: "erfüllte Atome."

adherents as well. *Nobody* has abandoned the idea of gravity! Ultimately even Mayer has a second force in the background, the *primum mobile*, God,—besides motion itself. And he certainly needs God!

Farewell, or, rather, flourish, my dear friend.

Loyally, your F. N.

95 · *To Lou Salomé*   [Naumburg, *ca.* June 10, 1882]

Yes, my dear friend, remote as I am, I do not overlook the people who must of necessity be initiated into what we intend; but I think we should firmly decide to *initiate* only the necessary persons. I love the hiddenness of life and heartily wish that you and I should not become subjects of European gossip. Moreover, I connect such high hopes with our plans for living together that all necessary or accidental side-effects make little impression on me now; and *whatever* happens, we shall endure it together and throw the whole bag of troubles overboard every evening *together*, shall we not?

Your words about Frl. von Meysenbug have made me decide to write her a letter soon.

Let me know how you plan to arrange your time after Bayreuth, and on what assistance of mine you will be counting. At present, I badly need mountains and forests—not only my health, but also *Die fröhliche Wissenschaft*, are driving me into solitude. I want to finish.

Will it suit you if I leave now for Salzburg (or Berchtesgaden), thus on the way to Vienna?

When we are together I shall write something for you in the book I am sending.[49]

Lastly, I am inexperienced and unpracticed in all matters of action; and for years I have not had to explain or justify myself to others in anything I have done. I like to keep my plans secret; let everyone talk of the things I have *done* as much as they please! Yet nature gave each being various defensive weapons—and to you she gave your glorious frankness of will. Pindar says somewhere, "Become the being you are"!

Loyally and devotedly,   F. N.

Note: This letter to Lou Salomé needs some commentary, as do the remaining letters of 1882. For many of the following details I am indebted to Schlechta's notes in vol. 3 of *Werke in drei Bänden* (pp. 1371 ff.). Others come from

49. *Morgenröte.*

E. Podach, *Nietzsches Zusammenbruch* (1930), especially pp. 36 ff. (English translation: *The Madness of Nietzsche*, London, 1931). Further details will be found in H. F. Peters, *My Sister, My Spouse*, New York and London, 1962. See, however, also Rudolph Binion, *Frau Lou* (Princeton, 1968), and W. Kaufmann, *Nietzsche*, 3d rev. and enlarged ed. (Princeton, 1968); neither could be seen before the present work went to press. Walter Kaufmann writes: "These two volumes will force Mr. M. to change some of his remarks about Nietzsche's relationship to Lou."

On March 13, 1882, Paul Rée arrived in Rome and met Lou Salomé in the home of Malwida von Meysenbug. Lou (1861–1937) was the daughter of a Russian general (of Huguenot stock, as Malwida was); her mother was German. In the events which ensued, she was to play for the first time her dominant role of intellectual *femme fatale*; she bewitched many eminent men during her lifetime, not least the young Rilke. N left Genoa for Messina on March 29; from Messina he traveled to Rome and met Lou. During the latter half of April he traveled with Lou, Rée, and Lou's mother to Orta, where they stayed for several days. On May 8 N arrived at the Overbecks for five days. From May 13 to 17 he was with Lou and Rée in Lucerne; they visited Tribschen. At this time N proposed to Lou, and she refused him. From May 23 to June 24 he was in Naumburg: during this period he went to Berlin but failed to meet Lou there. From June 25 to August 27 N was in Tautenburg; on July 26 Lou and N's sister attended the first performance of *Parsifal* at Bayreuth, and on August 7 they arrived together at Tautenburg (near Dornburg, in Saxony). On August 26, Lou left. Elisabeth refused to return to Naumburg with N; not much later, N broke with his mother and sister and went to Leipzig, in about mid-September, in flight from "Naumburg virtuousness." Of this episode and its consequences, Schlechta writes: "N's sister, through her ceaseless intriguing interference in N's relationship with Lou and Rée—which was difficult enough in any case—practically drove her brother to suicide; in connection with this affair she persecuted Lou von Salomé (later Frau Andreas) for as long as she lived, also Paul Rée [died 1901], in numerous publications which distorted the facts and even falsified them; she also tried to throw suspicion on the Overbeck couple, who attempted to intervene in order to clarify and ease matters." At the beginning of October in Leipzig, Lou, Rée, and N met again; it had been their plan to set up a studious platonic *menage-à-trois* there or in Vienna. N now appears to have alienated Lou by disparaging Rée. The plan was abandoned. During this time Peter Gast also came to Leipzig, and was much impressed by Lou. Toward the end of October, Lou and Rée left Leipzig. On November 15 N goes to Basel and visits the Overbecks, traveling on to Genoa on November 18. From November 23 to February 23, 1883, N in Rapallo; in January he writes Part 1 of *Zarathustra*. On December 24 he had decided to stop writing to his mother; on February 19, 1883, he writes to Gast, "This winter was the worst in my life"; and in mid-February to Overbeck, "My whole life has crumbled under my gaze. . . ."

In June, 1882, N had anticipated the opening of a new phase in his life. In a letter to Overbeck (dated summer, 1882) he wrote: "A mass of my vital secrets is involved in this *new* future, and I still have tasks to solve, which can only be solved by action. Also I am in a mood of fatalistic "surrender to God"—I call it *amor fati*, so much so, that I would rush into a lion's jaws, not to mention— As regards the summer, everything is extremely uncertain. . . ." It is certain that N saw in Lou a perfect disciple, and the days in Tautenburg were rapturous, momentous, and crucial for him in this regard, not least because Lou came there fresh from Wagner's triumphant 1882 festival (the last in his lifetime); and N was painfully aware that Wagner's triumph threatened his own claim to intellectual leadership (cf. letter to Gast, February 19, 1883).[50] It is likely that N's motives in wooing Lou were mixed—and incompatible. Throughout their correspondence he uses the formal "Sie" address, not the intimate "Du." Lou's own account of the affair appears in her *Lebensrückblick* (ed. E. Pfeiffer), Zürich-Wiesbaden, 1951.

96· *To Lou Salomé* [Tautenburg, July 2, 1882]

My dear friend:

Now the sky above me is bright! Yesterday at noon I felt as if it was my birthday. *You* sent your acceptance, the most lovely present that anyone could give me now; my sister sent cherries; Teubner sent the first three page proofs of *Die fröhliche Wissenschaft;* and, on top of it all, I had just finished the very last part of the manuscript and therewith the work of six years (1876–82), my entire *Freigeisterei.*[51] O what years! What tortures of every kind, what solitudes and weariness with life! And against all that, as it were against death *and* life, I have brewed this medicine of mine, these thoughts with their small strip of *unclouded sky* overhead. O dear friend, whenever I think of it, I am thrilled and touched and do not know how I could have *succeeded* in doing it—I am filled with self-compassion and the sense of victory. For it is a victory, and a complete one—for even my physical health has reappeared, I do not know where from, and everyone tells me that I am looking younger than ever. Heaven preserve me from doing foolish things—but from now on!—whenever you advise me, I shall be well advised and do not need to be afraid.

As regards the winter, I have been thinking seriously and exclusively of Vienna; my sister's plans for the winter are quite independent of mine, and we can leave them out of consideration. The south of Europe is now far from my thoughts. I want to be lonely no longer, but to learn again to be a human being. Ah, here I have practically everything to learn!

50. Later his sister told N what Wagner had said to her in Bayreuth: "Tell your brother that I am quite alone since he went away and left me." She also claims that this statement gave rise to the aphorism in *Die fröhliche Wissenschaft* called "Stellar Friendship" (*The Nietzsche-Wagner Correspondence,* pp. 311–12); if this was true, N must have been told of the remark before the summer of 1882; possibly Wagner had said it the year before.

51. Somewhat deprecatory term for "freethinking," the radical, critical kind of nineteenth-century thinking which N drives to a special pitch of intensity in *Menschliches, Allzumenschliches, Morgenröte,* and *Die fröhliche Wissenschaft.*

Accept my thanks, dear friend. Everything will be well, as you have said.

Very best wishes to our Rée!

Entirely *yours*,   F. N.

97· *To Peter Gast*   Tautenburg, July 13, 1882

My dear friend:

There are no words from you I hear more gladly than "hope" and "holi-day"—and now I impose this grueling task of proofreading on you, just at the moment when you should be feeling as if you were in paradise.

Do you know the harmless little poems I wrote in Messina?[52] Or have you said nothing about them out of politeness toward the author! No, nevertheless, as the woodpecker says in the last poem, my poetry writing is not going very well. But what does it matter! One should not be ashamed of one's follies; otherwise one's wisdom has little value.

That poem "An den Schmerz" ["To Pain"] was *not* by me. It is among the things which quite overpower me; I have never been able to read it without tears coming to my eyes; it sounds like a voice for which I have been waiting and waiting since childhood. This poem is by my friend Lou, of whom you will not yet have heard. Lou is the daughter of a Russian general, and she is twenty years old; she is as shrewd as an eagle and brave as a lion, and yet still a very girlish child, who perhaps will not live long. I am indebted to Frl. von Meysenbug and Rée for her. At present she is visit-ing Rée; after Bayreuth she is coming here to Tautenburg, and in the autumn we are going together to Vienna. She is most amazingly well prepared for *my* way of thinking and my ideas.

Dear friend, you will surely do us both the honor of keeping far from our relationship the idea of a love affair. We are *friends*, and I shall keep this girl and this confidence in me sacrosanct; what is more, she has an in-credibly definite character, and knows herself exactly what *she* wants with-out asking all the world or troubling about the world.

This is for you and nobody else. But if *you* were to come to Vienna, it would be *fine!*

Loyally, your friend   F. N.

52. Refers to the "Idyllen aus Messina" (written April, 1882).

98 · *To Erwin Rohde* Tautenburg, near Dornburg,
Thuringia [July 15, 1882]

My dear old friend:

It is no use—I must prepare you today for a new book of mine; you still have four weeks at the most before it disturbs your peace![53] One comfort is that it will be the last for many years, for in the autumn I am going to the University of Vienna and starting again as a student, after the somewhat abortive earlier student years with their one-sided emphasis on classical philology. Now I have my own study plan and behind it my own secret aim, to which the rest of my life is *consecrated*—it is too difficult for me to live unless I do it in the grandest style. I tell you this in confidence, my old comrade. Without an aim, which I thought to be indescribably important, I would not have kept myself up in the light and above the black torrents! This is actually my only excuse for the kind of things which I have been writing since 1876; it is my prescription and my home-brewed medicine against weariness with life. What years! What wearisome pain! What inner disturbances, revolutions, solitudes! *Who* has endured as much as I have?— certainly not Leopardi. And if I now stand above all that, with the joyousness of a victor and fraught with difficult *new* plans—and, knowing myself, with the prospect of new, more difficult, and even more inwardly profound sufferings and tragedies and *with the courage to face them!*—then nobody should be annoyed with me for having a good opinion of my medicine. *Mihi ipsi scripsi*[54]—and there it stands; and thus everyone should do for himself his best in his own way—that is my morality, the only remaining morality for me. If even my physical health reappears, whom have I to thank for that? I was in all respects my own doctor; and as a person in whom nothing stands separate, I have had to treat soul, mind, and body all at once and with the same remedies. Admittedly, others might perish by using the same remedies; that is why I exert everything in *warning* others against me. Especially this latest book, which is called *Die fröhliche Wissenschaft*, will scare many people away from me—you too perhaps, dear old friend Rohde! There is an image of myself in it, and I know for sure that it is *not* the image which you carry in your heart.

53. *Die fröhliche Wissenschaft*. In 1881 Rohde had not acknowledged the copy of *Morgenröte* which N had sent him. In a letter dated October 21, 1881, N had written: ". . . I suppose you will have found it difficult to write. Therefore I ask you today . . . without any embarrassing *arrières pensées*: do not write now. It will make no difference between us. . . ." (*Briefe und Berichte*, pp. 254–55.)

54. = "I have written for myself."

So, have patience, even if only because you must understand that with me it is a question of *aut mori aut ita vivere*.[55]

With all my heart,   your Nietzsche

99 · *To Lou Salomé*   Tautenburg [*ca.* July 20, 1882]

Well, my dear friend, all is well till now, and a week from Saturday we shall see each other again. Perhaps you did not receive my last letter? I wrote it on Sunday two weeks ago. That would be a pity; in it I describe for you a *very happy moment*—several good things came my way all at once, and the "goodest" of these things was your letter of acceptance! [—][56]

I have thought of you much, and have shared with you in thought much that has been elevating, stirring, and gay, so much so that it has been like living with my dear friends.[57] If only you knew how novel and strange that seems to an old hermit like me! How often it has made me laugh at myself!

As for Bayreuth, I am satisfied not to *have* to be there, and yet, if I could be near you in a ghostly way, murmuring this and that in your ear, then I would find even the music of *Parsifal* endurable (otherwise it is not endurable). I would like you to read, beforehand, my little work *Richard Wagner in Bayreuth;* I expect friend Rée has it. I have had such experiences with this man and his work, and it was a passion which lasted a long time—passion is the only word for it. The renunciation that it required, the rediscovering of myself that eventually became necessary, was among the hardest and most melancholy things that have befallen me. The last words that Wagner wrote to me are in a fine presentation copy of *Parsifal:* "To my dear friend, Friedrich Nietzsche. Richard Wagner, Member of the High Consistory."[58] At precisely the same time he received from me my book *Menschliches, Allzumenschliches*—and therewith everything was perfectly clear, but also at an end.

How often have I experienced in all possible ways just this—everything perfectly clear, but also at an end!

55. = "To live thus or die."

56. Dash indicates a cut of one and a quarter lines in original edition perpetuated in *Briefe und Berichte*, pp. 267–68.

57. Original: "mit meinen verehrten Freunden."

58. Original: "Oberkirchenrat." The word shows Wagner's slightly self-mocking susceptibility to N's anti-Christianity ("especially too much blood in the Holy Communion," Letter No. 79).

And how happy I am, my beloved friend Lou, that I can now think
of the two of us—"Everything is beginning, and yet everything is perfectly
clear!" Trust me! Let us trust one another!
With the very best wishes for your journey.

Your friend Nietzsche

Geist?[59] What is *Geist* to me? What is knowledge to me? I value
nothing but impulses—and I could swear that we have this in common.
Look through this phase, in which I have lived for several years—look
beyond it! Do not deceive yourself about me—surely you do not think that
the "freethinker" is my ideal![60] I am . . .

Sorry, dearest Lou!

F. N.

100 · *To Peter Gast*   Tautenburg, Tuesday, July 25, 1882

My dear friend:

So I shall have my summer *music* too!—the good things have been pouring down this summer, as if I had a victory to celebrate.[61] And indeed,
just think: in many ways, body and soul, I have been since 1876 more a
battlefield than a man.

Lou will not be up to the piano part; but at just the right moment,
as if heaven-sent, Herr Egidi turns up, a serious and reliable man and
musician, who happens to be staying here in Tautenburg (a pupil of Kiel's);
by a coincidence, I met him for half an hour, and, by another coincidence,
when he arrives home from this meeting, he finds a letter from a friend,
beginning, "I have just discovered a splendid philosopher, Nietzsche. . . ."

You, of course, will be the subject of the utmost discretion; introduced as an Italian friend whose name is a secret.

Your melancholy words, "always missing the mark," have lodged
in my heart. There were times when I thought precisely the same of *myself;*

---

59. The German word "Geist" connotes values which no English word does.
Even "spirit" would not be exact here. "Geist" here certainly denotes an anti-world to
impulse and unreflected emotion. Whatever may be said of N's claim here to value only
impulse, Lou did not rise to it before she met Friedrich Pineles (1895–96).

60. See note 51 to No. 96.

61. Gast had sent him the first half of the piano score of his opera *Der Löwe von
Venedig* (*The Lion of Venice*).

but between you and me, apart from other differences, there is the difference that I no longer let myself be "pushed around"—*sich schubsen lassen*, as they say in Thuringia.

On Sunday I was in Naumburg, to prepare my sister a little for *Parsifal*. It felt strange enough. Finally I said, "My dear sister, precisely this kind of music is what I was writing when I was a boy, at the time when I wrote my oratorio"; and then I took out the old manuscript and, after all these years, played it—the *identity* of *mood* and *expression* was fabulous! Yes, a few parts, for example, "The Death of the Kings," seemed to us more moving than anything we had played from *Parsifal*, and yet they were wholly Parsifalesque! I confess that it gave me a real fright to realize *how* closely I am *akin* to Wagner. Later I shall not conceal this curious fact from you, and you shall be the ultimate court of appeal on the matter—it is so odd that I do not quite trust myself to decide. You will understand, dear friend, that this does not mean I am praising *Parsifal!!* What sudden *décadence!* And what Cagliostroism![62]

A remark in your letter makes me realize that all the jingles of mine which you know were written before I met Lou (*Die fröhliche Wissenschaft* too). But perhaps you also feel that, as "thinker" and "poet" as well, I must have had a certain presentiment of Lou? Or is it "coincidence"? Yes! *Kind* coincidence.

The *comédie* we must read together; my eyes are now already too much occupied.[63] L. arrives on Saturday. Send your work as soon as possible—I envy myself the distinction which you confer on me!

Cordially, your grateful friend   Nietzsche

101 · *To Jakob Burckhardt*   Naumburg, August, 1882

I hope, *mein hochverehrter Freund*—or how should I address you?—that you will accept with goodwill what I am sending you—with a goodwill decided in advance; for, if you do not do that, you will have nothing but ridicule for this book, *Die fröhliche Wissenschaft* (it is so personal, and everything personal is indeed comic). ·

Apart from this, I have reached a point at which I *live* as I *think*, and perhaps I have meanwhile learned really to express what I think. In this

62. Cagliostroism would mean here "bogus magic" (from the notorious wizard who toured Europe at the end of the eighteenth century).

63. Gast was writing incidental music to the vaudeville play *Michel Perrin*, by Mélesville and Duveyrier; he had sent the text of the play to N.

respect I shall regard your judgment as a verdict; in particular, I would like you to read the "Sanctus Januarius" (Book 4), to see if it *communicates itself as a coherent whole.*

And my verses?

Trusting in you, with best wishes   Your   Friedrich Nietzsche

N.B. And what is the address of Herr Curti, of whom you spoke at our last and so very pleasant meeting?[64]

102 · *To Lou Salomé*   Naumburg, end of August, 1882

My dear Lou:

I left Tautenburg one day after you, *very* proud at heart, in *very* good spirits—why?

I have spoken very little with my sister, but enough to send the new ghost that had arisen back into the void from which it came.

In Naumburg the *daimon* of music came over me again—I have composed a setting of your "Prayer to Life"; and my friend from Paris, Louise Ott, who has a wonderfully strong and expressive voice, will one day sing it to you and me.

Lastly, my dear Lou, the old, deep, heartfelt plea: *become the being you are!* First, one has the difficulty of emancipating oneself from one's chains; and, ultimately, one has to emancipate oneself from this emancipation too! Each of us has to suffer, though in greatly differing ways, from the chain sickness, even after he has broken the chains.

In fond devotion to your destiny—for in you I love also *my hopes.*[65]

F. N.

64. N had met Burckhardt in Basel during his five days there in May (8–13).

65. Lou's description of N at this time appears in her book *Friedrich Nietzsche in seinen Werken* (1894), p. 11: "This secludedness, the sense of a secret solitariness—that was the first, strong impression made by N's appearance. The casual observer would not have noticed anything striking; of medium height, very simply dressed, but also very carefully, with his calm features and his brown hair neatly brushed back, he could easily have been overlooked. The fine and highly expressive lines of his mouth were almost completely covered by the large mustache combed forward over the mouth; he had a soft laugh, a soundless way of speaking, and a cautious, pensive way of walking, with rather stooping shoulders; one could hardly imagine this man in a crowd—he bore the stamp of the outsider, the solitary. Incomparably beautiful and noble in form, so that they could not help attracting attention, were N's hands, of which he himself believed that they disclosed his mind. . . ."

103 · *To Lou Salomé*   [Leipzig, probably September 16, 1882]

My dear Lou:

Your idea of reducing philosophical systems to the status of personal records of their authors is a veritable "twin brain" idea. In Basel I was teaching the history of ancient philosophy in just this sense, and liked to tell my students: "This system has been disproved and it is dead; but you cannot disprove the person behind it—the person cannot be killed." Plato, for example.

I am enclosing today a letter from Professor Jakob Burckhardt, whom you wanted to meet one day. He too has something in his personality which cannot be disproved; but because he is a very original *historian* (the foremost living historian), it is precisely this kind of being and person which is eternally incarnate in him that makes him dissatisfied; he would be only too glad to see for once through other eyes, for example, as this strange letter reveals, through mine. Incidentally, he expects to die soon, and suddenly, from a cerebral stroke, as happens in his family; perhaps he would like me to succeed him in his chair? But the course of my life is decided already.

Meanwhile Professor Riedel here, president of the German Musical Association, has been captivated by my "heroic music" (I mean your "Prayer to Life"); he wants to have it performed, and it is not impossible that he will arrange it for his splendid choir (one of the best in Germany, called the Riedel Society). That would be just one little way in which we could both *together* reach posterity—not discounting other ways.

As regards your "Characterization of Myself"—which is true, as you write—it reminded me of my little verses from *Die fröhliche Wissenschaft* with the heading "Request." Can you guess, my dear Lou, what I am asking for? But Pilate says: "What is truth?"[66]

Yesterday afternoon I was happy; the sky was blue, the air mild and clear, I was in the Rosenthal, lured there by the *Carmen* music. I sat there for three hours, drank my second glass of cognac this year, in memory of

66. The verses (in the "Prelude" section) run as follows (they are rhymed in the original):

> I know what many people think,
> And do not know just who I am.
> My eyes are much too close to me,
> I am not what I see and saw.
> I'd like to be more use to me,
> And could be, were I further off.
> Yet not as far as is my foe!
> Too far away my closest friend—
> Yet halfway here twixt him and me!
> Now guess what thing I'm asking for.

the first (ha! how horrible it tasted!), and wondered in all innocence and malice if I had any tendency to madness. In the end I said *no*. Then the *Carmen* music began, and I was submerged for half an hour in tears and heart beatings. But when you read this you will finally say yes! and write a note for the "Characterization of Myself."

Come to Leipzig soon, very soon! *Why* only on October 2? Adieu, my dear Lou.

Your   F. N.

104 · *To Franz Overbeck*   Address: Leipzig, Auenstrasse 26, 2d floor [September, 1882]

My dear friend:

So here I am, back in Leipzig, the old book town, in order to acquaint myself with a few books before going far afield again. It seems unlikely that my winter campaign in Germany will come to anything—I need clear weather, in every sense.[67] Yes, it has *character*, this cloudy German sky, somewhat, it seems, as the *Parsifal* music has character—but a bad character. In front of me lies the first act of the *Matrimonio Segreto*—golden, glittering, good, *very good* music.[68]

The Tautenburg weeks did me good, especially the last ones; and on the whole I have a right to talk of recovery, even if I am often reminded of the *precarious balance* of my health. But there must be a clear sky over me! Or else I lose all too much time and strength.

If you have read the "Sanctus Januarius" you will have remarked that I have crossed a tropic. Everything that lies before me is new, and it will not be long before I catch sight also of the *terrifying* face of my more distant life task. This long, rich summer was for me a testing time; I took my leave of it in the best of spirits and proud, for I felt that during this time at least the ugly rift between willing and accomplishment had been bridged. There were hard demands made on my humanity, and I have become equal to the hardest demands I have made on myself. This whole interim state between what was and what will be, I call "in media vita"; and the daimon of music, which after long years visited me again, compelled me to express this in tones also.

67. In her book on Nietzsche (2d. ed., pp. 17, 128), Lou wrote that N was planning at this time to give up writing for ten years and study natural sciences, in order to give his philosophy a firm foundation.

68. By Peter Gast (after Cimarosa).

But my most useful activity this summer was talking with Lou. There is a deep affinity between us in intellect and taste—and there are in other ways so many differences that we are the most instructive objects and subjects of observation for each other. I have never met anyone who could derive so many *objective insights* from experience, who knows how to deduce so much from all she has learnt. Yesterday Rée wrote to me, "Lou has decidedly grown a few inches in Tautenburg"—well, perhaps I have grown too. I would like to know if there has ever existed before such *philosophical candor* as there is between us. L. is now buried behind books and work; her greatest service to me so far is to have influenced Rée to revise his book on the basis of one of my main ideas. Her health, *I fear*, will only last another six or seven years.[69]

Tautenburg has given Lou an *aim*—she left me a moving poem, "Prayer to Life."

Unfortunately, my sister has become a deadly enemy of Lou; she was morally outraged from start to finish, and now she claims to know what my philosophy is all about. She wrote to my mother: "In Tautenburg she saw my philosophy come to life and this terrified her: I love evil, but *she* loves good. If she were a good Catholic, she would go into a nunnery and do penance for all the harm that will come of it." In brief, I have the Naumburg "virtuousness" against me; there is a real *break* between us—and even my mother at one point forgot herself so far as to say one thing which made me pack my bags and leave early the next day for Leipzig. My sister (who did not want to come to Naumburg as long as I was there, and who is still in Tautenburg) quotes ironically in this regard, "Thus began Zarathustra's Fall."[70] In fact, it is the beginning of the start. This letter is for you and your dear wife—do not think that I am a misanthropist. Most cordially,

Your   F. N.

Very best wishes to Frau Rothpletz and her family![71] I have not yet thanked you for your good letter.

69. In fact, Lou was to become one of the most amazingly robust of all the distinguished and active women of her time. These "six or seven years" are exactly the length of time left before N's own breakdown. Here too, as in the question of "impulse" (Letter No. 99, postscript), she appears to have been something of a *Doppelgänger* to N, and he a lover tripping over his own shadow. What he saw of her was a crystallization of his own as yet unrecognized (?) drives, dreams, desires.

70. N wrote a friendly letter to his sister soon after he arrived in Naumburg (dated beginning of September). Here he expressed his hope that she might come to like Lou, and thanked her for the kindness she had done him during the summer. Her letter that he quotes here was presumably a riposte. (I have retained the original's indirect speech between quotation marks.)

71. Louise Rothpletz was Overbeck's mother-in-law.

105 · *To Franz Overbeck*   [Leipzig, October, 1882]

My dear friend:

That is how things are! I did not write, because I was waiting for several things to be decided, and I am writing today only to tell you as much, for as yet *nothing* has been decided—not even regarding my plans for traveling and for the winter. Paris is still in the offing,[72] but there can be no doubt that my health has become worse under the impact of this northern sky; and perhaps I have never spent more melancholy hours as this autumn in Leipzig—although things *around me* give reason enough for me to be happy. Enough—there have been days on which I have traveled in mind via Basel toward the *sea.* I am somewhat afraid of the noisiness of Paris, and want to know if it has enough clear sky. On the other hand, the renewal of my Genoese solitude might be dangerous. I confess that I would be *extremely* glad to tell you and your wife at length about this year's experiences—there is much to tell and little to write.

I am very grateful to you for Janssen's book; it defines excellently all that distinguishes his view from the Protestant one (the main point of the whole matter is a defeat of *German* Protestantism—in any case, of Protestant "historiography").[73] It has not required me to revise my views on the matter. For me, the Renaissance remains the climax of this millennium; and what has happened since then is the grand reaction of all kinds of herd instincts against the "individualism" of that epoch.

Lou and Rée left recently—first, to meet Rée's mother in Berlin; from there they go to Paris. Lou is in a miserable state of health; I now give her less time than I did last spring. We have our share of worry—Rée is just the man for his task in this affair. For me personally, Lou is a real *trouvaille;* she has fulfilled all my expectations—it is not possible for two people to be more closely related than we are.

As for Köselitz (or rather Herr "Peter Gast"), he is my second marvel of this year. Whereas Lou is uniquely ready for the till now almost undisclosed part of my philosophy, Köselitz is the musical justification of my whole new praxis and rebirth—to put it altogether egoistically. Here is a new Mozart—that is the sole feeling I have about him; beauty, warmth, serenity, fullness, superabundant inventiveness, and the light touch of mastery in counterpoint—such qualities were never combined before; I already want to hear no other music than this. How poor, artificial, and

---

72. In September, N had written to Louise Ott asking her about the chances of finding a room in Paris.

73. Cf. Letter No. 82.

histrionic all that *Wagnerei* now sounds to me! "Will Scherz, List und Rache" be performed here? I think so, but I don't yet know.[74]

This picture which I enclose might be shown on your birthday-gift table (its quality as a photograph is much admired).

Did Frau Rothpletz receive my last book? I forgot her exact address.

With warmest best wishes for your coming year,

Your friend   Nietzsche

106 · *To Paul Rée*   Santa Margherita [End of November, 1882]

But, dear, dear friend, I thought you would feel just the opposite and be quietly glad to be rid of me for a while! There were a hundred moments during this year, from Orta onward, when I felt that you were "paying too high a price" for friendship with me. I have already obtained far too much from *your* Roman discovery (I mean Lou)—and it always seemed to me, especially in Leipzig, that you had a right to be rather taciturn toward me.

Think of me, dearest friend, as kindly as possible, and ask Lou to do the same. I belong to you both with my most heartfelt feelings—I believe I can show this more through my absence than by being near.

All nearness makes one so exacting—and I am, in the last analysis, an extremely exacting man.

From time to time we shall see each other again, shall we not? Do not forget that, *from this year on*, I have suddenly become poor in love and consequently very much in need of love.

Write me *precise details* of whatever concerns us now—of what has "come between us," as you say.

All my love   Your   F. N.

107 · *To Heinrich von Stein*[75]   [Santa Margherita] Beginning of December 1882

But, my dear Dr. von Stein, you could not have answered me more pleasantly than you have done—by sending your manuscript. That was a lucky co-

74. This was a *Singspiel* by Gast. The title is the same as that of the sixty-three verse epigrams which constitute the "Prelude" to *Die fröhliche Wissenschaft*.

75. On Heinrich von Stein, see note 42 to No. 127.

incidence! And there should always be just such a good omen at first meetings.

Yes, you are a poet. I feel the emotions, their changes, not least the
scenic arrangement—it is effective and credible (everything depends on
that!).

As for "language"—well, we shall discuss that when we meet one
day; that is not for a letter. Certainly you *read* too many books still, particularly German books! How can one possibly read a German book!

Ah, forgive me! I was doing that just now myself, and it made me
weep.

Wagner once told me that I wrote Latin, not German: which is quite
true—and sounds good to my ear. I can after all have only a share in German
things, no more than that. Consider my name: my forebears were Polish
aristocrats—even my grandfather's mother was Polish.[76] Well, I regard it
as a virtue to be half-German, and I claim to know more about the *art* of
language than is *possible* for Germans. So here, too—until we meet again!

As for "the hero"—I do not think so highly of him as you do. All
the same, it is the most acceptable form of human existence, particularly
when one has no other choice.

One gets to love something, and one has hardly begun to love it
profoundly when the tyrant in us (which we are all too ready to call our
"higher self") says, "Sacrifice precisely *that* to me." And we surrender it
too—but that is cruelty to animals and being roasted over a slow fire. What
you are dealing with are problems of cruelty, nothing more or less—does this
give you gratification? I tell you frankly that I have in myself too much of
this "tragic" complexion to be able not to *curse* it; my experiences, great and
small, always take the same course. What I desire most, then, is a high point
from which I can see the tragic problem lying *beneath* me. I would like to
take away from human existence some of its heartbreaking and cruel character. Yet, to be able to continue here, I would have to reveal to you what
I have never yet revealed to anyone—the task which confronts me, my

76. On N's ancestry, see M. Oehler's publications in *Jahresberichte der Stiftung
N-Archiv* (Weimar, 1937), under the heading "Berichte über die Gesellschaft der
Freunde des N-Archivs" (I have not had access to this source). N's forebears on his
father's side may well have come from Poland in the eighteenth century; but the claim
that they were aristocrats can have little weight, since poor country gentry, and even
peasants, had in those days titles which meant next to nothing. The Polish "aristocrat"
of the early eighteenth century was a far cry from the aristocrat of *virtù* who was N's
ideal. (For these suggestions, I am indebted to Czeslaw Milosz.) Hereafter, N consistently uses his supposed Polish ancestry as a standpoint from which to attack things German,
including the German in himself.

life's task. No, we may not speak of this. Or rather, being as we are, two very different persons, we may not even be silent together on *this* point.

Cordially and gratefully yours   F. Nietzsche

I am once more in my Genoa residence or near to it, more of a hermit than ever: Santa Margherita Ligure (Italia) (*poste restante*).

108 · *To Lou Salomé and Paul Rée* [*fragment*][77]

[Mid-December, 1882]

My dears, Lou and Rée:

Do not be upset by the outbreaks of my "megalomania" or of my "injured vanity"—and even if I should happen one day to take my life because of some passion or other, there would not be much to grieve about. What do my fantasies matter to you? (Even my truths mattered nothing to you till now.) Consider me, the two of you, as a semilunatic with a sore head who has been totally bewildered by long solitude.

To this, I think, *sensible* insight into the state of things I have come after taking a huge dose of opium—in desperation. But instead of losing my reason as a result, I seem at last to have *come* to reason. Incidentally, I was really ill for several weeks; and if I tell you that I have had twenty days of Orta weather here, I need say no more.

Friend Rée, ask Lou to forgive me everything—she will give me an opportunity to forgive her too. For till now I have not forgiven her.

It is harder to forgive one's friends than one's enemies.

Lou's "justification" occurs to me . . .

109 · *To Franz Overbeck*   [Postmarked Rapallo, December 25, 1882]

Dear friend:

Perhaps you never received my last letter? This last *morsel of life* was the hardest I have yet had to chew, and it is still possible that I shall *choke* on it. I have suffered from the humiliating and tormenting memories of this sum-

---

77. This fragment is one of the first signs of the repercussions from Elisabeth's scheming and gossip against Lou and Rée.

mer as from a bout of madness—what I indicated in Basel and in my last letter concealed the most essential thing. It involves a tension between opposing passions which I cannot cope with. This is to say, I am exerting every ounce of my self-mastery; but I have lived in solitude too long and fed too long off my "own fat," so that I am now being broken, as no other man could be, on the wheel of my own passions. If only I could sleep!—but the strongest doses of my sedative help me as little as my six to eight hours of daily walking.

Unless I discover the alchemical trick of turning this—muck into gold, I am lost. Here I have the most splendid chance to prove that for me "all experiences are useful, all days holy and all people divine"!!!

All people divine.

My lack of confidence is now immense—everything I hear makes me feel that people despise me. For example, a recent letter from Rohde. I could swear that if we had *not* happened to have earlier friendly relations, he would now pronounce the most contemptuous judgments on me and my aims.

Yesterday I also broke off all correspondence with my mother; I could not stand it any more, and it would have been better if I had not stood it for as long as I have. Meanwhile, *how* far the hostile judgments of my relatives have been spread abroad and are ruining my reputation—well, I would still rather know than suffer this uncertainty.

My relation to Lou is in the last agonizing throes—at least that is what I think today. Later—if there will be any "later"—I shall say something about that too. Pity, my dear friend, is a kind of hell—whatever the Schopenhauerians may say.

I am not asking you, "What shall I do?" Several times I thought of renting a room in Basel, of visiting you now and then, and attending lectures. Several times too I thought of the opposite: to press on in my solitude and renunciation, till I reach the point of no return, and—

Well, let that be as it may! Dear friend, you with your admirable and sensible wife, you two are practically my last foothold on firm ground. Strange!

May you flourish!   Your F. N.

IV

1883-89

Zarathustra;
Transvaluation
of
Values;
Turin

IV · 1883–89: Zarathustra; Transvaluation of Values; Turin

1883

January: writes *Zarathustra I*. February: "My whole life has crumbled under my gaze: this whole eerie, deliberately secluded life, which takes a step every six years...." February 13: death of Wagner in Venice. March: "I no longer see why I should live for another six months—everything is boring, painful, *dégoûtant*." To Malwida: "I am ... the Antichrist." Contemplates spending the next winter in Barcelona. May 4 to June 16: in Rome with Malwida von Meysenbug and Elisabeth, reconciliation. Writing: *Zarathustra II*. June 24: arrives in Sils Maria. Renewed rupture with Elisabeth over her persistent slandering of Lou and Rée. Publication of *Zarathustra I*. Plans (abandoned) for lecturing in Leipzig. September: in Naumburg. Sister is officially engaged to Bernhard Förster, Wagnerite anti-Semitic schoolmaster. October (?): publication of *Zarathustra II*; visits Overbeck. Return to Genoa. End of November: via Villafranca (Villefranche) to Nizza (Nice). Winter 1883–84: conversations with Julius Paneth, from Vienna.

1884

January 18: finishes *Zarathustra III* (published *ca.* end of April): "the terrific exuberant daring of this whole mariner's tale." In Nice until April 20. April 21 to June 12: in Venice with Gast. June 15 to July 2: visits Overbeck in Basel and falls ill. July 12–15: in Zürich, visits Meta von Salis and Resa von Schirnhofer. July 16 to *ca.* September 25: in Sils Maria. Conversations with Frl. Mansurov, once a pupil of Chopin's. August 26–28: visit from Heinrich von Stein. October: in Zürich with Elisabeth (reconciliation again). Meets Gottfried Keller. Friedrich Hégar arranges special private performance of the overture to Gast's opera *Der Löwe von Venedig*. November: in Mentone (Menton); writing *Zarathustra IV*. Beginning of December: arrives in Nice. Letter to Carl Fuchs on *Tristan*, rhythms of *décadence*.

1885

Private printing of *Zarathustra IV*. "R. Wagner's music ... How horrid I find this cloudy, sticky, above all histrionic and pretentious music. As horrid as . . . for example Schopenhauer's philosophy." Reading: St. Augustine, *Confessions*. Contemplates spending summer in a Roman monastery. April 10 to June 6: in Venice with Gast. May 22: marriage of Elisabeth and Bernhard Förster. June 7 to middle of September: in Sils Maria. Writing: *Jenseits von Gut und Böse*. Mid-September: to Naumburg, with some short stays in Leipzig (till end of November). Publication of Rée's *Entstehung des Gewissens* and Lou's *Im Kampf um Gott*. Beginning of November: visits Reinhart and Irene von Seydlitz in Munich. Mid-November: to Nice. Christmas Day walk to Cap St. Jean.

1886

Writing: *Jenseits von Gut und Böse* and prefaces to new editions of earlier books (appearing 1886–87). Sister and husband leave for Paraguay. May: a week alone in Venice, then for a short stay to Munich. Mid-May until June 27: in Naumburg and Leipzig. His mother reads him Keller's *Das Sinngedicht*. Last meeting with Rohde in Leipzig. Also meets Gast there and hears his septet. End of June: in Chur. July to September 25: in Sils Maria. Printing of *Jenseits von Gut und Böse*. Companionship with the Fynns, Helen Zimmern, and Frl. Mansurov. September: laudatory reviews of *Jenseits von Gut und Böse*, by J. V. Widmann. October: letter from Taine. Travels to Genoa and Ruta. October 22: in Nice. Massive work on systematizing his philosophy.

1887

January: hears at Monte Carlo the *Parsifal* prelude and is profoundly impressed. Epictetus read as proto-pseudo-philosopher ("country-parson") of Christianity: "It is all Plato's fault. He is still Europe's greatest misfortune." Reading: Dostoevski (*L'esprit souterrain*); also Renan's *Origines de la Chrétienté* and Sybel on the French Revolution. "Present-day Germany . . . represents the most stupid, broken-down, bogus form of *Geist* there has ever been." February 23–24: earthquake in Nice. May: Lou Salomé announces her engagement to Friedrich Carl Andreas. April–June: travels to Cannobio, Zürich, Ammden, Chur, Lenzerheide. June 12 to September 19: in Sils Maria. Particularly bad health and depression: "Effects like those of a severe psychological disease." July 7: writes to Hippolyte Taine. July 10–30: writes *Zur Genealogie der Moral* (published September?). Death of Heinrich von Stein. Meta von Salis and her friend Frl. Kym spend several weeks at Sils Maria. September: visit from Deussen and his wife. September 20: visits the Fynns at Menaggio on Lago di Como.

October 22: in Nice. Gast's orchestration of his "Hymn to Life" is printed. Interest in eighteenth-century Italian and French music (Gluck,

Piccini) : reading Abbé Galiani; also the Goncourt brothers' *Journal* (vol. 2).
November 26: letter from Georg Brandes. Renewal of friendship with Gers-
dorff (correspondence sporadic since 1877). Last letter (*à propos* Taine) to
Rohde. Mother sends natron-carbon smokeless stove. Letter to Gast on
Rousseau *versus* Voltaire.

1888

Letter to Seydlitz: "I am alone now . . . in . . . my relentless underground
struggle against everything that human beings till now have revered and
loved." Discovery of Baudelaire and Wagner as kindred spirits. Writing:
Der Fall Wagner (published October). Leaves Nice on April 2 and travels
via Genoa to Turin.

April 5 to June 5: first period in Turin. Hears of Brandes's lectures
on him in Copenhagen. Gast accepts appointment as music-tutor in the von
Krause household in Berlin. May: reading French translation of the "Laws
of Manu" (*Mānava Dharmaśāstra*). June 6 to September 20: in Sils Maria.
Health very bad. Renewed reading of Stendhal. Deussen sends anonymous
gift of 2,000 marks, to help with printing expenses; Meta von Salis gives
1,000 francs for the same. Visit from Deussen. Writing: *Götzen-Dämmerung*
(published January 1889). Conversations with Karl von Holten on Wagner
and Riesmann. Letters to Fuchs on classical and "barbarous" metric.
September 21: returns to Turin. Writing: *Der Antichrist*—"the first book
of the transvaluation of values." October: writing *Ecce Homo*. "I am now
the most grateful man in the world . . . it is my great harvest-time." Sudden
return of physical health. November: rupture with Malwida von Meysenbug
over Wagner. Writing: *Nietzsche contra Wagner*. Contemplates spending
winter in Bastia on Corsica. Laudatory reviews of *Der Fall Wagner* by Gast
and Carl Spitteler. Reading: Strindberg's *Les mariés* and *Le père*. Frequent
attendance at concerts. End of November–December 7: first exchange of
letters with Strindberg—question of criminal genius (Prado, Chambige).

Fails to find French translator for *Ecce Homo* (finally sent to printer
on December 8). "Occasionally nowadays I see no reason why I should
accelerate the tragic catastrophe of my life, which begins with *Ecce* . . . I
never write a sentence now in which the whole of me is not present."
"Since the old God has abdicated, I shall rule the world from now on." "I
am treated here as a little prince . . . my peddler-woman . . . will not rest
until she has found the sweetest of all her grapes for me." Corrects proofs
of *Der Antichrist*. December 31: beginning of breakdown. Messages to
Umberto, King of Italy, the House of Hohenzollern, and to the Vatican
State Secretary.

1889

January 3: collapse in the Piazza Carlo Alberto. January 4: last postcards to Gast, Brandes, Overbeck, Burckhardt, Cosima Wagner. January 5: writes last letter to Burckhardt. January 8: Overbeck arrives in Turin. January 9–10: N is brought back to Basel by Overbeck and Miescher and taken to the Psychiatric Clinic. January 13: N's mother arrives in Basel. January 17: N travels with his mother from Basel to the Jena Psychiatric Clinic.

110· *To Franz Overbeck*   [Received on February 11, 1883, from Rapallo]

Dear friend:

I have received the money; and once again I thought what unpleasant troubles I have been giving you all these years.[1] Perhaps it will not be for much longer now.

I will not conceal it from you, I am in a bad way. It is night all around me again; I feel as if the lightning had flashed—I was for a short time completely in my element and in my light. And now it has passed. I think I shall inevitably go to pieces, unless something happens—I have no idea *what*. Perhaps someone will drag me out of Europe—I, with my physical style of thinking, now see myself as the victim of a terrestrial and climatic disturbance, to which Europe is exposed. How can I help having an extra sense organ and a new, terrible source of suffering! Even to think thus brings relief—it saves me from accusing people of causing my misery. Though I *could* do this! And all too often I *do* do it. Everything that I have indicated to you in my letters is only by the way—I have to bear such a *manifold* burden of tormenting and horrible memories!

Not for a moment have I been able to forget, for instance, that my mother called me a disgrace to my dead father.[2]

I shall say nothing of other examples—but the barrel of a revolver is for me now a source of relatively pleasant thoughts.

My whole life has crumbled under my gaze: this whole eerie, deliberately secluded secret life, which takes a step every six years, and actual-

1. It was Overbeck who sent N the installments of his annual pension from Basel University.

2. Original: "dass mich meine Mutter eine Schande für das Grab meines Vaters gennant hat." This would have wounded N, on his almost permanent "quest for the father," in a most vulnerable spot.

ly wants nothing but the taking of this step,[3] while everything else, all my human relationships, have to do with a mask of me and I must perpetually be the victim of living a completely hidden life. I have always been exposed to the cruelest coincidences—or, rather, it is I who have always turned all coincidence into cruelty.

This book, about which I wrote to you, the work of ten days, now seems to me like my last will and testament.[4] It contains an image of myself in the sharpest focus, as I am, *once* I have thrown off my whole burden. It is poetry, and not a collection of aphorisms.

I am afraid of Rome,[5] and cannot decide. Who knows what torture is waiting for me there! So I have set about making myself my own copyist.

What can I do under this sky and with this changing weather! Ah, this fearfulness! And at the same time I know that, relatively, "it is for the best" by the sea!

With the warmest thanks, wishing you and your dear wife all the best,

F. N.

111 · *To Peter Gast*   Rapallo, February 19, 1883

Dear friend:

Each of your last letters was like a blessing for me; I thank you for this with all my heart.

This winter was the worst in my life; and I regard myself as the victim of a disturbance in *nature*. The old Europe of the Great Flood will kill me yet; but perhaps somebody will come to my aid and drag me off to the plateaus of Mexico. Alone, I could not undertake such travels: my eyes and other things forbid it.

3. The (roughly) six-year phases would be 1864–69 (student years at Bonn and Leipzig); 1869–76 (Basel professorship, Wagner, the break with Wagner); 1876–82 ("Freigeisterei," Lou); 1883–89 follows—from Zarathustra to the breakdown. This letter, by a curious coincidence, was written about four days before Wagner's death on February 13 in Venice.

4. *Also sprach Zarathustra, I* (the first sketches date back to August, 1881, in Sils Maria).

5. In a letter to Overbeck, dated February 22, N wrote that his sister was expected in Rome—presumably at Malwida von Meysenbug's. He was in Rome himself from May 4 to June 16. During this time he wrote the second part of *Zarathustra;* and his sister patched up their quarrel—until the new rift in relations which occurred in the late summer of 1883.

The enormous burden which lies on me as a result of the weather (even Etna is beginning to erupt!) has transformed itself into thoughts and feelings whose pressure in me was *terrible;* and from the sudden *shedding* of this burden, as a result of ten absolutely clear and fresh January days, my "Zarathustra" came into being, the most *liberated* of all my productions. Teubner is already printing it; I made the fair copy myself. Incidentally, Schmeitzner reports that during the past year *all* my writings have sold better, and I am hearing all sorts of things in the way of growing interest. Even a member of the Reichstag and Bismarck supporter (Delbrück) is said to have expressed his displeasure that I do not live in *Berlin* but in Santa Margherita![6]

Forgive this gossip—you know what other matters are now on my mind and in my heart. I was *violently* ill for several days, and my landlord and his wife were most concerned. Now I am all right again, and even think that Wagner's death brought me the greatest relief I could have had.[7] It was hard to be for six years the opponent of a man whom one has admired above all others, and I am not built coarsely enough for *that*. Eventually, it was the old Wagner against whom I had to defend myself; as for the real Wagner, I shall be in good measure his heir (as I often used to tell Malwida). Last summer I felt that he had taken away from me all the people in Germany worth influencing, and that he was beginning to draw them into the confused and desolate malignancy of his old age.

Naturally, I have written to Cosima.

As for your remarks about Lou, they gave me a good laugh. Do you think then that my taste in *this* differs from yours? No, absolutely not! But in this case it has damned little to do with "charming or not charming"; the question was whether a human being of real stature should perish or not.

Can I send you the proofs again, my old helpful friend? Many thanks for everything.

F. N.

6. Hans Delbrück (1848–1929) was Treitschke's successor to the chair of history at Berlin. An early arch-conservative ("For the emperor, against the Pope, against federalism, against parliamentarism, and against capitalism"), he became, after the turn of the century, more liberal in outlook, and was throughout his active life a severe critic of unethical practices in politics, especially as regards policy on minorities (e.g., the Poles). His biography has been written by Annelise Thimme.

7. Wagner had died in Venice on February 13. Not the least of N's torments during the winter (the "tormenting memories" [of the summer]; No. 110) would have been his fear of ridicule from the Wagner circle following the Lou episode. His sister's machinations must have made him suspect that he had been mistaken in Lou and that his most secret thoughts, divulged to her in Tautenburg, might have been misconstrued and mockingly blabbed about by her in all the capitals of Europe—cf. his fear for his "reputation" in No. 109.

112 · *To Franz Overbeck*   [Postmarked Rapallo, February
                                22, 1883]

Dear friend:

Things are very bad indeed. My health is back where it was three years ago. Everything is kaput, my stomach so much so that it even refuses the sedatives—in consequence of which I have sleepless, terribly tormented nights and, a further consequence, a profound nervousness. Ah, nature has outfitted me terribly well to be a self-tormentor! Of course, from outside it looks as if I am leading a most reasonable life. But my imagination *et hoc genus omne* of mind are stronger than my reason.

As for Rome, I wrote off to them yesterday; I do not want to speak to anybody just now. Also I have heard deviously that my sister is expected in Rome, and that she is going there via Venice.

On Saturday I am moving to Genoa; my address hereafter is (*please do not give it to anyone*): Genova (Italia), Salita delle Battestine 8 (interno 6).

I mean to find my health by the same means as before, in complete seclusion. My mistake last year was to give up solitude. Through ceaseless contact with intellectual images and processes I have become so sensitive that contact with present-day people makes me suffer and forgo incredibly much; eventually this makes me hard and unjust—in brief, it does not suit me.

Wagner was by far the *fullest* human being I have known, and in *this* respect I have had to forgo a great deal for six years. But something like a deadly offense came between us; and something terrible could have happened if he had lived longer.

Lou is by far the *shrewdest* human being I have known. *But* and so on and so on.

My *Zarathustra* will be getting printed now.

I wrote to Cosima as soon as I could—that is to say, after some of the worst days in bed that I have ever spent.

No! *This* life! And I am the advocate of life!

As soon as the time of year allows, I mean to go into the mountains, the southern slopes of Mont Blanc.

Nothing helps; I must help myself, or I am finished.

How is your health and your dear wife's?

                                        Your friend   F. N.

113 · *To Franz Overbeck*   [Received March 24, 1883, from
                                    Genoa]

My dear friend:

I feel as if you had not written to me for a long time. But perhaps I am
wrong; the days are so long I do not know any more what to do with a
day—I have no "interests" at all. Deep down, a motionless black melancholy. And fatigue. Mostly in bed—that is the best thing for my health.
I had become very thin—people were amazed; now I have found a good
trattoria, and will feed myself up again. But the worst thing is: I no longer
see *why* I should live for another six months—everything is boring, painful,
dégoûtant. I forgo and suffer too much, and have come to comprehend,
beyond all comprehension, the deficiency, the mistakes, and the real disasters
of my whole past intellectual life. It is too late to make things good now;
I shall never do anything that is good any more. What is the point of doing
anything?

This reminds me of my latest folly—I mean *Zarathustra*[8] (can you
read my handwriting? I am writing like a pig). Every few days I forget it;
I am curious to know if it has any merit; this winter I am incapable of making a judgment, and could be most crassly wrong either way. Incidentally, I
have heard and seen nothing of it: maximum speed was my stipulation for the
printing. Only my general fatigue has stopped me, day by day, from telegraphing to cancel the whole printing; I have been waiting more than four
weeks for the proofs—it is rude to treat me like this. But who nowadays is
polite to me? So I let it pass.

Winter this year has dragged on—one month extra or two. Otherwise I would be able to think of going soon into the mountains and trying the
mountain air. Genoa is *not* the right place for me; that is what Dr. Breiting
says.

I have not been for a single walk. I sweat at night. The daily headaches are less severe, but they still come regularly.

Recently I visited the Liebermeisters in the Hotel de Gênes; they are
in Santa Margherita now.[9]

I hope that you and your dear wife are happy; your life is certainly
not a failure—I think of it with pleasure.

                                    Your friend   F. N.

8. Still the *first* part of *Also sprach Zarathustra*.

9. Karl Liebermeister was a professor in the medical school at Basel University.

114. *To Malwida von Meysenbug*

[Genoa, end of March, 1883]

Verehrte Freundin:

In the meantime I have taken my decisive step—everything is in order. To give you some idea what it is about, I enclose a letter from my *first* "reader" —my excellent Venetian friend, who is once again my assistant with the printing.[10]

I am leaving Genoa as soon as possible and going into the mountains —*this* year I do not want to talk to anybody.

Do you want to know a new name for me? The language of the church *has* one—I am . . . the *Antichrist.*

Let us not forget how to laugh!

In all devotion, your   F. Nietzsche

Genova, Salita delle Battistine 8, interno 4.

115. *To Peter Gast*   Genoa, April 6, 1883

Dear friend:

As I read your letter, a shudder ran through me. If you are right, then my life would not be a mistake? And least of all precisely now, when I was thinking it most?

On the other hand, your letter gave me the feeling that I now have not long to live—and that would be right and just. You would not believe, dear friend, what an abundance of suffering life has unloaded upon me, at all times, from *early* childhood on. But I am a soldier—and this soldier, in the end, did become the father of Zarathustra! This paternity was his hope; I think that you will now sense the meaning of the verse addressing Sanctus

10. The letter enclosed must have been from Peter Gast, who was living in Venice. The "end of March" date for this letter to Malwida is not accurate if the Gast letter in question is one dated April 2 which Gast wrote on receipt of the first proofs of *Zarathustra I.* In this letter, Gast wrote gushingly on N's new work as one whose circulation should surpass that of the Bible. "There is nothing like it—because the aims which you indicate have never been, could never be, given to mankind before now" (cf. *Briefe und Berichte*, p. 292).

Januarius: "You who with the flaming spear split the ice of my soul and make it thunder down now to the sea of its highest hope."[11]

Also the meaning of the heading "Incipit tragœdia."

Enough of that. Perhaps I have never in my life known greater joy than that which your letter brought.

Now give me some advice. Overbeck is worried about me (you must trust him also as regards *Zarathustra*), and recently he suggested that I should return to Basel, not to the university but perhaps as a teacher at the Pädagogium again (he suggests that I should be a "teacher of German"). This shows good and fine feelings on his part—it even almost tempts me; my reasons against it are reasons of weather and wind and so on. Overbeck thinks that there would be "openings," were I to agree; people remember me kindly, and, to tell the truth, I was not the worst of teachers. My eyes and my incapacity for long stretches of headwork should be taken into consideration, likewise the proximity of Jakob Burckhardt, in whose company I really do feel happy and well. This summer I mean to write a few prefaces to new impressions of my earlier writings: not that there is a prospect of new editions, but simply to get done in good time what has to be done. I would also very much like to clean up and clarify the style of my older writings; but that can only be done within certain limits.

How is the Apulian shepherd's dance coming?

It disgusts me to think of *Zarathustra* going into the world as a piece of literary entertainment; who will be serious enough for it! If I had the authority of the "later Wagner," things would be better. But now nobody can save me from being cast among the writers of belles lettres. Hell!

Devotedly and gratefully, Your friend Nietzsche

116· *To Carl von Gersdorff*   Sils Maria [June 28, 1883][12]

My dear old friend Gersdorff:

I have meanwhile learned that you have had a great sorrow—the loss of your mother. When I heard this, it was a real comfort to know that you were not

11. The first four of eight lines of verse preceding the "Sanctus Januarius" section (book 4) of *Die fröhliche Wissenschaft* (the section is dated January, 1882, and N set great store by it, as the record of "crossing a tropic"; cf. No. 104; also No. 101).

12. N had arrived at Sils Maria on June 24. From May 4 to June 16 he had been in Rome, where there was a reconciliation (later much regretted) between him and his sister; they had traveled north together as far as Como.

alone in life, and I remembered the warm and grateful words in which you spoke of your wife when you last wrote to me. We have had a *hard* time of it in our youth, you and I—for various reasons; but it would be beautiful and right if, in the years of our manhood, some gentleness and comfort and heartening experiences came our way.

As for me, I have a long, difficult period of intellectual asceticism behind me, which I took upon myself willingly and which not everyone might have expected of himself. The past six years have been in *this* respect the years of my greatest self-conquest—which is leaving out of account my rising above such matters as health, solitude, incomprehension, and execration. Enough—I have risen also *above* this stage of my life—and what remains of life (little, I think!) must now give complete and full expression to that for which I have endured life at all.[13] The time for silence is *past:* my *Zarathustra,* which will be sent to you during the next few weeks, may show you *how* high my will has flown.[14] Do not be deceived by this little book's having a legendary air: behind all the plain and strange words stand my *deepest seriousness* and my *whole philosophy.* It is the beginning of my disclosure of myself—not more! I know *quite* well that there is nobody alive who would do anything the way this *Zarathustra* is—[15]

Dear old friend, I am now in the Upper Engadin again, for the *third* time, and again I feel that here and nowhere else is my real home and breeding ground. Ah, how much there is still hidden in me waiting to be expressed in words and form! There is no limit to the quiet, the altitude, the solitude I need around me in order to hear my inner voices.

I would like to have enough money to build a sort of ideal dog kennel around me—I mean, a timber house with two rooms, and it would be on a peninsula which runs out into the Sils lake and on which there used to be a Roman fort. For in the long run I cannot go on living in these farmhouses, as I have done till now; the rooms are too low and cramped, and there is

13. Original: "was jetzt noch vom Leben übrig ist (wenig, wie ich glaube!), soll nun ganz und voll das zum Ausdruck bringen, um dessentwillen ich überhaupt das Leben ausgehalten habe."

14. Publication of *Zarathustra I* had been delayed, to N's great annoyance, by the printing of 500,000 hymn books. He had sent advance copies, with letters enclosed, in May and June to Karl Hillebrand, Jakob Burckhardt, and Gottfried Keller. The printing of *Zarathustra II* was also held up in August and September while Schmeitzner was traveling on anti-Semitic business. On July 10 N wrote his sister a furious letter, threatening to break with Schmeitzner unless she could get him to start setting the book at once. Elisabeth tended to take Schmeitzner's side—Bernhard Förster, soon to be her husband, was one of the anti-Semites whom Schmeitzner published. Relations between N and Schmeitzner were just as bad again in 1885.

15. Original: "das niemand lebt, der so etwas machen könnte, wie dieser Zarathustra ist—."

always some disturbance or other. The people of Sils Maria think very kind-ly of me, and *I* like them. I eat in the Hotel Edelweiss, a very excellent inn, alone, of course, and at a price which is not entirely out of keeping with my small means. I have brought a large basket of books up with me, and the next three months are taken care of. Here *my* muses live: in "The Wanderer and His Shadow" I was already saying that this region was "blood kin to me and even more than that."

Well, I have told you something of your old friend, the hermit Nietzsche—a dream I had last night prompted me to do so.

Be well disposed and loyal to me!—we are old comrades and have shared much!

Your   Friedrich Nietzsche

117 · *To Franz Overbeck*   [Summer, 1883, from Sils Maria]

My dear friend Overbeck:

I would like to write you a few forthright words, just as I did recently to your dear wife. I have an *aim*, which compels me to go on living and for the sake of which I *must* cope with even the most painful matters.[16] *Without this aim* I would take things much more lightly—that is, I would stop living. And it was not only this past winter that anyone seeing and understanding my condition from close at hand would have had the *right* to say: "Make it easier for yourself! Die!"; in previous times, too, in the terrible years of physical suffering, it was the same with me. Even my Genoese years are a long, long chain of self-conquests for the sake of that aim and not to the taste of any human being that I know. So, dear friend, the "tyrant in me," the inexorable tyrant, *wills* that I conquer this time too (as regards physical torments, their duration, intensity, and variety, I can count myself among the most experienced and tested of people; is it my lot that I should be equal-ly so experienced and tested in the torments of the soul?). And to be con-sistent with my way of thinking and my latest philosophy, I must even have an absolute victory—that is, the transformation of experience into gold and use of the highest order.

Meanwhile I am still the incarnate wrestling match, so that your dear wife's recent requests made me feel as if someone were asking old Laocoön to set about it and vanquish his serpents.

16. This letter to Overbeck is evidently connected with the resurgence of hostility between N and his sister, brought about by her continued slandering of Lou. See also No. 118.

My relatives and I—we are too different. The precaution I took against receiving any letters from them last winter cannot be maintained any more (I am not hard enough for that). But every contemptuous word that is written against Rée or Frl. Salomé makes my heart bleed; it seems I am not made to be anyone's enemy (whereas my sister recently wrote that I should be in good spirits, that this was a "brisk and jolly war").[17]

I have used the strongest means I know to take my mind off it, and in particular have determined on the most intense and difficult personal productiveness. (In the meantime, I have finished the sketch of a "Morality for Moralists.") Ah, friend, I am certainly a cunning old moralist of praxis and self-mastery; I have neglected as little in this area as, for instance, last winter when treating my own nervous fever. But I have no support from *outside;* on the contrary, everything seems to conspire to keep me imprisoned in my abyss—last winter's terrible weather, the like of which the Genoese coast had never seen, and now again this cold, gloomy, rainy summer.

But the danger is extreme. My nature is all too concentrated, and whatever strikes me moves straight to my center. The misfortune of last year is only as great as it is in proportion to the aim and purpose which dominates me; I was, and have become, terribly doubtful about my right to set myself such an aim—the sense of my weakness overcame me at just the moment when everything, everything should have given me courage!

Think of some way, dear friend Overbeck, in which I can take my mind off it absolutely! I think the strongest and extremest means are required—you cannot imagine how this madness rages in me, day and night.

That I should have thought and written this year my sunniest and serenest things, many miles above myself and my misery—this is really one of the most amazing and inexplicable things I know.

As far as I can estimate, I *need* to survive *through next year*—help me to *hold out* for another fifteen months.

17. See E. F. Podach, *The Madness of Nietzsche* (London and New York, Putnam, 1931), pp. 87–88, for an account of Elisabeth's campaign against Lou and Rée (Podach, *Nietzsches Zusammenbruch,* Heidelberg: Niels Kampmann, 1930, pp. 44–46) during 1883: "After she had prepared him . . . by 'lighting the candles,' he lent himself to a step which the break in his friendship alone would never have induced him to take: he wrote a wounding letter, in his sister's name as well as his own, to Lou Salomé's mother. His sister wrote to Rée's mother, and, to crown everything, N offended Rée's brother [Georg], whom he had met no more than casually in Leipzig. It is well known that the incident nearly led to a duel with pistols. . . . N felt himself being dragged into an abyss. He was overcome by the sense that he had been faithless to his true self" (translated by F. A. Voigt). To his sister he wrote (summer, 1883; Podach-Voigt, p. 88): "I never hated anyone till then, not even Wagner, whose perfidies went far beyond anything achieved by Lou [about which, by the way, he had only been informed by his sister]. It is only now that I feel truly humiliated."

If you can see any way of realizing your idea of a meeting in Schuls, just let me know—I am extremely grateful anyway for your suggesting it.[18]

Loyally,   Your Nietzsche

118 · To Malwida von Meysenbug

Sils Maria, Engadin, Switzerland,
August, 1883

Meine liebe hochverehrte Freundin:

Or is it impudent to call you this? One thing is certain—I have boundless confidence in you; and so it does not depend much on the words.

I have had, and am still having, a *bad* summer. The sorry tale of last year has started all over again; and I had to hear so much that has ruined for me this glorious solitude of nature and has practically turned it into a hell.[19] According to everything I have heard *now*—ah much too late!—these two people Rée and Lou are not worthy to lick my boots. Excuse this all too manly metaphor! It is a protracted misfortune that this R., a thorough liar and crawling slanderer, should have ever crossed my path. And for how long have I been patient and sympathetic with him! "He is a poor fellow, and one must drive him on"—how often have I told myself this whenever his impoverished and dishonest manner of thinking and living have disgusted me! I am not forgetting the annoyance I felt in 1876 when I heard that he would be coming with you to Sorrento. And this annoyance returned two years later—I was here in Sils Maria, and my sister's announcement that he would be coming made me *ill*. One ought to trust one's instincts more, even the instincts of revulsion. But Schopenhauer's "pity" has always been the *main* cause of trouble in my life—and therefore I have every reason to be well disposed toward moralities which attribute a few other motives to morality and do not try to reduce our whole human effectiveness to "fellow feelings." For this is not only a softness which any magnanimous Hellene would have laughed at—it is also a grave practical danger. One should *persist* in one's *own* ideal of *man*; one should impose one's ideal on one's fellow beings and on oneself overpoweringly, and thus exert a creative influence! But to do this, one has to keep a nice tight rein on one's sympathy, and treat anything that goes *against* our ideal (for instance, such low characters as L. and R.) as

18. They did meet, in August.

19. In June (?), 1884, N wrote to Malwida apologizing for the present letter; see the translation of the forgery and suppressed section of that June, 1884, letter—No. 125.

enemies. You will observe this is how I "read a moral lesson" to myself— but to attain this "wisdom" has almost cost me my life.

I should have spent the summer with you and in the noble circle of your friends—but now it is too late!

With the warmest devotion and gratitude   Nietzsche

119. *To Peter Gast*   Sils Maria, end of August, 1883

First, dear old friend, another reminiscence of the time when I was working, zealously enough, on Democritea and Epicurea—a world of research that is still not exhausted, even for classical philologists!

You know, the Herculaneum library, whose papyri are being slowly and laboriously made to talk, is the library of an Epicurean; so there *are* hopes for the discovery of authentic writings by Epicurus! Part of one has been deciphered, for example, by Gomperz (in the *Reports* of the Vienna Academy); it concerns "the freedom of the will" and (probably) shows that Epicurus was a violent opponent of fatalism but, at the same time, a *determinist*—which will please you!

(In those days I was studying the atomist doctrine up to the quartos of the Jesuit Boscovitch, who was the first man to demonstrate mathematically that, for the exact science of mechanics, the premise of *solid corporeal* atoms is an *unusable* hypothesis: an axiom which now has *canonical* validity among natural scientists trained in mathematics.[20] For research practices, it is neither here nor there).

Yesterday the page proofs of *Zarathustra II* arrived from Naumann; on reading them I found four misprints. Apart from that, the book is nice and tidy. I do not yet have an objective impression of the whole thing; yet I feel that it presents a not insignificant *victory* over the "spirit of gravity," considering *how* difficult it is to present the problems in it. That the first part comprises a circle of feelings which *forms a basis* for the circle of feelings in the second part, this seems to me easily recognizable and a "good job of work" (to talk like a carpenter). Aside from that, I have all the difficulties and the worst difficulties still before me.

To give a fairly accurate estimate of the whole architecture, there will be just about as much again—roughly two hundred pages. If I can achieve this, as I *seem* to have achieved the first two parts (despite terrible feelings of hostility that I have toward the whole Zarathustra configuration),

20. See note 47 to No. 94.

then I shall give a party and die of delight in the midst of the festivities. Excuse me!

Probably I would, from artistic motives, have chosen darker and more somber and garish colors for the first two parts, if I had kept my soul serene and bright this year—for the sake of what happens at the end. But this year the solace of more serene and airy colors was *vitally* important to me; and so in the second part I have cavorted about like a clowning acrobat almost. The detail contains an incredible amount of personal experience and suffering which is intelligible only to me—there were some pages which seemed to me to drip with blood.

It is for me a most enigmatic fact that I really could do both parts this year. A figure that occurs in practically all my writings—"risen superior to oneself"—has become reality. O, if only you knew what *this in itself* means! You think a hundred times too well of me, friend Gast!

[no signature]

120 · *To Franz Overbeck*   [From Sils Maria, received
                                                         August 28, 1883]

(This letter is for you alone.)
Dear friend:

Leaving you threw me back into the deepest melancholy, and during the whole return journey I was possessed by evil, black feelings; among them there was a real hatred of my sister, who has cheated me of the success of my best acts of self-conquest for a whole year, by keeping silent at the wrong times and by speaking at the wrong times, so that I have finally become the victim of a relentless desire for vengeance, precisely when my inmost thinking has renounced all schemes of vengeance and punishment. This conflict is bringing me step by step closer to *madness*[21]—I feel this in the most frightening way—and I hardly think that a journey to Naumburg would lessen this danger. Quite the opposite—this might give rise to dreadful moments; and also that long-developing hatred could break out in word and deed, and *I* would be the one to come off worst. Then too, letters to my sister are not advisable now—except the most harmless ones (recently I sent her one letter full of amusing verses). Perhaps my reconciliation with her

21. *N's footnote:* Could *you* perhaps impress this strongly on my sister? *Note:* There exists a letter (dated beginning of August, 1883) in which N thanks Elisabeth for being so considerate, and claims that Rée had behaved far worse than Lou in the affair. Schlechta regards this as a forgery of Elisabeth's.

was the most fatal step in the whole affair—I *now* see that this made her
believe she was entitled to take revenge on Fräulein Salomé.²² Excuse me!
After we had agreed on the dubiousness of the Leipzig plan, it did
me good to receive a letter from Heinze which has put an end to the whole
thing—which was an act of desperation on my part.²³ I enclose the letter,
also the first public statement on *Zarathustra I;* strange to relate, the letter
was written in a prison. What pleases me is to see that this first reader has
at once felt what it is all about: the long-promised Antichrist. There has
not been since Voltaire such an outrageous attack on Christianity—and, to
tell the truth, even Voltaire had no idea that one could attack it in *this* way.
As for *Zarathustra II,* Köselitz writes: "Z. is most impressive; but it
would be audacious for me to say anything about it: it knocked me over.
I am still floored."
You see!
In the meantime, during our time together my old school friend Krug
tried to pay me a visit (he is "Director of the Royal Railways Administra-
tion in Cologne," it says on his visiting card).
Köselitz's letter contains remarks on *Epicurus* (an earlier one concerned *Seneca*) which show an incomparably profound and human grasp of
this philosophy; he indicates that he has "personal philologists,"²⁴ whom he
herds into the library to find what there is of Epicurus in the patristic writers
and other pen pushers.
What a blessing it was to have you and your warm confidence so
close at hand for once! And how well we understand and understood one
another! May your more stable good sense be and remain a prop to my now
precariously balanced head!

Cordially, your friend   Nietzsche

121 · *To Erwin Rohde*   [Nice, February 22, 1884]²⁵

My dear old friend:

I do not know why, but when I read your last letter, and particularly when
I saw the charming picture of your child, it was as if you pressed my hand

22. Refers to the reconciliation in Rome, May, 1883.

23. N had been planning to give a lecture in Leipzig in the autumn, as a pre-
liminary to teaching at Leipzig University for not less than four semesters. This plan was
part of a broader scheme to exert more influence on intellectual circles in Germany.

24. Original: "Leibphilologen," analogous to "Leibarzt," the personal physician
of a monarch.

25. In September, N had been to Naumburg, where his mother and sister had
pestered him to return to university teaching and had accused him of consorting with

and looked at me sadly—sadly, as if you wanted to say: "How is it possible that we have so little in common and live as in different worlds! And yet once—"

And that is how it is, friend, with all the people I love: everything is *over*, it is the past, forbearance; we still meet, we talk, so as not to be silent; we still exchange letters, so as not to be silent. But the look in the eyes tells the truth: and this look tells me (I hear it often enough!), "Friend Nietzsche, you are completely alone now!"

And that is really where I have arrived.

Meanwhile I go my way; actually it is a journey, a sea journey—and not for nothing have I lived for years in the city of Columbus.

My *Zarathustra* is finished, in its three acts: you have the first. I hope to be able to send you the other two in four or six weeks.[26] It is a sort of

---

people who were "not nice." In September too, his sister became engaged to Bernhard Förster, schoolmaster, Wagnerite, and anti-Semitic propagandist. Early in October, N spent a few days with Overbeck in Basel, and then went to Genoa. At the end of November he moved to Nice, then an Italian town (Nizza). On February 1 he was complaining to Gast of his sister's "maltreating" him with anti-Semitic letters. Her anti-Semitism then and thereafter was most painful to him—"the reason for a radical break between me and my sister," as he wrote to Overbeck on April 2, 1884.

N's appearance and bearing at this period, winter, 1883–84, were described by Dr. Julius Paneth, a young Viennese-Jewish zoologist who visited him in Nice: "He was unusually friendly, and there is not a trace of false pathos or any pose of the prophet about him, despite what I had feared from his latest works; his manner is, on the contrary, innocuous and natural, and we began quite a banal conversation about climate, accommodation, and such things. Then he told me, but without the slightest affectation, and quite un-self-consciously, that he always felt he had a mission and that now, as far as his eyes would allow it, he wanted to work out what was in him. [. . .] You would probably be just as amazed as I by his appearance—there is nothing *schwärmerisch* or put-on about it. He has an unusually clean-cut and high forehead, neat brown hair, cloudy deep-set eyes—as might be expected from his being half blind—bushy eyebrows, a fairly full-cheeked face, and an immense mustache, otherwise clean-shaven" [describing a visit on December 26, 1883]. "He said that he had the capacity for seeing images when he closed his eyes, very vivid ones, which would keep changing; physical discomforts made these images become ugly ones. Also that this proved his imagination was restlessly active, with only a fraction of it coming into consciousness. And that he wanted to write some musical compositions [. . .] to go with his writings. For he could say some things in music which could not be expressed in words. . . . We spent six hours in excited conversation; N seemed very lively and not at all tired. Everything he said was put very simply and gently. His behavior is thoroughly natural and unassuming, serious and dignified; he is most responsive to humor, and a smile suits his features very well" [describing a visit on January 3, 1884]. "N shows many contradictions, but he is a profoundly sincere man with an immense strength of will and endeavor" [visit of January 29]. (*Briefe und Berichte*, pp. 335–37.)

26. N had finished *Zarathustra III* on Friday, January 18, according to a letter which Overbeck received on January 26. N wrote to Overbeck, "The last two weeks have been the happiest ones in my life: I have never sailed with such sails across such a sea, and the terrific, exuberant daring of this whole mariner's tale, which has been going on for as long as you have known me, since 1870, reached its climax" (*Briefe und Berichte*, p. 329).

abyss of the future—something to make one shudder, especially the joy in it. Everything in it is my own, without model, kindred, precursor; a person who has lived in it will return to the world seeing things differently. But I must not speak of this. From you, however, as a *homo literatus*, I will not keep back a confession—it is my theory that with this *Z* I have brought the German language to a state of perfection. After *Luther* and Goethe, a third step had to be taken—look and see, old chum of mine, if vigor, flexibility, and euphony have ever consorted so well in our language. Read Goethe after reading a page of my book—and you will feel that that "undulatory" quality peculiar to Goethe as a draftsman was not foreign to the shaper of language also.[27] My line is superior to his in strength and manliness, without becoming, as Luther's did, loutish. My style is a dance—a play of symmetries of every kind, and an overleaping and mockery of these symmetries. This enters the very vowels.

Forgive me! I shall take care not to confess this to anyone else, but you did once (I think you are alone in this) express delight in my language.

In any case I have remained a poet, in the most radical sense of the word—although I have tyrannized myself a great deal with the antithesis of poetry.

Ah, friend, what a crazy, silent life I live! So alone, alone! So "child"-less.

Think of me with affection, as I truly do of you.

Your   F. N.

122 · *To Franz Overbeck*   [Nice, April 7, 1884] Monday

Very many thanks, my dear friend! Your Mickiewicz reference also came opportunely: I am ashamed to know so little about the *Poles* (who, after all, are really my "ancestors"!)—how much I would like to find a writer who goes with Chopin and does me good in the way that Chopin does! Some *very* precise information about Lipiner recently came my way: outwardly a "successful man."[28] In other respects the typical *present-day* obscurantist, has had himself baptized, is an anti-Semite, *pious* (not long ago he made a vicious attack on Gottfried Keller, and accused him of lacking "true Chris-

---

27. Original: "auch dem Sprachbildner nicht fremd blieb." The construction allows either Goethe or N to be intended as the "language shaper" in question. It is a curiously oblique piece of self-congratulation. Goethe as "draftsman" refers to Goethe's drawings.

28. Siegfried Lipiner, the Viennese writer, was mentioned in No. 79 (postscript).

tianity and faith"!). Lipiner is said to be the ruin of all the young people who come under his influence—he drives them into "mysticism" and makes them contemptuous of scientific thinking—a man whose intentions on the side are purely "practical," who exploits the "signs of the times." My information comes from a Viennese natural scientist who has known him since he was a child.[29]

I have no news about Schmeitzner. The question is most awkward for me, for I thought I would have a good opportunity to do a real service to my *mother* and so improve things between us somewhat, and then this anti-Semitism gets under my feet again![30]

Very soon now I shall be leaving Nice: I mean to wait until the first copies of my *Zarath.* arrive. I hope they will come, but there could be a month's delay again, as there was last year. I anticipate, *confidentially*, Schmeitzner's going bankrupt. Then what will happen to our books!

Next winter is fairly certainly taken care of: possibly the same house and the same room. Perhaps I shall succeed in forming my own society here, in which I shall not be entirely the "recluse." The climate of the *littoral provençal* suits my nature marvelously well; I could only have put the finishing touch to my *Zarathustra* on this coast, in the homeland of the "gaya scienza." Lanzky (a poet, by the way) is already determined to come; I would like to persuade Köselitz, perhaps Dr. Rée and Frl. Salomé too, with whom I would like to right certain wrongs that my sister has done.[31] I have had news of both of them, and pleasing news too (they are in Meran). Frl. S. is said to be publishing something this spring on "religious emotions" —it was I who discovered this theme in her, and I am extraordinarily pleased that my Tautenburg efforts should be bearing fruit after all.

My company this winter was provided by the people staying in the house in which I live: an old Prussian general with his daughter, in all practical things my adviser; an American parson's elderly wife, who translated from the English for me about two hours a day; recently Albert Köchlin and his wife (from Lörrach) have been extremely kind to me. At

29. His source would have been Julius Paneth. In conversation with Paneth, N observed this opportunism in Wagner too: "He then talked of Wagner, and said that Wagner had gone through all the variations of the general mood of the time but had always been a few years ahead of everyone else. When he had known Wagner, Christianity had only been talked of ironically [an allusion to *Parsifal*]. . . . Wagner had always wanted to be enthusiastic about Bismarck, but had not managed it—he had been jealous of Bismarck" [visit of March 26]. (*Briefe und Berichte*, pp. 337–38.)

30. N had wanted Schmeitzner to turn over to his mother the royalties accumulated from his writings until April 1. His postcard of April 2 to Overbeck suggests that Schmeitzner's anti-Semitic propaganda was using up not only his (Schmeitzner's) time but also the income from his (including N's) publications.

31. Paul Lanzky was a German writer living at Vallombrosa, near Venice.

the moment I have a visitor, for about ten days, from Zürich, a girl student; you will find this amusing—it does me good, quietens me somewhat, after the "great surgings" inside me during the last months. She is a friend of Irma von Regner-Bleileben; she and Frl. Salomé seem to be mutual admirers; she is also *very intimate* with Countess Dönhoff and her mother, naturally with Malwida too, so that we have enough personal things in common. Yesterday we went to a Spanish bullfight together.[32]

Heavens! I am starting to receive a pretty odd type of letter—this kind of adulatory style was introduced among the German youth by Richard Wagner; and what I long ago prophesied is now beginning—my becoming in some ways Wagner's heir.

The last few months I have been reading "world history," with great delight although with some horrifying results. Have I ever shown you the letter from Jakob Burckhardt which pushed me headfirst into "world history?"

If I get to Sils Maria in the summer, I mean to set about revising my metaphysical and epistemological views. I must now proceed step by step through a series of disciplines, for I have decided to spend the next five years on an elaboration of my "philosophy," the portico of which I have built in my *Zarathustra*.

On reading the *Morgenröte* and *Fröhliche Wissenschaft*, I happened to find that hardly a line there does not serve as introduction, preparation, and commentary to the aforesaid *Zarathustra*. It is a *fact* that I did the commentary *before* writing the *text*.

How are Emerson and your dear wife?

Your friend   N.

How is it you say nothing about your health?

123 · *To Franz Overbeck*   Venice, San Canciano calle nuova
                                   5256 [received on May 2, 1884][33]

My dear friend Overbeck:

It is at root *very* wonderful that we have not been estranged from one another during these last years, and not even, it seems, by *Zarathustra*. That I would be *alone* by the time I was about forty—about this, I have never had any illusions; and I know another thing too—that many bad things will be

32. The girl was Resa von Schirnhofer.
33. N stayed with Gast in Venice from April 21 to June 12.

still coming my way; I shall soon discover the price one has to pay, to use the foolish and false language of the *ambitiosi*, for *"reaching after the highest garlands."*

Meanwhile I shall use and exploit the situation I have seized: I am now, very probably, *the most independent man in Europe*. My aims and tasks are more embracing than anyone else's; and what I call grand politics gives at least a good standpoint and bird's-eye view for things of the present.

As regards all practical matters in life, I ask you, my loyal and proven friend, to guarantee me hereafter one thing—precisely the greatest possible independence and freedom from personal considerations. I think you know what Zarathustra's warning, "Be hard!" means in my own case. My idea that justice should be done to every particular person, and that I should in the last analysis treat precisely what is most hostile to me with the greatest gentleness, is disproportionately developed and involves danger upon danger, not only for me but also for my task: it is *here* that the hardening is necessary and, with a view to educating others, an occasional cruelty.

Sorry! It does not always sound good when one talks of oneself, also it does not always smell good.

With my health, it seems that I am over the hill. I shall spend the winters in Nice; for the summer I need a city which has a big library and where I can live incognito (I thought of Stuttgart—what do you think?).

This year I am still thinking of going to Sils Maria, where my book basket is—on the assumption that I shall know better than last year how to defend myself against interferences from my sister. She has really become a very malicious person; a letter full of the most poisonous imputations about my character, which I received from her in January, a nice companion piece to her letter to Frau Rée, has made me see this clearly enough—she must go to Paraguay.[34] For my part, I mean to break off relations with everyone

34. Not figurative. She did go to Paraguay with her husband, and they founded the Nueva Germania colony there (later, Bernhard Förster embezzled money raised for the colonists and committed suicide when questions began to be asked). Cf. N's letter, or draft of a letter, to his mother (probably written in February, 1884): "My sister, incidentally, is a wretched creature; this is the sixth time in two years that she has broken in on my most sacred feelings, feelings such as have hardly existed on earth, with a letter that smells most meanly of the Human All-Too-Human. [. . .] In Rome, and in Naumburg too, I marvelled that she so seldom says anything that does not go against my grain. [. . .] After every letter I am indignant over the dirty, libellous manner in which my sister speaks of Fräulein Salomé." Cf. also the letter, or draft, to his sister (spring, 1884): "Must I go on doing penance for having become reconciled with you? I am thoroughly tired of your pretentious moral chatter. [. . .] And this much is certain, that you and no one else have endangered my life three times in one twelve-months. [. . .]" (Quoted in F. A. Voigt's translation, slightly emended, from E. F. Podach, *The Madness of Nietzsche*, pp. 94–95. These letters or drafts were first published by J. Hofmiller in 1909 in 'N und seine Schwester,' in *Süddeutsche Monatshefte*, Vol. 6, Heft 2 [Munich]).

who sides with my sister; from now on, there can be no half-measures for me.

Here I am staying in Köselitz's house, in the peace and quiet of Venice, and am listening to music which is itself in many ways a sort of ideal Venice. But he is making progress, toward a more virile art: the *new* overture to the *Matrimonio* is bright, precise, and fiery.

Your friend   N.

124 · *To Franz Overbeck*   Venice, May 21, 1884

Dear friend:

My latest letter troubled you more than I would have liked: altogether I write very foolish letters. I must put an end to this business with my relatives—for two years I have been wearing myself out with the most good-natured efforts to put things right and to put their minds at rest, but in vain. As far as I know, moreover, this sort of incompatibility is the normal thing for men of my rank. It is bad enough for me to realize—at last! I must say—that nearly all my still existing relationships suffer from, and have been made absurd by, an irreparable fault at the root. Ultimately, though, my real *distress* lies elsewhere and not in my consciousness of this absurdity: a distress so great and deep that I am always asking if any man has ever suffered so. Who, indeed, feels as I do what it means to feel with every fiber of one's being that "the weights of all things must be decided anew." That from this situation, in the twinkling of an eye, all kinds of physical danger, prison and suchlike, could arise is the least important thing; or rather, it would comfort me if things were to go that far. I require so much from myself that I am ungrateful vis-à-vis the best work that I have done till now; and if I do not go to such an extreme that whole millennia will make their loftiest vows in my name, then in my own eyes I shall have achieved nothing. Meanwhile, I do not have a single disciple.

Onward! Let's talk of other things.

It was high time for me to come to Venice; for our maestro can hardly be persuaded to leave the place, and he thinks he really need do no more than write a score now and then. He hardly considers performance and performability, and in retrospect I realize how important it was that I summoned him to Leipzig in the fall eighteen months ago—even though it seemed at first to have been pointless. But it was not pointless; if he had not gone there, he would have spent another two years writing *impossible* music. I showed him at once that his "plan" with the Milanese firm of Lucca was just as impractical as his Venetian one, proving it with the firm's letter, which was an unconditional no. Also that his music, meanwhile, is impossible for Italians, and would, moreover, offend their piety toward their Cimarosa. In short, there was a revolution in *all sorts of ways*, including the libretto—Finali's—and many questions of form, which concern the music's effect. To summarize the result, look at this theater advertisement:

The Lion of Venice
Comic Opera in Five Acts by Peter Gast

Probable first performance in Dresden toward Christmas. Wasn't that well done?

In *general*, everything is going excellently with him, even amazingly well—I mean, as far as the development of his powers is concerned; and if, step by step, he can purge himself of the vestiges of *petty* taste, the Saxon-Chinese hypertrophy of good-naturedness and suchlike, then we shall live to see the birth of a new classical music, which will be *entitled* to summon up the spirits of *Greek* heroes. Meanwhile, he has given Venice a monument with the aforenamed work; and it is possible that twenty enchanting melodies from it will one day blend with the name and idea of "Venice." Here I have a fine opportunity for preaching my esthetic morality, and truly not to deaf ears! One must liberate R. W.'s great cause from his personal defects, defects which became converted into principles; in this sense I mean to lay hand, gladly, on *his* works and to prove, retrospectively, that we did not come together merely by "accident."

I welcome with joy your speaking of the "mystical separatists"; recently I was telling Köselitz that no "German culture" exists or ever has existed—except among mystical hermits, Beethoven and Goethe *very much* included!

Your friend and your wife's
Nietzsche

Note: The following letter is one of Elisabeth's forgeries. The text used is from *Gesammelte Briefe, Bd. V* (Leipzig, 1907), reprinted in *Briefe und Berichte* (Leipzig, 1932, ed. A. Baeumler, pp. 345–46).

125 · *To Elisabeth Nietzsche*   Venice, mid-June, 1884

Dear sister:

Our mother writes that you were so possessed with the third part of *Zarathustra* and could find no words to express your thanks for the gift. You must have received it long ago—at least I long ago instructed the publisher to send it. But it is not the sort of gift for which one can express thanks without more ado—I require the reader to relearn his most cherished and respected feelings, and much *more* than relearn them! Who knows how many generations must pass before people will come who can feel the whole depth of what I have done! And even then I am frightened by the thought of what unqualified and unsuitable people may invoke my authority one day. Yet that is the torment of every great teacher of mankind: he knows that, given the circumstances and the accidents, he *can* become a disaster as well as a blessing to mankind.

This being so, I myself will do everything I can to avoid encouraging all too crude misunderstandings; and now that I have built the portico to my philosophy, I must start working tirelessly until the main edifice also stands finished before me. People who understand only the language of ambition may say of me that I reach only for the *highest garland* that mankind has to give. Well then!

Thus the scaffolding for my main edifice must be erected this summer; or, in other words, during the coming months I mean to draw up the outline of my philosophy and the plan for the next six years. May my health last out for this!

Your brother

What reasons are there for believing this to be a forgery? One might have thought that there were internal stylistic ones. It contains some of the phrases which N used in his letter that Overbeck received on May 2 (No. 123): for example, the "portico" figure, the "highest garlands" cliché ("nach den höchsten Kronen" in the letter to Overbeck; "nach der höchsten Krone," singular, in this letter). The "ambitiosi" phrase in the letter to Overbeck ("die dumme und falsche Sprache der *ambitiosi*") is ironic, cosmopolitan, urbane; in the forgery, its parallel, "die Sprache der Ambition," is an owlish banality. The letter has a flat perfunctory tone, which Elisabeth might not have been able to avoid though it would not have been to her advantage. The loss of irony would indicate that she was incapable of capturing any of the finer shadings of N's vocabulary and tone.

However, Overbeck was the one correspondent of N's who refused to let Elisabeth acquire his letters from N (other correspondents had less reason to suspect her motives in tracking down the letters). So she cannot have used his letter as a basis for her forgery.

In fact, what she did was to take a letter of N's to Malwida von Meysenbug, adapt the first third of it, and suppress the rest. The conjectural date of that letter is June, 1884. A copy of it was discovered, after Elisabeth's death, in her Nietzsche Archive by Karl Schlechta, who reprinted it in his critical apparatus to *Werke in drei Bänden*, 3: 1420–22. The phrases in question occur in this letter too; the loss of irony is probably due to N's attuning his language to Malwida's ear. The perfunctory tone is absent after the first third; the remainder of the letter shows what N really had on his mind. To this first third, Elisabeth added to her own typewritten copy the words "Lie̶be Schwester," plus an opening sentence of her own invention (which includes the word "erfüllt," translated as "possessed"—a thoroughly *schwärmerisch* locution), and the concluding paragraph ("Thus the scaffolding . . ."). This forgery is one of the (at least) thirty letters in *Gesammelte Briefe, Bd. 5* (five of them dated during 1888) which appear there addressed to Elisabeth but for which no corresponding manuscripts or typewritten originals addressed to her exist (see *Werke in drei Bänden*, 3: 1410–12). Elisabeth had given N a typewriter early in 1882; it was brought to N in Genoa by Paul Rée, through whose negligence it was damaged; it was eventually "cured" by N's doctor (see N's letter to Elisabeth of April 27, 1883). Elisabeth later typed her forgeries on the same machine.

The letter to Malwida (from Venice, San Canciano, calle nuova 5256, where N stayed with Gast from April 21 to June 12 1884), begins: "Meanwhile, *meine hochverehrte Freundin*, I hope you have received the last two parts of my *Zarathustra* [i.e., *Zarathustra II* and *III*]; at least, I long ago instructed the publisher to send them." Then follows the central section translated above, from "But it is not the sort of gift . . ." to "Well then!" The paragraph ending "Well then!" is followed by four more paragraphs, which I now translate. These are of interest on two counts: they show what Elisabeth wanted to suppress, in order to make out that N loved and trusted her as a kindred spirit who could transmit his ideas, and they reveal more of N's view of the Lou and Rée affair. Thus, he continued in his letter to Malwida:

But this solitude, ever since my earliest childhood! This secretiveness, even in the most intimate relationships! There can be no breaking it, even by kindness. Recently when Frl. von Schirnhofer visited me in Nice, I often thought of you with great gratitude, for I guessed that this was due to your kindness; and truly her visit came at the right time, and was a gay and useful one (especially since there was no conceited goose there—excuse me! I meant my sister). But by and large I do not believe there is anyone who could rid me of this deep-rooted feeling of being alone. I have never found anyone to whom I could talk as I talk to myself. Forgive this kind of confession, *meine verehrte Freundin!*

I would like to know two things; first, where you are spending this summer; second, I need Liszt's address, the one in Rome (not for myself).

I am troubled about that *inhuman* letter which I sent you last summer;[35] this unspeakably nasty harrying had really made me ill. Meanwhile the situation has been changed by my radical break with my sister; for heaven's sake, do not think that you should mediate between us and reconcile us—there *can* be no reconciliation between a vindictive anti-Semitic goose and me. Beyond that, I am showing as much forbearance as possible, because I know what can be said to excuse my sister and what is at the back of her (to me) so despicable and undignified behavior—love. It is essential that she should leave for Paraguay as soon as possible. Later, very much later, she will come to realize how much her ceaseless filthy suspicions

35. Refers to No. 118.

about my character (it has been going on for two years!) have damaged the most decisive period in my life. Ultimately there remains for me the very uncomfortable task of righting the wrong that my sister has done Dr. Rée and Frl. Salomé (soon Frl. Salomé's first book will be appearing—on "religious emotion"—the very theme for which I discovered in Tautenburg her extraordinary talent and experience; it gladdens me that my efforts at that time should not have been entirely wasted). My sister reduces a rich and original creature like her to "lies and sensuality"—she sees in Dr. Rée and Frl. Salomé nothing but two "rotters"; it is of course against this that my sense of justice revolts, whatever good reasons I may have for thinking that the two of them have deeply offended me. It was very instructive for me that my sister, in the end, brought just the same blind suspicion to bear on me as on Frl. Salomé; only *then* did I realize that all the bad qualities which I had ascribed to Frl. S. went back to that squabble which occurred before I knew Frl. S. more closely—how much my sister must have misunderstood and added to what she heard then! She has no understanding of human beings at all—heaven forbid that one of Dr. Förster's enemies should ever get into a discussion with her about *him!*

Once more asking your forgiveness for bringing up this old story again! I wanted only to prevent you from having your own feelings influenced by that horrible letter which I wrote you last summer. Extraordinary people like Frl. Salomé deserve, especially when they are as young as she, to be treated with every consideration and sympathy. And even if I myself, for various reasons, am unable to *wish* for any new approach toward closer relations from her side, I shall nevertheless disregard all personal considerations in the event of her position becoming difficult and desperate. I now understand only too well, through this complicated experience, how easily my own life and destiny could come into the same disrepute as hers—deservedly *and* undeservedly, as always seems to be the case with such natures.

> With affection, devotion and gratitude   Nietzsche

126. *To Peter Gast*   Sils Maria, September 2, 1884[36]

Ultimately, *mein lieber verehrter Freund*—whatever unpleasant things may stand in our way—we two belong once and for all to the knightly brother-

---

36. N had reached Sils Maria on July 16, after having visited Resa von Schirnhofer and Meta von Salis in Zürich between July 12 and 15. He remained in Sils Maria until about September 25.

hood "of the *gaya scienza*" and can take deep comfort from this good year, which has shaken your *Lion* and my *Zarathustra* from one and the same tree.[37] The rest is—waiting, for you as for me.

For the future, I am nursing the hope that a small, extremely *good* society of this faith in the *gaya scienza* will take shape in Nice, and in my thoughts I have already dubbed you as the first knight, by way of consecrating that order. We ought to curse and swear "By the Mistral!"—I can think of no other duty, since among people like us everything "is understood."

At the moment I am being kept away from Nice by a double quarantine (that is, by twice seven days), and considering that the cholera will disappear only with the autumn rains—thus in about the second half of October, my longings are very much oscillating toward the north—more specifically, to Dresden. As soon as you yourself receive news of the "prospect of performance" (or even of the probability of this prospect), please send me a telegram. Here, without a stove, frozen through, with blue hands, I can hardly hold out much longer—unless I buy a stove.

Apart from that, I have practically finished the main tasks which I set myself for this summer; the next six years will be for working out a scheme which I have sketched for my "philosophy."[38] It has gone well and looks hopeful. *Zarathustra* has for the present the personal significance of being my book of "edifying and encouraging discourses"—beyond that, it is dark and hidden and ridiculous to everyone.

Heinrich von Stein,[39] a splendid person and man, in whom I have *rejoiced*, told me frankly that he understood "twelve sentences and no more" of *Zarathustra*. That pleased me very much.

Let me know about your translation.[40]

As for my health, it is uncertain; it was better in Venice, and still better in Nice. One good day in every ten—these are my statistics, the devil take them!

Nobody to read to me! Every evening melancholy in my low-ceilinged room, teeth chattering with cold, waiting three or four hours for permission *to go to bed!*

Today my best acquaintance of the summer is leaving me, my partner at table, Frl. von Mansurov, *dame d'honneur* to the empress of Russia—ah, we had so much to talk about, it is miserable that she is going away! Just

37. Refers to Gast's opera *Der Löwe von Venedig*.

38. Cf. the letter received by Overbeck on July 25: ". . . I am in the midst of my problems; my doctrine, that the world of good and evil is only a world of appearance and perspective, is such an innovation that I sometimes lose hearing and sight at the thought of it. . . ." *Jenseits von Gut und Böse* appeared in 1886; *Zur Genealogie der Moral*, in 1887.

39. See note 42 to No. 127.

40. Gast was translating the libretto of Cimarosa's *Matrimonio Segreto*.

think, an authentic Chopin pupil and full of love and admiration for this "arrogant and modest" man![41]

Sils Maria is first class as landscape—and hereafter too, as I have been told, because of the "hermit of Sils Maria."

You see—there I go again with a "first-class arrogation."

Loyally, your friend　Nietzsche

127. *To Heinrich von Stein*[42]　　Sils Maria, September 18, 1884

Dear Dr. von Stein:

A last greeting from Sils Maria, where it has become *very* autumnal—even the hermits are leaving.

Your visit was one of the three things for which I am deeply grateful to this *Zarathustra* year.

Perhaps *you* came off worse? Who knows—you may have come far too close to finding Philoctetes on his island—and even something of that belief of Philoctetes, "Without my arrow, Ilium will not be taken!"

In meetings like ours, much of consequence is always latent—much fatality. And believe one thing: from now on, you are one of the few people whose fate is involved, for good or ill, with mine.

Loyally yours,　　Nietzsche

N.B. In case you should need anything, here is my perennial address: Nizza, *poste restante.*

41. Meaning Chopin.

42. Heinrich von Stein (1857–87) had first written N toward the end of 1882, when he had sent him the manuscript of his *Helden und Welt*. He was a Wagnerite and an esthetician; in a letter to Overbeck, of September 14, 1884, N wrote of him: "At last, at last a new man, who belongs to me and instinctively respects me! Admittedly, at the moment too *wagnerisé*, but thanks to the rational discipline which he has acquired from being close to Dühring, very well prepared for me. In his presence I kept feeling most acutely what a *practical* task is contained in my life's work, if only I can possess enough young people of a very particular quality." Stein had promised to move to Nice as soon as his father died. From Berlin, however, he wrote a few months later inviting N to join him with two other friends of his own, in a discussion, by letter, about Wagner; they were to read and discuss articles in a Wagner encyclopedia. N now suspected that Stein might have been a Wagnerite decoy, commissioned to bring him back into the Wagner circle. In December, 1884, he wrote to Stein: "Do not let your love of Richard Wagner grow any less on my account. You must consider that I decline to be identified or compared with him—I am not for histrionics. . . ." During 1885, the relationship cooled; their last meeting was in the autumn of that year. Later, N said that he had only met three men whom he regarded as his peers: Rohde, Wagner, and Stein (see *Briefe und Berichte*, pp. 353–58).

128 · *To Franziska Nietzsche*   Zürich, October 4, 1884,
                                                        Pension Neptun

My dear mother:

In the meantime you will have had ample news that your children are now getting on nicely together again and are well and happy in every way.[43] But it cannot be said at the moment how long they will be together; the work which I plan requires solitude at all costs, and the clubfoot which I drag around with me—I mean my 104 kilos of books—will not let me fly too far away from here.

So it is impossible that *we* shall see each other again this year; I deeply hope that this will not upset you at all.

I welcome with gratitude the good intentions expressed in your last letter—that I should go about in the world somewhat more splendidly *dressed*; as a matter of fact, I am rather lacking in this regard, and, as a result of so many travels and changes, I am somewhat *too* scraped, like a mountain sheep.

My health gives me continuous trouble: a strange place and any food or daily routine to which I am not accustomed always maltreat me. But my appearance is good and not different from what it was last year.

With many thanks, Your   F.

129 · *To Carl Fuchs*   Nice, rue St. François de Paule 26,
                                                        II [Winter, 1884–85]

Werter und lieber Herr Doktor:

Believe me, even if I do not show it in writing (my eyes forbid this more every year), hardly anyone can be following your investigations and niceties with more sympathetic interest than I do. If *only* "sympathetic interest" were enough! But I lack knowledge and competence in all those areas where your remarkably various talent lies. Above all, years pass with nobody playing music for me, myself included. The last work I studied thoroughly

43. N spent most of October in Zürich, where he met his sister and they made up their quarrel (she married Förster on May 22, 1885; the departure for Paraguay could have encouraged N to bury the hatchet). In Zürich, N also met Gottfried Keller, whom he greatly admired; not surprisingly, nothing transpired between the new, self-appointed shaper of German prose and the almost septuagenarian master of Goethe's undulatory line. From mid-September until the end of November, N was in Naumburg; then he returned to Nice.

is Bizet's *Carmen*—and not without many thoughts, partly illicit ones, about all German music (which I judge in rather the same way as I judge all German philosophy); moreover, it is the music of an undiscovered genius, who loves the south as I do, and has the need for *melody* and the gift of melody in addition to the naïveté of the south. The deterioration of the melodic sense, of which I seem to catch a whiff at every contact with German musicians, the increasing attention to the *particular* gesture of emotion (I believe that you, my dear Dr. Fuchs, call it the "phrase"?), likewise the increase of skill in the performing of particulars in the *rhetorical* means of music, in the histrionic art of shaping the moment as convincingly as possible—these things, it seems to me, are not only compatible; they are also interdependent. That is bad enough! Everything good in this world has to be bought at rather *too high* a price! Wagner's expression "infinite melody" voices most sweetly the danger, the ruination of instinct and of good faith, of good conscience. Ambiguity in rhythm, the effect of which is that one does not know, and *should* not know, whether something is this way or that way round, is doubtless a technique which can procure wonderful effects— *Tristan* is full of it—but as symptom of an entire art, it is and remains the sign of dissolution. The part dominates the whole, phrase dominates melody, the moment dominates time (also the *tempo*), *pathos* dominates *ethos* (character, style, or whatever you want to call it); finally, even *esprit* dominates "sense." Forgive me! but what I think I can detect is a change in perspective; the particular is seen too sharply, the whole is seen too dully—and the *will* to this kind of optics is apparent in music, above all, the talent for it is there! But this is *décadence*, a word which, we agree, does not reject something but merely describes it. Your Riemann is a sign of this, likewise your Hans von Bülow, likewise yourself—you as the most subtle interpreter of needs and changes in the *anima musica* which, all in all, may ultimately be the best part of the *âme moderne.*[44] I am expressing myself damned badly—quite unlike you; what I mean is that, even in *décadence*, there is an immense number of qualities that are attractive, valuable, new, most admirable—our modern music, for example, also anyone who may be its true and brave apostle, like the three people just named. Forgive me if I add: decadent taste is furthest of all from one thing, and that is the *grand style:* which the Palazzo Pitti has, for example, but *not* the Ninth Symphony. The grand style is the most intense form of the art of melody.[45]

44. Hugo Riemann, the musicologist, had invented the word "Phrasierung" ("phrasing") and advocated the use of phrasing in musical scores. N mentions him as a creditable Wagnerite in *Der Fall Wagner*, section 11.

45. The views in this paragraph are developed in N's letter to Fuchs dated August 26, 1888; the analogy with visual-spatial art occurs in the July, 1877, letter (No. 76) as well as in the 1888 letter.

Finally, a word about a very big theoretical difference between us—
that is to say, as regards classical metric. Admittedly, I am hardly entitled
to talk about these matters any more, but I was entitled to in 1871, the year
I spent reading terrifying books on Greek and Latin metric, with a very
peculiar result. At that time I felt that I was the most sequestered metrician
among all classical philologists, for I demonstrated to my students that the
whole development of metrical theory from Bentley to Westphal was the
history of a fundamental error. I most vigorously resisted the idea that, for
example, a German hexameter had affinities to a Greek one. What I maintained was (to use the same example again) that a Greek reciting a Homeric
line used no accents other than the *word accents*—that the rhythmical interest
lay precisely in the *time quantities* and their relations and not, as with the
German hexameter, in the dum–di–di of the ictus [beat]—quite apart from
the fact that the German dactyl differs fundamentally from the Greek or
Latin dactyl in its time quantity. For we say "Pfingsten, das liebliche Fest,
war gekommen, es grünten und blühten ["Whitsun, the lovable feast, was
arriving, with leaf and with blossom"] with the feeling of ♩♪ | ♫ ♩ |,
perhaps even as triplets but certainly not solemnly in groups of twos[46] with
a long syllable having the duration of two short ones. What made the line
stand out from everyday speech in the ancient world was precisely the strict
observance of the duration of a syllable, which is not at all the case with us
northerners. For *us* it is hardly possible to feel our way into a purely quanti-
tative rhythmic pattern, because we are too accustomed to the emotional
rhythmic pattern of strong and weak beats, *crescendo* and *diminuendo*. But
Bentley (he is the great innovator; G. Hermann is only the next-comer), as
well as the German poets who thought they were imitating classical meters,
quite innocently made our kind of rhythmic sense seem to be the only one
and the "perennial" one—the rhythmic pattern per se—somewhat as we are
likely to regard our humane and sympathetic morality as *the* morality and to
project it into older, fundamentally different moralities. There can be no
doubt that our German poets "in classical meters" brought thereby into
poetry a variety of rhythmical interest which was missing from it (the tick-
tock of our rhyme poets is, in the long run, a terrible thing). But an in-
habitant of the ancient world would have heard none of *these* charms; even
less would he have thought that he was hearing *his* meters. The French more
easily understand the possibility of a purely time-quantitating metric: they
feel the count of the syllables as time. *Ecco*, the longest letter I have written
for years; accept it as such and also in every other sense as a sign that I do
not forget "the gratitude," *mein werter Herr Doktor*, you who have now

46. Original: "zweiteilig-feierlich."

treated me twice with specially select dishes. Where on earth did you acquire your talent *à causer en littérature?* is there any French blood in your veins? Finally, a word of anger about your publisher and printer. What! "Stitched"? Stitches which do not stitch!—*lucus a non lucendo.*[47] Pardon this joke from an old classical scholar and remember nevertheless kindly

Your most faithful Dr. Friedrich Nietzsche

formerly Professor of Classical Languages, including Metric

Read, I ask you, a book that few people know—St. Augustine's *De musica*—to see how people in those days understood and enjoyed Horace's meters, how they heard them "beat time," where they put the pauses, and so on (arsis and thesis are mere signs for the beats).

My address for all times is: Naumburg an der Saale. Everything is forwarded from there. I myself am a "fugitive and a vagabond on earth."

130 · *To Carl von Gersdorff*　　Nizza, pension de Genève, petite rue St. Etienne, February 12, 1885

My dear old friend:

I live such a sequestered life and see and hear no more of you. But this year I must, for family reasons, come to Germany again.[48] I think that we should, in anticipation of this, think out a little rendezvous, perhaps in Leipzig.

Today I want to give you, not without hesitation, some news which entails a question to you. There is a fourth (last) part to *Zarathustra*, a sort of sublime finale, which is not intended for the public (for me, the word "public," in connection with my whole *Zarathustra*, comes to sound rather like "whorehouse" and "strumpet"—forgive me!).[49] But this part should and must now be printed—twenty copies, for me and for distribution among my friends, and with every discretion. The expenses of such a printing (by C. G. Naumann, who printed the last parts) cannot be very high; but I am myself, owing to the great [—] of my publisher, as hard up as ever

47. Original: " 'Hefte'? Hefte, die nicht haften, die nicht geheftet sind!" "Heft" = "pamphlet"; "haften" = "fasten," "stick" (here "stitch," for lack of a word which is both verb and noun). The pamphlet sent by Fuchs must have fallen apart. N's word play is untranslatable.

48. In connection with Elisabeth's wedding; in the end, N did not go.

49. On his way back to Nice, where he arrived early in December, N had spent a few days in Menton (then Mentone), where he was already working on *Zarathustra IV*.

(that is to say, he owes me six thousand francs, and my attorney tells me that it would hardly be possible to bring a successful suit against him).[50] In other words, until my fortieth year, I have actually "earned" not a penny by my numerous writings—which is the humorous side (and, if you like, the proud side) of the whole thing.

More I will not say. Let me have, my dear old friend, as soon as possible, your answer to this, a frank answer (one can be as frank with me as with the "Lord God" himself—presuming there is such a one).

And, above all, let us be and remain in good spirits: there are a hundred reasons for being courageous in this life.

Your friend   Nietzsche

131 · *To Malwida von Meysenbug*

Nizza, Thursday, March 13, 1885

Verehrte Freundin:

Have you been wondering why I have stopped writing to you? I have been wondering about it too, but every time I began, I eventually put my pen down again. If I knew why, I would not wonder any more, but—I would perhaps be sad.

I have not been well the whole winter (I missed the dry air, thanks to this year's abnormal weather), and when your kind letter came I was very ill in bed. But that is an old story, and I had really had enough of writing letters about my health. "Help"—whoever could help me! I am by far my best doctor. And the positive side of it—that I can endure it and assert my will against so much resistance—is my proof for that.

Throughout the winter there was a German around me, who "holds me in reverence"—thank heaven he has gone! He bored me, and in our talks I was obliged to keep silent about so many things.[51] O the moral *tartufferie* of these blessed Germans! If only you could promise me an Abbé Galiani in Rome! There's a man for my taste—Stendhal too. As for music, I tested last autumn, conscientiously and curiously, how I *now* stand regarding R. Wagner's music. How horrid I find this cloudy, sticky—above all,

---

50. Dash indicates deletion (presumably by Elisabeth) from the original. Schmeitzner used two printers: Teubner and Naumann. Teubner had printed *Zarathustra I;* Naumann, the next two parts. Forty copies of *Zarathustra IV* were privately printed in 1885.

51. Paul Lanzky, on whom N had been counting for his "good society" or brotherhood of the *gaya scienza.*

histrionic and pretentious music! As horrid as—as—as a thousand things—for example, Schopenhauer's philosophy. It is the music of a musician and man who has gone astray—but of a *great actor*—I'll swear to it. But I applaud the brave and innocent music of my pupil and friend Peter Gast, an *authentic* musician; he will see to it that the actors and pseudo-geniuses will not ruin people's taste for much longer. Poor Stein! He even thinks that R. Wagner is a philosopher!

Why am I talking about *this?* It is only to give you some kind of example. It is the humor of my situation that I should be mistaken for the former Basel professor Dr. Friedrich Nietzsche. The devil take him! What has this fellow to do with me!

To be sure, *meine verehrte Freundin,* this letter is "between ourselves."

Do give me the address of that monastery! It could be that I should attempt to visit Rome sometime in the autumn, assuming that I can live there *incognito* and that nothing unnatural is imputed to my hermit's nature.[52]

You know, surely, how devoted I am to you?   Your   N.

I do not like this coast. I despise Nice, but in the winter it has the driest air in Europe.

132 · *To Franziska and Elisabeth Nietzsche*

Nice, March 31, 1885
Saturday

At last, my dears—that is to say, since an hour ago—I am in a position to tell you what my plans are for this spring. Zürich is no longer on the program, because of a sudden decision on the part of Herr Gast; this morning I heard from him that he *absolutely cannot* bear it there any longer and is on the way to *Venice.* But I do need to meet Herr G. now, for we have common plans; also, for the present state of my eyes, Venice is the best of places—enough; I am very pleased with this turn in events, which will spare me the journey to Zürich.

---

52. Malwida had told N of a monastery where he could stay in Rome. "Nothing unnatural" ("nichts Widernatürliches") would seem to be a mild joke at his own expense (as long as people do not think the hermit is queer). Sensing that this might be inappropriate in a letter to Malwida, N covers it over by the next sentence, which implies, "You will surely understand if I keep my distance from you, should I ever stay in this monastery." In effect, the question in the latter sentence is not very appropriate either: "wie sehr ich Ihnen zugetan bin?"

Herr Gast has the same troubles in Zürich as I once had in Basel (that means, for about ten years of my youth!) : the climate in these cities goes contrary to our *productive* powers, and this constant torment makes us ill. In this respect Basel was a *very great* misfortune for me, and I am still suffering from the terrible after-effects of that time (and shall never be rid of them).

One is thoroughly punished for one's ignorance; if I had, at the right moment, concerned myself with medical, climatic, and similar problems, instead of with Theognis and Diogenes Laertius, I would not be the half-ruined person that I am.

And thus one loses one's youth, and now one is past forty and still making the first experiments with what one does need and should have needed twenty years ago.

You will notice that I am once more in my more serene state of mind; the main reason for this is the departure of Herr Lanzky. A *very* estimable man and *very* devoted to me—but what do I care for either of these things! For me he means what I call "cloudy weather," "German weather," and the like. Really, there is nobody living about whom I care *much;* the people I like have been dead for a long long time—for example, the Abbé Galiani, or Henri Beyle, or Montaigne.

About my sister's future, I have my own thoughts—that is to say, I do not think it would be a good thing for Dr. Förster to return to Paraguay. Europe is not so small; and if one does not *want* to live in Germany (and in this I am like him), one still does not need to go so very far away. But of course I do not have his enthusiasm for "things German," and even less for keeping this "glorious" race *pure.* On the contrary, on the contrary—

Forgive me—you can see how serene I am. Perhaps we shall meet again this year. But *not* in Naumburg; you know that it does not suit me, and the place does not strike any chords in my heart; I was not "born" there and have never been "at home" there.

This winter Nice has for once been less bright and dry than usual. But I shall hardly be able to leave before the end of March.

With love, your F.

I forgot, my dear mother, to thank you for your letter which crossed with mine. It never for a moment occurred to me to "take" anything "badly"—on the contrary!

133 · *To Franz Overbeck*   [Nice, March 31, 1885]

Everything has arrived safely. Thank you, dear old friend, for all this trouble and care that you are taking on my account. You write nothing about your health and that of your wife. I take it as a good sign that you have borne this winter with better fortune than I have. For me there was much to overcome, many days of sickness. My eyes keep getting worse. Schiessen's medicines have not helped. Since last summer there has been a new development, which I do not understand—spots, blur, and watering too. I really ought not to stay in Nice again: the danger of being run over in the street is too great. Someone always had to serve me at table; I do not *want* to eat in company as long as the state persists.

Probably I shall spare myself the journey northward; the dangers and excitements of traveling alone have now become too great for me. Dr. Förster is back from Paraguay—great jubilation in Naumburg. Perhaps my sister's marriage will bring some benefit to me also; she will have much to do and will have somebody else whom she can trust completely and to whom she really *can* be useful, which two things were not always possible as far as concerns myself.

I have heard no news of the proceedings against Sch[meitzner]. Finally he had set himself a deadline for January 1, but, as before, he had passed it without so much as a murmur. Perhaps I can still manage to withdraw from him, and thus from the "public," the first three parts of my *Zarathustra*, which is what I want most of all.

Naturally I have not found a publisher for the fourth *Zarathustra*. Well, *I* am satisfied with it, and even enjoy it as a new stroke of fortune. What a lot of diffidence I always have had to overcome, in all my publications! If a man draws up the sum of a deep and hidden life, as I have been doing, then the result is meant for the eyes and consciences of only the most select people. Enough, *all in good time.* My desire for pupils and heirs makes me impatient now and then, and it has even, it seems, made me commit during recent years follies that were mortally dangerous. Eventually the immense gravity of my task always restores my equilibrium, and I know perfectly well what the foremost necessity is.

I have been reading, as relaxation, St. Augustine's *Confessions*, much regretting that you were not with me. O this old rhetorician! What falseness, what rolling of eyes! How I laughed! (for example, concerning the "theft" of his youth, basically an undergraduate story). What psychological falsity! (for example, when he talks about the death of his best friend, with whom he shared a *single soul*, he "resolved to go on living, so that in this way

his friend would not wholly die." Such things are revoltingly dishonest).
Philosophical value zero! *vulgarized* Platonism—that is to say, a way of
thinking which was invented for the highest aristocracy of soul, and which he
adjusted to suit slave natures. Moreover, one sees into the guts of Christianity in this book. I make my observations with the curiosity of a radical
physician and physiologist.

The sudden disappearance of our "relapsed" musician, who flum-
moxed me too with a postcard, made me angry. It is no use—I must go to
Venice again, as last year, and see what the matter really is. After all, we
must be fair; for years he has been leading an undignified dog's life as a
music copyist—it is not surprising that he should for once run wild in a way!
The copying of immense scores, the making of piano scores, during the productive years of a productive man's life, when something quite different was
needed, is a misery to me. Richard Wagner never had such a bad time, and
even Herr Bungert uses other musicians and copyists for such purposes. He
has no money—*voilà tout!* And therefore this "Lion of Venice" *must* first
publicly roar. And I want to do what I can to help.

I laughed about Frl. von Salis's precautions. That belongs among the
subtleties of the *agents provocateurs*; she wanted exactly what she achieved—a
refusal—in order to make capital for "agitation."[53]

Friendly greetings to yourself and your dear wife; as ever

Yours   F. N.

Nice, March 31, 1885

134. *To Elisabeth Nietzsche*   Venice, May 20, 1884[54]

My dear Lama:

On the decisive day in your life (and the day on which nobody could wish
you happiness and prosperity and good omens and good spirits more than
I do)—on this day I must draw up a sort of account of my life.[55] From now
on, your mind and heart will be, first and foremost, taken up with quite
other things than your brother's concerns, and that is right and good—and
likewise it is natural that you will more and more come to share your husband's way of thinking—which is not my way at all, whatever I may find

53. She had asked to be admitted to Jakob Burckhardt's lectures at Basel;
Burckhardt strongly supported the request at a regents' meeting on March 19, but it was
voted down. No women were admitted to university lectures at that time.

54. N stayed with Gast in Venice from April 10 to June 6.

55. Elisabeth married Bernhard Förster on May 22.

in it to honor and applaud. So that you may in the future have a kind of indication as to how far your brother's judgment will require from you much prudence and perhaps also forbearance, I am describing for you today, as a sign of great affection, the bad and difficult nature of my situation. I have found until now, from earliest childhood, *nobody* who had the same needs of heart and conscience as myself. This compels me still today, as at all times, to present myself, as best I can, and often with a lot of bad feeling, among one or another of the sorts of human being who are permitted and understandable nowadays. But that one can only really grow among people of *like mind* and like will is for me an axiom of belief (even down to diet and the body's demands); that I have no such person is my misfortune. My university existence was a wearisome attempt to adapt to a false milieu; my approach to Wagner was the same—only in the opposite direction. Almost all my human relationships have resulted from attacks of a feeling of isolation: Overbeck, as well as Rée and Malwida—I have been ridiculously happy if ever I found, or thought I had found, in someone a little patch or corner of common concern. My mind is burdened with a thousand shaming memories of such weak moments, in which I absolutely could not endure solitude any more. Not omitting my illness, which always discourages me in the most horrifying way; I have not been so profoundly ill for nothing, and am ill on the average now still—that is, depressed—as I say, simply because I was lacking the right milieu and I always had to playact somewhat instead of refreshing myself in people. I do not for that reason consider myself in the least a secret or furtive or mistrustful person; quite the reverse! *If I was that, I would not suffer so much!* But one cannot just simply communicate, however much one wants to; one has to find the person to whom communication can be made. The feeling that there is about me something very remote and alien, that my words have other colors than the same words from other people, that with me there is much multicolored foreground, which is deceptive —precisely this feeling, of which testimony has lately been reaching me from various sides, is nevertheless the subtlest degree of "understanding" that I have till now found. Everything I have written hitherto is foreground; for me the real thing begins only with the dashes. I am dealing with the most dangerous matters; that I commend the Germans between times, in a popular manner, to Schopenhauer or Wagner or think up Zarathustra—these things are for me recreation but, above all, hiding places, behind which I can sit down again for a while.

Do not therefore think me mad, my dear Lama, and especially forgive me for not coming to your wedding—such a "sick" philosopher would be a bad person to give away the bride! With a thousand affectionate good wishes,

Your F.

135. *To Franziska Nietzsche*   [Venice, end of May, 1885]

My dear good mother:

I have been feeling, all this time, much as you have; the whole thing went through me like a knife. And because your son has bad health, he was ill; this spring is one of the most melancholy in my life. I lack distractions and sympathetic people. On the wedding day, I had the good luck to go on an excursion to the Lido with a Basel family known to me from Nice; it was a real relief to be compelled to talk with people who were kindly disposed and halfway strange to me.

Perhaps everything has turned out just as it should be; also the two of us (I mean Dr. Förster and myself) have behaved correctly and with a very good will toward one another. But it is a dangerous situation, and we must be a bit careful; for my personal taste, such an agitator is an impossible person to have more intimate dealings with. He probably feels the same; he wrote to me in his latest letter, "I venture to doubt if a personal relationship before our departure would leave us enduring satisfaction." You understand.

I do *not* understand the shaping of his future, and for my own part I am too aristocratically inclined to be legally and socially on the same footing as twenty farming families, as he states in his program. In such circumstances, the person with the strongest will and the best intelligence comes out on top; for these two qualities in particular, German men of learning are badly prepared. The vegetarian diet, which Dr. Förster requires, makes such natures even more susceptible to irritation and gloom. Just look at the "meat-eating" English—till now, that was the race which knew best how to found colonies. *Phlegm* and roast beef—that was till now the receipe for such "undertakings."

I still do not know what I shall do this summer. Probably my old Sils Maria, even though I have horrible memories of all my stays there. I was always ill, had none of the food which I really needed, was immensely bored, owing to lack of eyesight and people—and was always in a sort of despair when September came. This time I have invited an old lady who lives in Zürich; I have still not heard from her about it. The young ladies—at least all the ones who sprout around Malwida von Meysenbug—are not to my taste; and I have lost all desire to seek my entertainment there. I would even prefer the company of German professors; at least they have *learned* something solid and honest, and consequently one can learn something from them.

My eyes get worse every day, and, unless someone comes along and helps me, I shall probably be blind by the year's end. So I shall decide not to read and write at all—but one cannot stick it out when one is completely alone.

Love as ever,   Your son

N.B. It always vexes me that my foolish health and your Naumburg and house do not get on with each other. It would be no small comfort for me if you could be with me.

Venezia (Italia) (poste restante)

136· *To Peter Gast*   Sils Maria, July 23, 1885[56]

Dear friend:

I could have taken a bet on it, that you yourself would reply to your own "cry of distress" letter in *this* way, as today's postcard shows—to my *great* joy, I happily confess. Only too well do I know from my own experience as a letter writer the phenomenon I call "answering oneself," also that one can be committing a foolish mistake, and an impropriety too, if, as the recipient of a letter, one intrudes with a quick avowal of sympathy upon this natural "resolution" (restoring of personal sovereignty). Ecco! Spoken like a pedant! but felt as a friend, believe me!

Yesterday I noted, in order to fortify myself along the course that I am taking through life, a quantity of traits by which I detect "distinction" or "nobility" in people—and, vice versa, what pertains to the "rabble" in us. (In all my states of sickness I feel, with horror, a sort of downward pull toward the weakness of the rabble, the gentlenesses of the rabble, even the virtues of the rabble—do you understand this? You picture of health!) It is distinguished to give a steadfast impression of frivolity, which masks a stoic hardness and self-control. It is distinguished to go slowly, in every respect, also to have the slow-paced eye. It is difficult for us to wonder at things. There are not many valuable things; and these come to us of their own accord, and *want* to come to us. It is distinguished to avoid small honors and to distrust anyone who is quick to praise. It is distinguished to doubt the communicability of the heart; solitude is distinguished—not chosen but given. To be convinced that one has duties only to one's equals, and acts toward others as one thinks fit; to feel always that one is a person who has honors to give, and seldom concedes that another has honors to give that are meant

56. N was at Sils Maria from June 7 until mid-September.

for us; to live almost always in disguise, to travel *incognito*, as it were[57]—
so as to spare oneself much shame; to be capable of *otium* [idleness], and not
only be busy as a chicken—clucking, laying an egg, clucking again, and so
on. And so on! Old friend, I am taxing your patience, and you can certainly
guess what pleases me and delights me in your life and what I would like to
see more and more firmly *underlined*.

Your idea about Herr Widemann[58] I welcome *most* warmly; send him
a copy[59] in a way that will show *my* sympathetic interest in him, as a sort of
congratulation on the completion of his work. I do not know it, but what
you indicate about "equilibriums" and the "indestructibility of force" belongs also among my articles of faith. Yet we have Dühring against us; by a
coincidence I have just found this fine sentence: "The aboriginal state of the
universe, or—more precisely—that of a changeless state of material being
entailing no temporal accretion of differences, is a question to be dismissed
only by a mind that sees the peak of wisdom in the self-multiplication of its
progenitive power."[60] So this Berlin "mechanician" regards us, *mein werter
Freund*, as *castrati;* at least I hope we have a sort of compensation for the
deficiency he indicates in our ability to "sing more beautifully" than Herr
Dühring. His tone and manner are the most repulsive I know. I have told
you in conversation my view: that *"finite"* space—that is, determinate
space—is an inevitable corollary to the mechanistic world view, and that to
me the impossibility of a position of equilibrium seems to hang together with
the question of how total space is shaped—it is certainly not "spherical."[61]

57. Cf. the sentence in a letter to Overbeck, dated July 2, 1885: "My life now
consists in wishing that everything may be *different* from the way in which I understand
it, and that someone may make my 'truths' incredible to me" (*Briefe und Berichte*, p. 368)*

58. Paul Heinrich Widemann was the musician with whom Gast had first come
to Basel to see N. Gast was responsible for sending out copies of *Zarathustra IV*.

59. *N's footnote:* I had been wondering that my fourth *Zarathustra* might have
resisted you. Indeed, it is inaccessible, with its remote situations and "world events";
yet they do exist, and are not merely arbitrary. This information for you, as my "individual."

60. Eugen Dühring (1833–1921) was a Berlin materialist philosopher.

61. See footnote on Robert Mayer and Ruggiero Boscovitch, letter No. 94. From
Mayer's theory of the conservation of energy, N developed a view of space which
Mittasch formulates as "finite force in finite space but infinite time" (*Ns Naturbeflissenheit*, p. 21). N wrote, "The *Gestalt* of space must be the cause of motion infinite in time"
(quoted by Mittasch, p. 21). Mayer's *Auslösung* theory—the realization of latent force,
or discharges of force—also had a strong appeal to N, who invoked Mayer also in support
of his theory of "eternal recurrence." Mittasch (p. 22) quotes, "The law of conservation
of energy requires the *eternal recurrence*." The following passage is from writings of the
late 1880's (*ca.* 1888): "If the world *may* be considered as a finite magnitude of force and as

My health, disturbingly uncertain—some cardinal danger or other. Frau Röder left two weeks ago, *bene merita!*[62] She helped through a bad month with the best of dispositions. Hot, absurdly hot, even here.

Your friend   N.

---

a finite number of centers of force—and every other conception is uncertain and therefore *unusable*—it follows that the world has to pass through a calculable number of combinations, in the great dice game of its existence. In an infinite period of time, every possible combination would at some time be attained; further, it would be attained an infinite number of times. And since between every combination and its next occurrence every other still possible combination would have had to have taken its course, and since each of these combinations conditions the whole suit of combinations in the same series, then this would be the proof of a cycle of absolutely identical series: the world as cyclical process, which has already repeated itself infinitely often and which plays its game *in infinitum*. This conception is not, without further ado, a mechanistic one; for, if it were that, it would occasion not an infinite recurrence of identical cases but a final state. *Because* the world has not attained this state, the mechanistic view must be considered as an imperfect and only provisional hypothesis." *(Werke in drei Bänden,* 3: 704.) During the same period, N wrote his description of the energy world as a "Dionysian" one also: "And do you know too what the 'world' is to me? Shall I show it to you in my mirror? This world—an immensity of force, without beginning, without end, a firm, brazen magnitude of force, which does not increase, does not decrease, does not consume itself, but only transforms itself, unchangeable as a whole in its magnitude, a household without expenses and losses, but likewise without additions, without income, surrounded by "nothingness" as its limit, nothing dissolving or wasting away, nothing infinitely extensive, but, as a definite force, inlaid into a definite space, and not in a space which is in any way empty, much more as force everywhere, as a play of forces and waves of force simultaneously one and many, here accumulating and simultaneously diminishing somewhere else, a sea of forces raging and flowing into each other, eternally changing themselves, eternally running back, with immense years of recurrence, with an ebb and flow of its forms, moving from the simplest to the most complex, from the uttermost of calm, rigor, cold into the uttermost of heat, wildness, self-contradiction, and then returning home from plentitude to simplicity, from the play of contradictions to the delight of concord, affirming itself even in this similarity of its courses and years, blessing itself as that which must eternally return, as a becoming which knows no satiety, no surfeit, no fatigue—this my *Dionysian* world of eternal self-creation, eternal self-destruction [. . .]" *(Werke in drei Bänden* 3: 916–17). Gast could not agree with this at all. He wrote in a letter dated 1913 (quoted by E. F. Podach, *Gestalten um N,* Weimar: Lichtenstein, 1932, p. 120): "I think that the belief that the present combination of atoms will repeat itself after so many milliards of years, and take the same course as now, is a prospect more joyous to the Philistine smoking his long pipe than to the hero and innovator who is fighting against a stupid environment. I find the doctrine of Eternal Recurrence sterile and comfortless—at least madly premature. His old, inherited theologian's instinct (belief in immortality) is playing a trick on N here. . . ." For a brilliant recent exemplification of N's theory of Eternal Recurrence, see Luis Buñel's film *El Ángel Exterminator* (1962).

62. Louise Röder-Wiederhold, from Karlsruhe.

137. *To Franz Overbeck*   Leipzig [October, 1885]
                                         Auenstrasse 48/II rechts

Dear friend:

Greetings from Leipzig! That will surprise you. But I could not resist coming to Germany again this fall (though there is nothing left here for me, body or "soul"), in order to see my mother and sister together again—who knows, perhaps for the last time. For in January or February the new "colonists" will be leaving, fortunately not alone but in company with others, all of them admirable and respectable people. I have not yet seen Dr. Förster, for he is in Westphalia, talking and riding alternately on his two horses (Paraguay and anti-Semitism), and will be doing the same in Saxony in November. People like us have no idea of the mass of work and excitement associated with such tasks. What consoles me is the unanimity in the praise of his *character* (for I was concerned to establish, on the sly, from friends and foes, the approximate reputation of my so unexpected "relative"). There are certainly good enough reasons for not generally trusting the anti-Semites any further than one can see them. And their case is much more popular than one supposes from afar—the whole Prussian nobility is indeed in raptures about it. The idea of colonization in Paraguay is something which I have personally studied, in case there might one day be a refuge for me there too. My conclusion is an unconditional no; my climatic needs are quite the contrary. In other respects, however, there is much good sense in the idea; it is a spendid soil for German farming people, and Westphalians and Pomeranians can take ship for the place with minds at rest though without actually fantastic expectations. Whether or not it is the right place for my sister and brother-in-law is another matter; and I confess that my mother and I are both often, and indeed terribly, *worried* about it. That my mother will be hereafter all alone is another worry for me. Perhaps she will end up spending at least a part of each year with me, possibly in Venice. That will be a great benefit for me, since, on account of my physical state and half-blindness, a considerate nurse (you will realize that my mother wants me to get married [—],[63] but she wishes it in vain) is becoming increasingly necessary, to say nothing of my inner isolation, from which the best will in the world could not now extract me. I accept this isolation as my lot, and I mean also to learn to bear it not as a misfortune. As a matter of fact, what I lack now is a person who would put the right space and distance around me, a sort of master of ceremonies, who would spare me the superfluous

---

63. Dash marks an editorial omission (as later in this letter); see *F. Ns Briefwechsel mit Franz Overbeck*, pp. 306–7.

malheurs to which I have been exposed during recent years, as I am exposed to them now once again. It seems that a big *bêtise* has to be committed against me at least once a month, especially by *messieurs les* women, who, in our age, are losing terribly their grace of heart and their modesty. Well, anyway, may heaven grant that people gradually forget me, and that my solitude may cease to be a pretext for shameless gossip. My plans for Sils Maria still hold: the needs of my eyes have been most graciously met there, by the creation of shady walks and a redisposition of the furniture in my room. Nothing is settled for the winter yet. Perhaps Venice, which will be possible for me as hermit after Köselitz's departure (for Vienna). Schmeitzner's case is my first concern [——]. How are you, dear old friend?

N.

In the middle of the month I shall be in Naumburg again. I cannot, at the moment, give you details of my monetary wishes.

138 · *To Heinrich von Stein*   Leipzig, October 15, 1885

Werter und sehr lieber Herr:

Your letter, which I discovered at the post office yesterday, was very touching—you are *right*, and what help would it be to prove that, on my part at least, an injustice has been done to you? I do as sick animals do and *hide myself away* in my "cave"—Leipzig is even more of a cave in this sense than Naumburg could be. The journey northward was not a success—my health was continuously dull and overcast; a few business matters, which seem to be urgent, refuse to be finally settled. And so forth.

Yesterday I saw Rée's book about conscience—how empty, how boring, how false![64] One really ought to speak only of things which are the stuff of one's experience.

I felt very differently about the seminovel by his *sœur inséparable* Salomé, whom I could at once jokingly picture.[65] Every formal aspect of it is girlish, soft, and—in the pretense that an old man is supposed to be telling the story—downright comic. But the *matter* itself has its serious side and its loftiness; and even if it is certainly not the eternal feminine which draws the girl on, then it is perhaps the eternal masculine.

I forgot to say how much I can appreciate the plain, clear, almost classical form of Rée's book. This is the "philosophical mantle."—A pity

64. *Die Entstehung des Gewissens* (Berlin, 1885).
65. *Im Kampf um Gott* (Berlin, 1885), under the pseudonym Henri Lou.

that there is not more content inside such a mantle! Yet no praise can be too high when, among Germans, someone abjures, as Rée has always done, the real German devil, the genius or *daimon* of obscurity. The Germans think they are profound.

But what am I doing? The cave bear is beginning to growl— let us all remain valiantly at our posts, also with some concern for one another; for what suits one does not suit two at all. Above all, let us growl as little as possible!

Loyally, your   N.

(In an hour, I am leaving for Naumburg; there I shall at last see Dr. Förster.)

139. *To Franz Overbeck*   [October 17, 1885]
                                   Leipzig, Auenstrasse 48/II rechts

Dear friend:

Everything is safely in my hands—and your birthday greeting, just arrived, safely in my *heart*. It was the only greeting on paper that I received this time; I thought about this fact of a forty-one-year-old life for a long time. It too is a sort of result and perhaps not an altogether sad one, at least when one has a right to avow that the meaning of one's life consists in knowing. To knowing belongs estrangement, distancing, perhaps a freezing too. You will have had ample chance to observe how the scale of "frost feelings" is now almost my specialty; that comes of living for so long "high up," "on the mountain," or also, like fair game, "up in the air"; one becomes sensitive to the subtlest charm of warmth, and more and more sensitive—O one becomes so thankful for friendship, my dear old friend!

Two days in Naumburg, for the "celebration" of my birthday. All the time unwell—I cannot make out whether from the outside inward or from the inside. Dense hazy sky and, perhaps, Naumburg for the last time.

I found Dr. Förster not unpleasant; there is something affectionate and noble about him, and he seems really made for *action*. It surprised me to see how many things he was always dealing with and how easy it was for him; I am different. His values are, as is only reasonable, not exactly to my taste. Everything is finished off too quickly—I think that we (you and I) find this kind of mind precipitate. A description of Förster which I read some time ago, published in *The Times*, I now find to have been a fair estimate.

Meanwhile the affair with Schmeitzner has been dragging on and on—I cannot say that it has been going "forward," not at all. Since last Monday, when a solemnly promised decision was to have been taken—the profoundest *silentium*. Compulsory auction is the prospect; since June his whole publishing concern has been legally impounded by me as a pledge. Assuming that the auction takes place, an attempt will be made to restore to me all my writings, so that I can transfer them to a new, worthier publisher (probably Veit and Company, i.e., Herr Credner in Leizpig). That is the plan. I cannot leave here until the matter is settled.

Yesterday I received, from the bookseller, a copy of Rée's *Entstehung des Gewissens*, and after a quick look at it I thanked my lucky stars that two or three years ago I refused to accept the dedication of this work, which was intended for me. Poor, incomprehensibly "senile."—At the same time, by a nice irony of chance, there arrived Frl. von Salomé's book, whose effect on me was the reverse. What a contrast between the girlish and sentimental form and the strong-willed and knowledgeable content! There is loftiness in it; and even if it is not really the eternal feminine which draws this pseudo-maiden ever onward, then perhaps it is—the eternal masculine. And there are a hundred echoes of our Tautenburg conversations in it.

Best greetings from me to your wife (by the way, Förster told me of a very pleasant meeting with you both—I thought that he was altogether a stranger to you?).

Loyally, your   N.

Leipzig, October 17, 1885

---

140 · *To Bernhard and Elisabeth Förster-Nietzsche*

Nizza, after Christmas, 1885

My dears:

The weather is glorious; so your animal[66] must make a happy face again, even though it has had very melancholy days and nights. But Christmas became a day of festival. I received your kind presents at noon, and at once the chain was hanging around my neck, and the nice little calendar crept into my waistcoat pocket. But while this was going on, the "money"

---

66. Original: "Euer Tier"; presumably this follows the German usage of the phrases "ein grosses Tier" or "ein berühmtes Tier," to designate a famous man, here in the context of a family joke. N might also have used "animal" with a certain irony in retrospect on Elisabeth's view of the Lou affair. His specifying the animal as a unicorn at the end of the letter turns the tables very astutely, considering Lou's ferocious virginity.

vanished, if, that is, there was money in the letter (our mother's letter says there was). Forgive your blind animal, who opened his things on the street; something may have slipped out, for I searched hard for the letter. I hope there was a poor little woman near by and that she thus found her present "from the Christ child" lying on the street. Then I went to my St. Jean peninsula, walked a long way around the whole coastline, and finally sat down among some young soldiers who were playing *boule*. Fresh roses and geraniums in the hedges and everything green and warm—not at all nordic! Then your animal drank *three* very large glasses of a sweet local wine and almost got *a bitzeli* drunk; at least, I afterwards said to the waves when they snorted up to me rather too impetuously, as one says to chickens, "Shoo, shoo, shoo!"[67] Then I went back to Nice again, and ate a *princely* supper in my *pension*; there was a big shining Christmas tree there too. Just imagine, I have found a *boulanger de luxe* who knows what curd cake is; he told me that the king of Württemberg has ordered one for his birthday. The word "princely" reminded me of this.

Unwell for a few days. So the letter was left unfinished. Meanwhile Overbeck has written that Rohde has been offered an appointment at Leipzig. Will he accept it, I wonder. Curious, I find it moving to think that everything which makes me feel not altogether homeless is gathering in Leipzig or nearby. Actually, it was nice to be in Leipzig again, this past autumn, a little melancholy, but in the way that spices all the pleasures of life for people like us—with the faint old rose fragrance of the irretrievable.

My eyes will hold out, in the long run, only in forests; but *old friends* must live near these forests. Would one not call that, all things considered, "Rosenthal"?[68] And just recently the Leipzig City Council declared war on *garlic* (the only form of anti-Semitism which smells sweet to your cosmopolitan unicorn)—excuse me![69]

Love as ever, Your F.

Heavens! I forgot to wish you *unlimited* good luck and health and strength and good thoughts and true friends for the new year.
N.B. I have learned to sleep again (without sedatives).

67. The *Schweizerdeutsch* phrase "a bitzeli" has the sense of "a little bit," with untranslatable homely overtones.

68. The name of a large park, at that time on the northwestern outskirts of Leipzig.

69. The city council had decided to do away with the garlic plants which infested the country surrounding Leipzig.

141 · *To Erwin Rohde*   [February 23, 1886] Nice (France)
                                rue St. François de Paule 26/II

Dear old friend:

My mother recently told me of your appointment at Leipzig; this news
made me happier than I have been for a long time. Since then I have been
thinking and thinking that this year must bring us together. Perhaps it can
be arranged for the spring; and, best of all, I would like to witness, with
eyes, ears, and heart, your inauguration. I cannot tell you how much this
hope cajoles and refreshes me. Last fall I spent a little time in Leipzig, as if
it were a foretaste; ah, quietly, almost in hiding, nearly always by myself,
but *warmed* as by the mere memory of you and of our old companionship in
this place. Chance willed that I should hear something of the project concerning yourself; immediately before the meeting at which the whole matter was
first discussed, I was together with Heinze and Zarncke. To me it is like a
dream that I should once have been a similar sort of hopeful animal, *philologus inter philologos*. Nothing came of it, or, as you and your colleagues now
perhaps tell one another, "nothing came of *him*." What is more, I have not
become any richer in friends; more and more, life has proposed my duty to
me with the terrible condition that I should fulfill that duty in *solitude*. It is
difficult for people to follow my feelings; I almost assume now, even among
acquaintances, that I shall be crassly misunderstood, and I cordially recognize any kind of delicacy of interpretation, even a goodwill to delicacy. I am
an ass—there is no doubt about that. Dear old friend Rohde, it seems to me
that you understand life better, by placing yourself in the midst of it; while
I see it more and more from a distance—perhaps also more and more clearly,
more and more terribly, more extensively, and with more and more attraction. But woe betide me if I should ever cease to be able to endure this
alienation! One grows old, one pines for things; already I need music like
that King Saul—Heaven has luckily given me also a kind of David. A man
like me, *profondement triste*, cannot endure Wagnerian music in the long
run. We need the south, sunshine "at any price," bright, harmless, innocent
Mozartian happiness and delicacy of tones. Really, I should also have around
me people who have the same constitution as this music which I love—the
kind with whom one can take a rest from oneself and laugh at oneself. But
not all can seek who would like to find—so I just sit and *wait*, and nothing
comes; and it has even come to this, that I should know no better than to tell
my old friend that I am alone.

Your latest letter is lying before me; possibly I am only now answering it, although a considerable amount of time has passed in the interim (the

letter is dated December 22, 1883). Be charitable to your taciturn friend, who in many ways has a difficult life and has learned to be afraid of opening his mouth. Before one knows it, a complaint comes out—and there is nothing sillier on earth than complaining. It humiliates us, even among the best friends.

Send me word to prove that you still love me, old friend Rohde. And once more, I rejoice at your fortune more than at my own. Give best wishes to your wife from the unknown bear and hermit, and caress your children in my name. With love

Your loyal friend   Nietzsche

February 23, 1886

142 · To Franz Overbeck

[Spring, 1886] Nice (France)
rue St. François de Paule, 26/II
Thursday

Dear friend:

A small red book which I sent you yesterday will tell you that my thoughts were with you in Basel at about the time when you were writing to me—how *good* it would be to be able to laugh together and with each other about such *curiosa* (even to be angry together)! Ah, my foolish health, which keeps me far from my friends! The news about your own health (from your two most recent letters), also about your eyes, makes me marvel at the way you bravely continue there in Basel. But of course, thanks to your wife, things are a hundred times better for you than for me—you have a nest together; I have, at best, a *cave*, however much I may toss and turn. People here tell me that I have been, throughout the winter, in a "splendid mood," in spite of many troubles; I tell myself that I have spent the winter feeling *profondement triste*, tortured by my problems day and night, really more in hell than in my cave—and that occasional contact with people is like a holiday for me, a redemption from "me." The way people misunderstand happy serenity! Malwida, the dear soul, who with her rosy superficiality has always kept herself "on top" in a difficult life, once wrote me, to my bitterest delight, that she could already see from reading my *Zarathustra* the serene temple beckoning from afar, the temple which I would build on this foundation. Well, it's enough to make one die laughing; and by now I am content that people do not pay attention and do not see *what* kind of "temple" I am building.

Recuperation, dear old friend—I now need nothing but recuperation; but it is getting more and more difficult to achieve. The light and refreshing music of Köselitz belongs there—how *much* I have to thank this lucky find of mine for! (But why did you say nothing about K's letter, which I enclosed with my latest letter to you? I hope nothing has been lost. I wrote as soon as the money arrived; since then I have heard nothing from you.) The poor fellow has had a bad time of it in Vienna, as in Dresden; he asked me to do what I could for him with Mottl in Carlsruhe.[70] The latter, though personally unknown to me, has meanwhile written a very kind letter; he placed great value on my recommendation ("the recommendation of a man whom I enthusiastically admire"). I hope he will match his words with deeds. What you say of your literary intentions delights me. I like reading you so much, even apart from what can be learned from you. You swallow your thoughts so nicely, I might almost say *craftily*, as a man of nuances, for that is what you are. Heaven bless you for it, in an age which is getting crasser every day.

Meanwhile people have been trying to urge me to resume academic activity. The idea is that I should lecture on cultural history—strange! The idea is quite familiar to me by now—merely as a way of recuperating. But it involves a miscalculation.

Please send to me here, as *soon* as you can, the money that is just becoming due (half in French currency, half in Italian, if that is not too much trouble). I shall be here until April 13. My eyes will not allow me to stay any longer. Thereafter, probably Venice, with its alley darkness; then the Engadin; in the fall, I must go and comfort my poor old mother somewhat.

Herr Credner is prepared to publish a "second volume of *Morgenröte*"; he wrote that he wanted to be "numbered among my admirers." I have never yet found such faith in Israel. All the same — — —

Ah, how much we might talk about, how much we might discuss together, dear friend! Give my best wishes to your wife and her relatives. This year will bring me once again to Munich.

Loyally, your friend Nietzsche

Working very hard. But do not be worried; there will not be a second volume of *Morgenröte*.

70. See note 129 to No. 161.

143 · *To Franz Overbeck* Sils Maria, August 5, 1886[71]

Dear friend:

Some news and a request! Fritzsch has just telegraphed from Leipzig: "Acquisition assured at last"—words which are a joy to hear.[72] A fatal mistake of my Basel years (somewhat "too much trust," as so often in my life) has thus been finally put right. What a good thing I went to Germany this spring! I have to repeat that, because it showed me at first hand my situation regarding publishers and public, also because I dealt *in person* with the excellent Naumann brothers. The new book, a result which could not have been settled from a distance, is now ready; a few days ago I gave instructions for a copy to be sent to you in Basel. Now the *request*, old friend: read it, from cover to cover, and do not let it embitter or estrange you—"collect all your strength,"[73] all the strength of your goodwill toward me, your patient and a hundred times proved goodwill; if the book is insufferable to you, perhaps a hundred *details* in it will not be! Perhaps too it will have the effect of shedding a few rays of light on my *Zarathustra*, which is an *unintelligible* book, because it is based on experiences which I share with nobody. If only I could give you an idea of my sense of *solitude!* Among the living, as among the dead, I have nobody with whom I have any affinity. It gives me the shudders—indescribably; and only my practice in enduring this sense and my gradual development of it from earliest childhood enable me to understand why it has not yet been the death of me. As for the rest, I can see clearly before me the task for which I live—as a *factum* of indescribable sadness,

71. This was N's fifth summer at Sils Maria. In May he had spent a week in Venice, and had then gone to Naumburg after a brief stay in Munich. He stayed in Naumburg until June 27; during this time he met Rohde in Leipzig, for the last time. He arrived in Sils Maria early in July, after a stay in Chur, and remained there until September 25. *Jenseits von Gut und Böse*, the "new book" of this letter, was being printed during this time, at N's own expense.

72. Fritzsch had been negotiating to acquire from Schmeitzner the rights for N's books. N expressed his annoyance with Schmeitzner in a letter to Overbeck dated summer, 1886: "During ten years, no copies have been sent to booksellers, also no review copies; not even a distributor in Leipzig; no *reviews*—briefly, my writings since *Mensch. Allzum.* [*Menschliches, Allzumenschliches*] are 'anecdota.' The parts of *Zarathustra* have sold sixty or seventy copies each, and so on, and so on." Fritzsch took over all the works published by Schmeitzner except *Zarathustra IV* and *Jenseits von Gut und Böse*. In 1888, just before his breakdown, N tried to buy back the rights from Fritzsch; it was only in his printers, the Naumann brothers, that he had any confidence.

73. Quotation from Ludwig Uhland's ballad "Des Sängers Fluch."

but transfigured by my consciousness that there is *greatness* in it, if ever there was greatness in the task of a mortal man.
I am staying here till the beginning of September.

In loyalty,   Your F. N.

144 · *To Jakob Burckhardt*   Sils Maria, Oberengadin,
September 22, 1886

Hochverehrter Herr Professor:
It grieves me not to have seen you and spoken with you for so long! If I may not speak to you, is there anyone left to whom I would *want* to speak? The "*silentium*" around me keeps gaining ground.
  I hope that C. G. Naumann has meanwhile done his duty and that my latest book, *Jenseits*, is now in your esteemed hands. Please read this book (even though it says the same things as my *Zarathustra*—only in a way that is different—very different). I know nobody who shares with me as many prepossessions as you yourself; it seems to me that you have had the same problems in view—that you are working on the same problems in a similar way, perhaps even more forcefully and deeply than I, because you are less loquacious. But then I am younger . . . The mysterious conditions of any growth in culture, that extremely dubious relation between what is called the "improvement" of man (or even "humanization") and the enlargement of the human type, above all, the contradiction between every moral concept and every scientific concept of *life*—enough, enough—here is a problem which we fortunately share with not very many persons, living or dead. To express it is perhaps the most dangerous venture of all, not for the person who ventures it but for those to whom he speaks of it. My comfort is that, for the time, there are no ears for my new discoveries—excepting yours, dear and deeply respected man; and for you again the discoveries will be nothing new!

Loyally,   Your Dr. Friedrich Nietzsche

Address: Genoa, *ferma in posta*[74]

74. N did pass through Genoa in October, on his way to Nice.

145 · *To Malwida von Meysenbug*

Sils Maria, September 24, 1886

Verehrte Freundin:

The last day in Sils Maria; all the birds have flown; the sky autumnally "murky"; the cold increasing—so the "hermit of Sils Maria" must be on his way.

I have been sending greetings in all directions, like someone drawing up his account of the year in company with his friends also. And while doing so it occurred to me that you have not heard from me for a long time. A request for your Versailles address, which I sent in a letter to Frl. B. Rohrl in Basel, was, unfortunately, not answered. So I am sending these lines to Rome, to which I also addressed a book not long ago. It is called *Beyond Good and Evil: Prelude to a Future Philosophy* (Forgive me! You should not read it, even less express to me your feelings about it. Let us assume that people will be *allowed* to read it in about the year 2000 . . .).

Warmest thanks for your asking after me in your letter to my mother, about which I heard this spring. I was in a bad way just then: the heat, to which as a neighbor of glaciers I am not accustomed, was almost crushing me. Moreover, in Germany I feel as if all the hostile winds are blowing at me, without feeling any joy or obligation to blow back *against* them. It is simply a wrong milieu for me. What concerns the Germans nowadays is of no concern to me—which is naturally no reason for fretting about them.[75]

So then old Liszt, with his flair for living and dying in the grand style, has had himself *buried*, as it were, inside Wagner's cause and his world—just as if he belonged there inevitably and inseparably.[76] This made my heart bleed for Cosima; it is just one more falsehood around Wagner, one of those almost insuperable misunderstandings in the midst of which Wagner's fame is growing and running riot today. To judge by the Wagner-ites I have known till now, the whole Wagner business seems to be an un-

75. N's hostility to Germany and the Germans appears also in the letter to Overbeck dated summer, 1886 (*Werke in drei Bänden*, 3:1239–41): ". . . I find life in present-day Germany is quite insufferable—it has a poisonous and paralyzing effect on me; and my contempt for human beings grows there to dangerous proportions. . . ." Here also he attacked German university life: "In this university atmosphere, even the best people deteriorate; I continually feel that the background and last resort, even to such natures as R[ohde], is an accursed pervasive don't-care attitude and a total absence of belief in what one is doing. . . ."

76. Franz Liszt had come to Bayreuth on July 21 for the Wagner performances, and had died there of double pneumonia on July 31. He had asked to be buried in Bayreuth. His funeral on August 3 was attended by many Wagnerites, aristocrats, and Roman Catholic dignitaries.

conscious approach to Rome, which is doing the same thing inwardly as Bismarck is doing outwardly.[77]

Even my old friend Malwida—ah, you do not know her!—is in all her instincts fundamentally Catholic, part and parcel of which is her indifference to formulas and dogmas. Only an *ecclesia militans* needs intolerance; every deep tranquility and certitude of faith *allows* scepticism, gentleness to others and other concerns . . .

To conclude, I shall write out for you a few words about me which appeared in *Der Bund* (September 16 and 17). Heading: "Nietzsche's Dangerous Book."[78]

"The stocks of dynamite used in the building of the Gotthard Tunnel were marked by a black flag, indicating mortal danger. Exclusively in this sense do we speak of the new book by the philosopher Nietzsche as a dangerous book. This designation entails no trace of reproach against the author and his work, as that black flag likewise was not meant to reproach the explosives. Even less could we think of delivering the lonely thinker up to the crows of the lecture room and the rooks of the pulpit by pointing to the dangerousness of his book. Intellectual explosives, like the material sort, can serve very useful purposes; it is not necessary for them to be used for criminal ends. Only one does well to say clearly, where such explosive is stored, 'There is dynamite here!' "

So be pretty grateful to me, *verehrte Freundin*, that I keep somewhat aloof from you! . . . and that I do not try to lure you along my ways and my "ways out." For, to quote *Der Bund* once more:

"Nietzsche is the first man to find a way out, but it is such a terrifying way that one is really frightened to see him walking the lonely and till now untrodden path!" . . .

In short, affectionate greetings from the *hermit* of Sils Maria.
Address shortly: Genoa, *ferma in posta*.

[no signature]

146 · *To Gottfried Keller*   Ruta ligure, October 14, 1886

Hochverehrter Herr:

In consequences of an old liking and custom, I recently took the liberty of sending you my latest book; at least, my publisher Naumann was instructed

77. Implies: "accumulating more and more hollow power."

78. The review was by J. V. Widmann, editor of *Der Bund*, a periodical published in Bern.

to send it. Perhaps this book, with its content a question mark, will not be to your taste; perhaps its *form* will be. A man who has seriously and devotedly concerned himself with the German language must give me a modicum of justice; it *is* something to give voice to such sphinxlike and mute problems as mine.

Last spring I asked my old mother to read me your *Sinngedicht*[79]— and we both heartily blessed you for it (throatily too, for we both laughed a lot), so pure, fresh, and firm was the taste of this honey.

> Your devoted admirer,
> Prof. Dr. Friedrich Nietzsche

147 · *To Franz Overbeck*   [Postmarked Nice, January 9, 1887]

Dear friend:

I posted my card to you shortly before your letter arrived, for which many thanks. I hope that your health is improving with the careful attention you are receiving; particularly when the eyes are affected, it seems to be least good for "man to be alone." It is a hard winter here too; instead of snow, we have had whole days of rain—the foothills have for some time been white (which looks like coquetry on nature's part, in a landscape so drenched in a variety of colors). This variety includes my *blue* fingers, as usual, likewise my *black* thoughts. I have just been reading, with thoughts of that kind, Simplicius's commentary on Epictetus; here one can see clearly before one the whole philosophical scheme in which Christianity became imbedded, so that this "pagan" philosopher's book makes the most Christian impression imaginable (except that the whole world of Christian emotion and pathology is missing—"love," as Paul speaks of it, "fear of God," and so on). The falsifying of everything actual by morality stands there in fullest array: wretched psychology, the "philosopher" reduced to the stature of "country parson." And it is all Plato's fault! He is still Europe's greatest misfortune!

> Your N.

79. Keller's novel *Das Sinngedicht* had appeared in 1882.

148 · *To Peter Gast*   Nice (France), rue des Ponchettes 29
au premier [January 21, 1887][80]

Dear friend:

It is a real relief for me to know that you are back to Venice. Your letter—
oh, it did me so much good! It seemed to contain a promise that things must
now be *better* for me too—better, that is, more bright, serene, more souther-
ly, less troubled, also I hope more "unliterary," for this whole "staging"
of my old writings has maltreated me cruelly and made me cruelly "personal."[81] I am not the sort of person to "chew over" life. I am now delighting and refreshing myself with the coldest kind of rational criticism, which
gives one blue fingers (and consequently takes away the pleasure of *writing*).
A full-scale attack on the whole idea of causality in philosophy till now will
be the result of it, and a few worse things besides.

If only you had had part of your opera performed. If one wants to
produce *oneself*, one has to produce what is most characteristic—that is, most
strange. That you should have played Levi your septet is, to my feeling,
more an act of politeness than anything else (something "Saxon"—forgive
me, old friend!).[82] The best part of the story is that your septet was received
in the way you have described; if people had liked it, I would have thought
something had gone wrong.

Levi made the best of impressions on me in the spring. Also, what I
have meanwhile heard from other Munich sources confirms that he has
neither lost nor *wants* to lose a kind of connection with me (he calls it
gratitude)—which is, incidentally, true of all Wagnerites (though I do not
know how to explain it). I was expected last autumn in Munich with
"feverish anticipation," as Seydlitz announced (now president of the Wagner
Society). In the Engadin, by the way, I shared a table with the Barber of
Bagdad's sister: do you understand this abbreviation?[83]

To end with—I recently heard for the first time the introduction to
Parsifal (it was in Monte Carlo!). When I see you again, I shall tell you precisely what it gave me to *understand*. But apart from all irrelevant questions
(what purpose such music *can* or *should* have?), and in purely esthetic terms:

80. N was in Nice from October 22, 1886, until April 2, 1887.

81. Refers to N's writing the prefaces for new editions of his earlier books.

82. In Leipzig the previous June, N had met Gast and had arranged for a private
performance of Gast's septet. To Overbeck he wrote that the music did not sound good
("much too thick"). Hermann Levi was a conductor in Munich.

83. Peter Cornelius's sister. Cornelius was the composer and librettist of the
comic opera *Der Barbier von Bagdad* (1858).

did Wagner ever compose anything better? The finest psychological intelligence and definition of what must be said here, expressed, *communicated*, the briefest and most direct form for it, every nuance of feeling pared down to an epigram; a clarity in the music as descriptive art, bringing to mind a shield with a design in relief on it; and, finally, a sublime and extraordinary feeling, experience, happening of the soul at the basis of the music, which does Wagner the highest credit, a synthesis of states which will seem incompatible to many people, even "loftier" people, with a severity that judges, an "altitude" in the terrifying sense of the word, with an intimate cognizance and perspicuity that cuts through the soul like a knife—and with a compassion for what is being *watched* and *judged*. Something of that sort occurs in *Dante*—nowhere else. Has any painter ever painted such a melancholy gaze of love as Wagner did with the last accents of his prelude?

Loyally, your friend Nietzsche

149 · *To Franz Overbeck*   (Wednesday) [Nice, February 23, 1887]

Dear friend:

Today, no more than my thanks for your letter and the money, which eased my mind considerably; I have never in my life been quite so much on my beam ends.[84] Moreover, I am unwell, cough *comme il faut*, shiver—and all the time the rowdy carnival of Nice is going on almost at my window . . .

Enclosed is a letter from the *maestro* of Venice,[85] which will please you, I think. I was so worried! But things are taking a turn for the better. A little scheme of mine—very indirect, to have Herr Hegar in Zürich do him a kindness—seems to have been successful.

Assuming I shall come to Zürich this spring and find Herr Hegar willing to perform the *Mizka-Czàrdas*[86] for me, I shall not fail to send you an invitation.

I also knew nothing about Dostoevski until a few weeks ago—uncultivated person that I am, reading no "periodicals"! In a bookshop my hand just happened to come to rest on *L'Esprit souterrain*, a recent French translation (the same kind of chance made me light on Schopenhauer when

---

84. N uses the idiom "so sehr am Ende meines 'Lateins,' " meaning additionally "at my wit's end."

85. Peter Gast.   86. A composition of Gast's.

I was twenty-one, and on Stendhal when I was thirty-five!).[87] The instinct of affinity (or what shall I call it?) spoke to me instantaneously—my joy was beyond bounds; not since my first encounter with Stendhal's *Rouge et Noir* have I known such joy. (The book consists of two novellas, the first really a piece of music, *very* foreign, very un-German music; the second a stroke of psychological genius, a sort of self-ridicule of the γνῶθι σαυτόν.) Incidentally, these Greeks have a great deal on their conscience—falsification was their real trade; the whole of European psychology is sick with Greek *superficialities*, and without the modicum of Judaism, and so on, and so on.

This winter I have also read Renan's *Origines* [*de la Chrétienté*], with much spite and—little profit. This whole history of conditions and *sentiments*[88] in Asia Minor seems to me to hang comically in the air. At root, my distrust goes so far as to question if history is really *possible*. What is it that people want to establish—something which was not itself established at the moment when it occurred? Dear friend, not a word about Germany, whose contemporaries we are! I am just reading Sybel's chief work, in French translation (after studying the relevant problems in the school of de Tocqueville and Taine), where I find, for example, this proud thought: "The feudal regime, and not its collapse, gave birth to egoism, avarice, violence, and cruelty, which led to the terrors of the September massacres."[89] I think that that is "liberalism" in the act of self-recognition; it is certain that such a blatant hatred of the whole social order of the Middle Ages consorts excellently with the most considerate treatment of Prussian history—for example, as regards the partition of Poland. (Do you know Montalembert's *Moines d'occident*? Or rather, do you know any work that is more solid and less partisan than this but with the same intention of showing what benefits European society owes to the monasteries?)[90]

---

87. In a letter to Gast, dated March 7, N tells some details of Dostoevski's life, and says of *The House of the Dead*, which he had read in French, that it is "one of the most human books ever written." The same letter shows that he read, on Overbeck's recommendation, *Insulted and Injured* (also in the French translation, *Humiliés et offensés*).

88. N uses the French word.

89. Heinrich von Sybel (1817–95); French title of the work in question: *Histoire de la période révolutionnaire de 1789 à 1795*.

90. The logic of this passage seems to be as follows: Bismarck's regime in Prussia is based on feudalistic premises; yet the liberals, who hate medieval feudalism, take a considerate view of Prussian history. How can this be so? The liberal *rapprochement* with Bismarck results from the liberals' *fear* of such power, fear which expresses itself as hatred when they deal with the medieval version of it. Thus in the liberals N is detecting the timidity of the hypocritical bourgeois; "egoism," "avarice," "violence," and "cruelty" would be the liberal distortions of the facts of medieval life; energy, pro-

This winter is treating me well—it is like an interval between scenes and a retrospect. Incredible! In the past fifteen years I have set an entire literature on its feet and finally "rounded it off" with prefaces and additions —so completely that I can see it as something quite detached from me, and can laugh about it, as I laugh fundamentally at all book writing. All in all, I have spent only the most miserable years of my life on it.

Loyally, your old friend
N. homo illiteratus

150 · To Reinhart von Seydlitz

Nizza, Thursday, February 24, 1887
rue des Ponchettes 29 au premier

Happily, dear friend, your letter did not at all prove in your own case *quod erat demonstrandum;* but in other respects I concede everything you say; the fatal effects of the cloudy sky, of the continuous damp cold, the presence of Bayovars and Bavarian beer—I admire any artist who can face enemies like these, not to mention German politics, which are simply another kind of permanent winter and bad weather. Germany seems to me to have become, during the past fifteen years, a real school of stultification. Water, mess, and filth everywhere [— —];[91]—that is how it looks from the distance. Forgive me, as I ask you a thousand times, if it hurts your finer feelings, but for this present-day Germany, bristling stiff with weapons though it may be, I no longer have any respect. It represents the most stupid, broken-down, bogus form of the German *Geist* that there ever has been—and this *Geist* has in its time certainly expected of itself all sorts of *Geist*-lessness. I forgive nobody who compromises with it, even if his name is Richard Wagner, and especially not if the compromise is made with such vile disingenuousness and prudence as that contrived in his last years by the clever and all-too-clever glorifier of "pure foolishness."

Here in *our* land of the sun, what different matters we have to think about! Nizza has just had its lengthy international carnival (with Spanish girls in the majority, by the way) and, immediately after that, six hours after its last *girandola*, new and more seldom tasted delights of life arrived. We

---

ductivity, exuberance, and creative genius were its true qualities (for N), as should be evident from any "solid and impartial" appreciation of the benefits accruing from the monasteries.

91. Dash indicates deletion from the original (presumably by Elisabeth).

are living, in fact, in the interesting expectation *that we shall perish*—thanks to a well-intentioned earthquake, which is making the dogs howl far and wide, and not only the dogs. What fun, when the old houses rattle overhead like coffee mills! when the ink bottle assumes a life of its own! when the streets fill with half-dressed figures and shattered nervous systems! Last night between two and three o'clock, *comme gaillard* as I am, I toured the various districts of the town to see where the fear is greatest. The population is camping out day and night—it looked nice and military. And now even in the hotels!—where there has been much damage and so complete panic prevails. I found all my friends, men and women, stretched out miserably under green trees, heavily flanneled, for it was bitterly cold, and thinking dark thoughts of the end every time a small shock came. I have no doubt that this will bring the *saison* to a sudden end—everyone is thinking of *leaving* (assuming that one can get away and the railroads have not been the first things to be "torn apart"). Already yesterday evening the guests at the hotel where I eat could not be persuaded to take their *table d'hôte* indoors— people ate and drank outside; and, except for an old, very pious lady, who is convinced that the good Lord is not entitled to do her any harm, I was the only cheerful person in a crowd of masks and "feeling hearts."

I have just found a page from a newspaper which will give you a much more picturesque account of last night than your friend can. I enclose it; please read it to your dear wife and remember me kindly.

Loyally, your   Nietzsche

(Forgive the hurry and sketchiness of my handwriting, but this letter has to leave by the next train.)

---

151 · *To Franz Overbeck*   [Nice, Thursday, March 24, 1887]

Dear friend:

I have just received your news—and since I am leaving (and must leave) at the end of next week, then that is one more good reason for answering your letter at once. I wish that I could have written "till we meet again," but my health forbids me, meanwhile, to visit Zürich and all that Zürich means. I am strangely unwell, all the time, tired, mentally and physically low, and good for nothing, also so impatient about noise and the whole small offence of life that I want to take refuge in some very quiet and remote place— namely, in a woody and walky place on Lago Maggiore, called Canobbio.

Nearby, there is a *pension*, Villa Badia, which has been well recommended to me; it is owned by Swiss people. I have booked a room there from April 4. Venice, which has tradition favoring it in the early spring, and which I earnestly love (the only place on earth which I love), has been bad for me every single year—the reason being certain definite meteorological factors, which I know only too well. Will it be possible for me to have the thousand francs by Wednesday or Thursday next week?

There is a Dr. Adams here; he has been here for about a month, an apparently gifted and able classical scholar, a former pupil of Rohde's and Gutschmidt's, but passionately disgusted with all classical studies and thoroughly determined to dedicate himself to philosophy—hence his pilgrimage hither, to visit his "master." Perhaps I shall manage to disillusion him and extract him from the vagueness of his intentions; I am gently guiding him toward the *history* of philosophy (he has worked on the *De fontibus Diodori*)—it is even not impossible that he may take up my abandoned *Laertiana!* The whole thing is really a toil for me, which reminds me of an earlier one (Tautenburg, summer, 1882); and, after all, I do know the world well enough to realize what is the world's reward in such cases. I do not like the "young people" at all.

Now a comic fact, which is coming more and more to my notice— I have an "influence," very subterranean, to be sure. I enjoy a strange and almost mysterious respect among all radical parties (Socialists, Nihilists, anti-Semites, Orthodox Christians, Wagnerians). The extreme candor of the atmosphere in which I have placed myself, is seductive . . . I can even abuse my outspokenness, I can vituperate, as in my last book—people are grieved by it; perhaps they "implore" me, but they cannot escape me. In the *Anti-Semitic Correspondence* (which is sent only privately through the mail, only to reliable "party members"), my name appears in almost every issue. The anti-Semites are smitten with Zarathustra, the divine man; there is a special anti-Semitic interpretation of it, which gave me a good laugh. By the way, I have made "in competent quarters" the suggestion that a list should be made of all German scholars, artists, writers, actors, musicians who are completely or partly Jewish—that would make a good contribution to the history of German culture, also to the critique of it. (In all this, between ourselves, my brother-in-law plays no part; my dealings with him are very polite but aloof and as infrequent as possible. His undertaking in Paraguay is prospering, it happens; my sister too.)

If things are no better for me in Cannobio, I am thinking of trying a small cold-water cure in Brestenberg. Ah, everything in my life is so uncertain and shaky, and always this horrible health of mine! On the other hand, there is the hundredweight of this need pressing upon me—to create a coherent structure of thought during the next few years—and for this I need five or six preconditions, all of which seem to be missing now or to be unattainable. The fourth floor of the Pension de Genève, in which the third and fourth parts of my *Zarathustra* were written, is now being dismantled, after the irreparable damage done to it by the earthquake. This transience of things hurts me. The ground still has an occasional tremor. With cordial greetings and wishes, also to your dear wife,

Your Nietzsche

I hope that there is good news from Teneriffe?[92]
[Marginal note:] I have a copy of Lecky—but Englishmen like him lack the "historical sense" and a few other things besides. The same is true of the much-read and -translated American Draper.

152 · *To Malwida von Meysenbug*

Address: Chur (Switzerland),
Rosenhügel, until June 10; there-
after, Celerina, Oberengadin
[May 12, 1887][93]

Hochverehrte Freundin:

Strange! The very kind idea which you have expressed, that we might both find it profitable and refreshing now to draw our two solitudes together and become close and friendly neighbors, is one that I have often had and contemplated in recent times. To spend another winter together, perhaps even with Trina looking after us both and waiting upon us—that is really a most enticing prospect and perspective, for which I cannot be too grateful to you! Preferably in Sorrento again (δὶς καὶ τρὶς τὸ καλόν, the Greeks say—"all good things come twice and three times!"). Or on Capri—where I shall make music for you again, and better than the previous time! Or in Amalfi, or Castellamare. Possibly even in Rome (although my distrust of the Roman climate and of all big cities is based on good reasons and is not easily reversed). Solitude with most solitary nature has been till now my solace, my

92. Early in December, 1886, Overbeck's brother-in-law, a geologist, had left for Teneriffe, together with his mother and two sisters, for reasons of health.

93. N's movements during the spring and summer months: April, in Cannobio on Lake Maggiore; April 28 to May 6, in Zürich (also a brief stay in Ammden, near the Wallensee); May 8 to June 8, in Chur; June 8 to 12, in Lenzerheide; June 12 to September 19, in Sils Maria. His health was again bad most of the summer; he was suffering also from states of depression.

medicine; such cities full of modern goings-on, like Nice and even Zürich (from which I have just come), make me in the long run irritable, sad, unsure, despondent, unproductive, unwell. What I have retained from that quiet stay *down there* is a sort of yearning and superstition, as if there, if only for a few moments, I had *breathed* more deeply than anywhere else in my life. For example, on that very first journey in Naples, when together we went toward the Posilippo.[94]

All things considered, finally, you are now the only person who could make me have this wish; for the rest, I feel *condemned* to my solitude and fortress. There is no choice any more. The unusual and difficult task which commands me to go on living commands me to avoid people and to bind myself to no one any more. It may be due to the state of extreme candor to which that task has brought me that I can now no longer *smell* "human beings," least of all the "young people," by whom I am not infrequently pestered (oh, they are importunate and clumsy, just like young dogs!).[95] That other time in Sorrento, Brenner and Rée were too *much* for me; I imagine that I was very taciturn toward them, even on subjects about which I would have spoken to nobody but them.

On my table is the *new* edition (in two volumes) of *Menschliches, Allzumenschliches*, the first part of which was being worked out at that time —strange! strange! close to your estimable self! In the long "prefaces" which I have thought necessary for the reissue of all my writings, there are curious things, of a ruthless frankness about myself. This is to keep the "crowd" once and for all at arm's length, for nothing annoys people so much as noticing something of the severity and hardness with which one treats, and has treated, oneself under the discipline of one's most individual ideal. To balance this, I have cast my book for the "few," and even then without impatience; the indescribable strangeness and dangerousness of my thoughts are such that a long time must pass before there are ears to hear them—and certainly *not* before 1901.

To come to *Versailles*—ah, if only that might somehow be possible! For I revere the circle of people whom you find there (a curious admission

94. Posilippo is a promontory nine miles southwest of Naples, reached by the coastal road. N writes "nach dem Posilipp zu," which could mean either "toward the promontory" or "toward the Posilippo Park," from which there is a view over the Bay of Naples to Vesuvius and the islands of Capri, Procida, and Ischia, and, in the other direction, across to Nisida and over the Gulf of Pozzuoli to Miseno. He is referring here to his drive with Malwida from Naples to Sorrento.

95. One such visit was that of Heinrich Adams (see No. 151), who came to N in Nice as a refugee from German classical philology in March, 1887. He told N that his books were being avidly read by theological students in the famous seminary at Tübingen, the "Tübinger Stift."

from a German; but I feel myself in Europe today to be related only to the intellectual *French* and *Russians* and not at all to my cultivated compatriots, who judge all things by the principle *Deutschland, Deutschland über alles*). But I *must* return into the *cold* Engadin air; the spring afflicts me incredibly—I do not like to confess what an abyss of despondency I am wandering in, under its influence. My body feels (as my philosophy does too) that it is committed to the *cold* as its *preserving* element—that sounds paradoxical and uncomfortable, but it is the most proven fact of my life.

This does not reveal in any way a *frigid* nature—you certainly understand that, *meine hochverehrte und treue Freundin!* . . .

Love and gratitude as ever　　　Your Nietzsche

Frl. Salomé also told me of her engagement; but I did not reply either, however much I sincerely wish her happiness and prosperity. One must avoid people like her, who have no reverence.

In Zürich I visited the excellent Frl. von Schirnhofer, just back from Paris, uncertain of her future, aim, prospect but, like me, most enthusiastic about Dostoevski.

153 · *To Hippolyte Taine*　Sils Maria, Oberengadin, July 4, 1887

Hochverehrter Herr:

There are so many reasons for me to be grateful to you: for the considerateness of your letter, in which your words about Jakob Burckhardt were especially pleasant to hear;[96] for your incomparably strong and simple characterization of Napoleon in the *Revue*,[97] which came into my hands almost by accident last May. (I was actually not ill prepared for you, thanks to my reading a recent book by M. Barbey d'Aurevilly,[98] the last chapter of which —on books about Napoleon—sounded like a sustained cry of longing—but for what? Without a doubt, for exactly the kind of explanation and solution of that immense problem of the inhuman and the superhuman that you have given us.) I should also not forget that I was glad to find your name in the dedication of the latest novel by M. Paul Bourget[99]—although I do not like

96. Taine had written a note in October, 1886, thanking N for *Beyond Good and Evil.*

97. *Revue des deux mondes*, vol. 79, 1887, pp. 721-52.

98. *Le XIXe siècle. Les œuvres et les hommes*, vol. 8 (Paris 1887), pp. 379-431.

99. *André Cornélis* (Paris, 1887).

the book;[100] M. B[ourget] will never be able to make a real physiological *hole in the chest* of a fellow being seem credible (that kind of thing is for him only *quelque chose arbitraire*, from which, I hope, his delicate good taste will hereafter restrain him. But it seems, does it not, that the spirit of Dostoevski gives this Parisian novelist no peace?). And now have patience, *verehrter Herr*, and kindly accept two of my books which have recently appeared in new editions. I am a hermit, you will know, and I no longer trouble much about readers and being read; yet, since I was in my twenties (I am now forty-three), I have never lacked a few excellent and very devoted readers (they were always old men), among them, for instance, the old Hegelian Bruno Bauer,[101] my esteemed colleague Jakob Burckhardt, and that Swiss poet whom I consider to be the only living *German* poet, Gottfried Keller.[102] I would be very happy if my readers were to include the Frenchmen whom I hold in the highest esteem.

These two books are dear to me. The first one, *Morgenröte*, I wrote in Genoa at a time when I was extremely and most painfully ill, given up by the doctors, face to face with death, and in the midst of incredible privation and isolation; but I wanted it no other way, and was nonetheless at peace with myself and sure of myself. For the other one, *Die fröhliche Wissenschaft*, I am indebted to the first glimpses of the sunlight of returning health; it was written a year later (1882), also in Genoa, during a few sublimely clear and sunny January days. The problems with which both books are concerned make one lonely. May I ask you to accept them with goodwill?

With every token of my deep and personal esteem, I am and remain

yours faithfully, Friedrich Nietzsche

100. *N's footnote:* "Unfortunately I do not know the title of it."

101. For an account of N's relation to Bauer, see the introduction to Ernst Barnikol, *Das entdeckte Christentum im Vormärz: Bruno Bauers Kampf gegen Religion und Christentum und Erstausgabe seiner Kampfschrift* (Jena, 1927).

102. N had sent Keller *Zarathustra I* from Rome in 1883, and *Beyond Good and Evil* in 1886. There is no sign that Keller read either of these books; it is even probable that he would have found *Zarathustra* bombastic at first glance and decided not to read N at all. He did not acknowledge either of the books. Keller's benign and beautiful smile is all that Elisabeth found noteworthy when she described the meeting between the two men in Zürich in October, 1884. The fact is that N was not being read by the writers he most admired; it is even doubtful that Burckhardt still read him. Bruno Bauer (born 1809) had died in 1882.

154 · *To Peter Gast*   Silas Maria, Monday [July 18, 1887]

Dear friend:

An immediate answer to your letter which just walked in, amid heavy rains which with their gentle darkness seem to me not unrefreshing. Perhaps you have them in Venice too—and have thus shed some of the nightmare laid across your soul by the summer. You are right; I ought really to appreciate my *cool* summer residence (this year I have sometimes suffered from the close heat even up here—how much worse it must have been for you!). Ordinarily, believe me, one can cope with anything as long as one is in good physical health, and, if one is physically unwell, nothing is any good and the best gifts from heaven are put aside coldly and sadly. A physiological constraint which has given me for the past year, without exaggeration, not a single good day, and which has shown itself in the form of all kinds of cowardice, vulnerability, distrust, inability to work—effects like those of a severe psychological illness, though I am certain that I am right to accuse the *phusis* as the guilty party—that is a *misère* which, dear friend, the good Lord has spared you. To be quite fair, I admit there has been a real change for the past week—but my distrust goes so deep and the extremely bad days of my attacks are so frequent that I feel tomorrow could be a return of the same old state of things.

I have at once vehemently exploited these better days and written a small polemical pamphlet[103] which, I think, sharply focuses the problem of my last book; everybody has complained that I am "not understood," and the approximately one hundred copies which have been sold have made it quite obvious to me *that* I am not understood. Just think, I have spent about five hundred talers on printing costs during the past three years—no honorarium has been paid me, of course—and this in my forty-third year, after I have published fifteen books! More—after a precise survey of all conceivable publishers and many most painful negotiations, one undeniable fact emerges—that no German publisher *wants* me (even if I do not claim an honorarium). Perhaps this small polemical pamphlet will help to sell a few copies of my older writings (honestly, it always hurts me when I think of poor Fritzsch, who is now carrying the whole burden). I hope my publishers will benefit from it; for myself I know only too well that I shall *have no benefit when* people begin to understand me . . .

Overbeck wrote that he had read the prefaces one after another as "the most exciting odyssey through the realm of ideas." Marie Rothpletz is

103. *Zur Genealogie der Moral.*

marrying a Major von der Marck (retired), whose sister I remember from Nice as a very good dinner-table companion.

A comical going back and forth—letters and inquiries between Weimar and the Goethe scholars there and our family; it has been discovered who "Muttgen" was (one of the enigmas in Goethe's diaries); the chief archivist Burkhardt has even published who it was—my grandmother. Meanwhile I have had some fun with these gentlemen by raising an objection; "it seemed to me improbable that 'Muttgen' (Erdmuthe Krause) was friendly with the young poet in 1778," because . . . Muttgen first saw the light of day only in December that year! Great astonishment! Now people are supposing that it must be Muttgen's mother. In any case, the relation to Goethe is certain beyond all doubt. It was Goethe who brought Muttgen's brother, the professor of theology Krause, from Königsberg to Weimar to be Herder's successor (as superintendent-general of the churches in the region).

Dear friend, not only is the printing in progress (with Naumann) but also the engraving (with Fritzsch)—do you feel the point?[104] . . . At least you will soon see it.

But do be angelic (as Countess Dönhoff used to say) and send to Bülow what must be sent . . . old friend—please—[105]

A curiosity for inclusion: Dr. Widmann of *Der Bund* has written me an enthusiastic letter, also concerning Brahms, with whom he is keeping company (the latter "most interested in *Jenseits [von Gut und Böse]*," now about to turn his attention to *Die fröhliche Wissenschaft*). Could I do anything *in this direction* for the *Lion of Venice*??? Question marks.[106]

Loyally, your   N.

104. N makes a pun here: "es wird gestochen . . . fühlen Sie den Stich?" *Den Stich fühlen* actually means "to feel the (unpleasant) effects of something." The reference is to N's composition *Hymn to Life*, for mixed chorus and orchestra, a setting of the poem which Lou had given him in August, 1882. He had received the score back from Gast in late June, 1887; his own setting for piano had been made in September, 1882.

105. Probably refers to Gast's *Der Löwe von Venedig*, the first part of which N himself eventually sent to Bülow thirteen months later.

106. N sent Brahms his own *Hymn to Life*, but the response was only a formal acknowledgment (see P. Gast, "N und Brahms," *Zukunft* [Berlin], vol. 19, 1897, pp. 266–69).

155. *To Franziska Nietzsche*   Venice, October 18, 1887

My dear mother:

Your letter, arriving on my birthday, found me doing a thing which would have pleased you: I was writing a little letter to the South American Lama. Your letter and birthday greetings were, by the way, the only ones that I received, which gives me a good idea of the "independence" to which I have now attained; the latter is the *foremost condition* for a philosopher. I hope that you did not overlook in my last letter the good mood with which I presented to you the menu of German judgments on me. It really did entertain me to know these; also I am well enough acquainted with human nature to know how the judgment on me will have been reversed in fifty years' time, and with what a splendor of reverence your son's name will then shine, on account of the same things as those for which I have till now been mishandled and abused. Never since childhood to have heard anything deep and understanding said about me—that is all part of my *fate;* also I do not remember ever having complained about it. As it happens, I do not take a fretful view of the Germans on this account; in the first place, they lack precisely the culture, the whole seriousness, with which to face the problems in which I place my seriousness; and second, they are really too occupied and they all have their hands too full to find time to concern themselves with something *absolutely foreign* to them. Incidentally, to put your mind at rest, you seem to think that the contradiction which I find has something to do, essentially, with my view of *Christianity.* No! Your son is not as "harmless" as that, and my opponents are not harmless either. The judgments which I wrote down for you derive without exception from the sphere of the most decidedly nonconfessional parties that now exist. Those were not the judgments of theologians. Almost every one of these criticisms (which came in part from very intelligent critics and scholars) was careful not to suggest that people wanted, because of the dangerousness of my book, to deliver me up to the "rooks of the pulpit and the crows of the altar." My opposition is a hundred times too radical seriously to involve religious questions and shades of difference between confessions.

Forgive me for this all too lengthy digression; but when I say that the most intelligent scholars have till now been *mistaken* about me, then it is self-evident that old P[lüss?] has not been any subtler.[107] He naturally felt that his views and mine were different—and regretted this.

The news from Paraguay is really very cheering; but I still have not

107. Possibly Theodor Plüss, formerly a teacher at Schulpforta.

the slightest wish to settle in the vicinity of my anti-Semitic brother-in-law. His views and mine are different—and I do *not* regret this.

The suitcase for my journey is already half packed; I leave late the day after tomorrow or early the following day. My state of health has remained steady, on the whole, except that my eyes have been troubling me.

With warmest and most grateful greetings,

your old creature

I shall write from Nice about the transportation of the little carbon-natron stove, which I shall need for my room there (with a hundredweight of fuel).

156. *To Peter Gast*   Nice, October 27, 1887
(blue fingers, sorry!)[108]

Dear friend:

Your letter has just arrived; I was reading Montaigne to extricate myself from a morosely gloomy and irritated mood—your letter helped even more effectively. Since yesterday evening I have had a fishbone in my throat; last night was gruesome; in spite of repeated attempts at vomiting, it is still stuck there. Curious, I feel there is an abundance of symbolism and meaning in this sordid physiological state.

What is more, it is cold, like January; my room, which faces north, does not allow me to make any jokes about myself—or about itself! Overbeck has just announced that he has rheumatism (he also sent news of Spitteler, his old student),[109] that he is deeply immersed in scholastic rubbish (on which he is lecturing for the first time this winter), also that R. Wagner's symphony has been performed in Basel. We must send him (as you suggest) the *Hymn* now, as something which calls for all kinds of courage. Incidentally, the conclusion, "Wohlan, noch hast du deine Pein" ["Well then, you still have your suffering"][110] . . . is the ultimate in hubris in the Greek sense, in its blasphemous challenging of destiny by an excess of spirit and exuberance—I still feel a slight shudder when I see (and hear) the phrase. It is said that the furies have ears for such "music."

108. N had left Sils Maria on September 19, and had stayed in Venice with Gast from September 21 to October 21. He was in Nice from October 22 until April 2, 1888.

109. See note 140 to No. 165, of February 26, 1888, to Gast.

110. The last two lines of Lou's poem read (translated): "If you have no more joy to give me, / Well then, still you have your suffering to give."

A sharp alleviates me, I cannot help you here, it forms the bridge to the "sweet" decisiveness of the final phrasings.[111] I would sustain A natural if it formed the start of a long, passionate, tragic, swelling, and diminishing cadence (in F sharp minor), possibly with the violins in unison; as it is, it stands there alone, dry, painful, without hope. Also, the melody moves through these bars in only small seconds—this unique large B-A sounds like a contradiction. You see, I cannot quite get away from the *moral contrariety* of this A.

The score, incidentally, gave me *great* pleasure; and it seems to me that Fritzsch has come out of it better than we thought he would. What good paper he has used! All in all, it is the most "elegant" score I have ever seen; and I am pleased that Fritzsch has actually arranged the *voices* for it (without mentioning anything to me beforehand); it reveals his faith that the *Hymn* can be performed. Oh, dear old friend, what a "service" you have done me with this! This small link with music and almost with composers, to which this *Hymn does* testify, is something of inestimable value, considering the psychological problem which I am; and now it will make people *think*. Also in itself the *Hymn* has some passion and seriousness and it defines at least one central emotion among the emotions from which my philosophy has grown. Last of all, it is something for *Germans*, a little bridge, which might enable even this ponderous race to become interested in one of its strangest monstrosities.

Nice, shaken up by its earthquake, is getting ready this winter to display all its seductive charms. It has never been cleaner; the houses are more beautifully painted; the food in the hotels is better. The Italian theater (Sonzogno as impresario is spending the winter here) promises, like Bülow, *I pescatori di perle* for a start (November 26);[112] after that, *Carmen;* then *Amleto* by [Ambroise] Thomas; then *Lakmé* (by Delibes)—all pieces for connoisseurs. We have just had a splendid congress of astronomers here, called *le congrès Bisch* (the rich Jew Bischoffsheim, amateur *in astronomicis*, has been paying all the *expenses* of the congress; and, indeed, people are delighted by the parties which he has arranged). Already Nice owes its observatory to him, likewise the maintenance of it, the salaries of its employees, as well as the costs of publications. *Ecco! Jewish usury in the grand style!*

Dear friend, I left you this last time not only with great gratitude but also with great respect. Remain true to *yourself*—I can wish you nothing better than that!

Affectionately, your N.

111. Gast had evidently proposed some changes in the *Hymn* while orchestrating it.

112. By Bizet.

157 · *To Peter Gast*   Nizza, November 10, 1887

Dear friend:

Chance has willed it (or is it not chance at all?) that I too found myself
dwelling last week on the Piccini-Gluck problem. Did you know that Gluck
died in November, 1787?—also perhaps that the greatest and most intelligent
expert on Piccini, the Abbé Galiani, died in the same year (October 30,
1787, in Naples)?[113] Thus we are celebrating the centenary of a great problem and of a fateful, probably *wrong* solution of the same. I am reading
Galiani; it really annoys me that this most fastidious and refined intelligence
of the last century should be so beside himself about his Piccini (somewhat
like Stendhal about Rossini, but more naïvely and with more "affinity," if
my feeling about it is right). He makes a sharp distinction between Piccini's
comic operas which are possible only for and in Naples, and the other ones,
which can just about be appreciated throughout Italy and even in France.
Only the former group, he says, show Piccini at the peak of his art; he says
to Mme d'Epinay that she can have no conception of them, so *supérieur* are
they to everything that she has heard. Piccini's great period is about 1770-71
(Galiani's letters were written in the latter year). At that time there were
performances in Naples of Piccini's *La finta giardiniera* and *Il Don Chisciotte*,
likewise of *La Gelosia per Gelosia*: Galiani's rapture must relate to one of
these, if not to all three ("he has taught me that we all sing, and always sing
when we speak. The difficult thing is to find our tone and our modulation
when we speak"). He laughs at Mme d'Epinay for wanting to bring these
things to Paris; he says, "Ils ne vont pas même à Rome." "You shall have
his *Italian* comic operas, like *La buona figlia* but none of the *Neapolitan* ones."
(This opera, *La buona figlia*, with Goldoni's libretto, was first performed in
Rome in 1760; in Paris, not until 1770, with great success. The French
critics said at that time: "Les oreilles françaises, habituées depuis quelques
années à un genre qui leur répugnait d'abord, ont reçu celle-ci avec la plus
delicieuse sensation. Les accompagnements surtout ont paru travaillés avec
un art infini."[114] Doesn't that sound very remarkable?)

    We must, it seems to me, discover afresh the whole opposition be-
tween Italian and French music, and lay aside for once the hybrid concept

---

113. In *Beyond Good and Evil*, section 26, N calls the Abbé Galiani "the profoundest, most perspicacious, and perhaps also the dirtiest man of his century" (*Werke in
drei Bänden*, 2:592).

114. "This was a delicious sensation for French ears, for several years accustomed
to a genre which at first displeased them. Above all, the instrumentation seemed to be
wrought with infinite art."

of "German music." It is a question of opposition between styles; where the composers come from is of no account here. Thus Händel is an Italian, Gluck a Frenchman (French critics are, for example, at this very moment celebrating Gluck as the greatest musician of the French spirit, as *their* Gluck). There are native-born Italians who honor the French style; there are native-born Frenchmen who write Italian music. But in what exactly does the great stylistic opposition consist? I recommend to you especially the *Mémoires* of Président de Brosses (his *Italian Journey*, 1739), in which this problem is continuously touched on, and with passion; for instance, *il Sassone*, your Venetian Hasse, appears there as being *fanatically* anti-French.

Can you get to see Piccini scores in Venice, especially his Neapolitan works? Is it possible that any of these works have been lost and forgotten? The *genius of gaiety* must be set in opposition to parochial "German seriousness" in music.

That reminds me of the *hymnus ecclesiasticus*—only one judgment on which has come in, Ruthardt's: "very dignified, pure in phrasing and harmonious."[115]

The second volume of the *Journal des Goncourts* has appeared—a most interesting new publication. It concerns the years 1862–65; in it, the famous *diners chez Magny* are described in an extremely vivid way, the dinners at which the most intelligent and skeptical troupe of Parisian minds at that time met together (Sainte-Beuve, Flaubert, Théophile Gautier, Taine, Renan, the Goncourt brothers, Schérer, Gavarni, sometimes Turgenev, and so on). Exasperated pessimism, cynicism, nihilism, alternating with a lot of joviality and good humor; I would have been quite at home there myself—I know these gentlemen by heart so well that I have actually had enough of them. One should be more radical; at root they all lack the principal thing—"*la force.*"

Loyally, your friend Nietzsche

158 · *To Erwin Rohde*   Nizza, November 11, 1887

Dear friend:

I still have to make amends to you, it seems, for what happened between us last spring.[116] As a sign that I do not lack the goodwill to do so, I am sending

115. Refers to N's *Hymn to Life*. Adolf Ruthardt was a professor of music in Geneva, later at the Leipzig Conservatory.

116. In May there had been a short exchange of letters between N and Rohde. Rohde had written unsympathetically about Taine; N had replied angrily on May 21, con-

you a book which has just appeared (perhaps I owe it to you in any case, for it is most closely connected with the last one I sent).[117] No, do not let yourself be estranged from me so easily! I at least shall not lose now, at my age and in my isolation, the few human beings in whom I once placed my trust.

Your N.

N.B. I ask you to come to your senses regarding M. Taine. Such crass things as you say and think about him annoy me. I would forgive Prince Napoléon for them,[118] *not* my friend Rohde. I find it hard to believe that a person who misunderstands this kind of austere and magnanimous mind (T. is the educator of all the more serious learned characters in France) can understand anything of my own task. Frankly, you have never mentioned anything to me that might have allowed me to suppose you *knew* what destiny it is that lies upon me. Have I ever reproached you for this? Never, not even in my heart, even if only because I do not expect it from anybody. Who has ever been concerned for me with even the slightest degree of passion and pain![119] Has anyone had even an inkling of the real cause of my long sickness, which I have perhaps mastered now, in spite of everything? I have forty-three years behind me, and am just as alone as when I was a child.

---

trasting the life of the lonely and ignored outsider with that of the scholar who has adjusted to society: ". . . His life, whether he will it so or not, takes on the character of a mission; there is a *necessity* which commands his attitude to all his problems (it is not a casual, random matter as it is for you and most classical philologists in your attitude to philology)." And on May 23, in a more conciliating letter, he had written: "With the exception of Burckhardt, Taine is the only man who has had something cordial and sympathetic to say about my writings, so that I sometimes think of him and Burckhardt as my only readers. We are at root all three committed to one another, as three radical nihilists— although I myself, as you perhaps feel, still do not doubt that I shall find the way out and the hole through which one arrives at 'something' " (*Briefe und Berichte*, pp. 417–19). Rohde sent no reply to this November letter.

117. *Zur Genealogie der Moral*. N sent a copy to Burckhardt, and in a letter to him (November 14, 1887) remarked that he regarded Burckhardt and Taine as the only readers who understood him.

118. Prince Napoléon, *Napoléon et ses détracteurs* (Paris, 1887), which included an attack on Taine.

119. In a letter to Overbeck, dated November 12, 1887, N used this same phrase but began it with an interesting addition: "With the exception of R. Wagner. . . ." Other sentences from the same letter: "This terrible decade that I have behind me has given me a plentiful taste of what it means to be alone—isolation such as I have known it, the isolation and exposure of a sufferer who has no means even of protecting, even of defending himself. [. . .] Moreover, I have a task which forbids me to think of myself much. [. . .] This task has made me sick; it will make me well again, and not only well but also more affable and all that that entails" (*Briefe und Berichte*, p. 429).

159 · *To Peter Gast*　　　　　Nizza, November 24, 1887

Dear friend:

This morning I am enjoying a *great* treat: for the first time there is a "fire idol" in my room, a small stove—I confess that I have already executed a few pagan leaps around it.[120] The time till now was a perpetual blue-fingered shiver, which meant that my philosophy too was not on a very good footing. It is hard to endure the icy breath of death in one's own room—not to be able to retreat into one's room as into one's fortress but to be *dragged back there as into one's prison.* There has been torrential rain for the past ten days: it is estimated that 208 liters have fallen to the square meter. This October was the coldest I have ever known, and November the rainiest. Nice is still fairly empty; yet there are twenty-five of us at table, friendly and kindly little people, to whom no objection can be taken.[121]

Meanwhile only Overbeck has written, full of joy at the *Hymn* and its "beautiful, uncommonly penetrating, and dignified melody" ("your present music seems to be extraordinarily simple"). He emphasizes the "rich, repeatedly so telling accent on the first 'pain' and the hush that comes in the last bars and sounds almost even more deeply into my heart." My friend Krug (who, by the way, asks me to reassess him not as Justizrat but as Regierungsrat)[122] speaks of being "deeply moved, to tears. I certainly hope that the chorus [*sic*] will be performed here. . . . The orchestration is excellent, as far as I can judge. It shows a pleasant intensity and variety, while being wisely moderated, as, for example, on page 8, where the words 'and in the heat of the struggle' are only softly indicated through the tremolo of the violins and the tenor trombone with the subsequent *piano* trumpet fanfare. On pages 6 and 10 the quietly descending flute notes will also stand out beautifully," and so on, and so on.

The fact that Rousseau was among the first admirers of Gluck makes one think; to me, at least, everything that Rousseau valued is a little questionable, likewise everyone who has valued *him* (there is a whole Rousseau family; Schiller belongs to it, Kant also, to some extent; in France, George Sand, even Sainte-Beuve; in England [George] Eliot and so on). Anyone who needs "moral dignity" *faute de mieux* has numbered

---

120. The stove had been sent to him by his mother.

121. He was living at this time in the Pension de Genève.

122. "Justizrat" was a title conferred on senior lawyers; "Regierungsrat" was a government councillor (equivalent of a senator in the United States and of a member of Parliament in England).

among Rousseau's admirers, down to our own favorite Dühring, who even has the good taste to present himself in his autobiography as the *Rousseau of the nineteenth century.* (Notice how a person stands vis-à-vis Voltaire and Rousseau: it makes the profoundest difference whether he agrees with the former or with the latter. Voltaire's enemies, for example, Victor Hugo, all the romantics—even the last sophisticated romantics, like the Goncourt brothers—are all gracious toward the masked plebeian Rousseau; I suspect that there is a certain amount of plebeian rancor at the basis of romanticism . . .) Voltaire is a glorious intelligent *canaille;*[123] but I share Galiani's opinion:

> un monstre gai vaut mieux
> qu'un sentimental ennuyeux[124]

Voltaire is only possible and sufferable in an aristocratic culture which can afford precisely the luxury of intellectual roguery . . .

Just look what warm feelings, what "tolerance," my stove is already beginning to flood me with . . .

Please, dear friend, keep this task in mind; you cannot get around it. You must, *in rebus musicis et musicantibus,* restore *stricter principles* to a position of honor, by deed and word, and seduce the Germans to the paradox which is only paradoxical today: that *stricter principles and gay music belong together* . . .

Loyally and gratefully, your friend N.

160 · *To Georg Brandes*[125]   Nizza, December 2, 1887

Verehrter Herr:

A few readers whom one personally honors, and no other readers—that is really one of my wishes. As for the latter part of the wish, I do of course

123. "Rogue."

124. The lines are by Voltaire; Galiani quoted them. Cf. *Werke in drei Bänden,* 3:453, where the quotation is used in support of a critique of the pessimism and sentimentality ushered in by eighteenth-century Enlightenment: "I guarded against the German and Christian narrowness and logical wrongness (*Folge-Unrichtigkeit*) of Schopenhauer's or even Leopardi's pessimism and sought out its most basic forms (Asia). But to endure *this* extreme pessimism (which sounds a note here and there in my *Birth of Tragedy*), to live alone 'without God and morality,' I had to find an antithesis for myself. Perhaps I know better than anyone why man alone laughs: he alone suffers so deeply that he *had* to invent laughter . . .'"

125. Brandes (actually Georg Cohen) was a Danish critic and literary historian (1842–1927). His first letter to N is dated November 26, 1887. His 1887–88 lectures on N appeared in his *Gesammelte Schriften,* vol. 1 (Munich, 1902).

see more and more that it is not being fulfilled. I am all the more happy that in my case the *pauci* are not lacking from the *satis sunt pauci*,[126] and never have been lacking from it. Of the living among these few, I would mention (to name such persons as you will know) my excellent friend Jakob Burckhardt, Hans von Bülow, H. Taine, the Swiss poet Keller; of the dead, the old Hegelian Bruno Bauer and Richard Wagner. It is a real joy to me that such a good European and missionary of culture as yourself should wish henceforth to belong among them; I thank you with all my heart for your goodwill.

Of course this will entail some difficulties for you. I personally do not doubt that my writings are still in some way "very German"; you will of course feel this much more strongly, being spoiled by yourself, as you are —I mean by your free and gracefully French manner of handling language (more sociable manner than my own). Many words have become for me encrusted with other crystals, and have another taste than for my readers— that must be taken into account. In the scale of my experiences and circumstances, there is a preponderance of notes that have a rarer, remoter, and thinner pitch than the normal ones in the middle. Also I have (to speak as an old musician, which I actually am) an ear for quarter tones. Lastly—and this is probably what most often makes my books obscure—there is in me a distrust of dialectic, even of reasons. What a man thinks to be true or not yet so, seems to me to depend more on courage, on the strength of his courage . . . (Only I seldom have the courage to acknowledge what I actually know).

The expression "aristocratic radicalism," which you use, is very good. That is, if I may say so, the shrewdest remark that I have read about myself till now.

How far this way of thinking has carried my thoughts, how far it will still carry me—I am almost too frightened to conceive. But there are paths which forbid one to travel them backward, and so I go forward, because I *must*.

So that I may do all I can to ease your access to my cave—that is, to my philosophy—I am asking my Leipzig publisher to send you my earlier writings *en bloc*. I recommend especially that you read their new prefaces (almost all the writings have been reissued). These prefaces, read in order, may perhaps shed some light on me, provided that I am not obscure *an sich* (obscure in and for myself), as *obscurissimus obscurorum virorum* . . .

—This might possibly be the case.—

Are you a musician? A choral and orchestral work of mine is just being published, a *Hymn to Life*. It is the one composition of mine that is

126. "A few are enough."

meant to survive and to be sung one day "in my memory"—assuming that enough remains of me in other respects. You see what posthumous thoughts I live among. But a philosophy like mine is like a grave—one does not live with others any more. *Bene vixit qui bene latuit*[127]—that is what is written on Descartes's tombstone—an epitaph if ever there was one!

I also wish to meet you one day.

Your Nietzsche

N.B. I am spending this winter in Nice. My summer address is: Sils Maria Oberengadin, Switzerland. I have given up my university professorship. I am three-quarters blind.

161 · *To Carl Fuchs*   Nice (France), December 14, 1887
                                          Pension de Genève

Dear and valued friend:

You chose a *very good* moment to write me a letter. For I am, almost without willing it so, but in accordance with an inexorable necessity, right in the midst of settling my accounts with men and things and putting behind me my whole life hitherto. Almost everything that I do now is a "drawing-the-line under everything." The vehemence of my inner pulsations has been terrifying, all through these past years; now that I must make the transition to a new and more intense form, I need, above all, a new estrangement, a still more intense *depersonalization*. So it is of the greatest importance what and who still remain to me.

What age I am? I do not know—as little as I know how young I shall become.

It is a pleasure for me to look at the picture of you; there seems to be much youth and courage in it, mixed, as is right, with beginnings of wisdom (and white hair?) . . .

In Germany there are strong complaints about my "eccentricities." But since people do not know where my center is, they will find it hard to know for certain where and when I have till now been "eccentric"—for example, being a classical philologist; this was being *outside* my center (which, fortunately, does not mean that I was a bad classical philologist). Likewise today it seems to me an eccentricity that I should have been a Wagnerite. It was an inordinately dangerous experiment; now that I know that it did

127. "He lived well who hid well."

not ruin me, I know also what meaning it has had for me—it was the strongest test of my character. To be sure, one's inmost being gradually disciplines one back to unity; that *passion*, to which no name can be put for a long time, rescues us from all digressions and dispersions, that *task* of which one is the involuntary missionary.[128]

Such things are very hard to understand from a distance. For this reason, my past years have been inordinately painful and violent. In case you want to hear more of this bad and problematic story, I recommend to your friendly interest the new editions of my earlier writings, especially the prefaces to them. (Incidentally, my publisher, who is with good reason rather desperate, is prepared to give away these new editions to anyone provided the recipient promises him a longish essay—on "Nietzsche *en bloc.*" The bigger literary periodicals, like Lindau's *Nord und Süd*, are ripe for needing such an essay, because a real disquiet and excitement about the meaning of my writings are becoming perceptible. Till now nobody has had enough courage and intelligence to *discover* me for the dear Germans; my problems are new, my psychological horizon is frighteningly extensive, my language bold and German, perhaps no other German books are as rich in ideas and as independent as mine.)

The *Hymn* also is part of the "drawing-the-line under everything." Could you not have it sung for yourself? I have had several prospects of performance (for instance, from Mottl in Karlsruhe).[129] It is of course really intended to be sung one day "in my memory": it is meant to be something of mine that will survive, assuming that I myself *survive*.

Remember me with kindness, my dear Dr. Fuchs. I thank you most cordially for *wanting* to remain loyal to me even in the second half of your century.[130]

Your friend Nietzsche

128. The substance of this letter to this point appears with some variations in the letter of December 20, to Gersdorff (cementing their renewed friendship), and in that of January 3, 1888, to Paul Deussen. In a postscript to the latter, N states that he still passionately wishes to spend a winter in some German university city ("a wish which, considering my need for intellectual nourishment, sometimes becomes a hunger and a torture"), but that his health has so far made this impossible (*Briefe und Berichte*, pp. 433–35 and 439–41).

129. Felix Mottl (1859–1911) was an Austrian conductor and composer, who also conducted at Bayreuth. One of his own works was an arrangement of dances from operas by Gluck, the incentive for which could have come from N.

130. Meaning, after Fuchs had passed his fiftieth birthday.

162 · *To Franz Overbeck*   Nice, February 3, 1888

Dear friend:

Here at last is the invoice from Herr C. G. Naumann: may I ask you to pay
it out of the money put aside? There is *no* hurry; I have a bad conscience to
be disturbing you at your peace and work with such a matter.

I am hard at work too; and the outlines of an unquestionably immense task before me are emerging more and more clearly from the mists.
There were dark moments meanwhile, whole days and nights when I did
not know any longer how to go on living and when a black despair attacked
me, worse than I have ever known before. Nevertheless, I know that I cannot escape by going backward or to the right or to the left; I have no *choice*.
This logic alone is now keeping me going; seen from any other side, my
state is untenable and so painful as to be a torture. My latest book showed
something of this; in the state of a bow strung to the highest possible tension,
any emotion is good for one, provided it is a violent emotion. No more
"beautiful things" are to be expected of me: no more than one should expect
a suffering and starving animal to attack its prey *gracefully*. The perpetual
lack of a really refreshing and *healing human love*, the absurd isolation which
it entails, making almost any residue of a connection with people merely
something that wounds one—that is all very bad indeed and right only in itself, having the right to be necessary.[131]

Do I have nothing better to say? There have been good signs of piety
and deep recognition from a number of artists, among them Dr. Brahms, H.
von Bülow, Dr. Fuchs, and Mottl. Likewise, an intelligent and combative
Dane, Dr. G. Brandes, has written me several letters showing his devotion,
astonished, as he says, by the original and new spirit which breathes in my

131. In a sketch for this letter, N had written: ". . . The first draft of my
'Transvaluation of all Values' is finished. The complete outline for it was by far the
longest torture that I have experienced, a veritable sickness. You other 'knowers,' you
have a better time of it, and are *not* so unreasonable! You do not know the truth as something that one has to tear, piece by piece, from one's heart, every victory taking its revenge
in a defeat." One of Elisabeth's forgeries (a letter to herself, dated January 25) makes N
seem to be hankering after female companionship at this time: "Believe me, for people of
my sort the best thing would still be a marriage like Goethe's—that is, marry a good
housekeeper! But even this idea gives me the shudders! No, definitely, it is not a wife that
I want, rather a young and gay daughter, for whom I would be an object of reverence and
loving care. But the best thing of all would be to have my good old Lama again. A sister
is, for a philosopher, a very beneficial arrangement, especially if she is serene, courageous, and loving (not an old sourpuss like G. Keller's sister). . . ." Earlier in this forgery,
Elisabeth had N cast aspersions on Overbeck's wife as a "clever goose who has no idea
how boring she is." (*Briefe und Berichte*, pp. 442-45.)

writings, the general tendency of which he describes as "aristocratic radicalism." He calls me the foremost writer in Germany by far. Did I write to you that Gersdorff has resumed his relations with us, in the most un-compromising and honest fashion?[132] I am sorry not to be able to say the same of Rohde. He has not replied to two letters which I wrote him with the warmest will to restore his good feelings and make him forget the out-burst that occurred; nor has he acknowledged my last book which I sent him. This does him no honor; but he is quite likely unwell, in a bad state. From Paraguay there is very calming news: the development of the whole project, which was certainly a daring one, can be described only as splendid. Already about a hundred persons are active in the new colony, among them several *very* good German families (for example, the Mecklenburg family of Baron Maltzan); my relations are among the biggest landowners in Paraguay [———][133] You can guess that [Dr. Förster] and I have to exert ourselves to the uttermost to avoid treating each other openly as enemies . . . The anti-Semitic pamphlets shower down wildly upon me (which pleases me a hundred times more than their earlier restraint). Enough for today! With best wishes to you and your dear wife.

Your   N.

163 · *To Reinhart von Seydlitz*   Nice, Pension de Genève,
February 12, 1888

Dear friend:

That was no "proud silence" which closed my mouth to almost everyone; it was much more—a humble silence, that of a sufferer who is ashamed to betray how much he is suffering. A sick animal retires to its lair; so does *la bête philosophe.* A friendly voice seldom reaches me nowadays. I am alone now, absurdly alone; and in the course of my relentless and underground struggle against everything that human beings till now have revered and loved (my formula for this is the "transvaluation of all values"), I have im-perceptibly become something like a lair myself—something hidden away, which people do not find, even if they go out and look for it. *But people do not go out in search of such things* . . . Between ourselves—the three of us—

---

132. Communication between N and Gersdorff had been sporadic since 1877, when a disagreement (involving Malwida von Meysenbug) had led to a break between them. N's letter of December 20, 1887 (not translated), marks the restoration of good relations.

133. Dash indicates an editorial omission (*Briefe und Berichte,* p. 447).

it is not inconceivable that I am the first philosopher of the age, perhaps even a little more, something decisive and doom-laden standing between two millennia. One is *always* doing penance for such an aloof position—by an ever increasing, more and more icy, more and more sharp isolation. And our dear Germans! . . . In Germany, though I am in my forty-fifth year and have published about fifteen books (including a *non plus ultra*, *Zarathustra*), there has not yet been a *single* even moderately reputable review of any *one* of my books. People help themselves out now with the phrases "eccentric," "pathological," "psychiatric." There are plenty of bad and slanderous gestures in my direction; an unrestrainedly hostile tone is paramount in the periodicals—learned and unlearned—but how is it that nobody protests against this? that nobody ever feels hurt when I am censured? And in all the years no solace, not a drop of humanity, not a breath of love—

In these circumstances, one must live in *Nice*. This time too it is seething with do-nothings, *grecs* and other philosophers, seething with "people like me"; and God, with the cynicism that is peculiar to him, lets his sun shine down particularly upon *us* more beautifully than upon the so much more reputable Europe of Herr von Bismarck (which is working with feverish virtue at its armaments, and entirely presents the aspect of a hedgehog with heroic inclinations). The days pass here in unashamed beauty; never was there a more perfect winter. And these colors of Nice—I would like to send them to you. All the colors permeated with a shining silver gray; spiritual, intelligent colors; no residue at all of the brutality of the dark tones. The advantage of this small piece of coast between Alassio and Nice is that it allows an Africanism, in color, vegetation, and the dryness of the air—this does not occur elsewhere in Europe.

O, how I would like to sit together with you and your dear and esteemed wife under some Homeric and Phaeacian sky . . . but I *may* not go any farther south (my eyes will soon compel me to leave for more northern and more stupid landscapes). Write, please, again during your stay in Munich, and forgive me for this *gloomy* letter!

Your devoted friend   Nietzsche

164 · *To Georg Brandes*   Nizza, February 19, 1888

Verehrter Herr:

You have put me under a most pleasant obligation to you with your contribution to the concept of "modernity"; for, this very winter, I have been circling this most crucial value problem, very much in the upper air, very much like a bird and with the best intention of looking down on the "modern" in as unmodern a way as possible . . . I admire—let me confess to you!—the tolerance of your judgments as much as the restraint with which you make them. How you suffer all these little children to come unto you—even Heyse![134]

During my next journey to Germany I plan to study the psychological problem of Kierkegaard, and also to renew my acquaintance with your earlier writings. This will be, in the best sense of the word, useful for me—and will serve to "bring home" to me the severity and arrogance of my own judgments.

Yesterday my publisher sent me a telegram to say that the books have been sent off to you. I will spare you and myself the story of why there has been such a delay. Do, please, make the best of a "bad job"—of these Nietzsche books, I mean.

My own pretension is that I have given to the Germans the richest, *most experienced*, and most independent books that they have; likewise, that my own person represents a crucial occurrence in the crisis of value judgments. But that could be an error; and stupid, too—I want not to *have* to believe anything about myself.

A few remarks here about my first writings (the *Juvenilia* and *Juvenalia*) :

The essay against Strauss, the wicked laughter of a "very free thinker" at the expense of one who thought he was free, caused an immense scandal. In spite of my twenty-seven years, I was then already a full professor, thus a kind of authority and something *substantial*. The fairest account of this affair, in which almost every "person of importance" took sides for or against me, and a ridiculous mass of paper went through the press, is given in Karl Hillebrand's *Zeiten, Völker und Menschen*, volume 2. What mattered was not my ridiculing the senile jottings of a remarkable critic but my catching the Germans red-handed in a compromising act of bad taste—German taste had unanimously admired Strauss's book *Der alte und der neue Glaube*, despite all religious and theological party factions, as a masterpiece of freedom and subtlety of thought (even of style!). My pamphlet was the first direct attack on German *Bildung* (that *Bildung* which people were celebrating as the conqueror of France). The word I coined, "Bildungs-

134. Paul Heyse (1830–1914) was widely known at the time for his stories. In his lifetime he published twenty-four books of novellas, and as many again of plays, poems, and translations. He was known principally as a "psychological" author, dealing with people in modern society; his characters and problems have not survived their epoch.

philister,"[135] survived the raging fluctuations of the polemics and has entered everyday language.

The two essays on Schopenhauer and Richard Wagner are, it seems to me now, confessions about myself—above all, they are avowals to myself, rather than, say, real psychological accounts of those two masters, to whom I felt as much kinship as I felt antagonism. (I was the first person to distill a sort of unity out of both of them; this erroneous belief is now very much in the forefront of German culture—all Wagnerites are adherents of Schopenhauer. This was not true when I was young. In those days it was the last Hegelians who adhered to Wagner, and even in the fifties the slogan was "Wagner and Hegel.")

Between the *Unzeitgemässe Betrachtungen* and *Menschliches, Allzumenschliches* come a crisis and a sloughing. Physically too, I lived for years next door to death. This was my great good fortune: I forgot myself, I survived myself . . . I have performed the same trick a second time.

Well then, we have given each other presents, perhaps like a couple of travelers who are glad they met each other on the way? . . .

I remain your most devoted   Nietzsche

165 · *To Peter Gast*   Nice, Pension de Genève,
                                            February 26, 1888

Dear friend:

Gloomy weather, Sunday afternoon, great solitude: I can devise no more pleasant occupation than talking a little to you and with you. I have just noticed that my fingers are blue: my handwriting will be decipherable only to him who deciphers my thoughts . . .

What you say of Wagner's style in your letter reminds me of a remark I found somewhere in writing: that his "dramatic style" was no more than a species of *bad* style, even of *non*-style in music. But our musicians see progress in this . . . Actually everything remains to be said, remains even to be thought, so I suspect, in this area of truths: Wagner himself, as man, as animal, as God and artist, surpasses a thousand times the understanding and the incomprehension of our Germans. Does he surpass that of the French as well?

Today I had the pleasure of finding the right answer, just when the question could seem extraordinarily hazardous: it is this—"who was most

135. "Culture-Philistine"—a central concept in N's analysis of culture as an incrustation over a vacuum.

ready for Wagner? who was most naturally and inwardly Wagnerian, in spite of and without Wagner?" For a long time I had been telling myself: it was that bizarre, three-quarters lunatic Baudelaire, the poet of *Les Fleurs du Mal*. It had disappointed me that this kindred spirit of Wagner's had not during his lifetime discovered him; I have underlined the passages in his poems in which there is a sort of *Wagnerian sensibility* which has found no form anywhere else in poetry (Baudelaire is a *libertine*, mystical, "satanic," but, above all, Wagnerian). And what did I find today! I was thumbing through a recently published collection of *Œuvres posthumes* by this genius—most deeply prized and even loved in France—and there, among some invaluable psychological observations relating to *décadence* ("Mon cœur mis à nu," of the kind which in Schopenhauer's and Byron's case has been *burned*) an unpublished letter of Wagner's catches my eye, on an essay by Baudelaire in the *Revue Européenne*, April, 1861. I'll copy it out for you:[136]

My dear M. Baudelaire, I called upon you several times without finding you in. You will understand how desirous I am of telling you how much satisfaction you have given me with your article, which does me more honor and gives me more encouragement than everything that has so far been said about my poor talent. Would it not be possible for me to tell you personally in the near future how intoxicated I felt on reading these beautiful pages, which told me—as the best of poems does—what impressions I can boast of having produced on a being with an organization as superior as yours? A thousand thanks for your beneficence and permit me to say I am most proud to be able to call you my friend. Until our meeting, then? *Tout à vous*, Richard Wagner.

(Wagner was at that time forty-eight years old, Baudelaire forty; the letter is touching, though written in miserable French.)
    In the same book I find sketches by Baudelaire for a passionate defense of Heinrich *Heine* against French criticism (Jules Janin). Even during the last years of his life, when he was half mad and slowly going to ruin, *Wagner*'s music was played to him as a *medicine;* Wagner's name had only to be mentioned to him, and he would "give a smile of delight."[137] (On only one other occasion, unless everything deceives me, did Wagner write a letter showing this sort of gratitude and even enthusiasm—after he had received the *Birth of Tragedy*.)
    (From a letter of Baudelaire's:[138] "I dare not speak of Wagner any

136. The original transcription is in French.
137. Original: "il a souri d'allégresse."
138. N translates into German here.

more: people have laughed at me too much. This music has been one of the great joys of my life; for a good fifteen years I have not experienced such exaltation—or rather *enlèvement*").

How are you now, dear friend? I have vowed to take nothing seriously any more for a while. But you should not think that I have been busy making "literature" again[139]—this manuscript was for *myself*; from now on, I intend to make a manuscript for myself every winter—the idea of "making it public" is out of the question.

The Fritzsch question has been settled by a telegram. Herr Spitteler has written, not badly, apologizing for his "impertinence" (as he says).[140]

The winter is a hard one; at the moment I have everything I want except perhaps a divine and tranquil music—*your* music, dear friend!

Your   N.

There has not been a single reply from the newspapers and periodicals among which Fritzsch circulated last autumn an offer of my collected works for review.

Overbeck's father has died, at the age of eighty-four. Overbeck has gone to Dresden on this account—to the detriment of his health, I fear, which is giving him difficulties again this winter.

Snowstorms everywhere, polar-bear humanity.

166 · *To Franziska Nietzsche*   Nice, March 20, 1888

My dear mother:

The money you sent and your accompanying letter brought me great pleasure—almost as if you had made me a present. My finances were in

139. Original: ". . . dass ich wieder 'Literatur' gemacht hätte." It is characteristic of N, in certain moods, to make ironic remarks about his writings; mere "Literatur," here as earlier, was the last thing he intended (cf., "No more 'beautiful things' are to be expected of me"; letter No. 162). The original of "manuscript" in what follows is "Niederschrift," with the raw sense of "something set down in writing." The work in question was eventually edited and arranged for publication as *Der Wille zur Macht*.

140. On September 17, 1887, N had written to Overbeck asking for information about Carl Spitteler (who had been a student of Overbeck's). Spitteler had written to N proposing to write an article on him. This article appeared in J. V. Widmann's periodical *Der Bund* during the winter (January 1, 1888). N found it "tactless and impertinent" (letter of July 20, 1888, to Overbeck). Spitteler later wrote an enthusiastic review of *Der Fall Wagner*, which also appeared in *Der Bund* (November 8, 1888). His memoirs of N were published in 1908: *Meine Beziehungen zu N* (*Gesammelte Werke*, vol. 6, Zürich, 1947). Widmann also published his own views on this relationship: "Carl Spitteler und F. N. in ihren persönlichen Beziehungen," *Der Bund*, October 6, 1907.

rather a bad way; and perhaps I have already told you that my hotel fees have been increased this winter. Nevertheless, my circumstances here are significantly less costly than those of the average hotel guest; and, moreover, this winter I have what I did not have before—a room which I like, a high one, with excellent light for my eyes, freshly decorated, with a large, heavy table, chaise longue, bookcase, and dark reddish-brown wallpaper, which I chose myself. It still seems to me that I must hold on to Nice: the climate has a better influence on me than any other. Precisely here I can use my eyes twice as much as anywhere else. Under this sky my head has become more free, year by year; here the uncanny consequences of being ill for years on end, in the proximity and expectation of death, are more mild in their effects. I would also mention that my digestion is better here than elsewhere; but above all, my mind feels more alert here, and carries its burden more easily—I mean the burden of a fate to which a *philosopher* is inevitably condemned. I walk for an hour every morning, in the afternoon for an average of three hours, and at a rapid pace—the same walk day after day—it is beautiful enough for that. After supper, I sit until nine o'clock in the dining room, in company mainly with Englishmen and English ladies, with a lamp, which has a shade, at my table. I get up at six-thirty in the morning and make my own tea and also have a few biscuits. At twelve noon I have breakfast; at six, the main meal of the day. No wine, no beer, no spirits, no coffee—the greatest regularity in my mode of living and in my diet. Since last summer I have accustomed myself to drinking water—a good sign, a step forward. It happens that I have just been ill for three days; today everything is all right again. I am thinking of leaving Nice at the end of March; the light is already too strong for me, and the air is too soft, too springlike. It is possible that I shall have a visitor before I leave: Seydlitz, who is on his way back from Egypt with most of his household in tow, and who means to come and see me. My old friend Gersdorff also wrote in a good mood; he has just completed his month of service in Berlin (he is chamberlain to the old empress). But the best thing was a long letter from Lama: eight pages of cordial and *very* sensible things. She wrote it while still in Asunción, but in very good spirits ("certainly I have a fate which suits me, and that is a good thing"). Yet she expresses anxiety that there will be too much to do in the months to come, because a mass of new colonists are registered and perhaps the preparations for them are not yet adequate. I forgot to tell you that an old school friend (my "junior"), Lieutenant Geest, is here being treated by the Red Cross sisters; I sometimes visit him. A very North German ambiance: Frau von Münchow, Frl. von Diethfurth, and so on. My table companion this winter is once again Baroness Pläncker, née Seckendorff, and, as such, she is very intimate with all the Seckendorffs at court and in the army (for example, with the Graf Seckendorff, who, as you know, is the new empress's "right hand"). She is also a close friend of Geheimrat von *Bergmann*, and is herself having treatment from him, so that I was very well informed about affairs in San Remo. I have even had in my hands some pages which the crown prince wrote, a few days before his departure. — — —

No more now, my dear good mother. Grateful embraces from

Your old creature

167 · *To Peter Gast*   Turin, April 7, 1888, Saturday[141]

Dear friend:

How good it was to hear from you! The first greeting I received here came from you; and the last to reach me in Nice was also from you. And what good and curious things you announced! That your quartet lies in front of you in a state of some calligraphic perfection, and that you now, on account of this, bless this last winter also! One certainly does become a very demanding sort of person when privately one *sanctions* one's life by works; it makes one forget, especially, to please people. One is too serious—you feel this—there is a devilish seriousness at the back of a man who *wants* to have *his work respected* . . .

Dear friend, I am using the first calm after a very stormy journey to write you a letter. Perhaps this will give me some peace and composure, for until now I was all in pieces and never have I traveled under such unfavorable circumstances. Is it possible to have so many absurd experiences between Monday and Saturday! Everything went wrong, from the very start. I was sick for two days—where? In Sampierdarena. Do not think I was wanting to travel there. Only my luggage held fast to the original course, to Turin; we others—that is, my hand luggage and I—dispersed in various directions. And how expensive the journey was! How rich my poverty will have made some people! I really am not fit for traveling alone any more; I get so worked up that I do stupid things. Here too, at the start everything

141. N left Nice on April 2; on April 3 he was in Sampierdarena, near Genoa, unwell; on April 4 he reached Genoa, and on April 5 he arrived in Turin, where he stayed until June 5. From June 6 until September 20 he was at Sils Maria. On September 21, he returned to Turin, and lived there until his breakdown in January, 1889. His address during both periods in Turin was Via Carlo Alberto 6, III (opposite the Palazzo Carignano, with a view over the Piazza Carlo Alberto), where he rented a room in the third-floor apartment of the newsvendor Davide Fino.

was every which way. I spent a sleepless night, amazed, not comprehending all the things the day had brought. When I see you again, I shall describe to you a scene in Savona which might have come straight out of the *Fliegende Blätter*.[142] Only it made me ill.

In Genoa I walked around like a mere shadow among memories. Five or six special places there which I loved appealed to me even more strongly; it seemed to me to have an incomparable pale *noblesse*, and to be vastly superior to everything else the Riviera offers. I thank my destiny for condemning me to live in this hard and gloomy city during the years of *décadence;* every time one leaves it, one has also left oneself behind—the will expands again, and one no longer has the courage to be pusillanimous. I never felt more grateful than during this pilgrimage through Genoa.

But Turin! Dear friend, I congratulate you! Your advice met my deepest wishes! This is really the city which I can now use! This is palpably for me, and was so almost from the start, however horrible the situation was for the first days. Above all, miserable rainy weather, icy, changeable, oppressive to the nerves, with humid, warm half hours between. But what a dignified and serious city! Not at all a metropolis, not at all modern, as I had feared, but a princely residence of the seventeenth century, one that had only a *single* commanding taste in all things—the court and the *noblesse*. Everywhere the aristocratic calm has been kept: there are no petty suburbs; a unity of taste even in matters of color (the whole city is yellow or reddish-brown). And a classical place for the feet as for the eyes! What robustness, what sidewalks, not to mention the buses and trams, the organization of which verges on the marvelous here! One can live, it seems, more cheaply here than in the other large Italian cities I know; also, nobody has swindled me so far. I am regarded as an *ufficiale tedesco*[143] (whereas I figured last winter in the official aliens' register of Nice *comme Polonais*). Incredible— what serious and solemn palaces! And the style of the palaces, without any pretentiousness; the streets clean and serious—and everything far more dignified than I had expected! The most beautiful cafés I have ever seen. These arcades are somewhat necessary when the climate is so changeable, but they are spacious—they do not oppress one. The evening on the Po Bridge—glorious! Beyond good and evil!

The problem remains the weather in Turin. I have suffered from it so far extraordinarily—I could hardly recognize myself.

With greetings and thanks, your devoted friend   Nietzsche

142. A popular humorous periodical of the time.

143. "German officer" (military, including retired); it could also mean "German functionary," but N understood it to mean the former; see his curriculum vitae, with its martial tone, at the end of the next letter.

168 · *To Georg Brandes*   Turin (Italy), *poste restante*,
April 10, 1888

But, *verehrter Herr*, what a surprise! Where did you find the courage to consider speaking in public about a *vir obscurissimus!* . . . Do you perhaps believe that I am known in my own dear country? I am treated there as if I were something way-out and absurd, something that one need not for the time being *take seriously* . . . Obviously you sense that I do not take my compatriots seriously either: and how could I today, now that German *Geist* has become a *contradictio in adjecto!*—I am most grateful to you for the photograph. Unfortunately nothing of the kind is to be had from my side: the last pictures I had are in the possession of my married sister in South America.

I enclose a small curriculum vitae, the first I have written.

As regards the chronology of the particular books, you will find it on the back flyleaf of *Jenseits von Gut und Böse*. Perhaps you no longer have that page.

Die Geburt der Tragödie was written between the summer of 1870 and the winter of 1871 (finished in Lugano, where I was living with Field Marshal Moltke's family).

The *Unzeitgemässe Betrachtungen*, between 1872 and summer, 1875 (there should have been thirteen of these; my health fortunately said No!).

What you say about *Schopenhauer als Erzieher* gives me pleasure. This little essay serves me as a signal of recognition: the man to whom it says nothing personal will probably not be further interested in me. It contains the basic scheme according to which I have so far lived; it is a rigorous promise.

Menschliches, Allzumenschliches, with its two continuations, summer, 1876–79. *Morgenröte*, 1880. The *Fröhliche Wissenschaft*, January, 1882. *Zarathustra*, 1883–85 (each part in about ten days). Perfect state of a "man inspired." All parts conceived on strenuous marches; absolute certainty, as if every thought were being called out to me. At the same time as the writing, the greatest physical elasticity and fullness—).

Jenseits von Gut und Böse, summer, 1885, in the Oberengadin and the following winter in Nice.

The *Genealogie* resolved on, written down, and the clean copy sent to the Leipzig printer between July 10 and 30, 1887. (Of course there are *philologica* by me too. But that does not concern either of us anymore.)

I am at the moment giving Turin a trial; I mean to stay here until June 5, and then go to the Engadin. Weather so far hard and bad as in winter.

But the city superbly quiet and flattering to my instincts. The loveliest sidewalks in the world.

Greetings from your grateful and devoted   Nietzsche

A wretched pity that I do not understand either Danish or Swedish. Curriculum vitae. I was born on October 15, 1844, on the battlefield of Lützen. The first name I heard was that of Gustav Adolf.[144] My forebears were Polish aristocrats (Niëzky); it seems that the type has been well preserved, despite three German "mothers."[145] Abroad, I am usually taken for a Pole; even this last winter the aliens' register in Nice had me inscribed *comme Polonais.* I have been told that my head and features appear in paintings by Matejko. My grandmother was associated with the Goethe-Schiller circle in Weimar; her brother became Herder's successor as superintendent-general of the churches in the duchy of Weimar. I had the good fortune to be a pupil at the distinguished *Schulpforta,* which produced so many men of note (Klopstock, Fichte, Schlegel, Ranke, and so on, and so on) in German literature.We had teachers who would have done honor to any University (or have done so). I was a student at Bonn, and later in Leipzig; In his old age, Ritschl, in those days the foremost classical scholar in Germany, picked me out almost from the start. At the age of twenty-two I was contributing to the *Literarisches Zentralblatt* (Zarncke). The establishment of a classical society at Leipzig, which exists to this day, was my doing. In the winter of 1868-69 the University of Basel offered me a professorship; I did not even have my doctorate. Subsequently the University of Leipzig gave me the doctorate, in a very honorable fashion, without any examination, without even a dissertation. From Easter, 1869, until 1879 I was at Basel; I had to give up my German citizenship, because as an officer (mounted artillery) I would have been drafted too frequently and disturbed in my academic duties. Nevertheless, I am versed in the use of two weapons: saber and cannon—and, perhaps, one other . . . At Basel everything went very well, in spite of my youth; it happened, especially with examinations for doctorate, that the examinee was older than the examiner. It was my great good fortune that friendly relations developed between Jakob Burckhardt

144. Lützen, in Saxony, close to which is Röcken, the village where N was born, was the scene of a famous battle in 1632, during the Thirty Years' War, in which Gustav Adolf, the Swedish king, and leader of the German Protestant side, lost his life in defeating the Catholic imperial forces. It was also the battlefield on which Napoleon defeated the allied Prussian and Russian armies in 1813. Lützen is about twelve miles northeast of Naumburg. Throughout this curriculum vitae N is striking a martial and heroic pose, creating an image of himself as anything but a Saxon provincial.

145. That is, three generations of maternal forebears: great-grandmother, grandmother, and mother.

and myself, a very unusual thing for this very hermetic and aloof thinker. An even greater good fortune that, from the beginning of my life at Basel, I became indescribably intimate with Richard and Cosima Wagner, who were then living on the estate at Tribschen near Lucerne, as on an island cut off from all their earlier associations. For several years we shared all our great and small experiences—there was limitless confidence between us. (In Wagner's *Collected Writings*, volume 7, you will find an "epistle" from him to me, written when the *Geburt der Tragödie* appeared). Through this relationship I met a wide circle of interesting men (and "man-esses")—actually almost everyone sprouting between Paris and Petersburg. Around 1876 my health grew worse. I spent a winter in Sorrento then, with my old friend Baroness Meysenbug (*Memoirs of an Idealist*) and the congenial Dr. Rée. My health did not improve. There were extremely painful and obstinate headaches which exhausted all my strength. They increased over long years, to reach a climax at which pain was habitual, so that any given year contained for me two hundred days of pain. The malaise must have had an entirely local cause—there was no neuropathological basis for it at all. I have never had any symptoms of mental disturbance—not even fever, no fainting.[146] My pulse was as slow as that of the first Napoleon (= 60). My specialty was to endure the extremity of pain, *cru, vert*, with complete lucidity for two or three days in succession, with continuous vomiting of mucus. Rumors have gone around that I am in a madhouse (have even died there). Nothing could be further from the truth. During this terrible period my mind even attained maturity: as testimony, the *Morgenröte*, which I wrote in 1881 during a winter of unbelievable misery in Genoa, far from doctors, friends, and relatives. The book is, for me, a kind of "dynamometer"—I wrote it when my strength and health were at a minimum. From 1882 on, very slowly to be sure, my health was in the ascendant again: the crisis was passed (my father died very young, at exactly the age at which I myself was nearest to death). Even today I have to be extremely cautious; a few climatic and meteorological conditions are indispensable. It is not by choice—it is by necessity—that I spend the summers in the Oberengadin, the winters on the Riviera . . . Recently my sickness has done me the greatest service: it has liberated me, it has restored to me the courage to be myself . . . Also I am, by instinct, a courageous animal, even a military one. The long resistance has exasperated my pride a little. Am I a philosopher? What does that matter! . . .

146. The last detail here might suggest that N wished to dispel all suspicion of his being an epileptic.

169 · *To Peter Gast*   Turin, Friday [April 20, 1888]
                          letters, as till now: *poste restante*

Dear friend:

How remarkable this all is! That now, after all, your star should rise over
Berlin![147] That there should be a small wingbeat of hope again. Really, your
recent "diversion," of which you write, is one of the most improbable and
unforeseen things possible on this earth. It makes one believe in *miracles*
again: a great step forward in the art of living! . . . It makes me extremely
happy, dear friend, that something gay and colorful should have flown across
your path, for it is exactly this which should have been done for you—but
what gloomy asses and owls the rest of us are! . . . That was something for
the Krause philosophy—and not for the Nietzschean one! . . .

As far as the latter is concerned, something of the kind must exist,
if one can trust a *Danish* newspaper which reached me recently. It announces
that a course of public lectures is being given at the University of Copenhagen, "om den tüske Filosof Nietzsche."[148] By whom? You can guess! . . .
What a lot one will have to thank these Jews for! Just think of my Leipzig
friends at the university—and how many miles they are from the idea of
lecturing about me!

Turin, dear friend, is a discovery of the *first importance*. I shall say
a few things about it; at the back of my mind is the thought that you also
might make use of it. I am in a good mood, at work from early in the day
until evening—a little pamphlet on music is keeping my fingers occupied—
my digestion is that of a demigod, I sleep despite the coaches rattling by at
night—all signs that Nietzsche has adapted himself eminently well to Turin.
It is the *air* that does it—dry, exhilarating, happy; there have been days on
which it had all the loveliness of the air in the Engadin. When I think of my
spring days in other places—for instance, in your incomparable magic sea-
shell; what a difference there is—the first place in which I am *possible!* . . .
And everything suiting me too, the people congenial and good-hearted. One
can live cheaply: twenty-five francs, including service, for a room in the
historic center of the city, opposite the grand Palazzo Carignano of 1680,
five paces from the great Portici[149] and the Piazza Castello, from the post
office, from the Teatro Carignano! In the last, since I have arrived, *Carmen*—

147. Refers to the invitation Gast had received to become music tutor in the
household of the Berlin banker Wilhelm von Krause.

148. "On the German philosopher Nietzsche"; these were Brandes's lectures.

149. The arcades.

naturally! . . . *Successo piramidale, tutto Torino carmenizzato!*[150] The same conductor as in Nice. Also *Lalla-Rookh*, by Félicien David. A young composer produced an operetta, with his own libretto—Herr Miller, Junior. In the residents' register there are listed: twenty-one composers, twelve theaters, an *Accademia filarmonica*, a school for music, and countless teachers of all kinds of instruments. Moral: almost a music center! The spacious tall Portici are the *pride* of the place: they extend over 10,020 meters, which means two good hours of walking. Big *trilingual* bookshops. I have never seen anything like them. The firm of Löscher is very attentive to me. Its present head, Herr Clausen, gives me all kinds of information (I am weighing the possibility of spending a winter here). An excellent *trattoria*, where people treat the German professor most courteously; I pay for each meal, including the tip, one franc, twenty-five centimes. (Minestra or risotto, a good portion of meat, vegetable, and bread—all good to eat!). The water is glorious; coffee in the foremost cafés costs twenty centimes a pot; ice cream of the highest quality, thirty centimes. All this will give you some idea.

Today the sky is overcast and rainy. But I do not seem to be depressed. They say of the summer that there are only four hot hours during any one day. The mornings and evenings refreshing. One can see beyond the town into the world of snow; there seems to be nothing in the way—the streets seem to run straight into the Alps. Autumn is said to be the most beautiful time. Really, there must be some energizing element in the air here—to be at home here will make one *king* of Italy . . .

So much and no more, my dear old friend! Most affectionate greetings.

Your N.

The moral I draw is this: you need a place where you can live all the year round, but under other meteorological influences than in Venice, perhaps also closer to music, possibilities of performance . . . And we must keep a hold on Italy!!!!!!

Tell me a little more about your quartet—where it is leading.

170 · *To Peter Gast*   Turin, Thursday [May 31, 1888]

If I answer your letter immediately once more, you will have no doubts about what I am missing: it is you yourself, dear friend! However well the

150. "Fabulous success, all Turin is Carmen-ized."

spring has treated me, it does not bring me the best thing, the thing which till now even the worst springs have brought—your music! The latter is closely interwoven—since Recoaro—with my idea of the "spring," somewhat as the gentle sound of bells across the city of lagoons is interwoven with my idea of "Easter." I dwell on these memories with long gratitude whenever a melody of yours occurs to me; nothing has ever made me so much aware of rebirth, exaltation, and ease as your music. It is my *good* music *par excellence*, for which I inwardly put on cleaner clothes than for any other.

I took the liberty of sending to you the day before yesterday some theater reviews by Dr. Fuchs. They contain much that is subtle and experienced.[151]

Dr. Brandes's lectures had a good conclusion—a great ovation, which, Brandes says, was not meant for him. He assures me that my name is now the topic in all intelligent circles in Copenhagen and is known throughout Scandinavia. My problems seem to have interested these northerners very much; individually they were better prepared, for instance, for my "master morality" as a result of the widespread precise knowledge of the Icelandic sagas, which provide extremely rich material for it. I am glad that the Danish philologists confirm and accept my derivation of the word *bonus*;[152] as a matter of fact, it is a tall order to trace the concept "good" back to the concept "warrior." Without my premises no philologist would have hit upon the idea.

It is really a pity that you made an excursion into paper and ink instead of into the Cadore.[153] It is plain that my bad example is spoiling your intrinsically better behavior. The weather was just right for such a mountain exploration; as a matter of fact, I made no use of it either, and am, like you, dissatisfied with myself for failing to do so.

I owe to these last weeks a very important lesson: I found *Manu*'s book of laws in a French translation done in India under strict supervision from the most eminent priests and scholars there. This absolutely *Aryan* work, a priestly codex of morality based on the Vedas, on the idea of caste

---

151. By July (see No. 172), N was exasperated by the mass of material which Fuchs kept sending him, and by Fuchs's vulgar self-seeking. Nos. 174–76 testify to an improvement in N's attitude toward him.

152. See *Zur Genealogie der Moral*, section 5: "The Latin *bonus* ["good"] I venture to interpret as warrior; providing that I am justified in deriving *bonus* from an older *duonus* (cf. *bellum* → *duellum* → *duen-lum*, which seems to preserve that *duonus*). *Bonus* would then spell the man of strife, of discord, the warrior. . . ." (*The Birth of Tragedy* and *The Genealogy of Morals*, translated by Francis Golffing, New York: Doubleday Anchor Books, 1956, p. 164.)

153. Pieve di Cadore, where Titian was born, is in the mountains behind Venice.

and very ancient tradition—*not* pessimistic, albeit very sacerdotal—supplements my views on religion in the most remarkable way. I confess to having the impression that everything else that we have by way of moral lawgiving seems to me an imitation and even a caricature of it—preeminently, Egypticism does; but even Plato seems to me in all the main points simply to have been well instructed by a Brahmin. It makes the Jews look like a Chandala race which learns from its *masters* the principles of making a *priestly caste* the master which organizes a people . . .[154] The Chinese also seem to have produced their Confucius and Lao-tse under the influence of this *ancient classic of laws*. The medieval organization looks like a wondrous groping for a restoration of all the ideas which formed the basis of primordial Indian-Aryan society—but with pessimistic values which have their origin in the soil of racial *décadence*. Here too, the Jews seem to be merely transmitters—they invent nothing.

So much, my dear friend, as a sign of how glad I always am to talk with you. I leave on Tuesday.

Affectionately, Your N.

171 · *To Karl Knortz*[155]   Sils Maria, Oberengadin,
                                              June 21, 1888

Hochgeehrter Herr:

The arrival of two works of your pen, for which I am grateful to you, seems to vouch for your having in the meantime received my writings. The task of giving you some picture of myself, as a thinker, or as a writer and poet, seems to me extraordinarily difficult. The first major attempt of this kind was made last winter by the excellent Dane Dr. Georg Brandes, who will

154. "Chandala" = "hybrid," not γενναῖος, not "pure caste." N develops these ideas in *Götzen-Dämmerung* and *Der Antichrist* (*Werke in drei Bänden*, 2:980–81 and 1224 ff.). Only in *Der Antichrist* does he give the least emphasis to the primacy, in the *Mānava Dharmaśāstra*, of the sage or "Mahātma" ("great Self or Spirit") as "mouthpiece of the timeless truth" (H. Zimmer, *Philosophies of India*, New York: Meridian, 1964, 8th printing, p. 40). Even in *Der Antichrist* he classifies the "sage" ("der Geistigste") as the "strongest man," not as the "magnanimous man" of original doctrine. Thus he confused the two castes of "sage" and "warrior"; the letters of this period enable one to see how this confusion, which had deadly historical consequences, had roots in N's own moribund state—with its concomitant compensatory urges. Also in *Der Antichrist* comes his identification of Chandala "mediocrities" and "Socialist rabble" (*Werke in drei Bänden*, 2:1228) as creatures of "weakness, envy, and *rancor*."

155. Knortz was an American journalist who planned to write an essay on N (see No. 174). Knortz did not publish anything on N in English, but published four pamphlets on him in German, between 1898 and 1913 (two in Switzerland and two in Germany).

be known to you as a literary historian. He gave, at the University of Copenhagen, a longish course of lectures about me, entitled "The German Philosopher Friedrich Nietzsche," the success of which, as I have been informed from there, must have been brilliant. He imparted to an audience of three hundred persons a lively interest in the audacity of the questions which I have posed and, as he says himself, he has made my name a topic of conversation throughout the north. In other respects, I have a more hidden circle of listeners and readers, to which also a few Frenchmen, like M. Taine, belong. It is my inmost conviction that these problems of mine—this whole position of an "Immoralist"—is still far too premature for the present day, still far too unprepared. The thought of advertising myself is utterly alien to me personally; I have not lifted a finger with that end in view.

Of my *Zarathustra*, I tend to think that it is the profoundest work in the German tongue, also the most perfect in its language. But for others to feel this will require whole generations to *catch up with* the inner experiences from which that work could arise. I would almost like to advise you to begin with the latest works, which are the most far-reaching and important ones (*Jenseits von Gut und Böse* and *Genealogie der Moral*). To me, personally, the middle books are the most congenial, *Morgenröte* and *Die fröhliche Wissenschaft* (they are the most personal).

The *Unzeitgemässe Betrachtungen*, youthful writings in a certain sense, deserve the closest attention for my development.[156] In *Völker, Zeiten und Menschen*, by Karl Hillebrand, there are a few very good essays on the first *Thoughts out of Season*. The piece against Strauss raised a great storm; the piece on Schopenhauer, which I especially recommend that you read, shows how an energetic and instinctively affirmative mind can accept the most salutory impulses even from a pessimist. With Richard Wagner and Frau Cosima Wagner, I enjoyed for several years, which are among the most valuable in my life, a relationship of deep confidence and inmost concord. If I am now one of the opponents of the Wagnerite movement, there are, needless to say, no mean motives behind this. In Wagner's *Collected Works*, volume nine (if I remember rightly) there is a letter to me which testifies to our relationship.

My pretension is that my books are of the first rank by virtue of their wealth of psychological experience, their fearlessness in face of the greatest dangers, and their sublime candor. I fear no comparison as far as

---

156. Original: "verdienen die höchste Beachtung für meine Entwicklung." The sentence telescopes, ungrammatically, two possible phrases: "verdienen die höchste Beachtung" and "sind höchst wichtig für meine Entwicklung." The ellipsis could be due to N's having to write with his eyes only about two inches above the paper.

the art of presentation in them and their claims to artistry are concerned. A love of long duration binds me to the German language—a secret intimacy, a deep reverence. Reason enough for reading hardly any books written in this language today.

I am, dear sir, yours truly, Professor Dr. Nietzsche

172 · *To Franz Overbeck*   Sils, July 20, 1888

Dear friend:

Nothing has improved, neither the weather nor my health—both remain *absurd*.[157] But today let me tell you something even more absurd: it is Dr. Fuchs. He has meanwhile written me an entire library (including a letter of twelve tall and narrow pages). This has gradually made me close up like a hedgehog, and all my old distrust has returned. His egoism is so crafty and, on the other hand, so timid and unfree that nothing helps him— his great talent does not, nor does his good measure of genuine artistic sense. He complains that he has had the whole world against him in Danzig for seven years; and there are a hundred signs that people there still have no confidence in him. He would like to get away; he is negotiating with Dresden, after failing to obtain an appointment at the Berlin School of Music. And on me he has tried every form of wooing (?) and adulation (?)! Yet another package of reviews tells the same story only too plainly. Much that is subtle and good, as long as he writes on matters of fact; as soon as persons come into account, the "infinitely small" dominates him. For me, he has written marginal notes. "This is much exaggerated; but I am indebted to *him* for this or that." Or: "*She* hates me for saying this—it was stupid of me." After the failure of his application for an appointment at the Berlin School of Music, three professors of that school came to Danzig and gave a concert. F. lauds them to the skies in a most impudent fashion. To excuse this, he writes to me that he did not want people to see how distressed he

157. Extracts from N's letter of July 4, to Overbeck: ". . . a recrudescence of my old sufferings . . ."; ". . . my life force is no longer intact . . ."; ". . . this extreme irritability under meteorological influences is *not* a good sign; it characterizes a certain pervasive exhaustion . . ."; ". . . I am not suffering from headaches or from stomach troubles but under the pressure of nervous exhaustion (which is in part hereditary—from my father, who also died from the consequences of a pervasive lack of life force). The only regimen which would have been suitable then would have been the American Weis-Mitchell treatment: extreme provision of the most nourishing foods (with absolute change of environment, company, interests). It is a fact that I have chosen, through ignorance, the diametrically opposite regimen, and I still cannot understand how I did not die in Genoa of total debility." (*Werke in drei Bänden*, 3: 1301–2.)

was by his failure. In fact, he was courting the three most influential supporters. He has offered me the prospect of an essay on my writings; at the same time he expresses a truly hellish fear that his advocacy of me as an atheist may prejudice his position as *organist* at St. Peter's. Naturally, he would use a pseudonym!! He has already sworn both my publishers to secrecy over this. For years the same F. went in fear of death lest his association with me might prejudice Wagner against him; a few years previously, when my influence in the Wagnerite world was incontestable, he had been courting my attentions only too zealously. I predicted that, on Wagner's death, he would find the courage again to write to me. And so it was, in an almost comical way.

He is also organist at the synagogue in Danzig; you can imagine, he makes fun of the Jewish services in the *dirtiest* way (but he gets *paid* for it!!).

Finally, he has written me a letter about his forebears, with so many disgusting and improper indiscretions about his mother and his father that I lost patience and forbade him most bluntly to write me such letters. I have absolutely no wish to have my solitude disturbed by chance arrivals of letters. That is how we stand. Unfortunately I know this sort of person too well to be able to hope that this is the end of it. Herr Spitteler wrote me a most grateful letter. I have managed to do something which he doubted would be possible—that is, to find a publisher [for him]. The book in question is on the esthetics of French drama: and, lo and behold, Herr Credner in Leipzig (Firma Veit, publisher for the imperial court) has most obligingly told me that he is willing.

This small act of human kindness on my part has a *humorous* background: it was my kind of revenge for an extremely tactless and impertinent article of Spitteler's on the whole of my writings, published last winter in *Der Bund.* I have far too high an opinion of this Swiss author's talents to be disconcerted by hooligan tricks of his (I respect his *character*—which is unfortunately not true with Dr. Fuchs). Sp. has also become, on my recommendation, a contributor to the *Kunstwart*, and, for my taste, he is its only interesting writer. Incidentally, I have done with that periodical; recently Herr Avenarius wrote bewailing my resignation, and I told him the truth in strong terms (the periodical is blowing the teutonic trumpet, and has betrayed Heine in the most *contemptible* fashion—Herr Avenarius, this Jew!!!)[158] At the moment, a small musical pamphlet is being printed, some-

158. In September, 1887, N had agreed to become a regular contributor to Ferdinand Avenarius's periodical *Der Kunstwart* ("because it is good to have a place where one can have one's say on esthetic questions from time to time"). Avenarius was at that time thirty-one years old, an anthologist of contemporary poetry; Gottfried Keller had spoken of him to N (*Werke in drei Bänden,* 3 : 1263). It would appear from this letter that N found infighting among German Jews as distasteful as anti-Semitism.

thing very jolly (written in Turin). Affectionate greetings and good wishes
to you and your dear wife.

Your Nietzsche

173 · *To Malwida von Meysenbug* Sils, end of July, 1888

Hochverehrte Freundin:

You will be thinking: at last!—won't you? But I involuntarily have no words
for anyone, because I have less and less desire to allow anyone to see into the
difficulties of my existence. There is indeed a great *emptiness* around me.
Literally, there is no one who could understand my situation. The worst
thing is, without a doubt, not to have heard for ten years a single word that
actually *got through* to me—*and* to be understanding about this, to understand
it as something necessary! I have given humanity its profoundest book
[———].[159] How one must atone for that! It places one outside all human
intercourse, it brings an unbearable tension and vulnerability—one is a
wild animal which is constantly being wounded. The wound is not hearing
any answer, and having to bear, most terribly, on one's own shoulders,
alone, the burden which one would have liked to share, to shed (why else
should one write?). One could die of being "immortal"! As chance would
have it, it is also my misfortune to coincide with a wretched impoverishment
and stagnation of the *German* mind. People in the "dear old Fatherland"
treat me like a man who ought to be locked up—this is the form of their
"understanding"! Moreover, the cretinism of Bayreuth obstructs me. The
old seducer Wagner, even after his death, is taking from me the few remaining people on whom I could have some influence.[160] But in *Denmark*—it is
absurd to say this!—-people last winter were celebrating me!! Georg
Brandes, a most intelligent man, has been brave enough to give a longish
course of lectures on me at the University of Copenhagen! And with brilliant success! A regular attendance of over three hundred! And a great ovation at the end! The prospect of something similar has just come to me from
New York. I am the most independent mind in Europe and the *only* German
writer—that is something!

159. Dash indicates editorial omission from original.

160. These words would have distressed Malwida, herself a staunch Wagnerite.
N's acrimony would have been directed against (among others) the Förster-Nietzsches:
Bernhard Förster was a zealous contributor to the *Bayreuther Blätter*. Not until November
are there the first signs of a definite German "Nietzsche movement"—with Spitteler's
article in *Der Bund* and an article by Gast in *Der Kunstwart*, both reviewing *Der Fall
Wagner*.

This reminds me of a question in your latest and much appreciated letter. You will realize that for books such as I write I receive no honorarium. But you will perhaps not realize that I have to pay the entire cost of printing and publication (about four thousand francs during the past few years). As result of my being outlawed and boycotted by the press and by booksellers, the number of copies sold does not reach one hundred. I have almost no capital—my pension from Basel is modest (three thousand francs a year); yet I have always saved some of the latter, so that till now I have no debts whatever. My trick is to simplify my life more and more, to avoid long journeys as well as living in hotels. So far it has turned out well; and I want it so. Only there are difficulties of one kind or another for one's *pride.*[161]

Under these manifold pressures from within and without, my health has, unfortunately, not been the best. In the past few years it has *not* improved. The past months, with the additional harassment of unfavorable weather, even seemed to be very similar to my worst times.

For my sister, things have meanwhile been going proportionately better. The project seems to be a splendid success—the festive, almost princely entry into the colony about four months ago made a great impression on me. There are about 120 Germans, plus a large appendage of native peons; there are good families among them, for example the family of Baron Maltzan from Mecklenburg.

Recently I was strongly reminded of you, *verehrteste Freundin,* thanks to a book which highlights a foreground figure in the first volume of *Memoirs of an Idealist.* Likewise Frl. von Salis wrote me, with much gratitude, a letter about her visit to you.[162]

With most affectionate wishes for your well-being, and the plea for your continuing, if silent, interest,

Your loyally devoted Nietzsche

It needs *greatness* of soul for a person to stand my writings at all. I have the good fortune to make all weak and virtuous people embittered against me.

161. At the Pension de Genève in Nice the previous winter, N had acquired a "real working room with special lighting and color scheme," which raised his daily rental to five and a half francs, including two meals: "But," he wrote to Overbeck (November 12, 1887), "between you and me, every other guest pays more (eight to ten francs). Incidentally, *a torture for my pride"* (*Briefe und Berichte,* p. 430). The November to April months each year at this price would have meant an expense of about one-third of his annual pension.

162. Meta von Salis, one of N's Zürich friends, visited him during the summer and gave him a thousand francs to help with his printing expenses.

174 · *To Carl Fuchs*   Sils, Sunday, July 29, 1888

Dear friend:

In the meantime I have given instructions for one of the few copies of my
ineditum to be sent to you, as a sign that all is well between us again and that
the *farouche* moment of an all too vulnerable and all too solitary soul is
past. The fourth part of *Zarathustra*: treated by me with that shyness vis-à-
vis the public, which I bitterly regret not having shown in the case of the
first three parts . . . More precisely, it is an entr'acte between *Zarathustra*
and what follows ("I name no names . . ."). The more exact title, the more
descriptive one, would be:

The Temptation of Zarathustra
An Entr'acte

Meanwhile, Herr C. G. Naumann will certainly have put at your
disposal everything of mine that he has in stock; I told him to do so. What
Herr Fritzsch has done I do not know; at the moment I can ask and obtain
nothing from him—for good reasons!

A really intelligent musician has introduced himself to me, Professor
von Holten of Hamburg, who remembered you with great interest and led
me into a discussion of the Riemann principles (also of other principles; we
are both very much anti-*décadence* musicians—that is to say, we are anti-
modern musicians).[163] He also wishes, as I do, that you had greater freedom
in your activities, and *not* in Danzig.

The weather is extremely irregular, and changes every three hours;
my health changes with it. Yesterday I received a letter from Bayreuth, written with overflowing Parsifal.[164] A Viennese admirer, unknown to me, who
calls me his "master" (oh!!!) and challenges me to perform a sort of act of
generosity toward *Parsifal*—I should be more magnanimous than Siegfried
was to the old Wanderer. He spoke, what is more, in the name of a whole
circle of my "disciples," as he put it, all of them "freethinkers" who are very
grateful for *Jenseits von Gut und Böse* . . . (he said that I had uttered so many
grand, deep, also *terrible* sayings . . .).

Of Dr. Georg Brandes's brilliant success in Copenhagen, I have
perhaps already told you. More than three hundred in the audience for his

163. Karl von Holten was a pianist. He was staying at Sils Maria, taking his
meals in the same hotel as N. See No. 175 (also for Riemann details). That summer Paul
Bourget also stayed at Sils Maria; N was disappointed to find him not interested in music
(letter of October 4, to Malwida von Meysenbug: *Werke in drei Bänden,* 3:1319–20).

164. Original: "aus vollem Parsifal geschrieben," a play on the phrase "aus
vollem Herzen" ("with an overflowing heart").

longish lecture course on me; at the end, a great ovation. He writes that my
name is now a topic of conversation in all intelligent circles in Copenhagen
and known throughout Scandinavia. From New York has come the prospect
of an English essay on my writings.[165]

If you should ever come round to writing about me (you lack the
time for this, my valued friend!!), be sensible enough—as nobody has been
till now—to characterize me, to "describe"—but not to "evaluate." This
gives a pleasant neutrality: it seems to me that in this way one can put aside
one's own passionate emphasis, and that it offers all the more to the more
subtle minds. I have never been characterized, either as a *psychologist*, or as
a *writer* (including *poet*), or as the inventor of a new kind of pessimism (a
Dionysian pessimism, born of strength, which takes pleasure in seizing the
problem of existence by the horns), or as an *Immoralist* (the highest form, till
now, of "intellectual rectitude," which is *permitted* to treat morality as illusion, having itself become *instinct* and *inevitability*). It is not necessary at
all—not even desirable—that you should argue in my favor; on the contrary,
a dose of curiosity, as in the presence of a foreign plant, with an ironic resistance, would seem to me an incomparably more intelligent attitude. Forgive me! I have written several naïve things here—a little prescription for
extracting oneself successfully from an *impossible* situation . . .[166]

.   Friendliest greetings,   Your N.

Die fröhliche Wissenschaft, "*la gaya scienza*," you certainly must read: it is my
most *medial* book—a great deal of subtle joy, a great deal of halcyonism . . .

175 · *To Carl Fuchs*   Sils, Sunday [August 26, 1888]

Dear friend:

A few days of peace. There were also a few days when I was unwell. But it
ought to be all right—and it is all right. This time it is my turn to talk—first,
about Dr. Brandes. He has done for me what he has been doing over the past
thirty years for all the independent minds of Europe: he has introduced me
to his compatriots. What I must highly honor in my case is his overcoming
here his passionate disgust with all present-day Germans. Just recently he

---

165. See No. 171.

166. No essay on N by Fuchs is on record, possibly to N's relief, though the postscript to his August 26 letter to Fuchs suggests that by that time he would not have been
averse to one. For an account of the relationship, see Hans Fuchs, "Carl Fuchs und sein
Verhältnis zu N," *Der Deutsche im Osten* (Danzig), October, 1938.

has once more, *after* the emperor's visit, expressed his contempt for all Germans, "in a veritably devilish mood," as the *Kölnische Zeitung* says. Well, anyway, they pay him back in plenty. In academic circles he has an extremely bad name: to be associated with him is thought to be a disgrace (reason enough for *me, as I am,* to give the widest publicity to his winter lectures). He is one of the cosmopolitan Jews who have the devil's own courage—in the north too he has hordes of enemies. He speaks many languages, has his best public in Russia, knows very personally the good intelligentsia in England and France—*and* is a psychologist (for which the German academics cannot forgive him . . .). His main work, which has run through several editions, *The Main Developments in Literature during the Nineteenth Century*, is still today the best *Kulturbuch*[167] in German on this big subject. To music, as he wrote last winter, he regrets having no relation.

Herr *von Holten* left us four days ago. We are all sad. Such a combination of kindness and mischievousness is a very rare thing. An old abbé, with the moods of a great actor. At the same time, very remarkably inventive in acts of kindness, in making people happy—everyone has his tale to tell of that. He must really be in a most fortunate situation, not as far as money is concerned, I mean, but his heart, for not a day passed without his committing some kind of "offense" out of the goodness of his heart. For me he had thought up the following kindness: he had studied a composition by the only present-day musician who has for me any significance, my friend Peter Gast, and he played it to me *privatissime* six times, from *memory*, enchanted by "the charming and intelligent work." *In rebus musicis et musicantibus* we got on very well—that is, we were quite without tolerance and analyzed the "one-eyed man" in the kingdom of the blind . . . As for *Riemann*, we discussed him seriously enough, but agreed, agreed that a published score in which the phrases are marked is worse than any other—because such phrasing is wicked pedantry. Phrasing which is "not right" can really be confirmed in countless cases; phrasing which is right, hardly ever. The illusion of the "phrasers" in *this* point seemed to us an extraordinary one. The premise on which they build—that there *is* a correct, that is, *one* correct exposition—seems to me to be psychologically and experimentally *wrong*. The composer, in the moment of creation as in that of reproducing, sees these subtle shadings only in a precarious equilibrium—every fortuitous intensification or relaxing of the subjective sense of power treats as unities fields which are one moment larger ones and the next moment are necessarily more *contracted* ones. In short, the old philologist says, on the basis of his whole philological experience: *there is no sole saving interpretation*, either for

167. This would seem to be a neologism of N's, for which no English equivalent exists—"book about culture."

poets or for musicians (a poet is absolutely *not* an authority for the meaning of his lines; the strangest proofs exist to show how fluid and vague the "meaning" is for them).

Another viewpoint which we discussed (perhaps I touched on it before, dear friend, a few years ago, in a letter to you). This animation and enlivening of the smallest articulations of music (I wish that you and Riemann would use the words known to everyone from rhetoric: *period* (sentence),[168] *colon, comma,* according to the size, likewise *interrogatory sentence, conditional sentence, imperative*—for the phrase marking is definitely the same as punctuation in prose and poetry)—anyway, we considered this animation and enlivening of the smallest articulations, as it enters Wagner's *practice* in music and has spread from there to become almost a dominant performance system (even for actors and singers), with counterparts in *other* arts—it is a *typical symptom of deterioration,* a proof that life has withdrawn from the whole and is *luxuriating* in the infinitesimal. "Phrase marking" would, accordingly, be the symptom of a decline of the organizing power, or, to put it differently, a symptom of incapacity to bridge *big* areas of relations rhythmically—it would be a decadent form of *rhythm* . . . This sounds almost paradoxical. The first and most passionate advocates of rhythmic precision and univocality would be not only the consequences of rhythmical *décadence* but also its *strongest* and *most successful instruments!* The more the eye is focused on the single *rhythmic* form ("phrase"), the more myopic it becomes with regard to the broad, long, big forms, exactly as in architecture in the manner of Bernini. An alteration in the optics of the composer—this is happening everywhere, *not only* in the surfeit of rhythmical life in the infinitesimal—also our capacity for enjoyment is restricting itself more and more to the tender, *small,* sublime things . . . as a result of which one only creates such things.

Moral: you are entirely on the "right track" with Riemann—that is, the only track *which still exists* . . .

We also discussed a point which concerns you especially. Von Holten's view was that phrase-marking concerts of the kind which you organize are absolutely ineffectual. They make the illusion of the performer complete. People do not *hear* the difference between the performance with phrasing and any other; even for the professional pianist, his accustomed and adopted interpretation is *by no means* so much a *conscious* matter, as clearly defined as might be desirable (a few instances excepted), as to make him constantly aware of a difference. Such concerts, he argued, convinced people of absolutely nothing, because they impressed no difference on the consciousness. It would be another matter, also of course only in the hands of

168. Original: "Satz"; also "phrase" or "movement" of a composition.

very sophisticated musicians, to present *different* kinds of performance one
after another; what von Holten denied was that this offered any proof as to
which performance was the right one. You had better take the vote on
this . . .

Everything that you write to me strengthens my wish that Danzig
delenda est; Bonn, that sounds much happier . . . I tacitly assume that the
benign Brambach, the Schumann admirer, is still functioning as conductor there (I sang in the choir under his direction in Cologne at the Gürzenich music festival—for example, Schumann's *Faust*). There are good people
living there, including women from abroad. The climatic difference is indescribably to your advantage . . . The whole color of the world changes
on the Rhine, in the "kind heart"—*crede experto.* Not least, there is a genuine
Rhineland *musical* life. You once saw my friend Krug in Naumburg; the
same, now an important fellow, with eighty employees under him, a
Justizrat[169] and director of the West Rhenish Railways, centered in Cologne,
very recently instituted in Cologne a Wagner society in the grand style; he
is its president.

With many good wishes, and hoping that you will forgive me for
anything unwelcome in this letter.

Your most devoted Nietzsche

P.S. In Sils till September 14. Leaving on 15th.
I hope you did not take my "literary prescription" seriously??
I do nothing but mischief when it comes to "publicity" and "fame."
—Some people are born posthumously.—

176 · *To Carl Fuchs*   [End of August, 1888]

Notes on differences between ancient metric
("time rhythm") and barbarous metric ("emotion rhythm")

1. The writers on rhythm (for example, Aristoxenus) offer no testimony, no definition, not the slightest verbal indication of there having been
any accent other than the word accent. Only since Bentley have *arsis* and
thesis been understood in the erroneous sense of modern theory of rhythm;
the definitions of these words given by ancient writers are completely unambiguous.

169. Cf. No. 159. N seems here to have reverted to thinking of Krug as Justizrat,
not Regierungsrat; likewise in No. 181.

2. In Athens, as in Rome, the rhetors, even the most famous ones, were reproached for having involuntarily spoken in verse. Numerous examples of such inadvertent verses are quoted. The reproach is, in terms of *our* usual way of speaking Greek and Latin verses, simply incomprehensible (for us, only the rhythmical *ictus* [beat] makes a sequence of syllables into a line of verse, but, in the judgment of the ancients, it was ordinary everyday speech itself which could very easily contain perfect verses).

3. According to explicit testimonies, it was not possible to hear the rhythm of spoken lines of lyrical verse unless a marking of the beat made the larger time units consciously felt. As long as dance was the accompaniment (and ancient rhythms grew out of dance, not out of music), one could *see* the rhythmical units with one's own eyes.

4. There are in Homer exceptional instances of a short syllable occurring at the start of a dactyl. Modern classical scholars suppose that in such cases the strength of the rhythmical *ictus* makes up for the missing time. Ancient scholars—the great Alexandrians, whom I have especially consulted on this point—offer not the least sign of any such justification of this *short* syllable (but they do offer five other justifications).

5. In the Greek sphere, as in the Latin sphere, a moment comes when the northern song rhythms dominate the ancient rhythmical instincts. There is invaluable material on this question in the main body of Christian-Greek hymnology (coming from a learned monastery in the south of France). The moment our kind of rhythmical accent invades classical verse, the *language* is lost in every instance; immediately the word accent and the distinction between long and short syllables go to the dogs. A step is taken toward the formation of barbarizing idioms.

6. Finally the main point. The two kinds of rhythms are *antithetic* in their most basic intention and derivation. *Our* barbarous (or Germanic) theory of rhythm understands by rhythm a series of equally strong heightenings of emotion, separated by unstressed syllables. This constitutes our oldest form of poetry; three syllables, each expressing a central idea, three impressive knocks, as it were, on the emotional sensorium—this forms our oldest metric. (In our language it is usually the syllable most pregnant with meaning, the syllable which dominates the emotions, which has the accent, a feature utterly different from anything in the classical languages.) *Our* rhythm is a *means of expressing emotion;* ancient rhythm—time rhythm—has the opposite task of mastering emotion and eliminating it to a certain extent. The delivery of the classical rhapsode was extremely passionate (in Plato's *Ion* there is a vivid description of the gestures, tears, and so on); the time symmetry was felt to be a kind of oil upon the waters. Rhythm to the ancient mind is, morally and esthetically, the reins which are put on passion.

In sum: our kind of rhythm relates to pathology; ancient rhythm relates to "ethos" . . .

Submitted to Dr. Carl Fuchs for his friendly consideration.

F. N.

177 · *To Paul Deussen*   Sils Maria, September 14, 1888
                                           Address until November 15: Turin
                                           (Italy), *poste restante*

Dear friend:

I do not want to leave Sils without pressing your hand once more, in re-membrance of the *greatest* surprise which this very surprising summer brought me.[170] Now too I can speak to you with more strength of spirit than my answer showed then; health has returned again, *with* the "better" weather (for the concept "good" is impractical for meteorologists and philosophers). Certainly we had last week the crowning *excess* of the year—a real opening of the heavens, which caused extremely serious flooding in the upper and lower Engadin. In four days there was a rainfall of 220 milli-meters, whereas the normal quantity for a whole month is 80 millimeters. You will receive something from me before this month is out: a small polemical pamphlet on esthetic matters, in which, for the first time and quite frontally, I attack the psychological problem of Wagner. It is a declaration of war to the knife on this whole movement; after all, I am the only person who has sufficient scope and depth to escape being uncertain here. The latest report from my publisher informs me that the promise of such a work by me, a pamphlet (if you like) *against* Wagner, is already causing some excite-ment. In response to a mere advance notice in the *Buchhändler-Börsenblatt*[171] so many orders have come in that the edition of a thousand copies can be regarded as sold out (that is, unless the copies ordered later fail to be col-lected . . .). Please do read it also from the standpoint of taste and style: *there is not a man in Germany today who can write as well as this.* It would be

170. Deussen had sent N two thousand francs during the summer, to help cover his printing expenses. C. A. Bernoulli, *Overbeck und Nietzsche*, 2: 260–61, quotes Deussen's account of how this money was raised by a young Privatdozent who had become inter-ested in N's work and had asked Deussen for information about him and his way of life. It is sometimes suggested that Rée was behind this.

171. Publishers' and booksellers' trade periodical.

as easy to translate it into French as it would be difficult, almost impossible, to translate it into German . . .[172]

My publisher already has another manuscript, which is a very stringent and subtle expression of my whole *philosophical heterodoxy*—hidden behind much gracefulness and mischief. It is called "Müssiggang eines Psychologen."[173] In the last analysis, both these works are only recuperations in the midst of an immeasurably difficult and decisive task which, *when it is understood*, will split humanity into two halves. Its aim and meaning is, in four words: the *transvaluation of all values*. Hereafter, much that was free will *not* be free any more; the realm of tolerance is reduced, by value decisions of the first importance, to mere cowardice and weakness of character. To be a Christian—one consequence among others—will be hereafter *improper*. Much is already astir in this most radical revolution that mankind has known. Only, to repeat, I need all kinds of diversions and caracols to be able to set the work up without any effort, like a game, like an act of "free will." My old friend, as you will guess, there will be something to print, this year and next—and that strange money magnanimity really did knock on my door at a *decisively good* moment. One must take joy in all things, even in acts of goodness . . . A few years ago—who knows what answer I would have given you! With most affectionate greetings.

Your friend   Nietzsche

I am also sending a copy to Herr Volkmar.[174]

172. N also wrote letters on *Der Fall Wagner* to Jakob Burckhardt (Autumn, 1888, from Sils Maria), Georg Brandes (September 13), and Malwida von Meysenbug (October 4). To Burckhardt he wrote: "The [Wagnerite] movement is now at its peak. Three-quarters of the world's musicians are entirely or half convinced Wagnerites; from St. Petersburg to Paris, Bologna, and Montevideo, the theaters are living off this art; recently the young German emperor described the whole affair as a national matter of the first importance, and placed himself at the head of it—reasons enough for permitting oneself to move into battle. . . ." To Brandes: "Europe will have to invent another Siberia for the author of these probings into values." And to Malwida: "You will see that I have not lost my good humor in the course of this duel. Frankly, to have done away with Wagner, in the midst of the inordinately difficult task of my life, is a really refreshing thing." He sent Malwida three copies, and suggested that she might be able to find someone to translate it; Malwida was very distressed by the book, and declined. Burckhardt did not acknowledge it. N's sister wrote that the book had deeply wounded her. Brandes put on a "kind expression" (as N wrote). Only Overbeck and Gast among N's friends were affirmative in their responses. (E. F. Podach, *Ns Zusammenbruch*, pp. 14 ff., gives details of reviews.)

173. Later entitled *Götzen-Dämmerung, oder: Wie man mit dem Hammer philosophiert* (preface dated Turin, September 30, 1888; published 1889).

174. Lothar Volkmar was a Berlin attorney, Deussen's father-in-law.

178 · *To Peter Gast*   Turin, October 14, 1888

Dear friend:

I shall be careful not to speak to you about my prescriptions for "heavenly and earthly convalescence," because you palpably understand this problem a hundred times better than I do, the "solution" included. In these circumstances, even Berlin is no problem; it gives me the greatest pleasure to know that you are *there*. Even Turin is really no longer a prospect.[175]

As regards *Der Löwe*, Bülow has not replied—which does him no credit. For this time it was *I* who wrote him a blunt and entirely justified letter, to break with him once and for all. I gave him to understand that the "foremost mind of the age had expressed a *wish*"; I allow myself such things nowadays.[176]

Today the sixth sheet came from Naumann; there will probably be two more. This work really puts me in a nutshell—a great deal in a small space.[177]

A letter has just arrived from Professor Deussen in Madrid; he plans to see the whole of Spain on his travels and still be back in Berlin for his lectures. "The air of Madrid, unique in purity, dryness, thinness and transparency—everything seems to be permeated with a colored ether, shining, like a painting under varnish."

Do you know who is to receive a copy of *Der Fall Wagner?* The widow of Bizet.[178] Because Dr. Brandes insisted on it most strongly—he calls her "the most charming, winsome woman, with a small nervous tic, which suits her curiously well, but completely genuine, completely true and fiery." He thinks that she knows some German. "Bizet's child is ideally beautiful and charming."

He has sent a copy of my book to the great Swedish writer August Strindberg, who (he says) is completely won over to me; he calls him a "true genius"—only rather mad. Likewise he requests copies for a few personalities in the highest St. Petersburg society, who have already had

175. Original: "Selbst Turin ist kein Gesichtspunkt mehr." Presumably refers to earlier plans for Gast also to live in Turin; see No. 169, postscript.

176. On October 9, N wrote to the Wagnerite von Bülow, to whom he had on August 10 submitted the first part of Gast's opera *Der Löwe von Venedig:* "You have not answered my letter. You shall hear no more from me—I promise you that. I think you do not realize that the foremost mind of the century had expressed to you a wish. Friedrich Nietzsche."

177. Refers to the proofs of *Götzen-Dämmerung.*

178. Bizet's music is favorably contrasted with Wagner's in *Der Fall Wagner.*

their attention drawn to me, as far as this is possible with the *ban* on my books in Russia—Prince Urussov and Princess Anna Dmitrievna Tenichev. They are "superior connoisseurs" . . .[179]

The French have put a version of Dostoevski's principal novel on the stage. I also recall an opera, *Bacchos*, music *and* words by the composer— the name escapes me. Not performed, only promised.

I have no faults to find with Turin: it is a glorious and strangely beneficent city. The problem of finding, in the *best* parts of the city, near, *very near* to its center, a quiet hermitage among amazingly beautiful and broad streets—this seemingly insoluble problem in big cities has here been solved.[180] Quietness is still the *rule* here; activity—"city life"—is the exception. Yet there are almost 300,000 inhabitants.

The weather for the past few days has had a Nice-like clarity and radiance of colors—only a little too *fresh* for me, terrified as I am of the coming winter, as a result of the winterlike enclosedness of the Engadin. I have been freezing ever since June—really freezing! Without any antidote! In addition, my health cannot get over a *choc* brought on by dysentery (*Kolik*, in German), which has been going on rather too long. At first I thought it was poisoning; yet the normal antidotes of bismuth and Dower powders did their duty. All the same, it saps one's strength, and that also makes one more susceptible to the cold.

Most affectionate greetings and embraces from your loyal friend

Nietzsche

I have just, on this morning of the 15th, received your kind *birthday letter*— many thanks! The more so, because it is the only one![181]

179. There appears to have been livelier interest in N's writings in Russia than in any other European country during the 1890's. According to details given in the Rei- chert-Schlechta *International N-Bibliography* (Chapel Hill: University of North Carolina Press, 1960), Russian publications, mainly articles, for N for the period 1890–1900 num- ber thirty-one; this figure includes two books (N. J. Abramovic, 1896, and L. Chestov, 1900 [on Tolstoy and N]); one book on Darwinism in Georg Simmel and N (Baratov, 1899); two translated books on N (Rihl, 1898, and Simmel, 1898); one book translated as several contributions to a journal (L. Stein, 1898); and one book, translated, on Stirner, N and Ibsen (Türck, 1898). The period 1901–14 produced seventy-one publications (includ- ing translations from Vaihinger, Fouillée, Lichtenberger, Riehl, Halévy. The earliest article is dated 1891 (anon., in *Novosti*, nos. 252 and 256; this was followed by two longer articles: P. E. Astaf'ev, 1892, and V. P. Preobrazensky, 1892, both in *Voprosy filosofii i psihologii* (Moscow).

180. See note 141 to No. 167. N's address, as earlier, was Via Carlo Alberto 6/III.

181. It was on this day, his forty-fourth birthday, that N began writing *Ecce Homo* (limited ed. 1908; 2d ed. 1911). It was finished on November 4. At the end of the foreword to *Ecce Homo*, he wrote: "On this perfect day, when all things are ripening and not only the grape darkens, a ray of sunlight fell upon my life: I saw backward, I saw outward,

I am more than delighted that an orchestra is making life pleasant for you. Your move makes more and more sense—even too much sense . . . Sheet 6 just sent to Naumann.

179 · *To Malwida von Meysenbug*[182]   Turin, October 18, 1888

Verehrte Freundin:

These are not things on which I allow anyone to contradict me. I am, in questions of *décadence*, the supreme court of appeal on earth; these present-day people with their miserably deteriorated instincts should think themselves fortunate to have someone who, in obscurer cases, can pour out unmixed wine for them. Wagner's knowledge of how to arouse faith (as you with your estimable innocence express it) in his being the "ultimate expression of creative nature," as if it were her "last word," that certainly required an act of genius, but a genius of *mendacity* . . . I myself have the honor to be the reverse—a genius of *truth*.

                                                            Friedrich Nietzsche

180 · *To Franz Overbeck*   Turin, October 18, 1888

Dear friend:

Yesterday, with your letter in my hand, I took my usual afternoon walk outside Turin. The clearest October light everywhere: the glorious avenue of trees, which led me for about an hour along beside the Po, still hardly

---

I saw so much and such good things all at once. Not in vain did I bury today my forty-fourth year; I was *entitled* to bury it—whatever was life in it has been saved, is immortal. The first book of the transvaluation of all values, the songs of Zarathustra, the *Götzen-Dämmerung*, my attempt to philosophize with the hammer—all gifts of this year, even of this last quarter of it! How should I not be grateful to my entire life? And so I shall tell myself the story of my life" (*Werke in drei Bänden*, 2: 1069). The first book of the "transvaluation" was *Der Antichrist* (1894); the "songs of Zarathustra" were the poems published under the title *Dionysos-Dithyramben* (1891: edited by Gast).

182. Written in reply to a letter from her protesting against his attack on Wagner in *Der Fall Wagner*. For example, "What has placed his movement in the foreground? What has reared it to greater and greater size? Above all, the pretensions of laymen, the art idiots [. . .] Second, an increasing indifference to any rigorous, noble, conscientious schooling in the service of art; usurping its place, faith in genius, or, more precisely, the impertinence of dilettantism [. . .] Third, and worst of all, the theatocracy—delusion of a faith in the primacy of the theater, in a right of the theater to *dominate* the arts, to dominate art [. . .]" (*Werke in drei Bänden*, 2:929).

touched by autumn. I am now the most grateful man in the world—autumnally minded in every good sense of the word; it is my great *harvest time*. Everything comes to me easily, everything succeeds, although it is unlikely that anyone has ever had such great things on his hands.[183] That the first book of the transvaluation of all values is finished, ready for *press*, I announce to to you with a feeling for which I have no words.[184] There will be *four* books; they will appear singly. This time—as an old artilleryman—I bring out my heavy guns; I am afraid that I am shooting the history of mankind into two halves. With that work which I gave you an inkling of in my last letter, we shall soon be ready; it has, in order to save as much as possible of my now invaluable time, been printed with excellent precision.[185] Your quotation from *Menschl., Allzumenschl* came just at the right time to be included.[186] This work amounts to a hundred declarations of war, with distant thunder in the mountains; in the foreground, much jollity, of my *relative* sort . . .[187] This work makes it amazingly easy for anyone to gauge my degree of heterodoxy, which really leaves nothing at all intact. I attack the Germans along the whole front—you will have no complaints to make about "ambiguity." This irresponsible race, which has all the great misfortunes of culture on its conscience and at all *decisive* moments in history, was thinking of "something else" (the Reformation at the time of the Renaissance; Kantian philosophy just when a scientific mode of thought had been reached by England and France; "wars of liberation" when Napoleon appeared, the only man hitherto strong enough to make Europe into a political and *economic unity*), is thinking today of the *Reich*, this recrudescence of the world of the petty kingdoms and of culture atomism, at a moment when the great question of value is being asked for the first time. There was never a more important moment in history—*but who knows a thing about it?* The disproportion here is altogether necessary; at a time when an undreamed-of loftiness and freedom of intellectual passion is laying hold of the *highest* problem of humanity and is calling for a decision as to human destiny, the general pettiness and obtuseness *must* become all the more sharply distinct from it. There is no "hostility" to me whatever—people are simply deaf to anything I say; *consequently* there is neither a *for* nor an *against* . . .

183. Original "unter den Händen."

184. *Der Antichrist.*   185. *Götzen-Dämmerung.*

186. Refers again to *Der Antichrist* (cf. section 55, which refers to *Menschliches, Allzumenschliches* I, aphorisms 54 and 483; *Werke in drei Bänden*, 2:1222).

187. *N's footnote:* With the immense tension of this period, a duel with Wagner was for me a perfect relaxation; also it was necessary, now that I am entering the lists in open warfare, to prove once and for all publicly that I have "one hand free" [N uses a singular form: "ein Handgelenk frei"].

Dear friend, please credit the Handwerkerbank account with the five hundred francs you mention. I must save with all my strength to be able to cope with the printing expenses of the next three years. (I assume that the thousand francs due on October 1 have also been deposited there). At the end of December I shall certainly need the five hundred francs very badly. My plan is to hold on here until November 20 (a somewhat frosty project, because winter comes early!). Then I shall go to Nice and establish the kind of existence which I now need, breaking completely with all my *usances* till now. I have had some thoughts even of Bastia on Corsica; yet I am afraid of the *experiment* and its dangers, my present deep self-contemplation being what I need.[188]

Herr Köselitz has moved to Berlin; his letters breathe the best state of mind one could wish for on earth. Also things are *happening* for him—I shall write to you about it later. Address: Berlin S.W., Lindenstrasse 116/IV/1.

Greetings to you and your dear wife, with very many thanks,

Your Nietzsche

188. Bastia is the chief port in north Corsica, on the east coast of the island. It was built by the Genoese in the fourteenth century, and became French in 1768. In 1906 the population was twenty-four thousand. By November 24, 1888, N had abandoned the idea of going there. But what prompted the idea in the first place? One reason could be the association of Corsica with Napoleon, of whom N thought most highly. It has been suggested that he envisaged Corsica as a sort of anti-Bethlehem. "Terrain privilégié de la 'bonne *éris*' qui exalte le courage et durcit les mains et les regards, climat de danger propice à une faune humaine exubérante, imbue de mépris et de ruse, pleine de candide cruauté. Scene d'une vie dont l'éclat est rehaussé par le sombre éclat de la mort,—une vie rouge sur noir" (Edouard Gaede, *N et Valéry*, Paris: Gallimard, 1962, p. 401). But why Bastia (why not, for instance, Ajaccio)? The name "Bastia" involves the group of phonemes which seems to have had a strong allure for N while his mind was breaking up. There is the word "Astu" (Greek, "city") in his last letter to Burckhardt. There, "Astu" follows an allusion to Alphonse Daudet's latest novel, *L'immortel* (1888), a satire against the Académie Française, and to its hero Astier. The name "Zarathustra" involves the same phonemes, in a different order. There is also the encomium, in *Götzen-Dämmerung*, on Greek *orgiastic* phallicism ("Was ich den Alten verdanke"): "To the Greeks, therefore, the sexual symbol was *the* symbol to be revered, the real depth of the whole of ancient religious piety." It happens that N does not once there use the adjective "orgiastisch," only the noun "Orgiasmus"; yet, farfetched as this may sound, the a-s-t-[u/ia/ier] series in his mind could have echoed against the Greek s-a-t-u-[ros] ("satyr"). It is a "coincidence" that the friend to whom N confided one of his last delusions—"The world is transfigured and all the heavens rejoice"—was Peter Gast. (The first physician who examined N in Turin reported, "Asks continually for women.") With or without the role of satyr (to be played perhaps on an island remote enough to prevent a *failure* of the "dangerous experiment" from becoming a source of ridicule), the name "Bastia" seems to have struck a deep chord in N's "mischievous" verbal imagination. Given the Greek derivation of the "mysterious" word "Astu" in the letter to Burckhardt, it is at least no longer necessary to believe, as Bernoulli did, that "Astu is, like the Alpa in Zarathustra, a pathological babbling sound which N might have recalled from dreams while under the influence of chloral" (C. A. Bernoulli, *Overbeck und N*, 2: 494).

181 · *To Georg Brandes* Turin, October 20, 1888

Werter und lieber Herr:

Once more there came with your letter a fair wind from the north; and, what is more, it was the only letter till now to show a "fair countenance," to countenance at all my attack on Wagner.[189] For nobody writes to me. I have spread helpless terror even among people who are near and dear to me. For example, my old friend Baron Seydlitz in Munich, unfortunately none other than the president of the Munich Wagner Society; my even older friend *Justizrat* Gustav Krug in Cologne, president of the Wagner Society there; my brother-in-law Dr. Bernhard Förster in South America, the not altogether unknown anti-Semite, one of the most zealous contributors to the *Bayreuther Blätter*—and my estimable friend Malwida von Meysenbug, author of *Memoirs of an Idealist*, thoroughly confuses Wagner with Michelangelo . . .

On the other hand, I have been told to be wary of the Wagnerite kind of woman—in certain cases she has no scruples. Perhaps people will defend themselves from Bayreuth in a German imperial manner, by banning my book as "dangerous to public morals" . . . People might even construe my sentence "We are all familiar with the un-esthetic concept of the Christian Junker" as being lèse-majesté.

Your doing Bizet's widow the honors gave me great pleasure. Please give me her address, likewise that of Prince Urussov. A copy has been sent to your friend Princess Dmitrievna Tenichev. When my next work appears, for which we shall not have to wait long (the title is now *Götzen-Dämmerung, or How to Philosophize with a Hammer*), I would like to send a copy to the Swede whom you introduced to me with such commendations. Only I do not know where he lives. This work is my philosophy in a nutshell—radical to a criminal extreme . . .

I too have wonders to announce on the effects of *Tristan*. A good strong dose of soul torment seems to me to be an excellent tonic to take before a Wagnerian meal. Judge Wiener in Leipzig told me that a course of treatment at the Karlsbad spa was also effective.

Ah, how hard you work! And, idiot that I am, I do not even know Danish! I quite believe it when you say that "in Russia one can come to life again"; any Russian book—above all, Dostoevski (translated into French, for heaven's sake not German!!)—I count among my greatest moments of pleasurable relief.

Affectionately, and with a *right* to be grateful, Your Nietzsche

189. Brandes had written after receiving a copy of *Der Fall Wagner*.

182 · *To Peter Gast*   Turin, Tuesday, October 30, 1888

Dear friend:

I have just seen myself in the mirror—never have I looked so well. In exemplary condition, well nourished and ten years younger than I should be. On top of it all, since choosing Turin as my home, I am much changed in the honors I do myself—I rejoice, for example, in an excellent tailor, and set value on being received everywhere as a distinguished foreigner. I have succeeded amazingly well in this. In my *trattoria* I receive without any doubt the best there is: they call my attention to things, and this is especially a success. Between ourselves, I have never known till now what it means to enjoy eating—also what I need to keep up my strength. My criticism of the winters in Nice is now very stringent: an inadequate and, especially for me, quite intolerable diet. The same, perhaps more so, is true, I am sorry to say, dear friend, of your Venice. I eat here with the serenest disposition of soul and stomach, probably four times as much as in the "Panada." In other ways too Nice was *pure foolery*. The Turin landscape is so much more congenial to me than this chalky, treeless, and stupid bit of Riviera that I am thoroughly annoyed at having been so late in putting it behind me. I shall say nothing of the contemptible and venal kind of people there—not excluding the foreigners. Here day after day dawns with the same boundless perfection and plentitude of sun: the glorious foliage in glowing yellow, the sky and the big river delicately blue, the air of the greatest purity—a Claude Lorrain such as I never dreamed I would see. Fruits, grapes in the brownest sweetness— and cheaper than in Venice! In every way, life is worth living here. The coffee in the best cafés, a small pot of remarkably good coffee, even the very best quality, such as I never found before, twenty centimes—and in Turin one does *not* pay a tip. My room, *best* position in the center, sunshine from early morning until afternoon, view on to the Palazzo Carignano, the Piazza Carlo Alberto, and across and away to the green mountains—twenty-five francs a month, with service and shoes cleaned.[190] In the *trattoria* I pay

190. The rent for this room compared very favorably with that of the room in the Pension de Genève in Nice (five and a half francs a day, including two meals). Visiting Turin twenty-five years later, Karl Strecker (*N und Strindberg*, Munich: Georg Müller, 1921, pp. 41 ff.) described the scene as follows: "The Via Carlo Alberto, where N lived, runs from the Corso Vittorio Emanuele—near the railway station—to the Piazza Carlo Alberto; it is long, but not broad, and darkened by very tall identical houses. In gloomy weather—and Turin has an average of 107 rainy days a year—a melancholy defile, comfortlessly long. To be sure, No. 6, where N lived on the third floor, stands on the corner of the Piazza Carlo Alberto, on to which he had a view. But the entrance has the monotony of a motor tire, and nobody would maintain that N, sensitive as he was to external impressions, to whom a fresh breeze, brightness, and a clear view were essentials of life,

for each meal one franc fifteen centimes and add—it is certainly regarded as an exception—an extra ten centimes. For this I get: a very large helping of *minestra*, dry or as bouillon—immense choice and variety—and Italian pastas of the first quality (only here am I *learning* the great differences); then an excellent portion of tender meat, above all, veal, better than any I have ever tasted, with a vegetable—spinach and so on; three rolls, very delicious here (for the fancier, *grissini*, the very thin little pipes of bread, which Turin people appreciate). A stove has been ordered, from Dresden; you know, natron-carbon heating—without smoke, consequently without chimney. I am also having my books sent from Nice. Moreover, it is wonderfully mild, even the nights. My shivery feeling, of which I wrote to you, has purely *internal* causes. It was at once all right again.

Your letter gave me great pleasure. I have never really heard from anyone how strong the effect of my thought is. The novelty—the courage of the novelty—is really of the first rank; as for the *consequences*, I sometimes look at my hand now with some distrust, because I seem to have the destiny of mankind "in the palm of my hand." Are you satisfied by my concluding with the Dionysus morality?[191] It occurred to me that this group of ideas should not at any price be absent from this *vade mecum* of my philosophy. With the few sentences about the Greeks, I take it upon myself to challenge everything that has been said about them. Finally, the Hammer speech from *Zarathustra*, perhaps, *after* this book, audible . . . I myself cannot hear it without feeling an icy shudder run through my body.

The weather is so glorious that there is no difficulty in doing something *well*. On my birthday, I began again with something that seems to be going well and has already made considerable progress. It is called *Ecce Homo, or How One Becomes What One Is*. It concerns, with great audacity, myself and my writings. Not only did I want to present myself *before* the uncannily solitary act of transvaluation; I would also just like to *test* what risks I can take with the German ideas of freedom of speech. My suspicion is that the *first* book of the revaluation will be confiscated on the spot— legally and in all justice.[192] With this *Ecce Homo*, I want to make the ques-

---

had chosen well to live here in his darkest time. His landlord, the newsvendor Davide Fino . . . was very happy when I told him I was following up the traces of Professor "Nitzky." And although customers kept coming and going, he found the time to tell me what he knew. . . . The burden of what he told me was always—N's lonely life, the darkness falling over his mind. . . . In the evenings, Davide Fino told me, he would improvise for hours at the piano, and Fino's daughter, who was musical, had said that he played mostly—Wagnerian music [. . .]"

191. Refers to *Götzen-Dämmerung*, of which Gast had read the proofs.

192. Refers to *Der Antichrist*, which finally appeared in 1894, edited by Peter Gast. It was not confiscated. Gast cut some words and sentences from sections 29, 35,

tion so intensely serious, and such an object of curiosity, that current and basically sensible ideas about what is *permissible* will here admit an exception for once. To be sure, I talk about myself with all possible psychological "cunning" and gay detachment—I do not want to present myself to people as a prophet, savage beast, or moral horror. In this sense, too, the book could be salutary—it will perhaps prevent people from confusing me with my anti-self.[193]

I am very curious about your *Kunstwart* philanthropy.[194] Did you know that I wrote Herr Avenarius in the summer an extremely blunt letter because of the way in which his paper dropped *Heinrich Heine?* Blunt letters —with me a sign of gay detachment . . .

With most affectionate greetings and all ineffable wishes on the side, behind and before ("*One thing* is more necessary than the other"—thus spake Zarathustra).

N.

183 · *To Franziska Nietzsche*   November 3, 1888
                                          Address: Turin (Italy),
                                          Via Carlo Alberto 6/III

Meine alte Mutter:

This is the most remarkable coincidence. For a moment, my mind boggled. Imagine, I was on the point of asking you to copy out for me a passage from Wagner's collected works—volume 9, in which there is a letter of Wagner's to me. I wanted the last sentence of it for a particular work on which I am engaged. *Your letter contains this sentence:* that third page, which gave you such pleasure. It's like a happening in a fairy tale!

---

and 38. On the title page of the proofs, N (end of 1888) crossed out the subtitle *Transvaluation of Values* and substituted *A Curse on Christianity*. Schlechta regards this as proof that N had by then ceased to regard it as the "first book in the transvaluation of all values" (*Werke in drei Bänden*, 3:1388).

193. Here I have adopted Michael Hamburger's (Yeatsian) translation of N's word "Gegensatz" as "anti-self" (*From Prophecy to Exorcism*, London, Longmans, 1965, p. 33). Hamburger comments: "The Nietzschean [. . .] is any reader of N who ignorantly, slavishly or dishonestly takes N's anti-self for the whole man, or its manic utterances for the whole of N's doctrine. That N quite frequently forgot or perversely disregarded the warning contained in that last letter [to Burckhardt] claiming absolute authority for himself and boasting of his ferocious predatory strength, merely testifies to the war between his self and his anti-self. Only a dialectic confrontation of both [. . .] can undo the mischief done by his sister, her scholarly abettors and all those Nietzscheans deficient in what N himself called the ultimate virtue, the will to honesty [. . .]"

194. Refers to Gast's undertaking to review *Der Fall Wagner* for *Der Kunstwart*.

To my regret, the envelope of that curious letter is missing: I have not the remotest idea where it comes from. If you had told me what was on the original postmark, instead of its wanderings from place to place, I would have some idea. It must be a close acquaintance; the joke in the address, "Röcken near Lützen," points to this. Was Vienna the place it came from?[195]

I have been suffering moderately still from the cold, except for a few days—it always makes one more sensitive. Now it is mild again, even at night. The coldest time was a *single* day in October when we did not reach the freezing point but almost did. Immediately after that, delightful autumn days came again. We still have an abundance of the most beautiful grapes: a pound of the very best ones costs twenty-four pfennigs in your money. The food is extremely good and wholesome. One is not living for nothing in the best cattle-breeding part of the country and, what is more, in its royal city. The tenderness of the *veal* is something absolutely new for me; also the *lamb*, which I like very much indeed. And how well it is prepared! What a solid, clean, even sophisticated cuisine! I never knew till now what it means to enjoy one's food; honestly, I eat four times as much as in Nice, pay *less*, and have not yet had any trouble at all with my stomach. Admittedly, there and in other ways, I receive preferential treatment; I definitely get the tidbits. But it is the same everywhere I go—people regard me as a person of distinction; you would be surprised how proudly and with what a dignified bearing your old creature walks about here. Things are quite the reverse of what they were in Nice. A light overcoat, lined with blue, is all I ever need over my suit.[196] Hillebrand's thick overcoat, still in good condition, will not be enjoying the privilege until this coming winter.[197] Two

195. This must have been a letter described by N's mother, presumably unsigned, which N could not identify. The joke "Röcken near Lützen" consists in this: Lützen (the battlefield referred to by N in No. 168) is to this day too small for ordinary maps, whereas Röcken, a slightly larger town, is on such maps. The writer of the letter had made Lützen seem the larger place, because it is the more famous place. Either way, it was not N's forwarding address.

196. Original: "Gesellschaftsanzug" or "going-out suit," which sounds considerably more imposing.

197. Perhaps N had acquired this overcoat through the mediation of Marchesa Emma Guerrieri-Gonzaga, his friend in Florence who had known Hillebrand. Karl Hillebrand (1829–84) had spent much of his life in Florence and had died there. N first mentions him in a letter of 1872 as the author of some newspaper articles on the French; N also admired his *Zwölf Briefe eines aesthetischen Ketzers* (*Twelve Letters of an Esthetic Heretic*), which he read on its appearance in 1874. In that year too, Hillebrand invited N to contribute to a review he was planning. His *Menschen, Zeiten und Völker* is also mentioned by N (for example, No. 171) in connection with his essay on David Friedrich Strauss.

pairs of laceable shoes. Immense English winter gloves.[198] Gold-rimmed
glasses (*not* when I'm out walking). Now you have a picture of your old
creature.

With love, F.

184 · To Malwida von Meysenbug   Turin, November 5, 1888

Just wait a little, *verehrteste Freundin!* I shall send you yet another proof that
"Nietzsche est toujours haissable."[199] Without any doubt, I have been
unjust to you; but since I am suffering from a surfeit of righteousness this
autumn, it was really salutary for me to do an injustice . . .

The Immoralist

185 · To Franz Overbeck   Turin, Via Carlo Alberto 6/III
November 13, 1888

Dear friend:

The fact that November 16 is a special day must excuse my writing so soon
after my previous letter to you.[200] Perhaps with you the winter has begun;
it is almost with us here—the nearest mountains are already wearing a
vestigial wig. I hope the winter will match up to the autumn; at least, the
autumn here was a real miracle of beauty and light—a permanent Claude
Lorrain. I have changed my ideas about what "good weather" means, and
think very poorly of my having clung to Nice. My books, which I left there,
are already on their way to Turin. While arranging for this I heard that my
jolly table companion of those days, Frau von Brandeis, has arrived at the
Pension de Genève. The carbon-natron stove is also on the way, at a very
decent price, for which I must give the Dresden man Nieske full credit.

---

198. In fact, N must have only had his eye on these gloves; he wrote to Overbeck
on November 13 that he had bought them on that day.

199. N adapts the Pascal saying (*Pensées* 455): "The ego is hateful; you, Miton,
cover it over, you do not shed it; so you are always hateful.[. . .] If I hate it because it is
unjust, because it makes itself the center of all things, I shall hate it always." This was
N's next to last letter to Malwida. Podach rejected Elisabeth's argument (*The Lonely
Nietzsche*) that Malwida's protest against *Der Fall Wagner* hurt N deeply and was one of
the things which hastened his breakdown (*Ns Zusammenbruch*, pp. 59–60).

200. November 16 was Overbeck's fifty-first birthday.

Today I bought a pair of superb English winter gloves. With the best will in the world, dear old friend Overbeck, I cannot find anything bad to tell you about myself. Things continue to go well at a *tempo fortissimo* of work and well-being. Also people treat me here *comme il faut*, as a person of extreme distinction; the way they open the door for me is something utterly new to me. Admittedly, I visit only very good places, and also I rejoice in a classical tailor. We recently had the melancholy pomp of a great funeral, in which the whole of Italy took part: that of Count Robilant, the most respected type of Piedmontese nobleman, actually also a son of King Carlo Alberto, as is well known here. In him Italy has lost an irreplaceable premier. Something gay at the very same time: the beauties of the Turin aristocracy were most elated when the pictures of the first beauties to be crowned in Spaa arrived here. They at once planned a *corso di bellezza*[201] of their own for January—I think they all have a right to it! At the spring exhibition I saw just such a *concours* in portraits. Even our new lady of Turin, the Princess Laetitia Buonaparte, newly married to the Duke d'Aosta, is happy to join in. Meanwhile I have received veritable acts of homage for my *Der Fall Wagner*. Not only has the work been called a psychological masterpiece of the first order, in a field where nobody till now has had eyes to see—in the psychology of the musician; also my revealing the *décadent* character of our music has been called an event of cultural and historical importance that nobody except me could have brought about—my remarks on Brahms are said to be the last word in psycholog. sagacity. Herr Spitteler expressed his rapture in the Thursday issue of *Der Bund*; Herr Köselitz, in *Der Kunstwart*; from Paris I am told that an article in the *Nouvelle Revue* is forthcoming.[202]

201. "Beauty competition."

202. Spitteler's review was more enthusiastic than substantial: "Six thinkers like N could do more good for a nation than myriads of scholars and philosophers could do in a whole century." Gast's review was also an encomium, but made a valiant attempt to define N's position and wealth of radical ideas: "Phenomena open out before him, and he divines primary things nobody has seen or heard of till now [. . .] Every one of his sentences is a survey and a judgment that is and can be only his own." Avenarius printed an editorial alongside Gast's review, disclaiming any anti-Wagner program and explaining that his periodical did not necessarily prefer the older anti-Wagner N to the younger pro-Wagner one. Avenarius also criticized N's style as being, in *Der Fall Wagner*, that of a *feuilletonist* with a head full of ideas but still only that of a writer of popular literary articles without much serious intent (cf. Podach, *Ns Zusammenbruch*, p. 19). N's own comments appeared in a letter of his which Avenarius published in *Der Kunstwart* 2, 1888/89, 6: Stück 89; he welcomed the remarks by both Gast and Avenarius, and concluded: ". . . and when I have, literally, to carry the destiny of man, it is part of my trial of strength to be able to be a clown, *satyr*, or, if you prefer it, *feuilletonist* to the extent that I have been one in *Der Fall Wagner*. That the profoundest mind must also be the most frivolous one is almost a formula for my philosophy." Podach remarks (p. 79), "The 'clown' becomes the final mask of self-control, the counterpoise to forces which are driving him to self-sacrifice."

There is other good news as well. The greatest Swedish writer—a "real genius," as Dr. Brandes writes—August Strindberg, has meanwhile announced that he is for me; also St. Petersburg society is seeking relations with me, which is made very difficult by the ban on my writings (Prince Urussov, Princess Anna Dimitrievna Tinichev [*sic*]). Lastly, the *charming widow of Bizet*! . . .

The printing of *Götzen-Dämmerung, oder Wie man mit dem Hammer philosophirt* is finished; the manuscript of *Ecce Homo: Wie man wird, was man ist* is already at the printer's. The latter, an absolutely important book, gives some psychological and even biographical details about me and my writings; people will at last suddenly *see* me. The tone of the work, one of gay detachment fraught with a sense of destiny, as is everything I write.[203] Then at the end of next year the *first* book of the *transvaluation* will appear. It is finished.

With most affectionate good wishes on your birthday for your flourishing in body and soul.

Your Nietzsche

186 · *To Meta von Salis*   Turin, November 14, 1888

Verehrtes Fräulein:

Since I am suffering permanently from a small surfeit of good humor and other blessings of fortune, you may forgive me if I write you an utterly senseless letter. Till now everything has gone more than well; I have carried my burden like a man born to be an "immortal" pack carrier. Not only was the *first* book of the transvaluation finished as early as September 30, but in the meantime an incredible piece of literature entitled *Ecce Homo: Wie man wird, was man ist*, has taken wing and is already flying, unless I am deceived, in the direction of Leipzig . . .[204]

This *Homo*, you will understand, is myself, including the *Ecce*; my attempt to shed a little light and *terror* as regards myself seems to have been almost too successful. The last chapter, for instance, has the dreary heading: "Why I Am a Man of Destiny." That this is indeed true is proved so strongly that, at the end, the reader is left sitting before me as a mere "mask," mere "feeling heart." The case of Malwida recently showed me

---

203. On the same day, N wrote to Gast and said of *Ecce Homo*, "The last sections are tuned to a mode which must have escaped from *Die Meistersinger*—the 'mode of the potentates'" (*Briefe und Berichte*, p. 493).

204. That is, to the printer.

that some explaining of myself was needed. I sent her, with a small ulterior motive, a copy of *Der Fall Wagner*, and suggested that she might make a few moves to arrange for a good French translation. Result: "declaration of war" against me—that is the word Malwida used.[205]

I have, between ourselves, convinced myself once more that the famous "idealism" in this case is an extreme form of immodesty—"innocently," of course. She has always been allowed to have her say, and, it seems to me, nobody has told her that every sentence she speaks is not only wrong but a *lie* . . . That is what they do, these *schöne Seelen*, who are not permitted to see reality.[206] Pampered her whole life through, she ends up sitting like a comic little Pythia on her sofa and says: "You are wrong about Wagner! I understand him better than you! He is just like Michelangelo." So I replied that Zarathustra wanted to do away with the good and the just people, because they are always *telling lies*. Her answer was that she agreed entirely, *for* there are so few *really* good people . . . And *that* is the argument which once served to *defend* me against Malwida!

Turin is no place to leave. I have put Nice behind me, likewise the *romantisme* of a Corsican winter (it is really not worth it any more; the bandits have in fact been done away with, even the kings, the *Bellacoscia*). Autumn here was a permanent Claude Lorrain—I often asked myself how such a thing could be possible on earth. Strange! For the misery of the summer up there, compensation did come. There we have it: the old God is still alive . . .

Also people are *very tender* toward me here; my situation has changed out of all recognition since the spring. I dare not speak of my health

205. He had written to Malwida on October 4, saying that three copies were on the way to her, and he himself had described the book as a "declaration of war *in aestheticis*." He suggested that she might ask Gabriel Monod, then professor of history at the Sorbonne, for advice about a French translator. Meta von Salis was a close personal friend of Malwida's; yet N chose to vent his bitter feelings about Malwida to her. His snobbery and self-congratulation in his letter to her, dated December 29 (No. 198), are just as full of puerilities and of the kind of rancor which N's "gay detachment" was meant to overcome. Only by contrasting the letters of the period with his other writings does one come to see some sense in Podach's analysis of these months. After debunking the writers who since 1900 have tried to explain away the psychological storm (with theories of drug addiction, paralysis, mental disease), Podach wrote: "At Turin a whole development was coming to a close—a development which, in his own words, resembles an accumulation of dynamite and makes the air pregnant with explosions. But it finds fulfilment in accordance with its own laws and is in no way affected by any reference to his final illness" (translated by F. A. Voigt, Podach, *The Madness of N*, p. 67; *Ns Zusammenbruch*, pp. 34–35).

206. The "schöne Seele" appellation derives from the age of Goethe, when it was used to describe characters who are "harmonious" and "integrated," but in a state of innocence, untested by—or unpermeated by—experience.

any more: that is a standpoint I have passed beyond. The work I finished while still in the Engadin, perhaps the most radical there is, has the title

Götzen-Dämmerung
oder Wie man mit dem Hammer philosophirt

The printing of it is finished. If I consider the things I have perpetrated between September 3 and November 4, I have my fears that there will soon be a small earthquake. In Turin this time; two years ago, when I was in Nice, it occurred, appropriately, in Nice. In fact, the last report from the observatory yesterday did mention a slight tremor . . .

We have had the melancholy pomp of a great funeral. One of the most estimable Piedmontese, Count di Robilant, was carried to his grave; the whole of Italy was in mourning. The country has lost a premier for whom people had been waiting with impatience—and whom nobody can replace.

With every devotion   Your Nietzsche

Herr Spitteler has uttered in *Der Bund* a cry of rapture over *Der Fall*.

187 · *To Georg Brandes*   Turin, Via Carlo Alberto 6/III
                                        November 20, 1888

Verehrter Herr:

Forgive me for replying at once. Uniquely curious things, meaningful coincidences, keep happening in my life now. The day before yesterday and again today. Ah, if only you knew what I had just written when your letter paid me its visit!

I have now told my own story with a cynicism that will make history. The book is called *Ecce Homo*, and is a ruthless attack on the crucified Christ; it ends by hurling such thunders and lightnings at everything Christian or infected by Christianity that one swoons. I am, after all, the foremost psychologist of Christianity, and can, as an old artilleryman, bring up some heavy guns, whose very existence no opponent of Christianity had ever suspected. The whole work is the prelude to the "transvaluation of values," of the work that lies finished before me; I swear to you that in two years we shall have the whole earth in convulsions. I am a man of destiny.

Can you guess who comes off worst in *Ecce Homo?* The Germans! I have told them terrible things . . . The Germans, for example, have on their conscience the fact that they robbed the last *great* period in history, the

Renaissance, of its meaning—at a moment when Christian values, the *décadence* values, had been defeated, when in the instincts of the highest priestly caste they had been overcome by counterinstincts—the vital instincts. To attack the Church—that meant restoring Christianity. (Cesare Borgia as Pope—that would have been the goal of the Renaissance, its real symbol.)

Also you should not be annoyed that you yourself appear at a decisive point in the book—I was writing it just now—in connection with my stigmatizing the conduct of my German friends toward me, their having been absolutely abandoned by honor and by philosophy. You suddenly appear, in a nice cloud of glory . . .

I completely believe what you say about Dostoevski; I prize his work, on the other hand, as the most valuable psychological material known to me—I am grateful to him in a remarkable way, however much he goes against my deepest instincts. Roughly as in my relation to Pascal, whom I almost love because he has taught me such an infinite amount—the only *logical* Christian.

Yesterday I read, with rapture and feeling altogether at home, *Les mariés* by Herr August Strindberg. My most unreserved admiration, which is marred only by the feeling that in admiring him I also admire myself a little. Turin remains my residence.

Your Nietzsche, now Monster

To what address shall I send you a copy of *Götzen-Dämmerung?* If you will be in Copenhagen for the next two weeks, no reply is needed.

188 · *To Peter Gast* Turin, December 2, 1888

Sunday afternoon, after four o'clock, wildly beautiful autumn day. Just returned from a big concert, which really made on me the strongest impression of any concert I have been to—my face kept making grimaces, in order to get over a feeling of extreme pleasure, including, for ten minutes, the grimace of tears. Ah, if you could have been there! In the main, it was the lesson of operetta *transferred to music.* Our ninety foremost musicians of the city; an excellent conductor; the largest theater we have here, with glorious acoustics; 2,500 in the audience—all the people, without exception, who live and talk music here. *Publico sceltissimo,*[207] I assure you; nowhere else have I had such a feeling that the *nuances* were being so well understood. All the things

207. "A most select audience."

played were extremely sophisticated ones, and I would look in vain for a more intelligent enthusiasm. Not one concession to average taste. The start was the *Egmont* overture—which made me think, to be sure, of Herr Peter Gast . . . Then Schubert's *Hungarian March*, splendidly explicated and orchestrated by Liszt. Immense success, *da capo*. Then something for strings alone: by the fifth bar I was in tears. A perfectly heavenly and profound inspiration—whose? A musician who died in Turin in 1870, *Rossoaro*—I swear to you, music of the first rank, with a goodness of form and *of the heart* which changes my whole idea of the Italians. Not a sentimental moment— I no longer know which names are the "great" ones . . . Perhaps the best things remain unknown. There followed the *Sakuntala* overture—storm of applause eight times. Devil of a fellow, this Goldmark! I would not have credited him with it. This overture is a hundred times better constructed than anything by Wagner, and has such a psychological scope, is so sophisticated, that I began to breathe the air of Paris again. Orchestrally planned and calculated, pure filigree. Now something else for the strings alone, Vilhac's *Cypriot Song*, again the utmost in delicacy of invention, again an immense success and *da capo*, though it is long. Finally *Patrie!* the overture by Bizet. How cultured we are! He was thirty-five when he wrote this work, a long, very dramatic work; you ought to hear how the little man becomes *heroic* . . .

Ecco! Can one have better nourishment? And the ticket cost one franc . . .

· This evening *Francesca da Rimini* at the Carignano. I enclosed a report on it in my latest letter. The composer Cagnoni will be there.

I am coming to think that Turin, in its musical judgments as in other things, is the most solid city I know.

Your friend N.

There will not be any proofs for a while: yesterday I asked for the whole manuscript to be sent back to me.[208]

189 · *To August Strindberg*   Turin, December 7, 1888

Sehr lieber und werter Herr:

Has a letter of mine been lost? The moment I had finished reading your *Père* for a second time, I wrote you a letter, deeply impressed by this masterpiece of hard psychology; I also expressed to you my conviction that your

208. *Ecce Homo.*

work is predestined to be performed in Paris now, in the Théâtre Libre of
M. Antoine—you should simply demand it of Zola!

The hereditary criminal is *décadent*, even insane—no doubt about
that! But the history of criminal families, for which the Englishman Galton
(*Hereditary Genius*) has collected the largest body of material, points constantly back to an excessively strong person where a certain social level
is the case.[209] The latest great criminal case in Paris, that of Prado, presented
the classic type: Prado was superior to his judges, even to his lawyers, in
self-control, wit, and exuberance of spirit; nevertheless, the pressure of the
accusation had so reduced him physiologically that some witnesses could
recognize him only from the old portraits.[210]

But now a word or two between ourselves, very much between ourselves! When your letter reached me yesterday—the first letter in my life
to reach me[211]—I had just finished the last revision of the manuscript of
Ecce Homo. Since there are no more coincidences in my life, you are conse-

209. N had studied Francis Galton's *Hereditary Genius* (1869) in English in 1884;
among his books there was also a copy of Galton's *Inquiries into Human Faculty and Its
Development* (1883) (Mittasch, *Ns Naturbeflissenheit*, p. 96). Strindberg had written to
him: "It seems to me that, for all your generosity of mind, you have flattered the criminal
type somewhat. Look at the hundreds of photographs which illustrate the criminals discussed by Lombroso, and you will concede that the criminal is a low animal, a degenerate,
a weakling, not in possession of the faculties necessary for getting round the paragraphs in
the law which are obstacles too strong for his will and his strength. Consider the stupidly
moral appearance of these candid beasts! What a disillusionment for morality!" (*Briefe
und Berichte*, p. 499). It does not appear that N was willing to concede anything here but
clung to his ideas drawn from one or two not very convincing cases. The Nietzschean
glorification of the "criminal type" is dealt with in the Moosbrugger episodes of Musil's
novel *Der Mann ohne Eigenschaften.*

210. Prado was tried in Paris on November 5, 1888; on November 14 he was
condemned to death. The story had been reported in the *Gazette des Tribuneaux*, 1888, on
the following dates: June 29; July 4, 22, 23; August 5; September 10, 11; October 10, 18;
November 1, 5, 6, 7, 8, 9, 10, 11, 12, 13, 14, 15 (and December 29 was to follow). Prado was
a Spanish subject who claimed that his real name was Linska de Castilon. He had lived
first in Peru, then in Spain, after exhausting his wife's fortune assessed at 1,200,000 francs.
Heavily in debt, he came to France and lived with a girl named Eugénie Forestier; the
couple has been without means since 1886. On November 28, 1887, Prado was arrested
for theft in Paris. The investigation proved that he had also been involved in another theft
outside Paris. During cross-examination, Eugénie asserted that Prado was the murderer
of a prostitute named Marie Agriétant, who had been killed during the night of January 14,
1886, in the rue Caumartin. This assertion proved to be true. In his last letter to Burckhardt, N identifies himself with Prado, also with Chambige, subject of another 1888 murder
trial. Henri Chambige was a law student who fancied himself a writer. He murdered the
English wife of a Frenchman living near Constantine in Algeria. He was tried in Constantine on November 8, 1888, and was condemned to seven years of hard labor (it was
a *crime passionel*).

211. Strindberg had expressed boundless admiration of N in his letter—for example, "I end all my letters to my friends with the words 'Read Nietzsche!' That is my
Carthago est delenda."

quently not a coincidence. Why do you write letters which arrive at such a moment!

Ecce Homo should indeed appear simultaneously in German, French, and English. Yesterday I sent the manuscript to my printer; as soon as a sheet is ready, it must go to the translators. *But who are these translators?* Honestly I did not know that you yourself are responsible for the excellent French of your *Père;* I thought that it must be a masterly translation. If you were to undertake the French translation yourself, I would be overjoyed at this miracle of meaningful coincidence. For, between ourselves, it would take a poet of the first rank to translate *Ecce Homo;* in its language, in the refinement of its feeling, it is a thousand miles beyond any mere "translator." Actually, it is not a thick book; I suppose it would be, in the French edition (perhaps with Lemerre, Paul Bourget's publisher!) priced at about three francs fifty. Since it says unheard-of things and, sometimes, in all innocence, speaks the language of the rulers of the world, the number of editions will surpass even *Nana*.[212]

On the other hand, it is anti-German to an annihilating extent; throughout, I side with French culture (I treat all the German philosophers as "unconscious counterfeiters"). Also the book is not boring—at points I even wrote it in the "Prado" style. To secure myself against German brutalities, I shall send the first copies, before publication, to Prince Bismarck and the young emperor,[213] with letters declaring war—military men cannot reply to that with police measures.—I am a psychologist.—

Consider it, *verehrter Herr!* It is a matter of the first importance. For I am strong enough to break the history of mankind in two.[214]

There is still the question of the English translation. Would you have any suggestion? An anti-German book in England . . .

Very devotedly,   Your Nietzsche

212. Zola's best-selling novel.

213. One wonders what would have happened if N had survived to do this. During 1889, there was already friction between Wilhelm II and Bismarck, the former pressing for social reform, the latter insisting on conservative stabilization, even at the expense of the 1871 constitution. On March 18, 1890, Bismarck was forced to resign. He could undoubtedly have used the book as a deterrent to the young emperor ("You see, this is what is waiting for us the moment we let up . . .").

214. Strindberg did at the time consider translating *Ecce Homo* into French. But in his reply he had to warn N that he would be expensive as a translator: he was living in poverty at Holtz, near Copenhagen, having to support a "wife, three children, two servants, debts, etc." (Podach, *The Madness of N*, p. 33; *Ns Zusammenbruch* has no counterpart to the Strindberg details in the English version.) Strindberg also warned N that he would not find much interest in England—"a country sunk in respectability and delivered over to women, which means the same thing as total decadence" (*The Madness of N*, pp. 33–34).

190 · *To Peter Gast*   Sunday, December 9, 1888
                                         Via Carlo Alberto 6/III

Dear friend:

I was about to write to you, then your letter came festively through the door, unfortunately *not* in company with the *Kunstwart*. But its coming can only be a matter of hours.[215] Your glorious news *in puncto* "Provence" gladdens me as few things could;[216] for, since things are going well for me, it is right and just that they should go even better for my "nearest and dearest." The first step, here as everywhere, is the most difficult—and only the females can help us with that . . .[217]

I have good news too. *Ecce Homo* went off to C. G. Naumann yesterday, after I had put my qualms of conscience to rest for the last time by weighing every word again from beginning to end. It so transcends the concept of "literature" that there is no parallel to it even in nature herself; it blasts, literally, the history of mankind in two—the highest superlative of *dynamite* . . .

Strindberg's first letter to me arrived yesterday—it was the first letter with a world-historical accent ever to reach me. He realizes something of the extent to which *Zarathustra* is a *non plus ultra*. Simultaneously a letter arrived from St. Petersburg, from one of the foremost women of Russia, almost a declaration of love, in any case a curious sort of letter—Princess Anna Dmitrievna Tenichev. Also the most intelligent man in St. Petersburg society, the old Prince Urussov, is said to be very interested in me. Georg Brandes is lecturing again this winter in these circles and will tell them wondrous things. Did I tell you that Strindberg and Brandes are friends, that both live in Copenhagen? Strindberg, by the way, regards me as the greatest psychologist of woman . . . *Ecco*, Malwida!!!

Yesterday I sent the *Götzen-Dämmerung* to M. Taine, with a letter asking him if he would be interested in doing a *French* translation of it. For the English translation too, I have an idea: Miss Helen Zimmern, who is now living in Geneva and is closely associated with my two friends Fynn and Mansurov.[218] She also knows Georg Brandes (it was she who discovered Schopenhauer for the English—so why not his opposite pole? . . .).

215. *Der Kunstwart*, Jg. 2, November, 1888, contained Gast's review of *Der Fall Wagner*.

216. Refers to a new composition by Gast, *Provençalische Hochzeit*.

217. Original: "über den [ersten Schritt] helfen nur die Weiblein hinweg . . ." Obscure.

218. Helen Zimmern had known N since 1886, when she had shared a table with him at meals in Sils Maria. She later published (anonymously) an article entitled "Memo-

I have got no further with E. W. Fritzsch; but I hope that, with patience, the price will go down by a few thousand marks. If I can buy back all my books for eight thousand marks, I shall have concluded the business. Naumann is advising me in this matter.[219]

Do visit, as soon as you can, my old friend Professor Paul Deussen (Berlin, W., Kurfürstendamm 142). You can tell him in plain terms what I am and what I am capable of. He is, to be sure, very devoted to me, and in the way which is most rarely found on earth: last summer he gave me two thousand marks, for the purpose of defraying my printing expenses (for the same purpose, listen! Frl. Meta von Salis gave me a thousand marks!!). *Between ourselves*, I implore you.

Now a serious matter. Dear friend, I want to recover all copies of the *fourth* part of *Zarathustra*, in order to secure this unpublished work against all the chances of life and death (I read it these past few days and almost died of emotion).[220] If I publish it later, after a few decades of world

---

ries of N" (*Living Age* [Boston], November, 1926), and was the first translator of *Beyond Good and Evil*. Emily Fynn, an Irishwoman (and her daughter, also called Emily) had known him from about the same time. Fräulein von Mansurov is mentioned by N in his letter of September 2, 1884, to Gast; he had shared a table with her at the Sils Maria hotel. All four ladies had been at Sils Maria in the summer of 1886, and they all lived in Geneva. An anecdote illustrates the relationship. In the summer of 1887, the Fynns and Fräulein Mansurov stayed at Maloja, where N visited them twice. Emily was a keen watercolorist; N once told her that she should put something ugly among the flowers she had painted, so they would look even more beautiful. Another anecdote: N knew that the Fynns were frightened of toads; so he caught one and put it in his trouser pocket one day when he came to visit them. When he left, they found it hopping about the room. In return, knowing that he liked sweets, the young Emily presented him, on his next visit, with a tin. The shortsighted N stooped low over the tin as he opened it, and a cloud of grasshoppers flew out into his face. It is also said that the ladies teased him once about the remark in *Zarathustra*, "Goest thou to women, forget not the whip," and that this troubled him; he did not want them to read any of his work, in case it offended them as Roman Catholics; so they stopped teasing him on that subject (C. A. Bernoulli, *Overbeck und N*, 2:7). He last met the ladies, who loved his finesse of feeling and the gentleness of his speech, at Menaggio on Lake Como in October, 1887. He wrote to them often, the last time in early December, 1888.

219. N was attempting to buy back from Fritzsch those works of his to which Fritzsch had the rights, especially *Zarathustra*. His "pretext" in doing this was that Fritzsch had published on October 25, in his *Musikalisches Wochenblatt*, an unctuous personal attack by Richard Pohl called "The Nietzsche Case: A Psychological Problem." This was a Wagnerite counterblow at N. Fritzsch was the Wagnerite publisher as well as the publisher of the new editions of N's writings until 1887. Fritzsch had asked for ten thousand marks (according to Podach); in his letter to Fuchs, dated December 27, N put the figure at "*circa* eleven thousand marks." N frostily ridiculed Pohl in *Ecce Homo*: "Nohl, Pohl, Kohl, *con grazie ad infinitum*. All the abortions are there. Poor Wagner, what he is doing in this galère?"

220. The fourth part of *Zarathustra* had been privately printed by C. G. Naumann in 1885; N had sent copies only to friends.

crises—wars!—then that will be the proper time.[221] Please try as hard as you can to remember *who* has copies. My memory tells me: Lanzky, Widemann, Fuchs, Brandes, probably Overbeck. Do you have Widemann's address? How many copies were printed? How many have we still got? There may be a few in Naumburg.

Weather incomparable, in every respect. Three crates of books arrived from Nice. I have been looking through my books, and *for the first time I feel ripe for them.* Do you understand this? I have done everything well, but had no idea this was so—on the contrary! . . . For example, these various prefaces, the *fifth* book of the "gaya scienza"—the devil, what things there are in them! In *Ecce Homo* you will read a discovery about the *third* and *fourth Unzeitgemässe* which will make your hair stand on end—mine stood on end too. Both speak of me alone, *anticipando.* . . . Psychologically speaking, neither Wagner nor Schopenhauer makes an appearance there . . . Both these pieces have become clear to me only during the past two weeks.

Signs and wonders!

Greetings from the   Phoenix

Menschliches, Allzumenschliches impressed me very strongly indeed; it has something of the tranquillity of a *Grand Seigneur.*

191 · *To Peter Gast*   Turin, Sunday, December 16, 1888

Dear friend:

Important extension of the concept of "operetta." *Spanish* operetta. *La gran via,* heard twice—main feature, from Madrid. Simply cannot be imported: one would have to be a rogue and the devil of an instinctive fellow—and *solemn* at the same time . . . A trio of three solemn [old gigantic villains is the strongest thing that I have heard *and seen*—also as music: genius cannot be formulated . . . Since I now know a great deal of Rossini—am familiar with *eight* operas—I took my favorite one, *Cenerentola,* as an example for comparison: it is a thousand times too kindhearted when compared with the Spaniards. You see, only a complete rogue could think out even the plot—

221. Cf. *Ecce Homo* (*Werke in drei Bänden,* 2:1152–53): "For when the truth goes into battle against the millennia-old lie, we shall have quakings, a convulsion of earthquakes, a moving of mountain and valley such as has never been dreamed of. The idea of politics will then merge completely into a war of spirits, all power structures of the old society will be exploded—they all rest on the lie: there will be wars such as the earth has never seen."

it is just like a conjuring trick the way the villains flash like lightning into view. Four or five pieces of music which must be *heard;* for the rest, the Viennese waltz in the form of larger *ensembles* predominates. Offenbach's *Schöne Helena* coming after it was a sorry falling-off. I left. It lasts exactly one hour.

This afternoon I plan to hear a requiem by the old Neapolitan Jommelli (died in 1774): *Accademia di canto corale.*[222]

And now the *important* thing. Yesterday I sent to C. G. Naumann a manuscript which must be dealt with at once, *before Ecce Homo.* I cannot find translators for *Ecce Homo;* I must postpone the printing for a few months. After all, there is no hurry. The *new* thing you will like—you appear in it, and in what a way! It is called

"Nietzsche contra Wagner

Documents of a Psychologist"[223]

Essentially it is a characterization of opposite poles, in which I have used several passages from my earlier writings, and in this way have written the *very serious* pendant to *Der Fall Wagner.* This has not prevented me from treating the Germans with *Spanish* mischievousness in it—the book (about three sheets in length) is extremely *anti-German.* At the end there is something of which even my friend Gast has no idea: a song (or whatever you want to call it) of Zarathustra, called "On the Poverty of the Richest"— you know, a little seventh heaven in which one-eighth is—*music . . .*

Occasionally nowadays I see no reason why I should accelerate too much the *tragic* catastrophe of my life, which begins with *Ecce.* The new work will perhaps, because of the curiosity aroused by *Der Fall Wagner,* be widely read—and since I never write a sentence now in which the whole of me is not present, then the *psychologist's antithesis* will also be a way for people to understand me—*la gran via . . .*

Avenarius, whose fingers I have touched with a mischievous little letter, has apologized most politely and kindly—I think I have dealt very well with this matter. (Ask for a few more copies of *Der Kunstwart!*)

Just think, dear friend! Piedmontese *cuisine!* Ah, my *trattoria!* I had no idea what experts the Italians were in the *art* of cooking! *and* in the quality! Not for nothing is one living in the most famous cattle-breeding part of the

222. The name of the choral society which performed the work.

223. Just before Christmas, N himself decided against publishing this (letter to Gast, dated December 22; not translated); he telegraphed Naumann to drop it and go ahead with *Ecce Homo.* However, he had been correcting the final proofs of it when Overbeck came to Turin in January, 1889. Overbeck insisted that the work should not be published at the time; Gast subsequently had a few copies privately printed for friends. First publication was in 1895 in the *Grossoktavausgabe* (ed. Fritz Kögel), volume 8.

country! And, altogether, though I eat like a prince—a *lot* too—I pay for each meal (ten centimes tip included!) one franc twenty-five. Evenings I sit in a spendid high room; a small, *very nice* orchestra plays so quietly, just as I would wish—there are three adjoining rooms. My paper is brought to me, *Journal des Débats;* I eat an excellent portion of ice cream; costs, including the tip (which I pay, since it is the custom here) forty centimes. In the *Galleria Subalpina* (into which I look down when I leave my lodging), the most beautiful, most elegant room of this kind I know; they play now, evening after evening, *The Barber of Seville*, and *excellently* too—one pays slightly more for what one eats. And how *good* the city looks when it is overcast! Recently I said to myself: to have a place that one does not want to leave, not even to go into the countryside—where one is glad to walk *the streets!* Earlier I would have thought it impossible.

In friendship.   Your N.

Last, *not* least: All the people who have anything to do with me now, right down to the peddler woman, who picks out glorious grapes for me, are people just as they should be, and very polite, serene, a little fat—even the waiter.

Prince von Carignano has just died; we shall have a great funeral. A glorious letter has just arrived from M. Taine![224]

192. *To Carl Fuchs*   Turin, Via Carlo Alberto 6/III
[December 18, 1888]

Dear friend:

Meanwhile everything is going wonderfully well. Never before have I known anything remotely like these months from the beginning of September until now. The most amazing tasks as easy as a game; my health, like the weather, coming up every day with boundless brilliance and certainty. I cannot tell you how much has been finished—*everything*.

The world will be standing on its head for the next few years: since the old God has abdicated, *I* shall rule the world from now on.

My publisher, no doubt, has sent you *Der Fall* and, most recently of all, the *Götzen-Dämmerung*. Would you perhaps be in something of a belliger-

---

224. Taine declined to translate *Ecce Homo*, on the grounds that his German was not good enough. He suggested Bourdeau, editor of the *Journal des Débats* and *Revue des deux mondes*. Bourdeau declined, on the grounds that he had no time, though he made it plain that he was greatly interested in N; he promised to publish an article by Gabriel Monod on *Der Fall Wagner* in the January *Journal des Débats*.

ent mood? I am extremely anxious that a—*the*—intelligent musician should now take sides with me as *anti-Wagner* and fling down the gauntlet to the Bayreuth people. A small brochure, in which entirely new and decisive things are said about me, applied in a special case, that of *music*—what do you think? Nothing tedious, something hard-hitting, trenchant . . . It is the right moment. One can still say truths about me which, in two years' time, might be almost *niaiseries*.

And *what* is going on in Danzig—or rather, *not*-Danzig? . . . Give me news of yourself again, dear friend—I have time, I have *ears* . . .

Most affectionate greetings,   The Monster

193 · *To Franziska Nietzsche*   Turin, Via Carlo Alberto 6/III
                                   December 21, 1888

Meine alte Mutter:

In a few days, unless I am deceived, it will be Christmas; perhaps my letter will reach you in time (perhaps, too, Herr Kürbitz has understood the signal I gave him a few days ago), with this request, that you should think of some present that would please you and by which to remember your old creature and, for the rest, apologizing that it is not more.[225] Here too we have a little winter, but not so much that I have had to light my stove. The sun and clear sky always return as masters again after a few days of fog. There has been a great funeral—one of our princes, the cousin of the king; he had done much for Italy, also for the navy, for he was admiral of the fleet.

I am in every way glad to be done with Nice; meanwhile three crates of books have been sent to me from there. Also the only congenial and pleasant company I had there, the excellent Köchlins, fine people and accustomed to the best society, are for the first time not spending the winter in Nice this year. Old Köchlin is unwell; Mme Cécile wrote me a long letter about it: he has a temperature continuously. They are near Genoa, at Nervi. But I had good and happy news from Mme Fynn and her Russian friend in Geneva.

But I have received the best news of all from my friend *Gast*, whose whole life has changed in an extraordinary way. Not only in that the foremost artists in Berlin, Joachim and de Ahna, are deeply interested in his work, the most exacting and pampered kind of artist that Germany has; above all, you would be amazed that he moves only in the wealthiest and

225. Kürbitz was N's banker in Naumburg.

most eminent Berlin society. Perhaps his opera will have its first performance in Berlin; Count Hochberg has to do with the circles which he frequents.

All in all, your old creature is now an immensely famous person ["Tier"]: not exactly in Germany, for the Germans are too stupid and too vulgar for the loftiness of my mind, and have always cast aspersions on me, but everywhere else. My admirers are all very *exclusive* natures, all prominent and influential people, in St. Petersburg, in Paris, in Stockholm, in Vienna, in New York. Ah, if you knew with what words the *foremost* personages express their devotion to me, the most charming women, not excluding by any means a Mme la Princesse Tenichev! I have real geniuses among my admirers—today no other name is treated with so much distinction and reverence as mine. You see that is the best trick of all: without a name, without rank, without wealth, I am treated here like a little prince, by everyone, down to my peddler woman, who will not rest until she has found the sweetest of all her grapes for me.[226]

Luckily, I am now ripe for everything that my task may require of me. My health is really excellent; the hardest tasks, for which no man was yet strong enough, are easy for me.

Meine alte Mutter, receive, at the year's end, my most affectionate good wishes, and wish me a new year which will match in every way the great things that must come to pass in it.

Your old creature

194. *To Franz Overbeck*   [Turin, Christmas, 1888]

Dear friend:

We must finish the business with Fritzsch quickly, for in two months I shall be the foremost name on earth.

I pluck up the courage also to tell you that in Paraguay things are as bad as they could be. The Germans who were lured over there are in rebellion, demanding their money back—there is none. Acts of violence have already occurred.[227] This does *not* prevent my sister from

---

226. "Without wealth": it is said that N used to spend much time in the Rosenberg and Sellier bookshop in Turin but did not buy books because he had no money for them (Podach, *Ns Zusammenbruch*, p. 82). Against the megalomania and rancorous puerilities elsewhere among the last letters, one should balance the almost clownish vanity and tenderness of this one.

227. Bernhard Förster's suicide followed early in June, 1889.

writing to me for October 15, with the utmost scorn, that she supposes I want to become "famous" too—that would be a nice state of affairs, to be sure! And what scum I had sought for company—Jews, who have been around licking all the plates, like Georg Brandes . . . And she calls me "sweet Fritz"? . . . This has been going on for seven years.

My mother still has no notion of this—that is *my* masterpiece. For Christmas she sent me a game: "Fritz und Lieschen[228] . . .

The remarkable thing here in Turin is the complete fascination which I hold for everyone, although I am the most unassuming person and ask *nothing*. But when I walk into a big shop, every face changes; the women on the streets look at me; my old peddler woman puts aside the sweetest grapes for me and *has reduced the price*! . . . Really it is ridiculous . . . I eat in one of the leading *trattoria*, with two immense floors of rooms large and small. For every meal I pay one franc twenty-five, including the tip—and I receive the most select items of the most select *cuisine*[229]—I never had any idea what either meat or vegetables or any of these Italian dishes *can* be like . . . Today, for example, the most tender *ossobuchi*—God knows how one says it in German!—the meat on the bones, where the glorious marrow is. Also *broccoli* cooked unbelievably well, and, to start with, the most tender macaroni. My waiters are radiant with elegance and helpfulness; the *best* part is that I do not make a fool of anyone . . . Since anything is possible in my life now, I make a mental note of all these individuals who have discovered me in my *undiscovered* period. It is not altogether impossible that my future cook is already attending to me.

Nobody yet has taken me for a German . . .

I read the *Journal des Débats*; the moment I entered the foremost café, someone instinctively brought it to me.

Also there are no coincidences any more: I need only to think of somebody, and a letter from him comes politely through the door . . .

Naumann is being splendidly zealous. I suspect that he was making the printers work over Christmas. In two weeks he has sent me five sheets. The end of *Ecce Homo* is a dithyramb of boundless invention—I cannot think of it without sobbing.

Between ourselves, I am coming to Basel in the spring—I need to! It is the very devil, not ever being able to speak a word in confidence . . .

Your friend N.

Dr. Fuchs is performing Köselitz's duet at a Danzig concert; he wants *Der Löwe von Venedig* for the theater there! But if Joachim continues to be inter-

---

228. The game's name combines the pet names of Friedrich and Elisabeth.

229. *N's footnote:* Moral: and I have never yet had an upset stomach.

ested, the work will very probably be taken on by Count Hochberg . . . K. fled to his parents for Christmas, to avoid receiving *presents* . . . The von Krauses make a princely display at Christmas (as at other times); they send, for example, a Christmas hamper to every family in their villages.[230] K. has introduced von Krause to his Venice friend the famous Passin, to help the latter earn a few thousand. P. is living in Berlin now.

195 · *To Elisabeth Nietzsche (draft)*   Turin, December, 1888

My sister:

I received your letter, and after reading it several times I see that I am compelled to part company with you for ever.[231] Now that my destiny is certain, I feel every word of yours with tenfold sharpness; you have not the remotest conception of what it means to be most closely related to the man and to the destiny in whom the question of millennia has been decided—I hold, quite literally, the future of mankind in the palm of my hand.

I know human nature, and am unspeakably far from judging in any individual case what the ultimate doom of mankind is; more, I understand how precisely you, out of your utter incapacity to see the things in whose midst I live, have had to take refuge in almost the opposite of what I am. What puts my mind at rest here is the thought that you have succeeded in your own way, that you have somebody whom you love and who loves you, that an important task is there for you to do, to which your ability and strength are dedicated; finally—and I shall make no secret of it—that this very task has led you rather far away from me, so that the next shocks of what will be occurring to me will not spread as far as you. This last I wish for your own sake; above all, I ask you fervently not to let yourself be seduced by any friendly and, in this case, actually dangerous curiosity into reading the writings which I am at present publishing. Such things could wound you terribly—and me, in my concern for you, also . . . In this respect, I regret having sent you the book about Wagner, which, in the immense tension which surrounds my life, was a real relief to me—as an honest duel between a psychologist and a pious seducer, whom people do not easily recognize as such.

To put your mind at rest, I will say of myself only that I am extremely well, with a certainty and patience which in my earlier life I never en-

230. Gast was a music tutor in the von Krause household.

231. Refers to the birthday letter mentioned in No. 194, in which Elisabeth had written, "It will be a fine lot of scum that believes in you [. . .]" In *Briefe und Berichte*, this draft is placed chronologically before the letter to N's mother dated December 21.

joyed for a single hour; that the most difficult things are coming easily; that everything to which I put my hand is turning out well. The task which is imposed *upon* me is, all the same, my nature—so that only now do I comprehend what was my predestined good fortune. I play with the burden which would crush any other mortal . . . For what I have to do is *terrible*, in any sense of the word; I do not challenge individuals—I am challenging humanity as a whole with my terrible accusation; whichever way the decision may go, *for* me or *against* me, in any case there attaches to my name a quantity of doom that is beyond telling . . .

In asking you, with all my heart, not to see any hardness in this letter, but the reverse—a real humanity, which is trying to prevent any unnecessary damage—I ask you, over and above this necessity, to keep on loving me.

Your brother

196. *To Carl Fuchs*   [Turin] December 27, 1888

All things considered, dear friend, there is no sense any more in talking and writing *about* me; I have settled for the next eternity the question as to who I am, with the book which we are having printed now, *Ecce Homo*. People should not trouble about me hereafter, but about the things for which I am there. [———]²³² First, *Nietzsche contra Wagner* will be published—if all goes well, also in French. The problem of antagonism is treated here at such a deep level that the Wagner question is actually settled. A page of "music" about music in the aforementioned work is perhaps the most remarkable thing I have written . . . What I say about Bizet, you should not take seriously; the way I am, Bizet does not matter to me at all. But as an ironic antithesis to Wagner, it has a strong effect; it would have been inordinately bad taste if I had used an encomium on Beethoven as my starting point. [———]

The stupid tactlessness which Fritzsch showed by mocking me in his own periodical has been very useful, insofar as it gave me a pretext for writing Fritzsch: "How much do you want for all my books? With sincere contempt, Nietzsche." Reply: *circa* eleven thousand marks. Assuming that in this way I can, at the last moment, become sole owner of my works (for even C. G. Naumann owns nothing of mine), Fritzsch's stupidity would be a first-rate stroke of luck.²³³ I shall see to it that you receive in good time all

---

232. Here, as at the end of this same paragraph, the dash indicates an editorial omission from the original edition (which Schlechta's edition perpetuates).

233. Though N does occasionally call Naumann his "publisher," the latter was publishing N's books only under commission; N had to cover the printing costs.

those books of mine which you do not have—only wait a little while! The idea of Rostock, assuming again that it would be only for an interim of two years, seems a very excellent one to me, especially for the practice and rehearsing of the real qualities of a conductor—in other ways, too . . .[234]

Dear friend, I urge you to send your pamphlet about Wagner to my publisher C. G. Naumann; you may dedicate it to me in a short preface. We must enrage the Germans with *esprit* . . .

Do not shirk *Tristan:* it is the central work and of a fascination which has no parallel, not only in music but in all the arts.

I suggest that your pamphlet on Wagner be preceded in the book by Herr Gast's excellent essay on me—makes a spendid impression.

Title: *Der Fall Nietzsche*
by Peter Gast and Carl Fuchs

[no signature]

197. *To Franz Overbeck*   [Received on December 28, 1888, from Turin]

Dear friend:

I could not help laughing just now: I suddenly remembered your old pay clerk, whom I still have to pacify. It will gladden him to hear that since 1869 I have had no rights of residence in Germany, and own a wonderful Basel passport which has been several times renewed by Swiss consulates.

I myself am working on a memorandum for the courts of Europe, with an anti-German league in view. I mean to sew up the Reich in an iron shirt and to provoke it to a war of desperation. I shall not have my hands free until I have the young emperor, and all his appurtenances, in my hands.[235]

Between ourselves! *Very much* between ourselves! Complete calm of soul! Ten hours of uninterrupted sleep![236]

N.

234. Having failed to get an appointment at Bonn, Fuchs was trying to get one in Rostock.

235. Overbeck replied to this letter anxiously, inquiring after N's health. N's reply (dated December 31) was altogether tranquil, and his explanation was: "I wrote the letter in very *bad* light—I no longer knew what I was writing."

236. This is the kind of detail which has been used—quite apart from the manic second paragraph of this letter—in support of Elisabeth's theory (which Podach rejected) that N had been taking excessive doses of chloral hydrate ever since the early autumn, causing excited mental states on the morning after; also that he had begun to take

198 · *To Meta von Salis*   Turin, December 29, 1888

Verehrtes Fräulein:

It is perhaps not forbidden to send you a greeting at the turn of the year.
I hope the coming year will be a *good* one. Of the old year, I shall say no
more—it was *too good* . . .

In the meantime I have begun to be quite unprecedentedly famous.
I think no mortal has ever received such letters as I have, and only from
exclusive intelligences, from characters with high duties and in high office.
From everywhere: not least from the highest St. Petersburg society. And
the French! You should hear the tone in which M. Taine writes to me! I have
just received an enchanting, and perhaps enchanted, letter from one of the
foremost and most influential men in France, who wants to make it his task
to become familiar with, and to translate, my writings—no less a person
that the editor-in-chief of the *Journal des Débats* and the *Revue des deux
mondes*, M. Bourdeau. He tells me too that a review of my *Fall Wagner* will
be appearing in January in the *Journal des Débats*—by whom? By Monod.
I have a veritable genius among my readers, the Swede August Strindberg,
who feels that I am the deepest mind of all times. I am sending you an
article in *Der Kunstwart*, requesting that you return it to me sometime, which

---

a "Javanese" sedative, which an "old Dutchman" had given him in Turin, the effect of
which was sedation only if the doses were small. One account tells of N's taking a few
drops too many of the latter and falling on the carpet in a paroxysm of laughter (Bernoulli, *Overbeck und N*, pp. 228–29). Writhing on the floor and paroxysms of euphoric
joy, followed by extreme lethargy, also characterized the early stages of N's breakdown.
However, the Javanese sedative ("Yauma") has never been identified; its existence has
been doubted. Possibly N slept his ten hours without sedation. Chloral hydrate, moreover, does not cause exhilaration. Elisabeth put out her theory (*Das Leben F. Ns*, 1904;
Der einsame N, 1910) about N's being disabled by drugs in order to allay and destroy suspicions that his madness could be "explained" as *paralysis progressiva* caused by syphilis
(as suggested by the Swedish doctor, Paul Bierre, author of *The Insanity of Genius*, 1905).
The *paralysis progressiva* diagnosis at the Basel clinic is not conclusive; Dr. Stutz, director
there during the 1920's, found that many cases on the records which had that diagnosis
would certainly be described as schizophrenic today. Podach warned in 1930 that neither
the Basel nor the Jena records provided *certain* evidence for either paralysis or syphilis,
even though there might have been some kind of luetic infection of the brain ("there can
be no certain verdict on the matter, because of the inadequacy of the data"—*The Madness
of N*, p. 235; *Ns Zusammenbruch*, pp. 158 ff.). Thomas Mann, who read Podach attentive-
ly and used him in his *Doktor Faustus*, thought differently (R. Blunck's 1953 findings [cf.
note to No. 2, 1865] may confirm his verdict) : "He [N] shared the fate of many artists and
pre-eminently of composers (one can number him among the latter, to some extent) : he
was destroyed by progressive paralysis, a malaise which is clearly and unambiguously of
sexual origin" (introduction to *The Short Novels of Dostoevsky*, New York: Dial Press,
1945, p. xii).

does indeed define the "Nietzsche case" perfectly. The most remarkable thing here in Turin is the complete fascination which I exert—over all classes of people. With every glance I am treated like a prince—there is an extremely distinguished air about the way people open the door for me or serve me food. When I enter a large shop, all the faces change. And since I make no demands and, with complete composure, am the same toward everybody, and also have a face which is anything but gloomy, I need neither name, nor rank, nor money to make myself always unconditionally the first.

So that there should be no lack of contrast, my sister announced for my birthday, with the utmost scorn, that she supposed I too was starting to be "famous" . . . A fine lot of scum it would be that believed in *me* . . . This has been going on for seven years . . .

Yet *another* case. I seriously regard the Germans as people of an utterly vulgar sort, and thank heaven that in all my instincts I am a Pole and nothing else. On the occasion of *Der Fall Wagner*, my publisher Herr E. W. Fritzsch printed in the *Musikalisches Wochenblatt*, which he edits, a most heinous article about me. I wrote him at once: "How much do you want for all my books? With sincere contempt, Nietzsche." Answer: eleven thousand marks. Think of it! That is German . . . the publisher of *Zarathustra*.

Georg Brandes is going to St. Petersburg again this winter, to give lectures on the savage beast Nietzsche. He is really an extremely intelligent man; never have I received such delicate letters. My writings are being zealously printed, with *fiery zeal* . . . Meanwhile, Herr Köselitz has become a famous person ["grosses Tier"]. Joachim and de Ahna are raving about this new "classic"—I add that he is wooing all too successfully a remarkably beautiful and interesting girl in one of the most spendid mansions of Berlin, although he has Count Schlieben for a rival. He spent the whole summer in his princess's woodland château in Pomerania, surrounded by Junkers and [*illegible word*].

Probably Count Hochberg will approach him to secure for Berlin the first performance of *Der Löwe von Venedig*. In short, Transvaluation of All Values . . . With best greetings and wishes,

Your N.

Did you hear that Mme Kovaleska in Stockholm (she is descended from the old Hungarian King Matthias Corvin) has received the topmost mathematics prize from the Paris Academy? She is regarded today as the only living mathematical genius.

199 · *To Peter Gast*   Turin, December 31, 1888

You are right, a thousand times over! Warn Fuchs yourself . . . You will find in *Ecce Homo* an astonishing page about *Tristan*, about my whole relationship with Wagner. Wagner is altogether the foremost name in *E. H.* Wherever I admit no doubts, here too I had the courage to go the whole way. Ah, friend! What a moment! When your card came, *what* was I doing . . . It was the famous Rubicon . . .[237]

I no longer know my address: let us suppose that it will soon be the Palazzo del Quirinale.

                                                                    N.

200 · *To August Strindberg*   [Undated]

Dear Sir:

You will soon have an answer about your novella—it sounds like a rifle shot. I have ordered a convocation of princes in Rome—I mean to have the young emperor shot.[238]

Auf Wiedersehen! For we shall see each other again.
Une seule condition: Divorçons . . .

                                                      Nietzsche Caesar

[Strindberg's reply:

                                        Holtibus pridie Cal. Jan.
                                                MDCCCLXXXIX
Carissime doctor!

θέλω, θέλω μανῆναι![239]

237. This phrase could be taken to indicate that N had gone out of his mind shortly before writing this note to Gast, thus before the date of his collapse on the Piazza Carlo Alberto on January 3 (the date established by Podach). The following postcard (No. 200) to Strindberg is likely to have been written on December 29th or 30th, since Strindberg's reply is dated (in Latin) January 1, 1889.

238. N did in fact write notes addressed to Umberto, King of Italy, to the Vatican State Secretary Mariani, and to the royal (Hohenzollern) house of Baden. He sent other notes to Rohde, von Bülow, Spitteler, and Malwida von Meysenbug.

239. Quotation from an Anacreontic poem, meaning: "I want, I want to be mad" (*Anacreontics*, ed. Isaac Bagg, Boston, 1895, Nos. III and IV, pp. 2-4). The Latin, from Horace, *Odes* II, X, lines 1-4, means: "Better wilt thou live, Licinius, by neither always pressing out to sea nor too closely hugging the dangerous shore in cautious fear of storms" (Loeb translation). The following phrase means "Meanwhile it is a joy to be mad."

Litteras tuas non sine perturbatione accepi et tibi gratias ago

> Rectius vives, Licini, neque altum.
> Semper urgendo neque, dum procellas
> Cautus horrescis nimium premendo
> Litus iniquum.
> Interdum juvat insanire!
> Vale et Fave!

> Strindberg
> (Deus, optimus maximus)

N's reply:

Herr Strindberg!
Eheu? . . . not *Divorçons* after all? . . .

> The Crucified]

---

201 · *To Peter Gast* [Postmarked Turin, January 4, 1889]

To my maestro Pietro.
Sing me a new song: the world is transfigured and all the heavens rejoice.

> The Crucified

---

202 · *To Georg Brandes* [Postmarked Turin, January 4, 1889]

To my friend Georg! Once you discovered me, it was no great feat to find
me: the difficulty now is to lose me . . .

> The Crucified

---

203 · *To Jakob Burckhardt* [Postmarked Turin, January 4, 1889]

Meinem verehrungswürdigen Jakob Burckhardt.

That was the little joke on account of which I condone my boredom at having created a world. Now you are—thou art—our great greatest teacher;
for I, together with Ariadne, have only to be the golden balance of all
things, everywhere we have such beings who are above us. . . .

> Dionysus

204 · *To Cosima Wagner*   [Beginning of January, 1889]

Ariadne, I love you.

Dionysus[240]

205 · *To Franz Overbeck*   [Received January 7, 1889][241]

To my friend Overbeck and his wife
Although till now you have had little faith in my ability to remain solvent,
I still hope to prove that I am a person who pays his debts.—For example, my
debts to you both . . .
      I am just having all anti-Semites shot . . .

Dionysus

206 · *To Jakob Burckhardt*   On January 6, 1889
                              [Postmarked Turin, January 5, 1889]

Dear Professor:

Actually I would much rather be a Basel professor than God; but I have not
ventured to carry my private egoism so far as to omit creating the world on
his account. You see, one must make sacrifices, however and wherever one
may be living. Yet I have kept a small student room for myself, which is

240. This message plays on the Cosima-Wagner-Nietzsche relationship, which
Charles Andler first detected beneath N's treatment of the mythic Ariadne-Theseus-
Dionysus relationship in N's "Empedocles" and "Naxos" fragments and *Zarathustra IV*.
N's poem "Lament of Ariadne" ends with Dionysus replying to Ariadne, "*I am your
labyrinth*" (*Werke in drei Bänden*, 2 : 1259). Podach writes: "Ariadne is the glittering symbol of the woman of N's heart's desire, a symbol that took root and grew up in his own
world of mythic experience. He does not reveal what experiences may have fostered its
formation and growth—out of deep need and also probably following his often all-too-
artistic impulse to put on a disguise. Yet beginning and end are certain: in Tribschen,
Cosima becomes for the young N the governing image of Ariadnean being; twenty years
later—in Turin—he turns back to the original realm of his Naxos dreams and sends a last
lover's greeting to his heroine" (*Ns Zusammenbruch*, p. 92; *Madness of N*, p. 148, where
Voigt's translation [not used above] is defective).

241. Overbeck received this undated note on Monday, January 7. On Sunday,
January 6, Burckhardt had received from N his long letter, postmarked January 5; both
letter and note (a postcard) could have been written on January 5.

situated opposite the Palazzo Carignano (in which I was born as Vittorio Emanuele[242]) and which moreover allows me to hear from its desk the splendid music below me in the Galleria Subalpina. I pay twenty-five francs, with service, make my own tea, and do my own shopping, suffer from torn boots, and thank heaven every moment for the *old* world, for which human beings have not been simple and quiet enough. Since I am condemned to entertain the next eternity with bad jokes, I have a writing business here which really leaves nothing to be desired—very nice and not in the least strenuous. The post office is five paces away; I post my letters there myself, to play the part of the great *feuilletonist* of the *grande monde*. Naturally I am in close contact with Figaro, and so that you may have some idea of how harmless I can be, listen to my first two bad jokes:

Do not take the Prado case seriously. I am Prado, I am also Prado's father, I venture to say that I am also Lesseps.[243] . . . I wanted to give my Parisians, whom I love, a new idea—that of a decent criminal. I am also Chambige—also a decent criminal.

Second joke. I greet the immortals. M. Daudet is one of the *quarante*.

Astu[244]

The unpleasant thing, and one that nags my modesty, is that at root every name in history is I; also as regards the children I have brought into the world, it is a case of my considering with some distrust whether all of those who enter the "Kingdom of God" do not also come *out of* God.[245] This autumn, as lightly clad as possible, I twice attended my funeral, first as Count Robilant (no, he is my son, insofar as I am Carlo Alberto, my nature

242. Vittorio Emanuele II, son of Carlo Alberto, died in 1878. He was father of Umberto I, who was king at this time.

243. On Prado (and Chambige), see note 210 to No. 189. Ferdinand de Lesseps (1805–94) was the French diplomat responsible for building the Suez Canal and who initiated the earlier stages of the building of the Panama Canal. He also fathered seventeen children. During the latter part of his life, he was involved in a scandal. N was offering Burckhardt these jokes with some reason: his own (*Der Antichrist*) idea of Cesare Borgia as pope—the total Renaissance secularization, absolute anti-Christianity—was culled from Burckhardt's *Civilization of the Renaissance in Italy.* In his (unpublished) note to Malwida, N identifies himself with Alexander Herzen: "In Natalie [Herzen] her father lives, and I was also him" (original in the Nationale Forschungs- und Gedenkstätten der klassischen deutschen Literatur in Weimar).

244. Greek for "city," with the connotation "hometown." The possible implication is "Alphonse Daudet's antiacademic hero Léonard Astier [in Daudet's novel *L'immortel*] is one of us." See footnote 188 to No. 180.

245. Presumably an allusion to N's writings as "children." The passage relates, somewhat obliquely, to his discovery (No. 190) that his *Thoughts out of Season* on Schopenhauer and Wagner were in fact essays about himself; by now, the author is both "God" and the total solipsist (without object world).

below), but I was Antonelli myself. [246] Dear professor, you should see this construction; since I have no experience of the things I create, you may be as critical as you wish; I shall be grateful, without promising I shall make any use of it. We artists are unteachable. Today I saw an operetta—Moorish, of genius[247]—and on this occasion have observed to my pleasure that Moscow nowadays and Rome also are grandiose matters. Look, for landscape too my talent is not denied. Think it over, we shall have a pleasant, pleasant talk together, Turin is not far, we have no very serious professional duties, a glass of Veltliner could be come by. Informal dress the rule of propriety.

With fond love   Your   Nietzsche

I go everywhere in my student overcoat; slap someone or other on the shoulder and say: *Siamo contenti? Son dio, ha fatto questa caricatura* . . . [248]

Tomorrow my son Umberto is coming with the charming Margherita whom I receive, however, here too in my shirt sleeves.

The *rest* is for Frau Cosima . . . Ariadne . . . From time to time we practice magic . . .

I have had Caiaphas put in chains; I too was crucified at great length last year by the German doctors. Wilhelm Bismarck and all anti-Semites done away with.[249]

You can make any use of this letter which does not make the people of Basel think less highly of me.

246. Antonelli was papal state secretary under Pius IX.

247. Podach (*Ns Zusammenbruch*, pp. 98–99) reads this as "quirinal-maurisch" ("Quirinal-Moorish"), which is doubtful; the original lacks, in any case, the middle letters "*ri.*" Schlechta's reading, "genial-maurisch" is, I think, correct. Presumably the reference is to the operetta *La gran via*, which N saw about December 15.

248. "Are we happy? I am God, I made this caricature . . ." The paragraphs following are written at various points in the margins of the original.

249. That is, Wilhelm (the emperor) and Bismarck. As early as 1881, N had anticipated farce and parody as a climax to his mental adventure; cf. *Die fröhliche Wissenschaft*, Bk. 3, sections 153 and 236; Bk. 4, section 342; Bk. 5, sections 382 and 383. Also *Jenseits von Gut und Böse*, section 223: "We are [. . .] ready, as no previous age was, for the grand carnival, for the laughter and recklessness of a mental Mardi Gras, for the transcendental heights of the highest idiocy and Aristophanic mockery of the world. Perhaps it is here that we shall discover the realm of our *invention*, that realm where we too can be original, perhaps as parodists of world history and clowns [*Hanswürste*] of God [. . .]" (*Werke in drei Bänden*, 2:686.)

Epilogue

Burckhardt took his letter to Overbeck during the afternoon of January 6. Overbeck wrote to N at once, insisting that he should come to Basel. On January 7 he went to see Professor Wille of the Basel Psychiatric Clinic, and took the train to Turin the same evening, arriving there on Tuesday afternoon, January 8. He described the situation in a letter to Gast, dated January 15:[1]

My dear Herr Köselitz:

[. . .] What I can say and want to say even to you at this moment will leave unanswered a thousand questions that you may have. First and foremost, you would like a factual report on what happened. I am obliged to be silent on a number of matters, only because the situation, in which I took action, was so urgent, and I would like not to have to mention such matters to any soul who was the sick man's friend, to you yourself especially, at least for now.

Until Christmas, I was bewildered by N's letters about his present situation; around Christmas the letters became more frequent, and at the same time the handwriting and contents most disquieteningly betrayed a peculiar exaltation. Yet what perplexed me most of all was a completely reasonable letter received on December 31 by my excellent colleague Andreas Heusler, whom N also knew from his Basel days. It concerned a demand for the return of [the rights of] those books of his which Fritzsch had published. The letters which I myself had received just before gave me cause to express [to N] insistence that he should desist in this as well as the anxiety which his letters were giving me. On the same December 31, I received a reply which gave me cause to believe that the plan to deal with Fritzsch was over and done with, but which dismissed my anxieties in a way that was anything but convincing. On January 6, Jakob Burckhardt received a letter, which he at once showed to me and which he has meanwhile given to me as the principal document which decided my intervention.[2]

1. C. A. Bernoulli, *Overbeck und N*, pp. 231–37.

2. Since Overbeck was not a relative, the law required that his intervention should be proved necessary. Elisabeth later caused a furor, challenging the legality of his action. She argued that the family and the family physician should have been called (that is, N's mother and Dr. Eiser of Frankfurt).

Now it was clear, between this letter and the previous one—on January 4, as his landlord later told me—N had gone out of his mind.[3] He was not only a king, but also father of other kings (Umberto and others), had even been to his own funeral (that of his son Robilant), and so on, and all this in the frenzied tone of a madman. In my helpless despair, I immediately wrote a most urgent letter to N, asking him to come to me at once, which was doubly foolish, as I learned on consulting the head physician of our insane asylum the next day, and whose possible consequences I cut short on the same day by telegraphing N that I was leaving at once for Turin. My colleague Wille—that is the physician's name—when I showed him that letter to Burckhardt and a short note which I had myself received on the Monday morning, left me in no doubt that no time should be lost, and said that I should leave at once if I felt it was my responsibility to do so. And for this I am now also very grateful to him, even though I was forced to undertake more than I knew I could do. In fact, it was fortunate that I did not arrive in Turin even an hour later than I did. On the same afternoon— the afternoon of my arrival, a week ago today—the affair became a public scandal there; the landlord, whom special circumstances prevented me from finding, was, when I had at least his wife before me at last, visiting the police station and the German consul—an hour before this, I had established that the police knew nothing. N, who had collapsed in the street on the previous day and had been picked up there, was now in danger of being committed to a private insane asylum and was at that very moment being surrounded by adventurers of the kind who in Italy gather around more quickly than anywhere else when such a thing occurs. It was the last possible moment for removing him without obstacles apart from his own condition. I shall pass over the touching circumstances in which I found N being looked after by his landlord and landlady—the former owns a newspaper kiosk on the Via Carlo Alberto—they too may be characteristic of Italy. The terrible moment at which I saw N again brings me back to my main concern, uniquely a terrible moment and quite different from all that followed. I see N crouching and reading in the corner of a sofa—the last proofs of *N contra Wagner*, as I later found—looking horribly worn out; he sees me and rushes

3. Podach makes January 3 the date of N's collapse (*Ns Zusammenbruch*, p. 82) and connects it with the well-known incident with the horse: "On January 3, as N is leaving his house, he sees on the Piazza Carlo Alberto, where the horsedrawn cabs are parked, a tired old horse being beaten by a brutal cabman. Compassion seizes him. Sobbing and protectively he flings his arms around the neck of the tormented animal. He collapses. Fortunately Fino comes by, attracted by the disturbance on the street. He recognizes his tenant, and with great difficulty brings him into the house." Karl Strecker (*N und Strindberg*, Munich, 1921, pp. 41 ff.), who visited Turin in 1913 and spoke to people who had known N, wrote that the incident with the horse occurred "several days" before the collapse (though he makes no claims to complete accuracy in his dating).

up to me, violently embraces me, recognizing me, and breaks into floods of tears, then sinks back on the sofa, twitching and quivering; I am so shaken that I cannot stand upright. Did the abyss open before him in that moment, on the edge of which he is standing, or rather into which he has plunged? In any case, nothing of this kind happened again. The whole Fino family was present. N was hardly lying there groaning and quivering again than they gave him a sip of the bromide water that was on the table. At once he became tranquil, and laughingly began to speak of the great reception which had been prepared for that evening. With this he was among the delusions from which he had not emerged by the time I left him—always lucid as regards me and all other persons, but completely in the dark about himself. That is, growing inordinately excited at the piano, singing loudly and raving, he would utter bits and pieces from the world of ideas in which he has been living, and also in short sentences, in an indescribably muffled tone, sublime, wonderfully clairvoyant, and unspeakably horrible things would be audible, about himself as the successor of the dead God, the whole thing punctuated, as it were, on the piano, whereupon more convulsions and outbursts would follow, but, as I said, this happened only at few fleeting moments while I was with him; mainly it was utterances about the profession which he had allotted to himself, to be the clown of the new eternities, and he, the master of expression, was himself incapable of rendering the ecstasies of his gaiety except in the most trivial expressions or by frenzied dancing and capering.[4] All the while the most childish innocuousness, which had never left him even during the three nights in which he had kept the whole household awake with his ravings, and precisely this innocuousness and this almost total docility, as long as one shared his ideas about kingly receptions and processions, music festivals, and so on, made the task of bringing him back here child's play, at least for the attendant whom, on Wille's strict advice, I had sought out and taken with me. The journey, including a stop of almost three hours in Novara, took from two-thirty on Wednesday afternoon until seven forty-five on Thursday morning, began with a terrible half-hour on the platform at Turin, with the usual platform confusion; in Novara too there was some trouble;[5] generally, though, we traveled alone, N sleepy with chloral, yet repeatedly waking up, though at most in his excitement he would sing loud songs, among them, during the night, the wonderfully beautiful gondola song (*N contra Wagner*, p. 7), the

---

4. N's assumed role of "Hanswurst" ("fool," "clown," "trickster,") during his last months is discussed at some length by Podach.

5. The attendant (a German-Jew named Miescher) who appears to have been a dentist by profession, cajoled N into believing that a regal reception was awaiting him in Basel, but that it would have to be called off if he did not behave himself.

origin of which I discovered later; it was a complete enigma to me, as I listened, how the singer could invent *such* words with such a wholly peculiar melody.[6] Also the transfer from the station to the hospital on the morning of the 10th, which I had feared most of all, was practically no trouble, except that for me the whole situation was quietly terrifying. A scene in the waiting room at the hospital (I preface this by saying that N *still has no idea* where he is; our attendant, in order to avoid the scenes we had in Turin, impressed upon the sick man before we left the train that he was entering Basel incognito to start with, and must therefore not greet anybody, or else the procession later on would not be so impressive; and so with the greatest composure N walks from the railway coach to the cab, where he crouches, for the most part, in a state of great prostration; also by saying that there has been a first meeting with Wille, the director, and the latter has just left the room again for a moment). Myself to our attendant of the journey: "Forgive me, doctor, for not introducing you" (I had omitted to do so, in my excitement). N (who must have known Wille from earlier years): "He hasn't yet introduced himself; we shall soon find out." (Wille has returned.) N (in the politest manner of his best times, and with great dignity): "I believe that I have seen you before, and am very sorry but at the moment I cannot recall your name. Would you —" W.: "I am Wille." N (without moving a muscle, continuing in the same manner and in a most quiet tone, without a moment's reflection): "Wille? You are a psychiatrist ["Irrenarzt"].[7] I had a conversation with you several years ago on religious insanity. The occasion was a madman [———],[8] who was then living here (or in Basel)." Wille has been listening in silence; he nods in affirmation.

6. This song appears in *Ecce Homo*, without a title:

> On the bridge I stood
> Not long ago in the brown night.
> From far away came song:
> In golden drops it poured
> Away across the quivering water.
> Gondolas, music, lights—
> Drunkenly swam into the gloom fading . . .
>
> And my soul, a stringed instrument,
> Sang, touched by invisible hands,
> To itself a secret gondola song,
> Trembling with all the colors of bliss.
> —Can someone have been listening?

7. The word "Irrenarzt" ("doctor for the insane") does not seem to have suggested to N that he himself was the patient.

8. The omission from Bernoulli's text was repaired by Podach; the patient's name, which N remembered, was Adolf Vischer. In 1875, he had given N an original engraving of Dürer's: *Ritter, Tod und Teufel*.

Just think with what a frozen feeling of surprise I heard this—being myself able to realize the literal exactness of this memory of seven years ago. And now the main thing: N does not bring this completely lucid memory into any relation whatever to his own present state; he gives no indication at all that the *Irrenarzt* has anything to do with him. Quietly he lets himself be handed over to the assistant physician, who walks in and orders breakfast for him and a bath to start with; and he leaves the room with the latter the moment he is told to do so—I can give you no clearer picture of the annihilating split in his personality. Since then I have not seen him again, not on Saturday either, when I went out there again. I was told that his condition has not significantly changed—much noise making and singing, sleep induced only artificially; I should not try to visit him for another week; the main thing is that he should have rest and quiet. On Thursday, when I was half demented myself, I had to write to his mother. The poor dear arrived on Sunday evening, saw her son yesterday afternoon [. . .]

On Wednesday, January 17, N traveled by train to Jena with his mother, an attendant, and Ernst Mähly (who had studied under N, was an adept of his later writings, and knew Otto Binswanger, head of the Jena Psychiatric Clinic). He enjoyed the cherries which Overbeck's wife had given him and a ham sandwich from his mother. On the journey N had a fit of rage against his mother; so she traveled in a different compartment from Frankfurt onward. During the last days of January, *Götzen-Dämmerung* was published. On May 13, 1890, N was allowed to leave the Jena clinic, and went to live in Naumburg with his mother. Six months later, his sister returned from Paraguay but went back there in June, 1892, for a year. At home, N's condition steadily deteriorated. Bernoulli (*N und die Schweiz*, Berlin, 1922), at that time a student at Jena, was present when N's mother brought him on a typical visit to the Gelzers there. "She usually brought her son, who followed her like a child. So as not to be disturbed, she took him into the drawing room, where at first he loitered by the door. She walked to the piano and played a few chords, whereupon he kept coming closer and eventually began to play himself—standing, at first, until his mother pressed him down on the stool (if I may use such an expression). Then he would improvise for hours. Frau Nietzsche in the other room always knew that her son was all right, without her having to watch over him, as long as she could hear him playing." As from early 1894, N was unable to leave the house. In 1895, there were signs of physical paralysis. On April 20, 1897, his mother died; soon afterward, his sister installed him, together with her Archive, in the Villa Silberblick in Weimar. His mother's old maidservant Alwine used to look after him. He died on August 25, 1900.

Sils-Maria
Engadin
(Schweiz)

Meine liebe hochverehrte

Freundin,

oder ist es überschreiten, wenn ich
Sie so nenne? Zunächst ist, dass
ich ein unbändig gutes Zutrauen
zu Ihnen habe; und so wird
es auch die Worte nicht sehr
ankommen.
Ich habe einen schlimmen Sommer
gehabt und habe ihn noch. Die
böse Geschichte des vorigen Jahres
stürzte noch einmal über mich her;
und ich habe so viel Böses müsst
was mir diese herrliche Natur=
Einsamkeit nur

... vorben und fast zur Hölle gemacht hat. Nach Allem, was ich nun erfahren habe, ach wie ist das spät! — sind diese beiden Instanzen Rée und Lou nicht würdig, meine Nießstiefeln zu lecken — Pardon für diese allzu männliche Zuversicht! Es ist ein langes Unglück, dass dieser Rée, ein lügnerischer und schleichender Verläumder von Grund aus, mir über den Lebensweg gelaufen ist. Und was habe ich lange Geduld und Mitleid mit ihm gehabt! "Es ist ein armer Bursch, man muss ihn vornehm behandeln" — wie oft habe ich mir das gesagt, nach seiner ärmlichen und unaufrichtigen Manier zu denken und zu reden. Mittlerweile ...

machte! Ich vergesse den Ingrimm nicht,
den ich 1876 empfand, als ich Rörek
zu machte mit Zu Ihnen nach Sorrent
kommen. Und nun zwei Jahren wie-
derholte sich nochmals dieser Ingrimm!
ich war hier in Sils-Maria und
wurde brauch bei der Nachricht meiner
Menschen, daß er hier her auch kommen
wollte. Man soll seinem Du'liebten
lassen nur wahr, auch den Du'liebten
des Mißbrauchs. Aber das Schopen-
hauerische "Mitleiden" hat immer in
meinem Leben bisher den Haupt=
Unfug angestiftet — und deshalb habe
ich allen Grund, Wesen Moralen
gut zu sein, welche nach ein ganz
andern Einfluss zur Moralität
rechnen und nicht unsern ganzen mensch=
liche Lüsterbeit auf "Mitgenüssen" ver=
dünnen wollen. Dies nämlich ist

nicht nur einem Menschen, sondern die
jeder gradgesinnte halten gelacht haben
würde — sondern einen rechten grade-
läufigen Gedanken. Man soll keinen Menschen
vom Menschen überschätzen, man soll
mit keinem Menschen keinen Mitmenschen
herein sich selber bringen und übermäß-
gezogen: und also schöpferisch wirken!
Dazu aber gehört, dass man seinen
Mitleiden hütet in jedem Fall, und
dass man, was unseren Ideale zuwider
geht (wie z.b. solches Gesindel wie
L. und R.) auch als feinde behandelt.—
Ein Herein, wie ich mir „die Moral Casa": aber dib ich dieser
Menschheit zu kommen, hat es mich
fast das Leben gekostet. —
Ich hätte den kommen mit Ihnen
und in dem edlen Sinne, der Sie aus-
zeichnet, leben sollen: aber nun ist es zu

Nietzsche

Index of Recipients

Numbers refer to letters, not to pages

General Index

Reference is to page numbers. Subentries are given for particularly constant or eminent subjects and names. In most cases their sequence is chronological, enabling the reader to scan a whole topic. Where multiple references occur, the sequence is alphabetical. The *Zarathustra* subentries are arranged on a chronological basis, with some double subentries intruding for ease of reference.